Family Therapy for Adolescent Drug Abuse

Edited by

Alfred S. Friedman and Samuel Granick

Foreword by

Otto Pollak

Lexington Books
D.C. Heath and Company/Lexington, Massachusetts/Toronto

Library of Congress Cataloging-in-Publication Data

Family therapy for adolescent drug abuse / edited by Alfred S. Friedman and Samuel Granick
; foreword by Otto Pollack.
   p. cm.
   ISBN 0–669–21461–2 (alk. paper)
   1. Drug abuse—Treatment. 2. Psychotherapy. 3. Teenagers—Drug use.
I. Friedman, Alfred S. II. Granick, Samuel, 1916–
   [DNLM: 1. Family Therapy. 2. Substance Abuse—in adolescence. 3. Substance
Abuse—therapy. WM 270 F1977]
RJ506.D78F36 1990
616.86—dc20
DNLM/DLC
for Library of Congress
89–13486
CIP

Published simultaneously in Canada
Printed in the United States of America
Casebound International Standard Book Number: 0–669–21461-2
Library of Congress Catalog Card Number: 89–13486

The paper used in this publication meets the minimum requirements of American National
Standard for Information Sciences—Permanence of Paper for Printed Library Materials, ANSI
Z39.48–1984. ∞™

Year and number of this printing:

90 91 92 10 9 8 7 6 5 4 3 2 1

Contents

Foreword

From a sociological or historical perspective, the use of chemicals for a change of consciousness is a universal. In Germany, it was beer; in Finland and Scandinavia, it was largely hard spirits; in the Soviet Union, vodka; in France, wine; in Mexico, peyote. Drugs have been used to change an ill feeling to at least no feeling or to a good feeling. The phenomenon is part of the human condition. Now why some people go from usage to something that we can qualify as destructive and therefore as abuse can be based on different hypotheses. It can have a genetic basis; it can result from parental influence; it can be part of adolescent culture, which more or less everywhere has a form of rebellion or admission to adult society by ritual.

But drug abuse is more than a ritual or a general cultural phenomenon. It is often used to avoid unpleasant aspects of life, and it becomes a dependency. We don't teach our children enough about how to cope with dissatisfactions, or how to handle misery and unhappiness or psychic pain. There is an expectation that life is just going to be pleasant. We convey our own wishes for ourselves to our children to expect a good life, although this expectation is often negated by everyday experience—for life is not always good, and it is very difficult to make it so; it is often frustrating, bothersome, or disappointing. The drugs are available, and if you are an adolescent, your friends are already using them. Drugs are attractive, offering relief and escape from some of the unhappiness, monotony, and boredom of the young person's life. An important part of the misery of daily life for many young people is the unhappiness of their family lives, where problems occur frequently. This is only one of the problems, but it is a very major one. Many families have not experienced enough open and honest talk among their members and have not been able to talk constructively about emotional issues. Some adolescent drug abusers do not trust their parents or feel betrayed by them. Some may have good reason for this attitude; others may not. If, however, they feel they have been betrayed, or believe that they cannot trust adults or society in general to care about them, they are more likely to turn to things—to chemicals—rather than to people, for an artificial solution to their problems, or to escape. Some adolescents have not had sufficient opportunity to experience legitimate "highs" within the family context, which may contribute to their tendency to seek chemical "highs" that are hazardous to their health and to their futures.

Two or three conditions contribute to adolescent involvement in drugs. One is the unhappiness and the pain present in many families. Another condition is found when the youngsters feel deprived after having been led to expect a better life, in terms of material and emotional satisfactions, and the parents have disappointed them. It is quite possible (if not as yet firmly established by hard data) that recent changes in the status and structure of the family have contributed to the increase in the drug problem (for example, the increase in the divorce rate and in single parenthood, and the sharp increase in the number of mothers who work outside the home). Such families have inevitably become less child-centered, as parents have begun to focus more on their work and careers. There is less time for and attention to the children and less supervision. By default this situation may enhance the influence of the adolescent peer group and its drug culture. There is also a family system theory popular among family therapists that when the parents don't have an adequate relationship, aren't getting satisfaction from each other, and don't want to face the problem in their marriage, they hold on to the child, to keep him or her dependent on them, and they do not foster the child's growth and autonomy. According to this theory, this situation predisposes children to substance abuse and other problems in late adolescence.

Interacting with the tensions generated by the dynamics of family life is the intrapsychic struggle of the adolescent, who needs to achieve a comfortable self-image and a sense of self-assurance in dealing effectively with the realities of approaching adulthood. The discovery that success requires hard work and diligent application can be unnerving, leading often to the impulse to find a seemingly easy solution through escapist behavior. Recourse to drugs at such times becomes a potent temptation.

When some kind of help is offered, such as therapy, some adolescents are attracted to the possibility of attaining a "better life." If you then apply family therapy you do at least one thing that is undoubtedly praiseworthy; you raise hope that something can be done. Even if this is only temporarily beneficial, it can be important in that it gives the family hope and can stimulate the abuser and the family to try to work in a new way to find a solution. Also, experiencing the family therapy process can be enriching and thus beneficial for the family. Improvement in communication and understanding by the family members of each other may occur, while some of the most intractable problems may continue unresolved.

—Otto Pollak
Department of Sociology
University of Pennsylvania

Preface and Acknowledgments

Our basic objective in organizing this volume has been to present clinical practice issues, research findings, case studies, and practical information to guide the thinking and clinical efforts of those attempting to help adolescent substance abusers and their families. Although clinical and research reports about these matters have appeared in increasing abundance over the past decade, most are scattered in a variety of publications (i.e., journal articles and book chapters); thus requiring the reader to search extensively in order to gain an in-depth acquaintance with the issues, background information, and intervention procedures that currently engage the attention of students and professional practitioners.

The family is the central focus in virtually all the chapters we have solicited for this collection. It reflects our orientation, which perceives substance-abusing behavior in the adolescent primarily as an aspect of the dysbalanced functioning of his or her family. This view has led us to explore the possibility of enabling the adolescent to overcome his or her substance abuse through family psychotherapy. Several of the chapters, therefore, report the findings of a research project we recently concluded on this matter. We do not mean to suggest that other approaches to this problem may not be useful, or even as effective, as family therapy; indeed, our research findings and those of other investigators support the potential effectiveness of other intervention procedures. Our working hypothesis primarily asserts that helping a family achieve improved functioning enables the adolescent to gain a more socially constructive orientation toward his life experiences—thereby overcoming the impulse to engage in substance abuse and related illicit behaviors.

Part I consists of chapters dealing with research considerations, programs, and clinical issues. Chapters one and four provide an extensive overview of much of the research reported in various journals and books on the relationship between substance abuse by adolescents and the structure and operational system of their families. Chapter two presents a survey and discussion of treatment needs and services for adolescent drug abusers.

In chapters three and four, observations based on clinical experience with families of substance-abusing adolescents are used to describe how families are affected by and interact with the abusing member. Factors in family functioning that prevent or overcome substance abuse are noted along with the rationale that family therapy helps families learn to cope effectively with and gain relief from the problem. Principles of family therapy for adolescent substance abuse are also described, illustrated with case materials and treatment vignettes.

Chapter eleven offers a summary of the basic results of our research project, which investigated the relative effectiveness of family therapy versus parent-group education and discussion in the treatment of drug-abusing adolescents. Chapter twelve reports the impact of father participation on outcome in the therapy process. Chapter eight, nine, and twelve also report findings on various characteristics of the families studied and treated in the project including data on mother/adolescent communication.

Because the Functional Family Therapy model was chosen as the intervention procedure for the project, we have included chapter ten by James Alexander and colleagues. Dr. Alexander is one of the originators of this system and is co-author of its manual of procedures. We wish to note also that one reason for choosing this approach to family therapy was that at the time it was the only system for which such a manual had been developed. This enabled us to introduce an element of standardization to the treatment procedures.

Chapters five, six, and seven are included because they deal with clinical treatment matters that often are either entirely neglected or are dealt with in only a summary or limited fashion. Chapter five is particularly important for mental health workers dealing with substance-abusing adolescents. It offers guidelines for helping parents deal with the teenager using illicit substances, thereby enabling the family to move toward treatment in a firm and sensitive fashion. The types of challenging, stressful, and frustrating situations faced by the parents are described as are the questions most frequently asked by such parents. Case vignettes and specific suggestions are presented that may be useful to the therapist who is responding to these questions and helping families gain relief from their difficulties.

In turn, chapters six and seven by Marks and Granick are oriented toward helping the therapist face his or her own personality functioning realistically during the family treatment experience. The authors recognize that all family therapists are likely to react personally in response to family-therapy dynamics, and they are thus in danger of losing sight of the needs of the family. Varied practical suggestions and examples from family-therapy sessions are offered to help clinicians deal with such problems in ways that can facilitate and help the family in treatment.

These three chapters serve to introduce Part II of the book, which consists mainly of specific detailed case studies. A unique feature is chapter fourteen, which consists of the reactions of three well-known senior level family therapists to the detailed presentation in chapter thirteen of a family therapy case involving an adolescent substance abuser in which the Structural Family Therapy model was systematically followed. Also included are the responses of the therapist-author to these critiques. The combination of the two chapters, therefore, provides the elements of a case conference.

Chapter fifteen presents a detailed description of the treatment of two black families by a black family therapist. The therapist's awareness of the cultural and ethnic aspects of the community to which the families belonged is of particular interest and value in this presentation. The implications such elements had on the conduct of the therapy are noteworthy.

The chapter by S.J. Marks that follows, is regarded by us as a unique contribution and one that may have considerable value to training programs in family therapy. Parallel to each intervention by the therapist is an interpretive comment by either the therapist-author or by another experienced family therapist (one of the editors of this book). These comments reveal that a dynamic and highly meaningful interplay of psychological forces occurs between the therapist and the family. We leave it to the reader to determine for him- or herself whether this interplay was therapeutic for the family, and more specifically, what aspects affected the family positively, negatively, or not at all. It may prove valuable to relate this case study to Marks' comments about the therapist's use of self in family therapy (see chapter six).

Chapters seventeen and eighteen present cases that come to the attention of family therapists, directly or indirectly, through the law enforcement system. How the two therapists dealt with the abundance of resistances should interest many readers, particularly relative newcomers to family-therapy work. The reader may note that having faith in the family therapy process may help both the clients and the therapist to persevere and work toward functional improvement. The presentations are also noteworthy because the therapists share their personal reactions to the clients and to the therapy as it unfolds.

Chapter nineteen presents a multigenerational orientation to the treatment of a dysfunctional family. Three generations were actively involved in the treatment experience, attempting to work through long-standing disturbances within the family system.

Chapter twenty reports on two separate courses of family therapy conducted by two different therapists over a period of eight to ten years. In this family, both the son and the daughter were severely drug addicted. An unusual feature of this report is the series of statements made by each of the four family members over a period of years showing the changes and inconsistencies that occurred in their perception of the situation.

Primarily, we aimed this book toward practical use by the broad array of workers who deal with drug-abusing adolescents. Our experience leads us to favor a family-oriented approach as the intervention of choice in these problems. We also believe, however, that the discussions and case presentations herein may also be instructive for those who deal solely with the addictive adolescent. To gain a proper understanding of the adolescent and to plan realistically to deal with the presenting problems calls for an in-depth awareness of the social/psychological system that shapes his or her behavior patterns, motivation, and personality. Toward this end, the family is a primary source. Accordingly, intervention should have an integral relation to the family system if it is to be realistic and effective. Moreover, the discussions and case histories dealing with the therapist's use of self and his or her reactions to the clients during the family process represent one of the central features of our plan for the book; one which is meant to be of interest to therapists in general.

One additional focus of this volume is to give recognition to the importance of scientific research in providing a firm, realistic base to clinical knowledge and procedures in the field of adolescent drug abuse. We recognize that, thus far, the field does not have solid scientific grounding. Our presentations show, however, that much serious and significant work has been accomplished. Hopefully, the material we offer will stimulate further effort and progress in the coming years.

We owe a sincere and grateful vote of thanks to all the authors who graciously contributed chapters to this volume. In addition, we wish to express our appreciation to Harriet M. Schwartz, our research secretary, for her conscientious efforts in preparing and editing the manuscript; and to Lynn Tomko for her careful proofreading and editing assistance.

We also wish to acknowledge that the inclusion of most of the family-therapy process reports in the "Case Book" section of the book, as well as the research findings reported on the families, was made possible by Grant No. 5R18 DA3184 from the National Institute on Drug Abuse entltled, "Assessment of Family Therapy for Adolescent Drug Abuse."

Alfred S. Friedman
Samuel Granick

I
Adolescent Drug Abuse and the Family

1

The Adolescent Drug Abuser and the Family

Alfred S. Friedman

Introduction

Adolescent drug abuse is acknowledged as a major problem in the United States, yet little is known about adolescent drug treatment programs and their effectiveness. More needs to be done in research of the treatment effects, to determine *what* treatment works for *whom*.

Meeting the challenge is not so simple. To understand adolescent drug abuse and how to treat it, one must understand the nature of adolescence as a time of experimentation and defiance. One also must understand the tremendous influence of peer pressure, the damaging effects of living in a family where children are misused, not properly supervised, or provided with poor role models, perhaps substance-abusing models, and of course the provocative appeal of the drugs themselves.

The Scope of the Problem

Adolescence is a complicated and often chaotic phase of life, involving efforts to resolve the counter-dependency struggle with parents, the challenge of the initial efforts to make the heterosexual adjustment, the challenges of graduating from high school and of planning or starting a career.

Of particular concern (for treatment) are the compulsive drug users who have serious personal problems and take drugs to avoid reality (to avoid the real problems in their life situation, or to get relief from the psychic pain, the anxiety, tensions, anger, and so forth). Unable to handle the pressure and responsibilities of growing up, many of these adolescents are confused and have a poor self-image.

On the other hand, this author has observed that many drug-using adolescents are more satisfied with their social lives and tend to have more peer and heterosexual relationships than do those who do not use drugs. For youngsters who use drugs to relieve the boredom they feel about school, attending school while "high" or while involved in drug use results in diminished school performance and failure. One controlled study showed that drug use contributes to a very significant degree to dropping out and to failure to graduate from high school—regardless of whatever other school behavior or learning problems the youngster might have (Friedman, Glickman, and Utada 1985). The failure in school and the problems with school authorities compound the problems that most of these adolescents already have in their relationships with their parents. This adds to other conflicts that already exist in the family. In a national survey of adolescent drug treatment programs, 49 percent of the clients reported at the time of admission to treatment that there were serious conflicts in their families, and they gave this as a reason for coming into treatment (Friedman et al. 1980).

The position of the adolescent drug abuser in relation to parents and other adult figures (such as treatment personnel) involves mistrust, misunderstanding, and fear of restriction, punishments, rejection, or abandonment.

Compared with the heroin addiction epidemic of the 1960s and early 1970s, adolescent drug abuse today is more broadly based; it cuts across all socioeconomic strata and involves a wider array of chemical substances. It also is the result of complex underlying problems inextricably bound to the psychology of adolescence, which is itself a challenge.

In 1986, 4 percent of high school seniors in the United States were *daily* users of either alcohol or marijuana. The majority of adolescents who come to drug treatment use more than one illicit substance. Marijuana is frequently used in combination with other substances. Approximately 51 percent of high school seniors had at some time in their lives experimented with or used marijuana, and some 24 percent had used stimulants. In addition, seniors had experimented with many other drugs: cocaine (17 percent), hallucinogens (10 percent), tranquilizers (11 percent), barbiturates (8 percent), phencyclidine (PCP) (5 percent), and inhalants (20 percent) (Johnston, O'Malley, and Bachman 1987).

Research shows that adolescents use drugs for a host of reasons: (1) they are often readily available; (2) they provide a quick, easy, and cheap way to feel good; (3) drugs offer a means of gaining acceptance in peer relationships; (4) drugs may help modify unpleasant feelings, reduce disturbing emotions, alleviate depression, reduce tension, and aid in coping with life pressures (Beschner and Friedman 1979).

For some adolescents, experimentation with drugs is merely part of a rite of passage through their challenging teen years (Feldman, Agar, and Beschner 1979). Most adolescent drug users fall into a category called "experimental," "situational," or "recreational" users. Such individuals, influenced to use drugs mainly by their peers, tend to use drugs infrequently and in small amounts to get high, have fun, and relax. They generally will not become habitual users or addicted, and will not have serious problems with drugs or require treatment. For others, however, drug use goes beyond experimentation and signals serious adjustment problems (Jalali et al. 1981). These others are generally compulsive, dedicated users with serious personal problems. They rely on drugs for self-medication to cope with their problems, not unlike some adults (Kandel 1981; Wesson et al. 1977). These adolescents— possibly up to 5 percent of teens aged fourteen to eighteen—have serious drug and drug-related problems and generally need treatment.

A recent longitudinal study (Newcomb 1988) found that heavy drug use by chronic users resulted in serious long-term harmful consequences: disrupted relationships, jobs, and education, and impaired physical and mental health. There was an apparent absence of measurable harmful consequences for most of the occasional or experimental users at follow-up evaluation after approximately ten years.

Why do some youngsters become more seriously involved in using drugs than others? Why do some become drug dependent? There is no single answer. Reasons for drug involvement and drug dependency are varied and complex. There are many different types of drug use patterns and many different types of drug users. One potent factor that seems to lead to drug dependency in adolescents as well as in adults is the psychoactive or tranquilizing effect of drugs that provide relief for pain.

Most popular drugs relieve stress and anxiety. Tranquilizers have become one of the most accepted and widely prescribed drugs because they calm anxiety. Heroin, like morphine and other opiate derivatives, is effective as a tranquilizing agent, also relieving feelings of worthlessness and despair. For addicts in ghetto communities, heroin provides a feeling of "normalcy"—a chance to feel good about themselves and to escape the feelings of hopelessness that come from living in poverty and lacking opportunities. Cocaine produces stimulation and euphoria. Marijuana can produce a dreamy, relaxed feeling similar to the effects that some get from alcohol. Alcohol can produce a wide range of effects; it can depress, stimulate, tranquilize, or agitate, depending upon the personality of the user, the environment, and the concentration and mixtures used.

So it is no wonder that in facing problems that sometime seem insurmountable many adolescents find drugs appealing. There is also a general tendency in our society to encourage escapist behavior (for example, the movies). Once adolescents start using drugs to relieve anxiety and stress and to escape from life's pressures there is an increased likelihood that they will return to such use, especially if problems persist and there are no alternative ways of relieving pressures and pain.

Drug use, however, can and usually does exacerbate the problems, especially if a youngster's performance is impaired or his or her behavior changes—which is likely with drugs. The youngster experiences more pressure from the parents and sometimes from school authorities and as a result is more likely to seek relief and escape through drugs.

Fewer adolescent abusers than adult addicts are physiologically addicted to narcotics (opioids). Consequently, their treatment is less likely to include the medical procedures that accompany addiction, such as detoxification, pharmacological substitution (such as methadone), and the use of narcotic blocking agents (such as naltrexone).

Nevertheless, since adolescence is a critical developmental period, heavy drug use and involvement in a drug life-style have a greater negative impact on the development, maturation, and the future of adolescents than they do on adults. Drugs divert the adolescent's interest, energy, and effort from more constructive life tasks and challenges.

Characteristics of Drug Abusers

About two-thirds of the adolescent males in residential treatment and one-half of the males in outpatient drug treatment (OPDT) committed crimes during the year prior to treatment. Although they may often engage in minor stealing and selling of drugs, it is unlikely that they will be imprisoned or will come into regular contact with the more hard-core criminal elements. As might be expected, adult drug abusers and addicts are more likely to have been arrested, convicted, and jailed. Thus, adolescent drug users who either seek or are referred to treatment usually present a multiplicity of problems beyond drug use per se. In any attempt to treat adolescent drug abusers, attention must be given to these underlying problems and usually to the family situation as well. Educational needs and the need for parental and family support, as well as the provision of education assistance and alternative activities and interests, play a large role in the treatment of adolescents.

In a study of high school students, drug users were more likely to be involved in gang activity, to have more problems with the police (including arrests for offenses of violence), and to have more problems in school (more grades repeated and less "enjoyment" and "satisfaction" with school; lack of motivation to achieve in school; suspension or expulsion from school). Adolescent drug users reported more time spent in "hanging out" with peers, more time sleeping, and less time spent discussing problems with parents, less time in reading, watching TV, or doing homework, and less time in religious activities. They expressed more satisfaction with the number of friends and the amount of social contact they had. Thus, these adolescent drug users appeared to be more dissociated from the adult world and more involved with their own particular peer group (Glickman, Utada, and Friedman 1983).

It has been our observation that the reason many of the adolescents using drugs express more sataisfaction with their social life, is that they actually have more peer relationships, more parties, more sex, etc., than most adolescents who do not use drugs and who tend to feel more lonely or isolated from peers.

These youngsters ostensibly seek pleasure in drugs, and for a period of time the drugs may work for them, but they are often miserable underneath—they hurt. Sometimes when you get to know them you see and hear their pain under their bravado and denial. As they struggle to achieve an identity, they frequently doubt whether they are going to make it in life.

The Role of the Family

By the time the parents discover the adolescent's drug problem it is likely to be serious. Like their adult alcoholic counterparts, teens confronted with their drug abuse almost always resort to denial, regardless of how long and how frequently they have been using drugs. Some parents, "buy into" this denial for a time, wanting to believe that there is no problem; some overreact and thus risk worsening the problem they are hoping to correct. Eventually, most parents begin to face the truth rationally and find their children's refusals to do so hard to understand.

Upon finding that their children are using drugs, many parents feel hurt, betrayed, or guilty. Some feel helpless because they have a limited understanding of adolescent rebellion or of drug abuse and do not know where to turn to or what to do. Others feel frustrated because after learning about the problem and reaching out for help, they find there is no simple (or "right") approach or answer. Each family's problem is unique in some ways.

Thus, adolescent drug users who seek or are referred to treatment usually present many problems beyond just drug use. In any attempt to treat adolescent drug abusers attention must be given to these underlying problems and usually to the family situation as well. Families of adolescent drug users differ significantly from families in which the adolescent offspring either do not use drugs or only have used marijuana experimentally. In contrast to experimental drug users or nonusers, adolescents with serious drug problems come from families with the following characteristics:

There is more discrepancy between how the parents would like their children ideally to be and how they perceive them actually to be (Alexander and Dibb 1977).

Parents are perceived as having relatively less influence than peers. Both parents are perceived to be more approving of drug use (Jessor 1975).

Offspring perceive less love and support from both parents, particularly fathers (Mellinger, Somers, and Manheimer 1975; Streit, Halstead, and Pascale 1974).

Kandel (1974) reported that adolescent initiation into the use of illicit drugs, other than marijuana, appears to be strongly related to parental influences. The adolescent's feeling of closeness to the family was associated with the low likelihood of initiation into these other illicit drugs, while strict controls imposed by parents and parental disagreement about discipline was associated with their likelihood of initiation. Use of drugs by parents was also found to be an important predictor.

Some of the findings of the National Youth Polydrug Study (Friedman, Pomerance, and Sanders 1980) on the relationship of family factors to adolescent drug abuse are as follows:

Adolescents whose parents had drug problems, alcohol problems, psychiatric problems, or problems with the law were found to be more heavily involved in drug abuse than adolescents whose parents were not reported to have such problems.

There is a significant positive correlation between the number of problems reported in the family and the number of different types of drugs abused by the adolescent offspring member.

There is less shared authority and poorer communication in the family (Cannon 1976; Hunt 1974).

There is less spontaneous problem solving in structured family interaction tasks (Mead and Campbell 1972).

In a study by Glickman, Utada and myself (1983), the most prevalent concerns expressed about the parent(s) by the adolescent clients in both outpatient and residential treatment settings were these: "Objects to my friends," "Is disappointed in me," "Complains too much," and "Does not trust me." Other concerns reported about their family situations by these adolescents were: "The family is too curious about what I do" (58 percent residential, 40 percent outpatient); "Fights with brothers and/or sisters" (48 percent residential, 34 percent outpatient); and "My friends are not welcome at home" (47 percent residential, 34 percent outpatient).

In addition to drug and alcohol problems and family problems (conflict with parents, and so on), the reasons given by adolescent clients in the National Youth Polydrug Study ($N = 1,750$) for applying for treatment were (in rank order): (2) school-related problems (39.5 percent); (3) legal problems—involvement in criminal justice system (35.3 percent); and (4) emotional or psychiatric problems—need for counseling, and so forth (27.7

percent). Almost a third (32.7 percent) of the adolescents surveyed had had one or more previous overdose episodes; 15.9 percent had had one or more previous suicide attempts; and 20.4 percent had had treatment for a mental health problem on one or more occasions.

There are probably multiple factors in the life of any given adolescent which determine whether or not that adolescent will become involved in drug use or abuse. The fact that there is a significant peer influence was established by research a number of years ago (Kandel 1974). More recently, research evidence has been accumulating to suggest that there is also a significant family influence in adolescent drug abuse. The report of the 1979 National Survey on Drug Abuse (Miller and Cisin 1979) concluded: "Among youth, family influence can either encourage or discourage drug use, as older family members 'set examples' of substance use or abstention." This report also stated that it found evidence to corroborate an earlier report by Miller and Rittenhouse (1980) that "teenagers appear to be influenced by the example of older family members." Drug use was also found to be "more likely among teenagers whose older brothers or sisters used alcohol and/or illicit drugs—and is less likely among those whose older siblings abstain."

There is evidence for drug use across generations in families—parents of adolescents who use illicit drugs are more often found to be involved in drug abuse themselves than are parents of adolescents who do not use drugs (Smart and Fejer 1979; Adler and Lotecka 1973; Velleman and Lawrence 1971; Kandel 1974; McKillip and Petzel 1973). Thus it is possible that one of the determinants of adolescent drug abuse is that specific aspects of parental behavior may operate as either a model for or an influence on adolescent offspring behavior.

In a national survey of adolescent drug treatment programs (Friedman, Pomerance, and Sanders 1980), the severity of the drug abuse problem of the adolescent clients was found to be significantly related to the following family factors: (1) certain demographic characteristics of their families (religion and educational level of parents); (2) the disruption and dissolution of the structure (lack of intactness) of their families; (3) certain family constellation factors (one interesting family constellation finding, which is apparently a new finding, is that young male drug users who have older brothers are more seriously or heavily involved in drug abuse than are young male drug users who have older sisters); (4) the number (and type) of problems that they perceived to be present in their families (in regard to the parents of the clients in this survey, 31 percent of the fathers and 23 percent of the mothers were reported to have at least one of the following types of problems: substance abuse, a legal problem, and/or an emotional, psychiatric problem).

Cooper and Olson (1977), who reviewed the literature on the association of parent/child relationships with drug use, concluded that:

researchers who have investigated the role of the family and illicit drug use emphasize the importance of the family process, and present evidence of differences between families whose members are drug-free and families whose members use drugs (Blum 1972; Annis 1974; Timms et al. 1973; Tec 1971; Anholt and Klein 1976; Prendergast and Schaefer 1974; Wechsler and Thum 1973). High levels of perceived parental support and perceived positive parent-child relationships have been found to be related to low drug use in adolescents in several studies (Blum 1972; Bethards 1973; Streit et al. 1974) but not related in another study (Prendergast and Schaefer 1974).

In their own study Cooper and Olson noted that high school students who reported no drug use or low drug use also reported that they perceived a high degree of parental supportiveness in their families and that they experience high personal esteem, whereas low perceived parental support and low self-esteem were related to frequent drug usage.

These findings should not necessarily be taken as specific to, or unique for, families with drug-abusing offspring because some of the just listed studies compared such families with volunteer "normal" control families; some of the same differences might be found if families whose offspring had behavior problems or symptoms other than drug use were compared with volunteer "normal" control families.

In addition to suggestive findings and "hard data" from controlled research studies, many clinical observations have been made over the years regarding the family system factors and the relationships of families with drug-using offspring, observations that were derived from psychodiagnostic evaluations of these families and from conducting family therapy with them. Some time ago the overinvolvement of male addicts with their mothers was observed by Mason (1958), Chein et al. (1964), and Vaillant (1966). In his literature review of these reports, Stanton (1980) lists five additional references in which the authors report how the other family members behave in such a way as to keep the drug abuser or addict in a dependent, incompetent role, or to undermine his or her self-esteem. Some clinical observers have speculated that, in spite of the fact that the parents and other family members have many difficulties and much suffering related to the adolescent member's drug abuse, they paradoxically need this drug abuse behavior to maintain the homeostasis and stability of the type of pathological family system to which they are accustomed or habituated. For example, the involvement of the parents in the drug abuse problems may serve to distract them from the fact that they are emotionally divorced from each other, or that they have an intensely conflictual marriage.

Very often parents seem to be trying to keep control over their youngsters, to avoid separation, by giving them money for drugs. They claim this protects the adolescent from having to steal for drug money. But in effect this keeps the youth dependent on his parents—which the parents may very much desire, without realizing it.

Kaufman and Kaufman (1979) have compiled the following list of the most frequently asserted clinical and theoretical speculations regarding the family system characteristics of families that have adolescent drug abuse members:

1. The addict is the symptom carrier for the family dysfunction.

2. The addict helps to maintain the family homeostasis.

3. The addicted member reinforces the parental need to control and continue parenting, yet he finds such parenting inadequate for his needs.

4. The addict provides a displaced battlefield so that implicit and explicit parental strife can continue to be denied.

5. Parental drug and alcohol abuse is common and is directly transmitted to the addict or results in inadequate parenting.

6. The addict forms cross-generational alliances that separate parents from each other.

7. Generational boundaries are diffuse—there is frequent competition between parents. Frequently the crisis created by the drug-dependent member is the only way the family gets together and attempts some problem solving, or is the only opportunity for a "dead" family to experience emotions.

Kaufman (1980) also pointed to the limitation of available knowledge about drug abuse families: the knowledge is based primarily on observations of families who volunteer for treatment, and not on sufficiently systematic studies. According to Kaufman, "It is reasonable to hypothesize that families who become involved in treatment are more enmeshed than those who do not" (p. 266).

Reilly (1976) has reported nine dysfunctional or pathological family interaction patterns and six "conflict themes" that he has found, in his family therapy work, to be characteristic of families with substance abuse members. He has proposed that these family characteristics may tend to maintain and exacerbate addiction. They are presented here, following, because most of them are consistent with observations made by this author from family therapy work with families of adolescent drug abusers. However, it is necessary to make the disclaimer that these characteristics are not unique or specific to substance abuse families, but are observed to occur more regularly and in more extreme or intense form in substance abuse families than in families with less severe problems. The additional disclaimer is made that clinicians may either observe such patterns and themes in families, or may elicit them, or may read them into families. Following are Reilly's nine dysfunctional family interaction patterns:

1. Negative interaction (family members give negative messages when they do communicate, such as criticisms, put-downs, complaints, and nagging).

2. Inconsistent limit setting or structuring by parents.

3. A cry for help or attention by the substance abuser (designated patient), advertising drug use and related problems as a way of getting some particular response or structuring or limit setting by parents.

4. Global or massive parental denial—for example, they manage not to see what is going on, either the evidence of substance abuse or accidents and other evidence that the problem is getting worse.

5. Offspring on drugs provide some vicarious gratification that parents need, either consciously or unconsciously.

6. Use of alcohol and drugs as self-medication or as disinhibitor by substance-abusing member who needs this aid for expressing or acting out certain reactions or feelings (such as destructiveness, violence, and so on).

7. Difficulty in expressing anger between parents and children (unexpressed rage). There is no appropriate continuum of expression, resulting in either no expression or violence.

8. Pathogenic parents' expectations of substance-abusing child, who is either perceived (represents or symbolizes) as a good or bad image of a grandparent or relative of the parent and is not seen as a real person for him- or herself.

9. "Incredible language." Family members make statements, such as promises about their behavior in the future, that are so unrealistic that they cannot be believed. They don't mean what they say.

Reilly's six characteristic "conflict themes" are

1. Attachment and separation
2. Ego diffusion (undifferentiated family mass, symbiosis) and individuation
3. Dependency and autonomy
4. Nurturance and deprivation
5. Control, leadership, limit setting versus freedom, permissiveness
6. Loss and restoration, death and rebirth

Family Therapy for Adolescent Drug Abuse

Since the family therapy approach has gained respect in recent years, not only from its practitioners but also from other clinical observers, as an effective change agent for adolescent behavior problems, determining the effectiveness of this intervention method for reducing drug abuse appears to be a matter of some significance and importance. Because adolescence is the time when the use of illicit drugs is usually initiated, and because adolescents are usually intensely involved in their relationships with their parents, it is natural to think of involving the family in the treatment of the adolescent drug abuser.

A major task for the adolescent and his family is to effect a healthy positive separation and individuation and to establish a separate identity of the adolescent apart from the family unit. As many family therapists have observed, one or both parents will tend to feel hopeless at the prospect of the adolescent's leaving the family unit if the parents' marriage is unsatisfactory, devitalized, or bankrupt. One or both parents in such a marriage will try to maintain a close, dependent, or enmeshed relationship with the adolescent child and will not foster independent growth. The adolescent who is rebelling against the parents or is trying to become independent may well see the family therapy process as an obstacle to his goal, as having the effect of keeping him involved in the family and under the parents' control. If such adolescents who are substance abusers accept the idea of obtaining professional help, they will tend to prefer individual or peer group counseling or therapy, rather than expose their thoughts and behavior to their parents in family therapy sessions. This situation challenges the family therapist to show the adolescent that family sessions can help him or her to make a more successful type of separation and to become more independent. If the family is polarized by an aggressive conflict between the adolescent and his or her parents, it will be difficult to make progress in family therapy and to maintain the family's motivation to continue in family therapy.

Use of the family therapy approach for a broad range of individual behavior and symptom problems, and for family relationship problems, has accelerated rapidly and spread widely in recent years. The confidence in and the expectation of the efficacy of family therapy as a treatment method of choice has also increased significantly. Nevertheless, the empirical support of these clinical impressions and theoretical convictions about family therapy, through well-controlled research evaluation studies of outcome, has been hard to come by.

Gurman and Kniskern (1978) reported optimistically from their review and appraisal of papers and studies on the outcome of family therapy oriented approaches as follows: "largely positive results emerge on the basis of a wide variety of criteria, on change measures from a number of evaluative perspectives, for many types of marital and family problems, from therapy conducted by clinicians of all the major therapeutic disciplines, and in therapy carried out in a number of treatment settings."

Hirsch (1961) was perhaps the first author in the literature to advocate family therapy as appropriate for adolescent drug abuse. Subsequently, a number of other practitioners made the same recommendation (Gottesfeld, Caroff, and Lieberman 1972; Kempler and MacKenna 1975; Wellisch and Kaufman 1975). Levy (1972) reported that in a five-year follow-up study, those narcotic addicts who successfully overcame their addiction most often had family support in coping with the problem. Ganger and Shugart (1966) conducted family therapy with more than one hundred male addicts and concluded that addiction is a "familia-genic disease" and that the "treatment of the addict within his family should constitute the treatment of choice." Auerswald (1980) stated that he could *not* recall, from his many years of working with families, "a single, openly communicating, mutually respecting, well-organized, lovingly close family in which an actively participating member had a serious and lasting drug habit . . . possibly only transient experimentation with occasional alcohol or marijuana." He recommended social programs to support family life and the construction of family support networks.

Stanton (1979) reviewed the literature on family treatment for drug problems and found information on sixty-eight different studies or programs. Most of the papers expressed the opinion or the conviction that the various forms of family-oriented therapy or marital therapy that were being reported on or described were beneficial and effective. However, most of the papers either reported only case studies or presented no quantitative data on outcome:

> Six of the studies involved comparisons with other forms of treatment or control groups. Four of the six (Hendricks 1971; Scopetta et al. 1979; Stanton 1978; Wunderlich et al. 1974) showed family treatment to be superior to other modes, while the remaining two (Winer et al. 1971; Ziegler-Driscoll 1977, 1978) obtained equivalent, or equivocal, results.

The author concludes that "family treatment shows considerable promise for effectively dealing with problems of drug abuse." It is the opinion of this author, however, that only Stanton's own study applied adequate research controls, including the appropriate application of the method of random assignment of subjects to treatment and/or treatment conditions.

There has been reported in the literature at least one systematic research study of the effects of a family-oriented approach with heroin addicts. This study (Stanton et al. 1979) indicated that a short-term family therapy approach, added to a methadone maintenance regime, was effective in reducing the drug abuse of heroin-methadone addicts, but was not more effective than a "family move" program or individual counseling in achieving vocational-educational improvement. Also, paid family therapy, in which payment to clients was contingent on attendance and clean urine, was found to be somewhat but not significantly superior to unpaid family therapy. Since the family therapy intervention in this study was conducted in conjunction with methadone maintenance treatment, the findings may not be generalizable to a situation in a "drug-free" treatment setting in which no drugs are administered to patients, and further, the specific effects of the family therapy intervention with the older heroin-methadone addicts may not be the same as they would be for younger polydrug, nonopiate users. (It is obviously easier to maintain subjects, in a treatment demonstration project, in a methadone maintenance clinic setting than in a drug-free clinic setting.)

There is, in fact, one report (Garrigan and Bambrick 1977) in the literature of a relatively small study ($N = 28$) that happened to use most of the same basic research design for evaluating the effects of family therapy which has been developed independently by the author of this chapter (and which will be reported and discussed in later chapters of this book): the comparison of the effect of a family therapy method with the effects of a "parent group discussion and seminar method." In a school for middle-class emotionally disturbed boys, cases assigned to a brief course of Zuk's "go-between" method of family therapy showed more improvement than did cases assigned to the parent group method. Since the report did not indicate whether or not all the control cases were actually included in the parent group procedure, it is not clear whether this might be a group of cases combining no treatment with an alternative treatment. The Zuk "go-between" method of family therapy has some features that are similar to the "functional" and "strategic" methods, to be discussed below.

Alexander (1973) reported the first reasonably adequate research controlled study to our knowledge of the outcome of family therapy intervention with delinquent families. This fact is relevant for this book, since many adolescent drug abusers are often considered to be "delinquent" or to engage in "deviant" behavior; and because the "functional" model of family therapy developed by Alexander and used in his study was also used in the family therapy demonstration for adolescent drug abuse that is reported in this book. These delinquent families were predominantly white and middle-class, and were characterized as "deteriorated family systems, with a runaway and ungovernable adolescent" member. The results of the study indicated that families that received a specific short-term, behaviorally oriented family intervention program demonstrated significant changes on three family interaction measures at the end of therapy, and also showed significantly reduced recidivism rates at follow-up when compared with families receiving no professional treatment. The treatment method was designed to increase family reciprocity, clarity of communication, and contingency contracting. The outcome measures showed that the behavioral-functional family intervention method demonstrated "more equality in talk time, less silence, and more interruptions among family members, and significantly less recidivism, compared to a no-treatment control group" (Parsons and Alexander 1973).

The classic controlled study of the effects of family therapy was the Langsley-Denver study (Langsley and Kaplan 1968) in which acutely disturbed psychiatric patients were randomly assigned to either immediate admission to a psychiatric hospital or to an outpatient family therapy procedure. The family therapy group of patients did as well as the hospitalized group on symptom relief, social functioning, and work functioning; they were superior, on follow-up evaluation, in avoiding the need for rehospitalization. Thus, the family therapy approach was considered to be an effective alternative to hospitalization and to be much most cost-effective.

Based on this author's own extensive clinical and study experience with the family-therapy modality over a twenty-two-year period, and the experience of a rather large staff of trained family therapists in the drug treatment program at the Philadelphia Psychiatric Center over a twelve-year period, we consider the family-therapy modality to be particularly relevant for effecting change in the relationship between the parents and their drug-abusing adolescent offspring. The position is consistent with the rationale presented by Fishman, Stanton, and Rosman (1982). In such families the degree of dysfunction, conflict, and discord is great, and the lack of a healthy, sustaining, stabilizing family milieu is conducive to serious, self-destructive drug abuse by the adolescent; in a vicious circle, the drug abuse behavior then leads to an intensification of the discord and conflict in the family. This unresolved conflict then often feeds into more acting out and to increased use of drugs by the adolescent.

Types of Family Therapy

Some of the labels or titles that have been assigned to the various types of family therapy are:

1. Psychodynamic
2. Experiential
3. Behavioral
4. Strategic
5. Structural

6. Communication
7. Family system approach
8. Problem-centered systems family therapy
9. Contextual family therapy
10. Functional family therapy
11. Integrative family therapy
12. Intergenerational (extended family) family therapy

The model or type of family therapy that was used in conducting the family therapy demonstration, the experience and findings of which are reported in the later chapters of this book, is the functional family therapy model. The rationale, and the procedures and techniques of this model are presented in detail in chapter ten of this book by James Alexander.

Siblings

It is generally assumed that it is appropriate and usually advantageous when conducting family therapy to include the siblings of the adolescent drug abuse client and the total nuclear family in the treatment unit. The idea that the parental pair triangle is so crucial in the family therapy of addicts that the role of siblings can be overlooked, Kaufman (1980) states is a myth. Also, it is reasonable to expect in those cases in which the family therapy intervention is successful that the therapy will have a positive effect, not only toward limiting or terminating the drug abuse of the identified patient (the adolescent drug abuse client), but also on the future behavior of the siblings of the identified client—specifically, drug abuse by younger siblings can be prevented, and any siblings who are already involved in drug abuse will improve. The importance and relevance of this potential secondary effect of the family therapy method is apparent simply from the fact that 65 percent of high school seniors in 1980 had already tried some type of illegal drug, and 39 percent had used an illegal drug other than marijuana (Johnston et al 1987). It can further be assumed that the younger siblings of adolescent drug abuse clients who apply for treatment are at greater than average risk, because of the influence of their older siblings, the characteristics of their family relationships, and, in some cases, the general socioeconomic conditions in which they live. The findings of the National Youth Polydrug Study (Friedman, Pomerance, and Sanders 1980) indicated that adolescents who apply for treatment have used, on the average, more than six different types of illegal drugs during the relatively brief period of their drug use histories. Furthermore, 60 percent of that adolescent drug abuse client sample reported that they had at least one younger sibling, and in 15.5 percent of the families at least one of these younger siblings (including all siblings from age one to seventeen) were already involved in illegal substance use. The drug problems of the younger sibling sample can be expected to be less serious, on the average, than those of the primary, older adolescent client sample. Nevertheless, some will have multiple severe problems.

As might be expected, the findings for the older siblings of the adolescent clients, in this national sample, were much more serious than were those for the younger siblings. In 37 percent of the families that had older siblings, at least one other sibling had a substance abuse problem. Older siblings are obviously more likely than younger siblings to exert a decisive influence on, or to be followed as a model by, the client-subjects; and older male siblings are more likely than older female siblings, according to the findings of the survey, to influence or provide a model for client-subjects to engage in drug abuse behavior.

It would be reasonable to postulate that the siblings assigned to the family therapy treatment condition who participate directly and actively in the treatment process will show improvement at posttesting and follow-up evaluation. Clinical experience demonstrates that when parents achieve positive change or improvement in their individual life adjustments and/or in their marital relationships, as a result of therapy, there is an additional positive spin-off effect for the parent-child relationships in the family and in the personal adjustment of the children.

In summary, the following points demonstrate the significance and importance of a systematic evaluation of the effects of family therapy for adolescent drug abuse:

1. Adolescent drug abuse is a major national problem.

2. There will be a continuing need for treatment rehabilitation services for adolescents seriously involved in drug abuse.

3. The use of the family therapy modality has spread across drug treatment programs, has gained popularity in recent years, and is increasingly being considered the treatment of choice for adolescent drug abuse.

4. There has been, heretofore, very little evidence of an adequately controlled systematic research evaluation of the effectiveness of family therapy with problems of adolescent drug abuse, nor of the comparative effectiveness of this modality in relation to other modalities.

5. It would be an additional contribution to the field to determine the relative costs and benefits of adding either a family therapy modality or a parent group modality to the modalities that are provided on a more regular and usual basis to adolescent drug abusers.

References

Adler, P.T., and L. Lotecka. 1973. Drug use among high school students: Patterns and correlates. *International Journal of the Addictions* 5: 257–78.

Alexander, B.K., and G.S. Dibb. 1977. Interpersonal perception in addict families. *Family Process* 16: 17–28.

Alexander, J.F. 1973. Defensive and supportive communications in normal and deviant families. *Journal of Consulting and Clinical Psychology* 40 (2): 223–31.

Anholt, H., and M. Klein. 1976. Drug abuse in junior high school populations. *American Journal of Drug Alcohol Abuse* 3: 589–603.

Annis, H.M. 1974. Patterns of intra-familial drug use. *British Journal of Addictions* 69: 361–69.

Auerswald, E.H. 1980. Drug use and families in the context of twentieth century science. In *Drug Abuse from the Family Perspective*. Rockville, Md.: National Institute on Drug Abuse.

Beschner, G.B., and A.S. Friedman. 1979. In Introduction. G.B. Beschner and A.S. Friedman, eds., *Youth Drug Abuse: Problems, Issues and Treatment*. Lexington, Mass.: Lexington Books, 10–11.

Bethards, J. 1973. Parental support and the use of drugs. *Humbolt Journal of Social Relations* 1: 26–28.

Blum, R.H. 1972. *Horatio Alger's Children*. San Francisco, Calif.: Jossey-Bass.

Cannon, S.R. 1976. *Social Functioning Patterns in Families of Offspring Receiving Treatment for Drug Abuse*. Roslyn Heights, N.Y.: Libra Publications.

Chein, I., D. Gerard, R. Lee, and El Rosenfeld. 1964. *The Road to H*. New York: Basic Books.

Cooper, D.M., and D.H. Olson. 1977. *Perceived Parental Support and Self-Esteem as Related to Adolescent Drug Use*. Minneapolis, MN: Multi-Resource Center.

Feldman, H.W., M.H. Agar, and G.M. Beschner. 1979. *Angel Dust: An Ethnographic Study of PCP Users*. Lexington, Mass.: Lexington Books.

Fishman, H.C., M.D. Stanton, and B.L. Rosman. 1982. In M.D. Stanton and T.C. Todd and Associates, eds.: Treating families of adolescent drug abusers. In *The Family Therapy of Drug Abuse and Addiction* New York: Guilford Press.

Friedman, A.S. 1982. Adolescent drug abuse treatment programs. *NIDA Treatment Research Notes*, Rockville, Md.

Friedman, A.S., N. Glickman, and A. Utada. 1985. Does drug and alcohol use lead to failure to graduate from high school? *Journal of Drug Education* 15(4): 353–364.

Friedman, A.S., E. Pomerance, R. Sanders, Y. Santo, and A. Utada. 1980. The structure and problems of families of adolescent drug abusers. *Contemporary Drug Problems* Vol. 9(3): 327–356.

Ganger, R., and G. Shugart. 1966. The heroin addicts' pseudoassertive behavior and family dynamics. *Social Casework* 47: 643–49.

Garrigan, J.J., and A.F. Bambrick. 1977. Family therapy for disturbed children: Some experimental results in special education. *Journal of Marriage and Family Counseling* 3: 83–93.

Glickman, N., A. Utada and A. Friedman. 1983. Characteristics of drug users in urban public high schools. *Clinical Notes,* grant no. H81-DA-01657. Rockville, Md.: National Institute on Drug Abuse.

Gottesfeld, M., P. Caroff, and F. Lieberman. 1972. Treatment of adolescent drug abusers. *Psychoanalytic Review* 59(4): 527–37.

Gurman, A.S., and D.P. Kniskern. 1978. Research on marital and family therapy: Progress, perspective and prospect. In S.L. Garfield and A.E. Bergin, eds. *Handbook of Psychotherapy and Behavior Change: An Empirical Analysis.* New York: Wiley.

Hendricks, W.J. 1971. Use of multifamily counseling groups in treatment of male narcotic addicts. *International Journal of Group Psychotherapy* 21: 84–90.

Hirsch, R. 1961. Group therapy with parents of adolescent drug addicts. *Psychiatric Quarterly* 35: 702–10.

Hunt, D.G. 1974. Parental permissiveness as perceived by the offspring and the degree of marijuana usage among offspring. *Human Relations* 27: 267–85.

Jalali, B., M. Jalali, G. Crocette, and F. Turner. 1981. Adolescents and drug use: Toward a more comprehensive approach. *American Journal of Orthopsychiatry* 51(1): 120–29.

Jessor, R. Predicting time of onset of marihuana use: A developmental study of high school youth. 1975. In D. Lettiere, ed. *Predicting Adolescent Drug Abuse: A Review of Issues, Methods and Correlates.* Washington, D.C.: U.S. Government Printing Office.

Johnston, L.D., P.M. O'Malley, and J.G. Bachman. 1987. *National Trends in Drug Use and Related Factors among American High School Students and Young Adults, 1975–1986.* Washington, D.C.: NIDA, U.S. Department of Health and Human Subjects.

Kandel, D. 1974. Inter- and intragenerational influences of adolescent marijuana use. *Journal of Social Issues* 30(2): 107–35.

———. 1982. Epidemiological and psychosocial perspectives on adolescent drug abuse. *Journal of American Academic Child Psychiatry* 21(4): 328–47.

Kaufman, E. 1980. Myth and reality in the family patterns and treatment of substance abusers. *American Journal of Drug and Alcohol Abuse* 7(3–4): 257–79.

Kaufman, E., and P. Kaufman. 1979. From a psychodynamic orientation to a structural family approach in the treatment of drug dependency. In E. Kaufman and P. Kaufman, eds. *Family Therapy of Drug and Alcohol Abuse.* Gardner Press, N.Y.

Kempler, H., and P. MacKenna 1975. Drug abusing adolescents and their families: A structural view and treatment approach. *American Journal of Orthopsychiatry* 42:223–24.

Langsley, D.G., and D.M. Kaplan. 1968. *The Treatment of Families in Crisis.* New York: Grime and Stratton.

Levy, B. 1972. Five years after: A follow-up of 50 narcotic addicts. *American Journal of Psychiatry* 7: 102–6.

Mason, P. 1958. The mother of the addict. *Psychiatric Quarterly Supplement* 32 (pt. 2): 189–99.

McKillip, G., and T.P. Petzel. 1973. Patterns and correlates of urban drug use. Paper presented at Illinois Sociological Association Annual Meeting.

Mead, D.E., and S.S. Campbell. 1972. Decision-making and interaction by families with and without a drug abusing child. *Family Process* 11: 487–98.

Mellinger, G.D., R.H. Somers, and D.I. Manheimer. 1975. Drug use research items pertaining to personality and interpersonal relations: A working paper for research investigators. In D.J. Lettieri, ed., *Predicting Adolescent Drug Abuse: A Review of Issues, Methods and Correlates.* DHEW publ. no. (ADM) 76-299, National Institute on Drug Abuse. Washington, D.C.: U.S. Government Printing Office.

Miller, J.D., and I.H. Cisin. 1979. Highlights from the national survey on drug abuse: 1979. Rockville, Md.: National Institute on Drug Abuse. U.S. Government Printing Office.

Miller, J.D., and J.D. Rittenhouse. 1980. Social learning and drug use in family dyads. In J.D. Rittenhouse, ed., *National Survey on Drug Abuse during the Seventies: A Social Analysis.* Washington, D.C.: U.S. Government Printing Office.

Newcomb, M. 1988. *Personal Communication.* Los Angeles.

Parsons, B.V., and J.F. Alexander. 1973. Short-term family intervention: A therapy outcome study. *Journal of Consulting and Clinical Psychology* 41: 195–201.

Prendergast, T., and E. Schaefer. 1974. Correlates of drinking and drunkenness among high school students. *Quarterly Journal of Studies on Alcohol* 35: 232–42.

Reilly, D.M. 1976. Family factors in the etiology and treatment of youthful drug abuse. *Family Therapy* 2: 149–71.

Scopetta, M.A., O.E. King, J. Szapocznik, et al. 1979. Ecological structural family therapy with Cuban immigrant families. Unpublished.

Smart, R., and D. Fejer. 1979. Drug use among adolescents and their parents: Closing the generation gap in mood modification. *Journal of Abnormal Psychology* 2: 153–60.

Stanton, M.D. 1978. Some outcome results and aspects of structural family therapy with drug addicts. In D. Smith, S. Anderson, M. Buxton, T. Chung, N. Gottlieb, and W. Harvey eds., *A Multicultural View of Drug Abuse: The Selected Proceedings of the National Drug Abuse Conference, 1977.* Cambridge, Mass.: Schenkman.

———. 1979. Family treatment approaches to drug abuse problems: A review. *Family Process* 18: 251–80.

———. 1980. Some overlooked aspects of the family and drug abuse. In *Drug Abuse from the Family Perspective.* DHHS Pub. No. [ADM] 80-910, Washington, D.C.: National Institute on Drug Abuse. U.S. Government Printing Office.

Streit, F., D. Halsted, and P. Pascale. 1974. Differences among youthful users and non-users of drugs based on their perceptions of parental behavior. *International Journal of Addiction* 9(5): 749–55.

Tec, N. 1971. Drugs among suburban teenagers: Basic findings. *Social Science Medicine* 5: 77–84.

Timms, M., P. Carney, and R. Stevenson. 1973. A factor analytic study of drug abuse in adolescents. *Irish Journal of Psychology* 2: 86–95.

Vaillant, G.E. 1966. A 12-year follow-up of New York narcotic addicts: Some social and psychiatric characteristics. *Archives of General Psychiatry* 15: 599–609.

Velleman, J., and T. Lawrence. 1971. Drugs in the high school: A student research report. In D.G. Wolk, ed., *Drugs and Youth.* Washington, D.C.: National Council for the Social Studies.

Wechsler, H., and D. Thum. 1973. Teenage drinking, drug use, and social correlates. *Quarterly Journal of Studies on Alcohol* 34: 1220–27.

Wellisch, D., and E. Kaufman. 1975. Family therapy. In E. Senay, V. Shorty, and H. Alksne, eds., *Developments in the Field of Drug Abuse*. Cambridge, Mass.: Schenkman.

Wesson, D.R., A.S. Carlin, K.M. Adams, and G.M. Beschner. 1977. *Polydrug Abuse*. New York: Academic Press.

Winer, L.R., J.P. Lorio, and I. Scrafford. 1974. *Effects of Treatment on Drug Abuser and Family*. Report prepared for the Special Action Office for Drug Abuse Prevention, Executive Office of the President, Washington, D.C.

Wunderlich, R.A., J. Lozes, and J. Lewis. 1974. Recidivism rates of group therapy participants and other adolescents processed by a juvenile court. *Psychotherapy: Theory, Research and Practice* 11: 243–45.

Ziegler-Driscoll, G. 1977. Family research study at Eagleville Hospital and Rehabilitation Center. *Family Process* 16: 175–89.

———. 1978. Family treatment with parent addict families. In D. Smith, S. Anderson, M. Buxton, T. Chung, N. Gottlieb, and W. Harvey eds., *A Multicultural View of Drug Abuse: The Selected Proceedings of the National Drug Abuse Conference 1977*. Cambridge, Mass.: Schenkman.

2

Treatment Needs and Treatment Services for Adolescent Drug Abusers

Alfred S. Friedman
George M. Beschner

C ompared with the heroin addiction epidemic of the 1960s and early 1970s, adolescent drug abuse today is more broadly based: it cuts across all socioeconomic strata and involves a wider array of chemical substances. It is the result of complex underlying problems inextricably bound to the psychology of adolescence, which is itself a challenge.

More than fifty thousand teenagers per year received treatment in federally sponsored treatment programs during the 1980s, according to the Client Oriented Data Acquisition process (CODAP) of the National Institute on Drug Abuse. Who were these teenagers, and what were their drug use patterns?

The Adolescent Drug Abuser

The vast majority (75.8 percent under twenty years of age) were white. A much smaller percentage of the older (twenty and over) drug clients (53.8 percent) were white. Blacks made up a much smaller percentage (11.5 percent) of the younger client group than of the older group (34.1 percent).

Recent studies also suggest that white adolescent drug abusers entering treatment are more likely than minority drug abusers to use multiple substances (Farley, Santo, and Speck 1979; Hubbard et al. 1983). In the National Youth Polydrug Study, of 2,750 clients, twelve to eighteen years of age, white clients reported using an average of 4.3 different drugs "regularly" (at least once per week), compared with 2.6 and 2.9 different drugs, on the average, for blacks and Hispanics, respectively (Farley, Santo, and Speck 1979).

The drug use patterns of young drug abusers (nineteen and under) entering treatment are considerably different from the patterns of adults (NIDA 1983a). Across ethnic/sex groups, more than half (55.1 percent) reported primary marijuana use (versus 10.6 percent for the older clients), and an additional 19.6 percent used marijuana as the secondary drug of abuse. Over a third (37.8 percent) of the young primary marijuana abusers smoked the drug one or more times daily, and 10 percent used it more than three times each day. Also, there are substantial differences in the patterns of youth drug abuse (distribution of types of "primary drug problems") across ethnic groups. For example, a much higher percentage of white adolescent clients (thirteen percent) compared with black clients (four percent) or Hispanic clients (five percent) had amphetamines as their primary drug problem, while a much lower percentage of white clients (two percent) compared with black clients (five percent) or Hispanic clients (eleven percent) had heroin or other opiates as their primary drug problem.

To understand adolescent patterns of drug use, one must go beyond the primary drugs reported. Most compulsive, dedicated users—particularly those who require treatment—are multiple drug users. Investigators studying "heavy" marijuana smokers report that the vast majority use other substances (Farley, Santo, and Speck 1979; Hubbard et al. 1983; Miller and Cisin 1983; Wish et al. 1983). Marijuana is frequently used with other drugs. For example, one of the common methods of using phencyclidine (PCP) is to sprinkle the powdered form on a marijuana cigarette and smoke it (Feldman, Agar, and Beschner 1979).

The 1982 National Household Survey findings show that most persons who use one illicit drug will also try others. Typically, persons who have a degree of experience with marijuana (used more than ten times) will become involved in the use of another illegal drug. In fact, those who use illegal drugs, other than marijuana, are likely to continue using at least three substances concurrently. Very few experienced marijuana users say that they have never combined alcohol with marijuana (Miller and Cisin 1983).

The National Youth Polydrug Study found that the average primary marijuana and alcohol users also used more than three other substances regularly. Only 9 percent of the adolescents in treatment had used a single drug (Farley, Santo, and Speck 1979).

Alcohol is the second most commonly used drug by adolescents entering drug abuse treatment programs. It was the secondary substance of abuse for 33.2 percent of the adolescent clients entering treatment during 1980 and was used by more than half (53.0 percent) of the young primary marijuana users (NIDA 1983). A comparatively small number (6.1 percent) reported alcohol as the primary drug of abuse. (This is probably because federally funded "drug" treatment programs were primarily oriented to treatment of drug abusers and some programs may have understated the extent of alcohol abuse by adolescents.)

Amphetamines are also popular among adolescents, and it appears that the use of these substances has been increasing. The percentage of clients in CODAP treatment who reported primary amphetamine abuse rose from 6.5 percent in 1978 to 10.7 percent in 1980. These findings are consistent with what has been found in the National High School Survey (Johnston, Bachman, and O'Malley 1982). Also, adolescent clients in drug treatment programs claiming cocaine as the primary drug of abuse increased from 1.1 percent to 4.1 percent (NIDA 1981).

White youth are far more likely to be primary amphetamine and barbiturate/sedative abusers than are the young clients in other ethnic groups. However, minority youth tend to be much more likely than whites to be using heroin and cocaine. Again, this may be due to availability. A relatively small percentage of young black males (3.4 percent) report that heroin or some other opiate is their primary drug of abuse. Black females (6.6 percent), Hispanic males (10.2 percent), and Hispanic females (13.3 percent) report much higher percentages of primary heroin abuse than do young white males (1.1 percent) or young white females (4.0 percent). Primary PCP abuse is more prevalent among Hispanic youth. Inhalant abuse, which involves use of a low-cost, readily available substance, is also more prevalent among Hispanic youth, particularly in the southwestern part of the United States.

In addition to drug and alcohol problems and family problems (conflict with parents, and so forth), the reasons given by adolescent clients in the National Youth Polydrug Study (N = 2,750) (Santo 1980) for applying for treatment were (in rank order): (2) school-related problems (39.5 percent); (3) legal problems/involvement in criminal justice system (35.3 percent); and (4) emotional or psychiatric problems/need for counseling, and so forth (27.7 percent). Almost a third (32.7 percent) of the adolescents surveyed had one or more previous overdose episodes; 15.9 percent had one or more previous suicide attempts; and 20.4 percent had treatment for a mental health problem on one or more occasions.

Upon admission to residential and outpatient treatment programs, adolescents were asked to identify (from a list of thirty-five items) their own personal problems (Glickman and Utada 1983). During this initial phase of treatment, most of the adolescents identified negative feelings/attitudes they have about themselves. For example, the most prevalent problems identified by adolescents in residential programs were: "hard to express feelings" (77 percent); "feeling bored" (72 percent); and "getting angry often" (58 percent). Adolescent outpatient clients, at admission, most often reported "feeling bored" (63 percent), "feeling restless" (56 percent), and "daydreaming a lot" (50 percent). Obviously, it is important for counselors to assess how adolescents, upon entering treatment, feel about themselves; to gain some impression of their self-concept; and to be prepared to engage these clients about feelings of alienation, anger, loneliness, and self-doubt.

Clearly, adolescent drug users who seek or are referred to treatment usually present a variety of problems beyond drug use per se. In any attempt to treat adolescent drug abusers, attention must be given to those underlying problems and usually to the family situation as well.

The Clinical Picture

The presenting clinical picture, at intake to treatment, includes poor school performance, lack of interest in extracurricular activities, nonstraight friends, loss of interest in or conflict with family, hostile-aggressive and resistant behavior, brushes with the law, and sometimes physical signs of being "high" or "stoned." Clients show negative feelings, alienation, anger, loneliness, and self-doubt. There is among them a fairly high rate of suicidal attempts and of crises related to drug overdoses. Counselors view their adolescent clients as presenting many complex problems, requiring different intervention strategies.

These youngsters ostensibly seek pleasure in drugs, and for a period of time the drugs may work for them, but they are often miserable underneath—they hurt. Sometimes, when a counselor gets to know them, he or she can see and hear their pain under their bravado and denial. As they struggle to achieve an identity, they frequently doubt whether they are going to make it in life.

In the early stages of treatment youngsters are usually defiant, angry, and distrustful of the adult staff. They can get through this stage, but the counselor has to work fairly long and hard to establish a relationship of trust and to get their cooperation in treatment. After engaging the adolescent client in a relationship of trust, the counselor tries to develop the experience of "being" and "staying" with the young client, of creating a holding relationship of listening and maintaining a secure treatment frame where the client can feel safe. At some point in the treatment process, the issue of the client's continuing to use drugs needs to be confronted. Also, most cases need a support system (usually the family, and sometimes a nonusing boyfriend or girlfriend, or some other caring, interested persons).

Gradually, the counselor helps the young client to express intense feelings—which may be under the surface—of fear, rage, sadness, anxiety, worry, frustration, despair, hopelessness, helplessness. Once these feelings have been expressed and are in the open, the counselor helps the adolescent to understand them, how and why they came about, and how to deal or cope with them without resorting to drugs.

Counselors agreed in a national survey of adolescent drug treatment programs (Friedman, Santo, and Hooper 1982) that the following are effective counseling approaches:

- Having an understanding and empathic attitude
- Confronting the client with his or her self-destructive and maladaptive behavior
- Providing emotional support
- Providing practical assistance in solving the client's real-life problems

These clients need to be helped to own responsibility for causing some of their own problems.

The number of counseling issues and considerations is almost unlimited, and it is difficult to identify them in any systematic way, because counseling is such a phenomenon. It is not just a method but also a skill, an art, and a personal experience that is unique for each client-counselor relationship. Any attempt to list the issues and the elements that are appropriate for the counselor's role and for the counseling process will be incomplete; nevertheless, it is important to recognize the basic elements. Here is a list of relevant drug counseling elements presented by Marks, Daroff, and Granick (1985):

1. Listening closely and intently to the client, keeping an open mind, and respecting the client's ideas and opinions.

2. Being warm, empathic, sensitive, responsive, genuine, relevantly self-disclosing toward the client, and confronting in an honest, assertive, but nonaggressive way.

3. Being reassuring regarding any doubts or fears the client may have about participating in the counseling relationship and process.

4. Encouraging and acknowledging the client's efforts to participate in the counseling process, including the efforts (*a*) to describe accurately, fully, and openly what's happening in the client's life; (*b*) to explore the client's feelings about whatever he or she is experiencing and perceiving; and (*c*) to give up self-critical and self-defeating tendencies that block the client from making progress.

5. Understanding and accepting any feelings that the client may express (including negative, distrustful, or angry feelings toward the counselor).

6. Having respect and concern for the difficult and challenging time the client is experiencing in his or her life.

7. Providing advice, guidance, and assistance in solving practice problems.

8. Presenting to the client and discussing in a calm, straightforward manner some of the options that appear to the counselor to be available to the client in regard to a given problem situation.

9. Maintaining the emotional flow of the sessions and avoiding the tendency to intellectualize.

10. Providing cognitive and attitudinal reorientation and values clarification (for example, shifting from a tendency to think in terms of labels of "good" or "bad" to planning for attitudes and behavior that will function, in the long run, for the client's life).

11. Allowing the client to be realistically dependent on the counselor, but at the same time encouraging and fostering the client's ability to become independent and autonomous.

12. Being very clear, specific, and concrete, rather than abstract, general, or vague, in talking with the client.

13. Teaching clients new communication and social coping skills via role playing and Gestalt experiences.

14. Role modeling via appropriate self-disclosure.

15. Giving the client enough time and avoiding pressuring the client to make any major decisions or major changes in his or her life.

16. Tolerating frustration as the client does not show much progress, or as the client fails or regresses after some initial efforts to change.

17. Appreciating the client's apprehensions in trying to make a significant change or improvement (such as cutting down on drug use, or giving up drugs, and trying to find a new way to cope with this loss).

18. Providing understanding and support for the loss and depression that may follow the client's efforts to give up a drug use life-style and the drug-using social peer network (friends); acknowledging the help as well as the fun and pleasure that the client has derived from using drugs in the past.

19. Acknowledging any improvement or achievement that the client makes in his or her life or in the counseling process.

There are differences of opinion and sometimes sharp controversy among professional treatment personnel about whether effective individual treatment or effective family treatment can occur while the adolescent patient is addicted or dependent on drugs, or whether abstinence must be achieved before effective treatment can take place. Many proponents of Alcoholics Anonymous (AA) and others believe that the substance abuser or addict must first take responsibility for achieving a drug-free, abstinent state. Other drug counselors and therapists believe that it is possible, although often difficult, to establish a relationship of trust and to provide support and assistance with other problems in the young client's life while the client is continuing to use drugs and alcohol; and that if this first phase of the therapy is successful it can lead gradually to the client's giving up the use of the drugs and the chemical dependency. Therapists in outpatient treatment programs obviously are more frequently faced with this type of challenge, since the residential program clients and the hospital patients do not have as ready access to drugs and alcohol as do the outpatient clients.

Edward Kaufman, a family therapist, discusses this issue in detail in chapter three of this book. He states that when the adolescent patient is physically dependent or addicted, the therapy is almost never effective if the goal is controlled drinking or controlled substance use, rather than abstinence. If the drug use is interfering with the individual's and the family's functioning, Kaufman first recommends abstinence as the initial goal; to stop substance abuse immediately by means of detoxification, and/or by means of the "one day at a time" AA approach, in order to facilitate individual rehabilitation and to restore family functioning. Since he sees the parents in such families as being quite confused by the situation, Kaufman provides structure and recommends for the initial phase of treatment the just described direct course of action, rather than a traditional form of family therapy. Kaufman also reports, however, that there are families in which the adolescent's "mild to moderate drug and alcohol abuse," without physical addiction, "can be controlled if both parents can agree on clear limits and expectations and how to enforce them."

Types of Treatment and Intervention Environments and Programs

The varied types of adolescent drug treatment resources and services that are available in many communities include the following:

1. Hotlines (emergency telephone services)
2. Hospital emergency units
3. Outpatient drug treatment programs ("drug-free" or OPDF)
4. Drug treatment units in community mental health centers (CHMCs) and psychiatric clinics
5. Nonhospital residential programs (therapeutic communities)
6. Day care, or day-school treatment centers
7. Halfway house programs
8. Hospital (inpatient) programs

Treatment Resources Available for Adolescents

Few drug treatment programs in this country are designed specifically to serve adolescents. Approximately 20.6 percent of all drug clients in treatment ($N = 173,479$) are nineteen years old and younger (NIDA 1983a). Of the 3,018 substance abuse treatment facilities in the National Drug and Alcoholism Treatment Utilization Survey in September 1982, only 155 (5.1 percent) had adolescents as their main clientele (at least 50 percent nineteen and under) (NIDA 1983b).

Most (75.2 percent) adolescents are admitted to outpatient drug-free programs (OPDF) (NIDA 1983a). These embrace a wide range of organizational types: unstructured drop-in centers, highly structured therapies (psychotherapy, family therapy) activity programs (such as stress challenge experiences and camping trips), and so on. In contrast, 49.5 percent of all clients (adolescents and adults) are treated in DFOP. Five percent of the young clients participate in day care programs, which provide more extended treatment activity than DFOP. One type of day program—offering educational services—can lead to high school certificates for dropouts from public schools.

Another 15.1 percent of adolescents enter residential programs. Compared to adolescents in DFOP, residential clients generally are (1) lower in education level; (2) more likely to have been referred to treatment by the criminal justice system; (3) more likely to have had previous treatment episodes; and (4) more likely to have been using drugs other than marijuana, such as heroin, other opiates, cocaine, hallucinogens, barbiturates, and inhalants (NIDA 1983a).

Few residential drug programs are specifically designed for adolescents, who therefore are likely to receive the same treatment as adults.

Small percentages of adolescent drug clients are treated in publicly supported inpatient (1.6 percent), prison (1.5 percent), and nonspecified programs. Methadone maintenance is generally restricted to drug abusers over age eighteen who show some evidence of physical addiction; consequently, few adolescents participate in such programs.

Many adolescents are seen for drug abuse–related problems by one or more organizations not primarily invested in drug abuse treatment, such as community mental health centers, family and child agencies, programs for court-referred juvenile delinquents, group homes, halfway houses, "alternative activity" programs, religious training programs, free clinics, family physicians, school counselors, and school-based programs. Some of these institutions, especially those used by the criminal justice system, may be unfamiliar with drug abuse and ill-equipped to treat it. Because these organizations are outside the normal drug treatment network, little is known about how many adolescents they treat or how well the adolescents fare.

Parents who decide, or are required by the school or the court, to seek professional treatment for their children have several options. A member of the clergy or family physician or school counselor may be able to provide some guidance for the family in finding an appropriate resource, since it is likely that professional help will be needed from someone who is trained to treat adolescent substance abusers. Initially, the family should seek the advice of someone who has an understanding of the overall problem and can provide information about the various treatment options that are available. Good diagnosis and a careful evaluation of the youngster are the key to selecting an appropriate approach and should be done before treatment is initiated. Substance abusers are more likely than nonabusers to be depressed, to have other emotional and psychological problems, or to have serious physical problems. These problems, in addition to family history and the youngster's social functioning, must be considered in developing a treatment plan.

If youngsters are not motivated to seek treatment and are outside the control of their parents, there are few treatment options. In extreme cases, they can be legally committed to a hospital (inpatient) facility that provides diagnostic services, detoxification treatment, and psychological counseling. In some states it is difficult to work out the involuntary commitment procedure.

In recognition of the growing need for detoxification and emergency treatment for overdoses, private hospital (inpatient) treatment programs have been started in many communities. But these programs are very expensive, costing as much as ten thousand dollars per patient per month, and therefore are available only to families with comprehensive health insurance. Some state and local governments support public inpatient treatment programs that are less expensive, but the capacity of these programs is usually limited.

Most hospital programs offer only short-term care, essentially to treat crisis situations and to diagnose medical and psychological problems. If long-term treatment is needed, the hospital will usually try to refer adolescents to less expensive outpatient, day care, or residential (nonhospital) programs.

Compared with inpatient programs, residential programs are far less costly, averaging between nine and ten thousand dollars per year. Residential programs generally provide individual and group therapy, educational classes, parent participation, confrontational meetings, recreational activities, and shared responsibility for managing the facility; they generally lack the medical, psychological, and diagnostic services offered by hospital programs.

Residential programs may not be appropriate for teens who are in treatment against their will. Most do not have closed, locked wards to prevent youngsters from running away. Many are located in remote areas to discourage escape attempts, but these locations make it difficult for parents to be involved in regular family sessions. For a number of reasons, residential programs tend to have high dropout rates (about 80 percent leave in the first few months), but those who do stay in these programs are likely to show improvement, and progress is roughly proportionate to the length of time in treatment (DeLeon and Schwartz 1984).

Day care treatment programs offer many of the same services as residential programs but without overnight accommodations. Some school systems support alternative education programs or day care programs for substance-abusing high school students. The drug treatment programs operate during school hours, serving adolescents until they are drug free and able to return to regular school classrooms. Unfortunately, only about fifty such programs have been established in the United States.

Almost all communities have outpatient drug treatment and counseling programs or community mental health centers supported by state, county, or city governments. These programs, which treat more than 80 percent of the adolescent substance abusers admitted to treatment, generally provide drug counseling services to adults and adolescents in addition to treating a broad range of psychological and behavioral problems. Outpatient clinics have very few controls and relatively little structure. Thus, patients must be highly motivated in order to benefit from the counseling provided and must make a personal commitment to attend regularly and participate actively. As in other treatment settings, family participation may be needed for treatment to be effective, and unfortunately, few adolescent outpatient programs have family therapy specialists.

Program Characteristics of Successful Outpatient Programs

The relationship to treatment outcome (as measured by reduction in drug use) of specific characteristics and elements of thirty drug-free outpatient programs for adolescents was reported in a study by Friedman and Glickman in 1986. The program, rather than individual clients, was the unit of analysis. The following characteristics of programs were found to predict the outcome criterion variable reduction in drug use to a statistically significant degree: treatment of a large number of adolescent clients; a special school for dropouts; a relatively large budget; employment of counselors or therapists having at least two years of work experience with adolescent drug abusers; provision of special services such as vocational counseling, recreational services, and birth control services; use of therapy methods such as crisis intervention, gestalt therapy, music/art therapy, and group confrontation; and perception of the program by the clients as allowing and encouraging free expression and spontaneous action.

Five percent of the young clients participate in day care programs, which provide more extended treatment activity than do outpatient clinics. One type of day program—which offers educational services—can lead to high school certificates for dropouts from public school.

Aftercare programs are based on the recognition that the treatment process should not end abruptly at discharge from a day care, inpatient, or residential program. Aftercare programs usually have professional counselors or other support persons available when problems arise, anxieties build, and peer pressure or temptation to use drugs increases. Some aftercare programs make use of peer groups to provide support during the reentry process.

These groups, consisting of other teens going through recovery, are organized and led by both professional and peer counselors. Teens often feel more comfortable talking openly to peers about their families, friends, and other relationships and also may be more receptive to feedback from their peers.

Choosing the Appropriate Type of Treatment Setting

There are different opinions on whether outpatient treatment is feasible when the young client (patient) has ready access to drugs. For those in the treatment community who believe that treatment for substance abuse should occur only in a setting where there is no access to the abusive substance, residential (nonhospital) settings and hospitals may be considered the only appropriate types of programs for adolescents who are involved in any serious degree of abuse. For such treatment personnel, outpatient sessions scheduled once or twice per week may allow too great a time interval between sessions to sustain a patient who has a tendency toward self-destructive behavior (such as overdosing or suicide) or prostitution, or even a patient who is not functioning adequately in school, in work, or in family or social relationships because of serious abuse of substances.

Comparison of Outpatient Drug-Free and Residential Programs

A national survey compared thirty-one adolescent residential programs with forty-three adolescent outpatient programs (Friedman and Utada 1983) and learned that:

> OPDF devoted more staff time to counseling and psychotherapy than did residential programs (69 versus 40 percent). OPDFs devoted more staff time to individual counseling and family counseling, and less time to group counseling, medical services, art therapy, vocational training, and IQ testing. The group counseling emphasis in residential treatment reflects the essential nature of residential programs—people who live together tend to work out their problems together.

> When asked to specify the most important attribute for a counselor of adolescent drug abuse clients, residential administrators most often selected "ability to project a positive role model," while DFOP administrators chose "natural ability and ease in relating to adolescents." "Having street savvy" and "experience as ex-drug abuser" were more important to residential than to OPDF administrators.

A greater proportion of DFOP program counselors have master's degrees or higher degrees than residential counselors (54 percent versus 29 percent)

The counselor groups in both settings reported using the reality therapy model more than any other in their counseling work. The residential counselors used "confrontation," "rap sessions," and "assertiveness therapy" more, while outpatient counselors used "long-term psychotherapy," "values clarification," and "gestalt therapy" more.

The Dual Diagnosis Factor (Comorbidity)

Some adolescent drug abusers may have serious psychiatric disorders and severe psychic symptomatology, particularly depression and personality disorders. Some even come to treatment in a confused or psychotic state that is not solely a toxic reaction to the drugs. Thus all the psychic symptomatology may not disappear with detoxification. For adult drug and alcohol abusers, a global measure of the severity of psychiatric problems at pretreatment was found by McLellan, Luborsky, Woody, O'Brien and Druley (1983) to be the single best predictor of treatment outcome, compared with five other types of problems at pretreatment: those adult abusers and addicts with relatively *severe* psychiatric symptoms showed lower levels of improvement, or improved relatively little from treatment, unless treated in a psychiatric hospital. On the other hand, abusers with *low* severity of psychiatric symptoms did quite well, regardless of what type of setting they were treated in, suggesting, therefore, that it is less cost-effective to admit the latter type of patient to a hospital. It would appear that a drug abuser with moderately severe or very severe psychiatric problems should be admitted to a hospital—unless, at least, the other types of treatment settings (outpatient, day treatment, or residential) develop a special staff well trained to treat psychiatric problems.

A Sampling of Innovative Treatment Programs for Adolescent Drug Abuse

The specific drug treatment programs for adolescents that are described briefly in this section were selected because they are unique or exceptional in some way. Obviously there are many other drug treatment programs that provide good services but could not be included here. These are not programs that use the family therapy modality as a control or as an important part of their treatment approach, as some adolescent drug treatment programs do. One of these programs, however (Straight, Inc.), temporarily places the young client with another family, away from his or her own family; another (Unitas) uses a "symbolic family" concept, by organizing its young clients into groups where the older ones assume the role of surrogate parents.

Straight, Inc.

This is a day treatment program for adolescent substance abuse clients which schedules twelve hours per day of program activity, including a modified version of AA, daily meetings, guided group interaction, and rational-emotive and reality therapy approaches. A unique feature is temporary placement of the client with the family of a client who has progressed further in the program.

Parents are required to follow a strict set of rules for the remainder of their child's involvement in the Straight program. For example, no drugs (including alcohol) are to be used by anyone in the home, and anyone visiting the home must be approved by the Straight staff. Parents are involved in therapy groups, both with other parents and with adolescents (though not their own children). The five phases of the program are as follows.

First Phase is the period immediately after the young person enters the program. It lasts for a minimum of fourteen days. The young person is working on "self." This involves developing honesty about one's past as a "druggie" and about one's "process" (thoughts and feelings). The youth lives with a more advanced person in the program, who is his "oldcomer," and is in the facility building from 9:00 A.M., Monday through Saturday, and for seven hours on Sunday.

The daily, twelve-hour program regimen (for Phases 1 and 2) is composed primarily of several large-group discussion and rap sessions of one hour's duration each, on the following topics:

Theme sessions regarding clients' behavior/activities during holidays during their previous, drug-using years

Rules sessions: learning the rules and traditions of the agency

Same-sex sessions on sexual issues

Exercise therapy, one hour

Lunch, forty-five minutes; dinner, forty-five minutes

"Fun therapy" sessions

Voting on other clients' advancement to the next phase

Review of open meeting sessions

Educational sessions (medical tapes, movies, and so forth)

Song sessions (learning a repertoire of group songs)

Second Phase is the exciting moment when the youth "comes home." Now he lives in his own home instead of the host home, and adds working on the family relationship to working on self. Family meetings are scheduled as needed or indicated. At least one such meeting is scheduled for each client, and some clients have several such meetings. This procedure is not planned as an ongoing family therapy process. Rather, families that are considered to have serious problems (such as sexual abuse), and significant treatment needs are referred out to a "consulting family psychologist."

During this phase, large, multiple-family meetings, in which both the parents and clients participate, are scheduled regularly. Some of the clients report at these meetings on their progress in the program, and the parents respond and comment. There are also separate meetings for the siblings of the clients, and these function as support groups for the clients. Also available are "rap" sessions for parents and individual counseling for family members. In addition to individual counseling sessions, a number of small peer group and large peer group sessions are scheduled for each client. These large-group sessions use both guided group interaction and group therapy methods.

During phases 1 and 2 the client is not in school. During phase 3, the client is back in school in the community, away from the Straight, Inc., facility, and is scheduled at the Straight, Inc., facility from 3:30 P.M. to 8:00 or 9:00 P.M. on weekdays, and all day on Saturday and Sunday. Most of this time is devoted to various types of group sessions and recreational group activities. Specific sessions on phase 3 are identical to phases 1 and 2 except that homework periods are granted those who have academic deficiencies.

Specific services include tutoring as required, educational evaluation, and group sessions about school problems and family problems.

Third Phase has to do with working on achievement through school, a job, or at home, while continuing to work on self and family. Some clients take part-time jobs off campus. Achievements also include written assignments called moral inventories, which are done on a daily basis, and they include responsibilities at home such as chores and respectful behavior, and responsibilities with newer clients who live in the homes of third, fourth, and fifth phasers. Work assignments at Straight include cleaning detail, helping pass out dinner trays, painting, functioning as "runners" to carry messages, helping volunteer parents, flagpole detail, accompanying phase 1 clients to the doctor or dentist as needed, and greeting visitors. This phase also represents the first time a youth faces "do drugs" peer pressure again. He has to face old friends at school and say no.

Fourth Phase is the time when the young person begins a gradual withdrawal from active involvement in the program. He comes to the building after school three weekdays and one of the two weekend days.

Fifth Phase involves only three days in the building, more personal freedom, and working on service to others—social responsibility. Fifth phasers assist the staff in working with the large group. During the Fifth Phase the client is encouraged to practice peer counseling to use the principles that he or she has learned. Out of the Fifth Phase clients, some are chosen to become staff trainees. Success in this position leads to a junior staff position, which is a paid, part-time job. The executive staff monitors the nonprofessional staff closely and continuously. There is a written procedure for withdrawal from the facility called "Withdraw"; it is instituted by the client or family.

The Door

The Door is a large outpatient facility—55,000 square feet of space that is bright and attractive, and it provides an open, warm, inviting environment that is also very functional. This very rich and impressive multimodality treatment program, which serves thousands of adolescent clients per year from the multi-ethnic population of the Lower East Side of New York City, is made up of five general components. The most central of these components is the counseling services and support activities, which include a full range of psychiatric and social services, comprehensive medical services, sex counseling, a complete educational program, and the "Learning Laboratory." The Learning Laboratory comprises remediation and tutoring in basic skills, high school equivalency and training, legal counseling services, a recreation program, vocational training workshops, creative and manual arts and crafts, life skills workshops, "alternative programs," "milieu" programs, youth awareness seminars, and a food and nutrition program. Some of the life skills workshops make use of videotape, psychodrama, creative dramatics, music, sensory awareness, creative writing, field trips, special guests, discussions, and debates. There are also yoga and martial arts programs— to provide instruction in self-defense, self-control, and "centering"—and techniques adapted from Eastern disciplines for relaxation, concentration, and problem solving. At follow-up evaluation, 43 percent of The Door's Learning Laboratory participants were involved in education or training programs, 56 percent had furthered their education, and 50 percent had decreased their drug use (Mai et al. 1980).

De La Salle Vocational School

In Bucks County, near Philadelphia, De La Salle Vocational School provides a treatment program for court-adjudicated, drug-abusing boys, fourteen to eighteen years of age, which set in a day-school treatment center that includes a vocational high school program, a counseling program, and a special "supportive life skills" program this is experience-based enrichment. Six earlier program models were adapted for the supportive life skills program:

1. Outward Bound
2. Project Alive
3. The Community Service Corps
4. Discovery Leadership Institute
5. The Parkway Program
6. The Foxfire Program

Three types of "courses" are provided:

1. Stress challenge (Outward Bound, Project Alive, and so on)
2. Service learning (day camp counselor, Operation Santa Claus, helping children, and so on)
3. Adventure learning and community-based historical-cultural (bicycle course, earth science, peoples of Philadelphia, workings of government, and so forth)

Some of the supportive skill-learning activities are conducted off campus in the Philadelphia community, and some involve travel and one- to three-week trips outside of Philadelphia.

One of the central rationales for the program is that it can help young men develop the social, affective, and intellectual support skills needed to secure and maintain employment, and can help them learn to view their community and its institutions as helpful and friendly rather than harmful and hostile.

This experience-based learning program tries to place client-students in situations that help them to understand themselves and their weaknesses and to gain confidence from their strengths as they grow in their abilities to absorb new experience and to change. Client-students are challenged to reach out and take hold of many new types of learning resources. They begin to use a wide range of information about themselves from formal and informal assessments and face-to-face interactions with staff and resource people. They get practice in planning, making decisions, and holding responsible positions.

Unitas

This is a community-based prevention and early intervention program for children and early teenagers ten to fifteen years of age, in a neighborhood that has a predominately poor Hispanic and black population. The program focuses on the personal-social and mental health needs of the children and their families, and provides support, to help them avoid or overcome inclinations toward substance use and other destructive behavior problems. The Maxwell Jones (1953, 1976) "therapeutic community" model includes the unique feature of creating "symbolic families," for which the older peer clients participate in a training program to prepare them to assume the role of parent surrogates.

All the children in the program, troubled and normal alike, are grouped into small symbolic families. The groups are made up of boys and girls living on the same street, usually eight to ten to a symbolic family. They are headed by older neighborhood teenagers, one or two to a group, who become the symbolic parents to that family. The symbolic mothers and fathers share the nurturing and disciplining role with older children in the family, who in turn care for the younger symbolic brothers and sisters. A particular street may have three or four such symbolic families.

Specific interventions of the teenagers who function as symbolic parents include the following: (1) providing exclusive parental attention on a daily basis to a troubled "son" or "daughter" by actively listening, tutoring, giving advice, encouraging, and following up therapeutic tasks; (2) taking their son or daughter for medical and dental attention as needed; and (3) reinstating truant children in school and reinforcing this through behavior modification techniques.

While many of these contacts take place informally (as, for example, a Unitas youngster chatting with his surrogate father outside his apartment building), others occur in large circle meetings held weekly during the academic year and four days a week in the summer. In these meetings, all of the symbolic families gather together into a symbolic extended family under the director's leadership. This network of symbolic families, sometimes having a total of one hundred members, helps build a feeling of *communitas* (a sense of being cared about) as well as a feeling of belonging to an extended family. The circle meetings also provide experience in developing problem-solving skills through discussion, modeling, and role playing of real-life and hypothetical situations. Other features of the program consist of play therapy, class therapy and discussion sessions, art therapy and individual counseling.

Kukulu Kumuhana

This is a cultural enrichment program in Hawaii found to be effective in treating young (ages fourteen to nineteen) inhalant abusers. The program combines education instruction, skills training, and group and individual counseling with a number of cultural activities. Six-month follow-up data showed that clients made significant gains in measures of self-esteem, psychological adjustment, and academic achievement. Even more encouraging, the evaluators found an almost total absence of inhalant use at follow-up (Winn 1981).

Channel One

One of the best known and most widely replicated youth-oriented substance abuse prevention and early intervention alternatives programs is Channel One. Its emphasis is on the process of local strategy formulation. Sponsored by the National Institute on Drug Abuse and by the Prudential and Metropolitan Life insurance companies, Channel One was derived from a local program called the Gloucester (Massachusetts) Experiment. A grass-roots effort, it involved high-risk young people in alternatives, with an emphasis on skill building in the area of hands-on work. More than one hundred Channel One projects were still operating in 1984 without federal funds, many of them with sufficient income-generating capability (through the sale of products or services) to be self-funding. The Channel One process may be instructive to program planners focusing on a public school population, since the process is so easily initiated by a catalyst person in the educational system, and because so many program activity examples have been catalogued and proved.

Outcome of Treatment for Adolescent Drug Abuse

There are relatively few reports in the research literature of systematic or controlled studies of the effects or outcome of treatment for adolescent drug abuse clients. The two best-known large-scale studies, DARP (Sells and Simpson 1979) and TOPS (Hubbard et al. 1985), reported significant reductions in drug use for adolescent clients in "drug-free" outpatient (OPDF) treatment, and less reduction for alcohol and marijuana. The OPDF treatment in the DARP study showed a slight decrease in mean frequency of marijuana use, no change in mean frequency of alcohol use, and a significant decrease in frequency of nonopioid drug use (other than marijuana and alcohol). In the OPDF subsample of the TOPS study there was a decrease in drug use except for clients seventeen years of age and younger who were in treatment for more than three months. The DARP and TOPS studies also reported significant improvement in employment and a significant degree of "satisfaction" with the treatment programs reported by the adolescent clients of the outpatient drug-free programs.

How much of the improvement reported by these two studies was due to the treatment per se and how much was due to other factors (maturation of the subjects, changes in their life situations, and so forth) is not clear, since neither of the two studies referred to above had a no-treatment control group. (Because of the ethical questions involved in deferring or denying treatment to those who apply for help, studies with no-treatment control groups, based on assignment to a waiting list, are difficult to arrange.) Szapocznik et al. (1983) reported adolescents who received four to twelve sessions of brief strategic family therapy, in addition to individual sessions, reported overall reductions in drug use and delinquent behavior at a six-month follow-up evaluation.

A follow-up study (Friedman 1989) of the clients of the Straight, Inc., program, which was described earlier in this chapter, showed the following encouraging outcomes: Only 35 percent of the clients reported using alcohol, and only 26 percent reported using marijuana during the follow-up period, compared with reports of 99 percent and 97 percent, respectively, for the period before admission to the program. There were also large reductions in the prevalence rates reported by the clients for all other types of illicit substances. Follow-up reports by parents agreed quite well with the clients' self-reports, indicating that a statistically significant decrease in the proportion of clients who were still involved in substance use at follow-up.

Statistically significant improvement at follow-up was also reported by the clients on seven of eight other selected outcome criteria (such as suicidal thoughts, physical violence, number of arrests). The majority of the clients reported that they were "satisfied" with the program (70 percent), that the program "helped" them (74 percent), and specifically that the program helped them with their relationship with their parents (69 percent).

Reports on a follow-up study of court-referred adolescent delinquent and drug-abusing student-clients in a private vocational high school with a day treatment program (Gaus and Henderson 1985) reported many statistically significant improvements and benefits: (1) improved attitudes toward school, satisfaction with and enjoyment of school; (2) an increase in positive family role tasks, and a decrease in negative family role tasks in the home; (3) a decrease in property offenses and victim offenses; and (4) a decrease in frequency of use of two of thirteen illicit substances, and in frequency of getting drunk. There was, however, relatively little change found in this study in drug use patterns overall.

Treatment tenure has been shown to be the most consistent predictor of successful outcome for residential therapeutic community (TC) programs (DeLeon and Jainchill 1986), as well as for some outpatient and day treatment programs for adolescent clients (Friedman, Glickman, and

Morrissey 1986). Sells and Simpson (1979) reported for the adolescent DARP study that time in treatment and completion of treatment were positive prognostic indicators of outcome. However, one adolescent outpatient study (Rush 1979) reported that time in treatment was negatively related to a "productivity" outcome criterion. The investigator's speculation regarding the unexpected finding was this:

> Probably some of the juveniles who have the best potential to become more productive in education and employment do not need to stay in treatment very long to achieve these particular goals. Juvenile outpatient clients who stay in treatment longer may have more severe problems and be less capable of making constructive changes in productivity. In contrast, juveniles in therapeutic communities had more serious problems on the average, and those who remained longer in the protective environment were apparently better able to restructure their lives and then become productive at discharge.

Dropping out, rather than completion or graduation, is the rule for most drug abuse treatment programs, for adolescent as well as for adult clients (DeLeon and Schwartz 1984). The method of evaluating the effectiveness of a treatment program by showing that clients who stay in treatment longer make relatively more improvement, however, has a limitation: the length of time a client stays in a treatment program and whether the client drops out of the program rather than graduating can be significantly influenced by the client's motivation, readiness, or suitability for the particular type of program at the time of admission. It is necessary to control for differences between the graduate and drop-out subgroups that might occur on these and other relevant client variables at admission (DeLeon and Jainchill 1986).

Stanton (1979) reviewed a number of treatment programs, outpatient and inpatient, that had involved families in a variety of ways in the treatment of adolescent and young adult drug patients and clients. An abbreviated (paraphrased) version of this review report by Stanton (1979) is as follows:

1. Hagglund and Pylkkanen (1974) in Scandinavia used family therapy concurrently with group and individual treatment in an inpatient unit. As therapy progressed, the family members shifted their aggression from the identified patient to others. At follow-up, 60 percent of the patients had stopped using drugs, and an additional 12 percent had decreased drug use.

2. In the "familization" therapy of Cantanzaro et al. (1973), members of the inpatient's natural family were admitted, at a particular phase of the therapy, for a period of several weeks as co-patients, with the idea that the identified patient would transfer the newly learned family relationship skills to the usual home relationships.

3. Weiland, Yarnes, and Bellows (1975) described a citywide system of

"family mediation centers" that provide short-term, crisis-oriented services to (primarily) families of polydrug abusers; techniques include improvement in communication skills, family negotiations, establishing achievable goals, and so on.

4. A "personalistic" approach to treatment, based in part upon systems and ecological concepts, was taken by Friedman (1974) in treating thirty white, working- and middle-class families. Most were polydrug users. Treatment revolved around emergent family alliances, loyalties, and conflicts and focused on creative problem solving and conflict resolution through negotiation. This ecological approach also involved the engagement of all relevant social systems, such as school, peer groups, and work setting.

5. Ziegler-Driscoll (1977) reported on a comparison of the outcome of the structural family method with two other treatment conditions, which was conducted at the Eagleville therapeutic community facility. Though this study was an early example of good research methodology for evaluating treatment outcome, it ran into a number of staff and other problems and did not finally report any significant advantage in outcome for family therapy.

6. Szapocznik et al. (1983) reported (more recently than the review by Stanton, 1979) on positive outcomes for "conjoint brief strategic family therapy" (four to twelve sessions). The types of improvement found included reductions in drug use and delinquent behavior of the client and such healthier family relationships as less blaming of the client, more appropriate distances between family members, increased family expressiveness, and better conflict resolution.

Most of these studies, plus a number of others that reported on family therapy with a relatively small number of young drug abusers, reported improvement for the identified patient in an encouraging percentage of the families treated. We agree, however, with the appraisal of these results by Stanton (1979): "Lack of control or comparison groups dictates that these findings be considered promising but tentative" (p. 138).

References

Catanzaro, R.J., V.D. Pisani, and E.R. Kennedy. 1973. Familization therapy: An alternative to traditional mental health care. *Diseases of the Nervous System* 34: 212–18.

DeLeon, G., and N. Jainchill. 1986. Circumstance, motivation, readiness and suitability as correlates of treatment tenure. *Journal of Psychoactive Drugs* 18(3): 203–8.

DeLeon, G., and S. Schwartz. 1984. Therapeutic communities: What are the retention rates? *American Journal of Drug and Alcohol Abuse* 10: 267–84.

Farley, E., Y. Santo, and D. Speck. 1979. Multiple drug-abuse patterns of youth drug abuse. In G.M. Beschner and A.S. Friedman eds., *Youth Drug Abuse: Problems, Issues and Treatment*. Lexington, Mass.: Lexington Books.

Feldman, H.W., M.H. Agar, and G.M. Beschner. 1979. *Angel Dust: An Ethnographic Study of PCP Users*. Lexington, Mass.: Lexington Books.

Friedman, A.S. and N.W. Glickman. 1986. Program characteristics for successful treatment of adolescent drug abuse. *The Journal of Nervous and Mental Disease* 174(11): 669–79.

Friedman, A.S., N.W. Glickman, and M.R. Morrissey. 1986. Prediction to successful outcome by client characteristics and retention in treatment in adolescent drug treatment programs: A large-scale cross-validation study. *Journal of Drug Education* 16(2): 149–65.

Friedman, A.S., R. Schwartz, and A. Utada. 1990. (in press). Outcome of a unique youth drug abuse program: A follow-up study of clients of the Straight, Inc. *Journal of Substance Abuse Treatment* 6.

Friedman, A.S., Y. Santo, and E. Hooper. 1982. *Characteristics of Clients and Staff of Residential and Outpatient Adolescent Treatment Facilities*. Report submitted to the National Institute on Drug Abuse, Rockville, Md.

Friedman, A.S., and A. Utada. High school drug use. 1983. *Clinical Research Notes*, National Institute on Drug Abuse.

Friedman, P.H. 1974. Family system and ecological approach to youthful drug abuse. *Family Therapy* 1: 63–78.

Gaus, S., and G. Henderson. 1985. Supportive life skills program for court-committed adolescent substance abusers. In A.S. Friedman and G.M. Beschner, eds., *Treatment Services for Adolescent Substance Abusers*. Rockville, Md.: National Institute on Drug Abuse, DHHS publ. no. (ADM) 85-1342.

Glickman, N., and A. Utada. August 1983. *Characteristics of Drug Users in Urban Public High Schools*. Project report to National Institute on Drug Abuse under Grant No. H81 DA 01657, Rockville, Md.

Hagglund, T., and K. Pylkkanen. 1974. Psychotherapy of drug-using adolescents as inpatients and outpatients in a hospital care unit. *Psychiatric Fenn*, 249–56.

Hubbard, R.L., E.R. Cavanaugh, S.G. Craddock, R.M. Bray, and J.V. Rachal. 1985. Characteristics, behaviors, and outcomes for youth in the TOPS Study. In A.S. Friedman and G.M.Beschner, eds., *Treatment Services for Adolescent Substance Abusers*. Rockville, Md.: National Institute on Drug Abuse, DHHS publ. no. (ADM) 85-1342.

Hubbard, R.L., E.R. Cavanaugh, S.G. Graddock, and J.V. Rachal. 1983. *Characteristics, Behaviors and Outcomes for Youth in TOPS Study*. Report submitted to NIDA, Contract No. 271-79-3611. Research Triangle Park, N.C.: Research Triangle Institute.

Johnston, L.D., J.G. Bachman, and P.M. O'Malley. 1982. *Student Drug Use, Attitudes, and Beliefs, National Trends, 1975–1982*. University of Michigan, Institute for Social Research, Rockville, Md.: National Institute on Drug Abuse, U.S. Department of Health and Human Services.

Jones, M. *Maturation of the Therapeutic Community: An Organic Approach to Health and Mental Health* (New York: Human Sciences Press, 1976).

Jones, M. 1953. *The Therapeutic Community* (New York: Basic Books, 1953).

McLellan, A.T., G.E. Woody, L. Luborsky, C.P. O'Brien, and K.A. Druley. 1983. Predicting response to alcohol and drug abuse treatments. *Archives of General Psychiatry*, 40: 620–25.

Mai, L., S. Pedrick, and M. Greene. 1980. *The Learning Laboratory, Treatment Research Monograph*. DHHS Publ. No. (ADM) 80-928 (Rockville, Md.: National Institute on Drug Abuse).

Marks, S.J., L.H. Daroff, and S. Granick. 1985. Basic individual counseling for drug abusers. In A.S. Friedman and G.M. Beschner, eds., *Treatment Services for Adolescent Substance ABusers*. Rockville, Md.: National Institute on Drug Abuse, DHHS publ. no. (ADM) 85-1342.

Miller, J.D., and I. Cisin. 1983. *Highlights from the National Survey on Drug Abuse, 1982*. Rockville, Md.: National Institute on Drug Abuse, DHHS publ. no. (ADM) 83-1277.

National Institute on Drug Abuse. 1983a. *Data from the Client Oriented Data Acquisition Process (CODAP)* Series E, No. 23 (Rockville, Md.: U.S. Government Printing Office, Department of Health and Human Services).

National Institute on Drug Abuse. 1983b. *Main findings for Drug Abuse Treatment Units: Data from the National Drug and Alcoholism Treatment Utilization Survey (NDATUS)* (Rockville, Md.: U.S. Government Printing Office, Department of Health and Human Services).

Rush, T.V. 1979. Predicting treatment outcomes for juvenile and young-adult clients in the Pennsylvania substance-abuse system. In G.M. Beschner and A.S. Friedman, eds., *Youth Drug Abuse: Problems, Issues and Treatment*. Lexington, Mass.: Lexington Books.

Sells, S.B., and D.D. Simpson. 1979. Evaluation of treatment outcome for youths in the Drug Abuse Reporting Program (DARP): A follow-up study. In G.M. Beschner and A.S. Friedman, eds., *Youth Drug Abuse: Problems, Issues, and Treatment*. Lexington, Mass.: Lexington Books.

Stanton, M.D. 1979. Family treatment approaches to drug abuse problems: A review. *Family Process* 18: 251–80.

Szapocznik, J., W.M. Kurtines, F. Foote, A. Perez-Vidal, and O. Hervis. 1983. Conjoint versus one person family therapy: Some evidence for the effectiveness of conducting family therapy through one person. *Journal of Consulting Clinical Psychology* 51: 881–89.

Wieland, W.F., A.L. Yarnes, and B.L. Bellows. 1975. Family mediation centers: A contribution to drug abuse prevention. In E. Senay, V. Shorty, and H. Alksne, eds., *Developments in the Field of Drug Abuse*. Cambridge, Mass.: Schenkman.

Ziegler-Driscoll, G. 1977. Family research study at Eagleville Hospital and Rehabilitation Center. *Family Process* 16: 175–89.

adolescents. The most common finding in the families of adolescent substance abusers is parents who are themselves substance abusers, specifically alcoholic fathers and prescription drug–abusing mothers. Parental abuse of drugs and alcohol is a much more important determinant of adolescent abuse than parental attitude toward the child's drug and alcohol use (Kandel et al. 1978). Even parents who use minor tranquilizers in prescribed doses have a greater incidence of drug- and alcohol-abusing adolescents (Kandel et al. 1978). Parental as well as adolescent smoking also predisposes adolescents to drug and alcohol abuse. Alcohol- and drug-abusing siblings also statistically predispose other siblings to substance abuse although it may at times spare them through the family dynamics described above. Parental mental illness, divorce, separation, and frequent moves (Gibbs 1982) also predispose to adolescent substance abuse. Another predisposing factor is birth trauma (Gibbs 1982), perhaps because it leads to diminished coping skills and the need for drugs as compensation.

In general, a traditional family structure insulates the adolescent from drug abuse (Blum 1972). Thus, in a family where there are greater degrees of parental control, a high premium on achieving, high expectations and structured, shared parent/child activities, there is a lower likelihood of substance abuse (Brook et al. 1978). However, if any of these attitudes are overdone and excessive, then the converse may be true, and these overconcerned attitudes may lead to or perpetuate substance abuse. The key to determining if these traditional values are overdone is the adolescent's response. If the child vigorously and repeatedly defies parental controls, is overwhelmed by expectations, and avoids activities, then the parents' escalating but ineffective demands may lead to drug abuse or secondarily be associated with it (Brook et al. 1978).

Family Factors That Prevent Adolescent Substance Abuse

A healthy family system will prevent adolescent substance abuse even in the face of heavy peer pressure to use and abuse drugs. As warm and mutual family ties diminish, the adolescent becomes more vulnerable to peer pressure. The key to healthy family functioning is the family's ability to adapt flexibly to different stresses with different but effective coping mechanisms. Thus, extreme closeness is necessary when children are small, but as they enter adolescence, the family must permit them to become autonomous without imposing excessive control and guilt. The healthy family requires a balance in the following processes: assertiveness, control, discipline, negotiation, roles, rules, and system feedback (Olson, Sprenkle, and Russell 1979). A family should be able to adapt not only to unexpected stresses in the life cycle, but to unanticipated stresses such as physical illness, accidents, job loss, relocations, deaths of family members, divorce, inclusion of new members (including stepfamilies), and external catastrophes.

General Principles in the Family Therapy of Adolescent Substance Abusers

Many of the techniques used in the family therapy of adolescent substance abusers are identical with those used in other adolescent disorders. My personal approach is a synthesis of six basic approaches to family therapy: psychodynamic, systems, structural, communications, experiential, and behavioral. The six approaches have borrowed greatly from one another to a point of substantial integration; however, there are discrete differences that have at times led to conflict between approaches. My major approach is a structural one which incorporates the other techniques. It is my impression that many different styles or systems of family therapy can be successful with adolescent substance abusers if the therapist understands substance abuse, can recognize typical patterns (described previously) and is cognizant of several basic "rules of thumb" in regard to the treatment of this group.

Basic Rules of Thumb in Treatment

Confused families of adolescent substance abusers need structure and guidance. Too many alternatives only confuse them. Simple, direct courses of action are most helpful.

A critical general principle deals with establishing a system for enabling the substance abuser to become free of abuse chemicals to a point where family therapy can take place effectively. The specific methods employed to achieve this vary according to the types of chemicals used and the extent of use, abuse, and dependence.

If a drug is interfering with family functioning but there are no signs of dependence, I will suggest abstinence as the goal that will best restore family functioning and facilitate individual rehabilitation.

My approach is to contract for abstinence, utilizing the "one day at a time" approach of Alcoholics Anonymous. If the IP is or has been physically dependent, then I will inform the family that therapy is generally quite successful when members work toward abstinence, but it almost never works (with me as the therapist) if controlled drinking or substance use is their goal. One problem with the approach of controlled drinking or substance use is that the individuals cannot take advantage of AA or NA (Narcotics Anonymous) as a support group while they are using any abusable substances.

Many adolescents are notable exceptions to this rule, which has been developed with more long-term substance abusers. Some adolescents may use substances in a peer-appropriate way without any impairment of function. In these families, the major problem may be the parents' overreaction or scapegoating. Here, the therapists' approach may need to go in quite the opposite direction from that described above; e.g., to normalize this level of substance use and join with the family sufficiently to focus on other problems. Thus, the therapeutic contract made in the beginning of treatment should focus on how the family will deal with substance abuse. Often, mild to moderate drug and alcohol abuse can be controlled if both parents can agree on clear limits and expectations and how to enforce them. However, if the substance abuser's intake is so severe that he or she is unable to attend sessions without being under the influence, if functioning is severely impaired, if there is substance-related violence, and/or if there is physical dependence on alcohol, narcotics, or sedatives, then the first priority in treatment is to stop substance abuse immediately. My first goal therefore is to persuade the family to pull together to initiate detoxification or at least some measure to achieve temporary abstinence. Generally, this is best done in a hospital and, if the abuse pattern is severe, I will require this in the first session or very early in the therapy.

If the substance abuse is only moderately severe or intermittent, and without physical dependence, such as binge alcoholism or weekend cocaine abuse, then the family is offered alternative measures to initiate this temporary substance-free state. I insist, however, that the family adopt some system that will enable them to continue to stay free of abuse substances such as teen-oriented AA groups and Al-anon for the rest of the family. Some moderate substance abusers who are resistant to self-help groups may find a system that helps them stay off of drugs through involvement in religion or dedication to a sports program. Even adolescent substance abusers who are not drug or alcohol dependent may benefit from hospitalization in a specialized drug-dependency program. Such programs may cool down high-conflict-level family systems, immerse the IP and family in educational programs as well as multiple therapeutic modalities, and permit establishment of a therapeutic alliance with the IP. For some severely dysfunctional families, long-term residential treatment such as that utilized in Phoenix House in New York City, Pride House in Los Angeles, or a specialized long-term hospital unit may be necessary. Most families will not accept this until other methods have failed. In order to accomplish this, a therapist must maintain long-term ties with the family, even through multiple treatment failures. On the other hand, it may be more helpful to terminate treatment if the substance abuser continues to abuse chemicals rather than continue treatment, which allows the family the pretense that they are changing when actually they are not. This excludes temporary "slips" into substance abuse, which are an expected part of the treatment. Treatment should not be terminated for these slips but may best be ended if the family does not adopt any workable system for enforcing abstinence.

When I have properly joined with such families and they truly believe that I am terminating in their best interest, they invariably return to treatment a few months or a few years later, ready and willing to commit to abstinence.

With a commitment and a system to achieve abstinence, the family therapy of formerly dependent substance abusers can take place. If the substance abuse is not so severe, then the family approach is very similar to that used with other acting-out adolescents. Thus, my method of treatment of adolescent substance abuse is based on a fusion of two approaches: restructuring the maladaptive aspects of the family system and establishing a method for controlling or eliminating substance abuse. This method is described in the following case examples:

A family entered treatment because Milt, age 16, and his brother, Doug, age 17, were arrested together for smoking marijuana in a car and treatment was a part of their probation. I invited the entire family to the first session in order to understand and work with the whole system. Thus, mother, 37, father, 37, sister, Carol, 18, and brother, Jimmy, 5, also attended. The teenagers' pot smoking was symptomatic of overall family and individual dysfunction. Mother had been in psychotherapy for a year for a weight problem and difficulties in relating to others. She was taking amphetamines for weight reduction and had been on them for an extended period of time. Father was a moderately successful small businessman who had difficulty asking for money that was owed to him, leading to frequent family financial crises. Carol was employed as a clerk and was on the verge of moving out of the house. Doug was described as having a personality change that was related to marijuana and admitted to smoking up to twelve joints a week, including smoking during school hours. He had become passive and irritable but generally responded to structure. Milt was much more assertive and had a very lucrative weekend job. He would involve the family in endless debates whenever they attempted to set limits for him. Jimmy had asthma and slept in his parents' bedroom. Doug and Milt had signed a probation contract in which they agreed not to be out after curfew and to abstain totally from alcohol and drugs. Dad generally let Mom take responsibility for every aspect of household and parental decision making. When Mom failed, Dad expressed extreme rage and prescribed rigid prohibitions that he later failed to enforce. One solution that Dad had tried in the past was to have the boys work in his business, but this generally failed because of their defiance and his inconsistency in setting limits. Although mother had most of the power in the family, she felt controlled by father.

I asked the parents to agree in this first session to establish clear limits about marijuana smoking. They came up with the following limits on their own: if they determined the boys were smoking pot (and that judgment was to be strictly up to them), then they were to work for five days without pay and be placed on restriction for one week. If they were caught a second time, the penalty would be doubled, and if a third offense occurred, they would be asked to move out. They were also asked to plan one meal a week where they would all eat together.

The family arrived for their second session with a suitcase full of Jimmy's toys and this helped focus that session on how the family interacts around the youngest child. Jimmy's sleeping in the parents' bedroom was focused on as a way of keeping the parents apart, and the first in a series of tasks to move him into Carol's soon to be vacated room was assigned, e.g., that they begin to talk about his moving out of their bedroom. The family was seen as they generally function when they were asked to deal with getting Jimmy's toys packed with fifteen minutes left in the session. The older siblings all put him down and said he could never do it himself. Mother defended him but father began to put the toys back himself. Dad was asked to support Mom in requiring that Jimmy do it himself and that neither parent do the job for him or leave it up to Mom. Jimmy's getting in between his parents and interfering with their closeness had to be dealt with, as well as how they undermined each other. If they could learn to function together to deal with Jimmy and reestablish their own intimacy, then they could handle their teenagers better. The teenagers were also asked to limit their parenting of Jimmy and to leave these functions to his natural parents.

It required two months of gradual practical steps, such as choosing and hanging wallpaper, to move Jimmy out of the parental bedroom and into his own room. During the exploration of these practical steps, many emotional issues between the parents were also explored, and they began to spend what they termed "quality time" together. Once the parents were able to function as a team sexually, as well as in decision making, the teenagers' marijuana problems abated substantially.

The family functioned well for over a year after the termination of their initial course of therapy, but returned when they learned that Milt was again smoking marijuana and the daughter was asking to come back home. At this point their functioning was at a sufficiently high level for them to agree readily that the daughter was not to come home because "she regresses and pulls the whole family back." They were also able to establish clear guidelines for Milt, who was now 17½, as to their expectations, and to state firmly that if he did not follow them he would be requested to leave the house even if he was in college and functioning well. I supported their position, even though Milt's use of marijuana at this time was apparently not interfering with his functioning. This was because both parents were clearly together on this issue, and because parents have the right to place limits on the drug and alcohol use of children living in their own home even after the age of eighteen.

In this case example, substance abuse was relatively mild and the situation could be resolved by direct structural approaches including strengthening the spousal bond, removing Jimmy from between his parents and from his overinvolvement with mother, strengthening Dad's confidence, facilitating Carol's moving out and staying out, and some normalizing of the other boys' behavior.

When substance abuse is more severe than in the above case, all early efforts in family intervention are directed toward cessation of substance abuse as a prerequisite for family therapy. A recent case in which the adolescent was addicted to heroin and his mother was directly and indirectly providing the money for his drugs is illustrative of the need for the therapist to take a much "harder line" about substance abuse early in the therapy.

The family consisted of Tom, age nineteen, his wife, Cora, age nineteen, their one-year-old son, John, and Tom's family of origin. The present household included Tom's family and the following members of his family of origin: brother Mel, age seventeen, Mom, a 54-year-old registered nurse, and Dad, a 56-year-old engineer and rodeo afficionado. Julie, a thirty-year-old sister who was living in the Midwest, joined us three weeks later for a pivotal session. Tom and Cora were both on methadone maintenance since the age of eighteen and both had used heroin since fourteen and been addicted for over two years. They had a very lucrative job in which they were given a daily percentage of the money they raised for a charity. Tom had difficulty with the ready, daily access of money and fell behind in the amount of money he was to turn back to the company because he was spending huge sums of cash to inject sufficient heroin to overcome his methadone blockade. Cora would argue with him about his wasting the money unless he shared his heroin with her, which would quiet her protests. Because of the money spent on heroin, Tom and Cora were unable to pay the fees of their private methadone program and were "borrowing" from Tom's Mom to pay their weekly fees. Mom had been holding Tom's money for him but he still managed to withhold enough to buy heroin. He had also stolen goods from everyone in the family and pawned them. Mom would then pay off the pawnbroker and return the goods to the household. Mom's protectiveness of Tom caused constant conflict between her and Dad, and reinforced their distance. Dad repeatedly threatened to kick Tom out but couldn't enforce it because of Mom's fears that Tom would die if he were outside of the family.

The therapist pointed out to Mom that her overprotectiveness keeps Tom an infant while her constant concern with Tom keeps her apart from her husband. She responded with, "I can't kick him out; what else can I do?" I suggested that a simple answer was to ask her husband for help, but she was not ready to do this yet because they had become so used to being polarized. Mom replied with, "I could send him to Phoenix House." I suggested that we evaluate the situation further and that in order to do that, I would have a session with Tom, Cora, and John, an individual session with Tom (to join with him and work toward his being an ally in his own individuation), and a family session with Julie when she returned home for Christmas. (Christmas week is often a time to hold a family session which includes significant members who have left the household.) I also assigned Mom and Dad the task of going out on a date the next time Tom got high on heroin. In the session with Tom, Cora, and John, Cora tended to manage and deal with John, leaving Tom on the periphery. They revealed one of the typical patterns in co-addicted pairs. Cora would never initiate using heroin on her own but would only use it when Tom provided it. Tom was able to state that he knew his mother would always bail him out if he got into trouble and this was one reason why he felt he could use heroin in safety. They also stated that all of their peer relationships were with fellow heroin addicts and that they felt this contributed to their problems. They were given a task to spend one evening with a drug-free couple and to keep in mind that this would be very frightening to them.

In the individual session with Tom, we explored his fears of success and independence as well as his guilt about manipulating his mother. We explored his feelings about Julie who had been seriously disfigured facially by a gunshot wound when Tom was nine. She had received a great deal of attention around the wounding and ten years of surgery to correct it. His mother felt guilty about the attention she gave Julie and tried to make it up to Tom. Tom denied that he was directly upset about Julie, stating that he did not start to use drugs until three years later, at age twelve.

The session which Julie attended was very poignant because of a powerful presence, despite her facial disfigurement and inability to speak. She communicated in writing. Her notes began with, "I know what you're going through" and "I don't have anyone who can help me by saying I've been there." She wrote to her mother, "You're killing Tom and keeping me alive." She suggested that the family establish a written agreement of ground rules that would permit them all to live together without conflict. When attempts at this failed, she wrote her last note, "I don't think Tom can get out of his habit alone. I think he needs a residential program." The family readily agreed that Tom would enter Phoenix House and Tom agreed to go. I reinforced this by stating that I was pleased they had all agreed to this and that no further therapy was necessary at this time, but that I would appreciate a call about how Tom was doing at Phoenix House and how the family was doing in general.

Four months later Tom called requesting an individual session. He informed me that he did not go to Phoenix House because it was too much like jail. He had quit his job which had solved the problem of having money available for heroin. His mother was now paying for his and Cora's new methadone program. However, he was now devoting himself to golf which was a great pastime of his father's. Thus, they were playing golf together at least three times weekly which was bringing them closer than they'd ever been. Unfortunately, he had pawned his golf clubs a few days before to get money to buy heroin. This permitted us to focus on his self-destructiveness as well as his fear of success.

Since Tom had a "system" for staying off of heroin, i.e., methadone maintenance, and he and his family expressed motivation for change, I agreed to resume outpatient treatment even though he had recently used heroin. I stated to the family that I had gone too fast the last time and that they were not ready to part with Tom because Mom and Dad needed him around to occupy their relationship and keep them apart. They readily agreed with the first part of the paradox, seemingly not hearing the interpretation of the need for the IP to continue his symptomatic behavior. I also suggested that both parents join Al-anon to help them learn to become less involved with Tom, as well as to have an activity that would unite them. Since that time Tom has remained free of heroin for two months and has registered for college. Cora has a job and infuriated the family by stating she wanted to buy an expensive ring before she paid off her debts. She is five months pregnant and a new child will reinforce her and Tom's dependency on the family. Tom got his own golf clubs out of hock with money earned from odd jobs. He began to explore his intense fear of his father and how the fear disappeared when he and his father played golf together.

Tom's stated goal, as well as that of every other family member, is for him and his own nuclear family to leave the household and establish one of their own. In order to achieve this, the tie between Tom and his mother will have to be further loosened. Tom's new relationship with his father is an important step in that direction. However, his mutual tie with Cora will have to be strengthened, as with the ties between his mother and father. Tom and Cora's getting off of methadone is a long-term goal of this therapy but neither expresses any motivation for detoxification at this point.

Although it is unusual for an adolescent to have a drug-abuse history as severe as Tom's, the description of his mother's overinvolvement is not at all atypical, nor is the triangulation between mother and father. Sedative-tranquilizer dependence, severe cocaine abuse, or alcohol dependence can be equally dangerous for the adolescent and devastating for the family. In this case, outpatient treatment was initially terminated to reinforce the family's decision for long-term residential treatment as the only system Tom could utilize to stop using heroin. However, without Julie's continual presence, the family was unable to implement that decision. Four months after that termination, Tom and his family returned to treatment, this time at Tom's urging. With some realignment of the family, particularly Tom's alliance with father, family, individual, and couple therapy had a better chance of being successful this time.

The initial intervention would have been more successful if I had available a multifamily group, which would support maternal letting go. However, unlike during most of my work with the families of substance abusers, such a group was not available to me at the time this family participated in treatment. Without this type of support, I worked paradoxically with the family's need to hold on to Tom. Cora's pregnancy certainly reinforces Tom's need to stay at home for financial and convenience reasons and offers their children more stable parenting through the grandparents.

These case examples illustrate that the actual family therapy of adolescent abusers is not appreciably different from the family therapy of other types of adolescent problems. There are some modifications of specific family therapy techniques that can be very helpful in working with these types of problems. The contract, which is made at the end of the first or second session, should deal with the substance abuse and how the family should react to it. This should include the system used by the IP to detoxify from substances as well as to maintain abstinence. The family's involvement in support groups such as Al-anon or a multifamily group should also be made a part of the contract. The family should also be coached to disengage from their reactivity to substance use or paradoxically to monitor it more closely as part of the contract. Involving all siblings in treatment should also be a part of the contract.

Joining with all family members may be too difficult for one therapist. I have often found it necessary to utilize a co-therapist who treats the adolescent individually and maintains an adolescent-advocate position in the family sessions. This enables me to join better with parents and facilitate their setting limits. In other cases, the adolescent is begging for limits underneath his bravado and a single therapist can easily join with the adolescent as well as the parental system.

Marking boundaries is very important with these families. After I have observed the adolescent's interfering role in parental decision-making during an actualization or enactment, I will work with the parents to restrict the adolescent from such interference while respecting the adolescent's right to his or her privacy. I will often ask the adolescent subsystem to leave the room while parents are agreeing on limits, in order to underline the importance of making such decisions without the adolescent being present or influencing his or her parents. Once decisions have been made, the adolescent can then participate in negotiations as long as an intergenerational coalition or triangle can be avoided. It is also important that all siblings not be treated exactly the same or bumped into categories regardless of whether these are "actor-outer," "good child," "bad child," "drug abuser," "alcoholic," or the like.

One situation which occurs frequently in these families is parental substance abuse, which may be more extensive than that of the adolescent. However, if the adolescent is clearly labeled "the problem" by the family, then it is very important that the family be given some relief from the adolescent's behavior and/or substance abuse before the drug/alcohol or behavior problems of the parent(s) are addressed. On the other hand, if the adolescent's problems are only a means to get the more seriously disturbed parent into the session and the family clearly labels the parents' problems as major, then primary parental difficulties can be addressed and even made a part of the initial treatment contract. In the former case, once there is some relief for the family from the adolescent's problems, then the parental substance abuse and other problems can be dealt with. When the parents themselves are dependent on drugs or alcohol, it is very difficult for them to acquire appropriate parenting skills; thus, their finding a system for abstaining becomes a very high priority in the treatment.

The therapist must become knowledgeable about the pharmacologic effects of drugs and alcohol, particularly about the dependence process and long- and short-term effects of usage. Frequently, educating the family and identified patient can be extremely helpful if not essential to the family in putting the substance abuse into proper perspective, whether they be exaggerating or minimizing these effects.

These above therapeutic techniques are examples of how structural family therapy can be modified to be implemented with the families of adolescent substance abusers. If the basic principles of working with this group of patients and their families and these modifications are kept in mind, the family therapist can readily adopt his or her own techniques to working successfully with this challenging but workable group of patients.

References

Attardo, N. 1965. Psychodynamic factors in the mother-child relationship in adolescent drug addiction: A comparison of mothers of schizophrenics and mothers of normal adolescent sons. *Psychotherapy and Psychosomatics* 13: 249–55.

Blum, R.H. 1972. *Horatio Alger's Children*. San Francisco: Jossey-Bass.

Brook, J.S., I.F. Lukoff, and M. Whiteman. 1978. Family socialization and adolescent personality and their association with adolescent use of marijuana. *Journal of Genetic Psychology* 133: 261–71.

Cleveland, M. 1981. Families and adolescent drug abuse: Structural analysis of children's roles. *Family Process* 20: 295–304.

Fort, J.P. 1954. Heroin addiction among young men. *Psychiatry* 17: 251–59.

Gibbs, J.T. 1982. Psychosocial factors related to substance abuse among delinquent females. *American Journal of Orthopsychiatry* 52(2): 261–71.

Hendin, H., A. Pollinger, R. Ulman, and A.C. Carr. 1981. Adolescent marijuana abusers and their families. *NIDA Research Monograph*, no. 40, 17–25.

Kandel, D.B., R.C. Kessler, and R.S. Margulies. 1978. Antecedents of adolescents, initiation into stages of drug use: A developmental analysis. *Journal of Youth & Adolescence* 7(1): 13–14.

Kaufman, E. 1976. The abuse of multiple drugs: Psychological hypotheses, treatment considerations. *American Journal of Drug and Alcohol Abuse* 3: 293–304.

———. 1977. Family structures of narcotic addicts. *International Journal of the Addictions* 12: 106–8.

Kaufman, E., and P. Kaufmann. 1979. From a psychodynamic to a structural understanding of drug dependency. In E. Kaufman and P. Kaufmann, eds., *The Family Therapy of Drug and Alcohol Abuse*. New York: Gardner Press.

Olson, D.H., D.H. Sprenkle, and C.S. Russell. 1979. Circumplex model of marital and family systems: 1. Cohesion and adaptability dimensions, family types, and clinical applications. *Family Process* 18: 3–28.

Reilly, D.M. 1976. Family factors in the etiology and treatment of youthful drug abuse. *Family Therapy* 2: 149–71.

4

The Family Scene When a Teenager Uses Drugs: Case Vignettes and the Role of Family Therapy

Arlene Utada
Alfred S. Friedman

T he purpose of this chapter is to show the effect on a family when an adolescent becomes a drug abuser, to elucidate how the parents may have been implicated in the development of the problem, and to present the rationale for family therapy. One of the methods utilized in the chapter is the presentation of three case vignettes about actual families in which drug abuse problems occurred.

Each year hundreds of thousands of families in the United States are challenged, distressed, and sometimes torn apart by a teenage family member using drugs. Parents, adolescent substance abusers, and the other family members are caught in a desperate situation that may escalate into a major crisis in the life of the family. Many of these families may be confronted with recurring crises over a period of years. What is perhaps most disconcerting about this situation is the likelihood that the parents themselves unwittingly contributed to the development or the escalation of the drug problem.

Although the fact that there are many harmful illicit drugs readily available to young people makes possible the drug abuse problem, the problem cannot be explained solely by this fact. One might say that even with the availability of the substances young people should be more enlightened or exercise more self-control or, at the least, should have been frightened away or deterred from use of these harmful substances. There is also the role of the family to consider in the development of this problem: Why have the parents not been effective in raising children or adolescents so that they do not become involved in substance abuse? The family has a lot at stake; it is the entity that often is hardest hit by the drug abuse problem—sometimes even devastated—when it happens to an adolescent member of the family. Some parents may actually experience more suffering

Reprinted from G. Beschner and A.S. Friedman, eds., *Teen Drug Use*. Lexington, Mass.: Lexington Books, 1985.

from the youngster's involvement in drug abuse than the adolescent abuser experiences himself or herself.

The parents unfortunately are in the front-line trenches in this battle against drug abuse and usually have the main responsibility for dealing with and solving the problem. Why this is so needs further explanation. The parents may feel that they didn't create this problem but that it was imposed upon them: if it were not for the fact that their youngster came under the influence of the wrong friends; if it were not for the government's failure to adequately control the large-scale trafficking in drugs; if it were not for a deterioration in the social and moral values of our society . . . On the other hand, if the problem is explained by the fact that this has become a drug-using society, and that using drugs has become a rite of passage for all adolescents, why have half the adolescents not tried drugs at all, and the majority who have experimented with drugs have only used them infrequently or occasionally at a party? Why have only approximately 10 percent become so seriously and heavily involved in regular substance abuse or addiction that it has become the central theme in their lives, and has negatively affected their development and careers, and the lives of their families? It is reasonable that the effort to understand the problems of this 10 percent should include not only the study of the adolescents as individuals, but the study of the families, and certain situations and conditions in the histories of these families, and the histories of the particular child growing up in these families.

Thus, blaming the peer group, or blaming the larger society, the schools, the churches, or the drug enforcement agencies, is not very realistic. No one or any single cause is to blame; not the parents, not the grandparents, not the peer group. All are caught up together in a complicated situation and the solutions are not easy to find. In many cases the ways that the parents have contributed to the development of the problem are subtle and hard to see. Was it just that they did not listen to the youngster in an understanding enough way, or they didn't pay enough attention, or were rejecting, or too strict or controlling, or not firm enough, or too permissive, or too indulgent? The parents need the help of someone not directly and emotionally involved in the family situation, who can perceive objectively what happens in the family, is skilled and wise and experienced, will listen with understanding and discernment, and will intervene in constructive ways that the family can accept and respond to.

Even relying on a psychiatrist or on the expertise of a specialized drug treatment program to solve the problem is not sufficient. The family almost inevitably has to be actively involved in the solution, since it may well have been part of the problem. The problem needs to be understood within the framework of the family, and in terms of the dynamics of the system of relationships and interactions that have developed in the family. Every family is unique in regard to the constellation of interrelationships that have developed during its history, and these relationships operate at more than one level. For example, one family can be described as having "pseudo-mutual" relationships: the family members appear on the surface to get along with each other, to be loyal and unified, to defend each other against outsiders; but this is partly a facade kept up at the price of suppression of resentments and hostilities felt toward each other. Another family may be openly argumentative and conflictual, but with deeper ties of affection and love than the first family. Given this and even greater degrees of complexity of each family's system, it requires time and understanding on the part of a skilled family counselor or therapist to enter into the various levels on which the family interrelationships are operating. From such empathic understanding one may find some clues for helping the family change its pattern of interactions or some of the attitudes and feelings that the members have toward each other.

There is a growing awareness that parents are not only inextricably involved, but that for the future welfare of the child it is essential that parents become involved in whatever treatment process is recommended. Adult drug abusers have more independent control of their life situations than young drug abusers. Most youngsters, even after successfully completing an inpatient or residential treatment program, must return to their families and the living conditions they were in when they used drugs.

Some adolescents abuse drugs to gain attention in a family that otherwise ignores them. Family therapists who specialize in treating substance-abusing young people have found that the families of their patients often are conflictual or disengaged, or lack open communication, mutual respect, reasonable organization, and close, loving relationships. The parents and children often are alienated and the parents may be poor models, or may be overly controlling. In such cases, expert assistance may be needed. The drug use itself is of deep concern but cannot be treated outside the context of these other factors.

Researchers (Friedman et al. 1980; Kandel 1982) found that initial use of illicit drugs by adolescents is related to parent-child relationships. Adolescents who feel close to their families are less likely than others to begin using illicit substances. Conversely, the children of parents who are perceived as maintaining strict controls and parents who tend to disagree about discipline are more likely to begin using illicit drugs. Use of drugs by parents has also been found to be an important predictor of adolescent drug use.

Findings produced by the National Youth Polydrug Study (Friedman 1980) show the relationship between family factors and adolescent drug abuse:

Adolescents whose parents had drug problems, alcohol problems, psychiatric problems, or problems with the law are more heavily involved in drug abuse than adolescents whose parents were not reported to have such problems.

There is a significant positive correlation between the number of problems reported in families and the number of types of drugs used by the adolescent offspring.

High school students who use drugs spend more time with peers who have similar drug use behavior patterns and are more likely to be estranged from parents and other adults than students who do not use drugs (Friedman 1983).

Absence of parent, lack of parental closeness, unconventional parents, excessively passive mothers, lack of perceived closeness to parents, and drinking and drug use patterns of parents have been positively correlated with drug use (Jessor and Jessor 1977; Brooke et al. 1980; Kandel 1982).

Families of adolescent drug users differ significantly from families in which the adolescent offspring either do not use drugs or have used marijuana only experimentally. In contrast to experimental drug users or nonusers, adolescents with serious drug problems come from families with certain characteristics:

Parents are perceived as having relatively less influence than peers. Both parents are perceived to be more approving of drug use (Jessor 1975).

Offspring perceive less love from both parents, particularly fathers (Streit et al. 1974; Mellinger et al. 1975).

Less shared authority and poorer communication characterize the family (Hunt 1974; Cannon 1976).

Less spontaneous problem solving occurs in structured family interaction tasks (Mead and Campbell 1972).

The following verbatim report of an individual ("one-to-one") interview with an adolescent drug abuser reveals clearly and in detail how this young client perceives his father's attitudes and behavior as the primary cause of his drug abuse.

Why do you think that you started using drugs?

"Well, I guess in my family my dad was always very, I would probably call it overbearing. He was always trying to control my life and he was always pushing very hard on school work. While I did very well in school he was never quite satisfied with it. I didn't really express resentment towards that early on, I started to express it more later as I got older. But I couldn't really do anything about it by the time I started to express myself. So I started to use drugs to escape from the bad feelings that I had, the problems that I couldn't express or that I couldn't deal with, my feelings towards him. I needed to escape from the difficulties I had dealing with people as a result of my upbringing. I hadn't been exposed to the situations where I had to open up and be vulnerable, I just escaped uneasiness and difficulties."

What were some of the feelings that you were trying to escape?

"Uneasy, just anger basically I guess and resentment later, because I hadn't expressed the anger at first. It was not just that I was angry at him for wanting me to do well in school. I was angry with him for not being satisfied when I did do well in school. He always seemed to be trying to be overly controlling my life at home and otherwise."

How did you use drugs? How did they help you?

"Well, I would just retreat into my own little world. I would go up into my room. They would generally be just watching TV or something at night. I would put on music and turn the lights down and get high and I wouldn't have to think about it. For me, drugs helped me get more along, help me be more comfortable with myself, because I didn't have to face the feelings that I had inside."

What kinds of feelings did you have?

"Sad, I guess, because he hadn't given me what I wanted. And because he hadn't given the rest of my family what they wanted. I also had a lot of fear. He wasn't showing any signs of changing, and I didn't want it to go on like that but I couldn't really do anything about it and I had some guilt for not doing or saying anything about it."

How often did you use drugs?

"Pretty much every day since I've, well when I first started I used it about every week for the first six to eight months, then I started doing marijuana every day for about the next few years. That took away the bad feelings without really taking away my ability to function as much as alcohol."

How did drugs effect your relationships with others?

"When I got high, I was more self-centered. It helped me withdraw into myself, so I didn't make it a point to go out in public, not to be seen in situations where people would be looking at me or noticing my eyes or noticing that I was high. And it made me uncomfortable in public not just among adults but among other kids my age. That's just one of the effects."

Did you use drugs more by yourself or with other people?

"Mostly, with a select group of close friends, who I could trust not to get down on me for doing it or notice me, just paying special attention to me cause I was high. After awhile I started doing it a lot alone, just sitting in my room playing guitar and getting high. It made me withdraw even more."

How have drugs affected different aspects of your life?

"They [drugs] made it hard for me to function with people a lot more than probably would have happened if I had not taken up the drugs. They definitely interfered with my ability to work at school, not so much at first because I would do my work and then get high, but later as I started getting high I enjoyed doing work while I was high, or thought I enjoyed it. I did enjoy doing it more but I didn't do it as well. They [drugs] kept me from dealing with my family as well, because they made me want to forget about everything and not deal with it, just get high, and forget about my problems. Yeah, not deal with things, a lot easier to get high and forget it."

What kind of person are you? How do you see yourself?

"Quiet, thoughtful I suppose, but I don't have very strong feelings one way or the other that I like to admit to myself. I don't like to show my emotions. It's just been so long since I've been able to express my true feelings to anybody or even myself that I kinda forgotten. I don't think I was really ever able or willing to express my feelings to my family since early childhood, I don't think I ever really."

Did you have trouble expressing feelings to your mother?

"Less trouble I suppose, because she was the object of control that my dad represented for me. She wasn't so much the authoritarian figure, so it was a lot easier to express myself to her. You know, I would express my emotions concerning my father to my mother, but they never really got relayed to him with the same intensity that I felt. I guess I didn't always express them to her in the same intensity."

Did you feel that you were more a failure or success when you were using drugs?

"It [drugs] definitely made my family see me as a failure. At first I didn't want to admit to myself that I was. My school work was suffering, or my summer employment would be suffering from it, but it became pretty obvious after a while. Definitely it caused me to drop out of school."

Do you think that the fact that your friends and acquaintances and other people your own age around you used drugs had any influence on your starting or continuing to use them?

"Yeah, one of my father's complaints at the beginning when I first started using drugs was that I was valuing my acquaintances more than I valued my family. I guess I was rebelling against him and against all structures more than I even knew, without basically thinking about why I was doing it, I was just going to my friends because they shared some of the same feelings I had that definitely had an effect on me socially. Pretty much all we would do after I started getting high was getting high when we were together. When we were together it naturally spurred us to get high."

How did drugs affect your relationships with girls?

"The problems that I had dealing with people were further injured by the drugs. I guess that I used it to withdraw into myself so I wouldn't have to face people. I always had problems dealing with girls more than guys. I didn't go around with as many girls as other guys so I certainly wasn't exposed to them. Anyway, I definitely had problems meeting girls. I thought I could deal with them more openly and equally because of drugs.

"The first girlfriend was very into drugs. We would always get into it. That's how we met, at parties getting high, and that, our relationship was based almost totally on sex and drugs. That didn't really work cause a relationship can't last on those for too long healthfully. So I kinda ended it. After that, well, I still dated girls that were using drugs, but they weren't using drugs as heavily as she was. The next girl I went out with was not into drugs as far as other people were concerned. She was very straight, she would drink once in a while, but she was really concerned with her schooling."

Do you think that school had anything to do with you using drugs?

"School was just another authority for me, I was at that time really rebelling against my father and all the structure that he imposed on me. I hadn't objected out loud, not to him. School was just another thing to rebel against and I was looking for anything that was there to rebel against. I was up for rebelling and drugs just helped me to rebel against authority. It was something I could do. I could do things that were strictly against their regulations and all."

How did your family react when they found out that you used drugs?

"They were aware of my abuse and they were scared that I was going to get caught and screw up my future. They were very angry with me for doing it, even though I made all these rationalizations to them about how all my friends do a lot more. I was very discreet about it [drug use] and only did it at times, very late at night, and only did it when I wouldn't be caught. They were still pretty gullible back then, but they were very angry with me. My dad more vocal about it than my mother."

What's your folks' attitude now?

"If I were to tell them that I was still using it every day I don't think they would probably let me stay in the house, they would probably want me to get out. They told me if I really wanted to smoke every day and wanted that to be my life-style then they would be much happier if I got out of the house. I pretended not to want to do that and stayed in the house just to please them, which is basically what I have done since I started smoking. That's their attitude. They don't want me to do it and they are willing to support me if I don't do it; but if I want to do it, they would rather have me doing it out of the house."

Have you been doing it?

"With one exception I haven't done it in the last nine weeks or so. So it's been a drastic change in my life. At first I wasn't really sure, that I wanted to stop at least for a while. I wasn't really sure how long I would want to stop, I mean after the second week I was talking it over with them and saying I wanted to be able to get high every once in a while. But then after five weeks I got high again and I wasn't really enjoying it. I didn't really know what to do because I was all alone again and I was high for the first time in a while, I felt guilty about getting high, about ruining the chance that I had started for myself. I didn't really enjoy it at all."

What do you want to get, if anything, from coming here for treatment?

"A better attitude I guess towards drugs, and towards dealing with my problems, that's basically all."

Do you feel like you are getting something out of the family therapy?

"Yeah, a lot more of the family therapy than the group therapy, cause I don't feel comfortable with the group yet and I don't really talk a lot. Family therapy stirs up the problems that already exist and makes us talk about them and deal with them. When we go home the problems are still there but it's helpful to get them out in the open, realize what they are, and try to face them. So it's been helping."

Today, most adolescent drug treatment programs (outpatient, residential, and hospital settings) provide family services. Increasingly, programs have come to realize that adolescent substance abuse impacts severely on the family and that the whole family may need assistance to cope with the problem.

Most families who come with or bring an adolescent member for drug abuse treatment see this adolescent as the only or main problem in the family. Their attitude is that the adolescent needs to be treated or controlled so that the family can get some relief from the problem, but not that the whole family needs treatment. If they agree to attend any family sessions they are likely to see their role as providing information about the behavior of the young client to the client's therapist. The family therapist, however, may view the adolescent drug abuser as an integral part of a dysfunctional, disturbed, or disorganized family. It follows from this view that the family needs to change. In some families it appears that the drug abuse behavior of the adolescent may serve the function, whether intentionally or not, to maintain the family homeostasis or status quo. For example, if the parents are in a state of emotional divorce, or have a very conflictual marital relationship, it may appear that the parents need to stay together to cope jointly with the continuing family crises posed by the adolescent's drug abuse problems. This deflects the parents from facing the problem of their relationship, and avoids the greater danger of the family breaking up. Or in another family it may appear that a parent needs to keep an adolescent dependent in such a way that the adolescent does not become self-sufficient and independent enough to move away from the parents. A mother may believe that she continues to give her adolescent child money to buy drugs so that he or she does not steal, and thus to avoid the risk of the child's going to jail. At the same time this parental behavior may operate to keep the child tied to the parent.

Even if it is assumed that the family was not significantly involved originally in the development of the adolescent's drug problem, the family can, with expert guidance, help the drug abusing youngster to overcome the problem. This may develop into a long-term endeavor, in the more severe cases, requiring patience, firmness, persistence, and tolerance of frustration on the part of the parents. For this reason the parents often need the support of a professional during the process.

A central concept of family therapy is to work with and attempt to change the family system rather than the individual family members. The family, rather than the identified drug-abusing client, is the main focus of treatment. In some cases, the emotional atmosphere is so consistently negative or pathological in the family that it is necessary to treat teenage drug users in a different living milieu, away from the family. Inpatient or residential treatment may also be needed by young clients who require a maximum degree of structure and control for their drug abuse and other problem behavior. The parents themselves may welcome the separation from the youngster, since it promises temporary relief from recurrent crises and behavior that they may feel helpless to control. In situations like these, the adolescent client is treated separately until it is determined that family interaction should begin. Where possible, programs have youngsters and their families participate in the same sessions, to help prepare them for the youngster's return home.

Not every family is available to participate in family therapy, and some are not willing to be involved. There are some families who are afraid of what might be exposed. In a recent case in our drug abuse treatment clinic, it was difficult to get the mother and the 15-year-old daughter, the drug client, together for a session. The mother showed up alone for the first scheduled family session, and stated that she was afraid to meet together with the daughter. She was very angry at her daughter's behavior, and was concerned that if she expressed her anger, it would be harmful to her daughter and would complicate the situation further. The daughter had started in individual counseling and was cooperating with the treatment. But she was adamant about not having joint sessions with her mother. It turned out that the mother had undergone major surgery several months earlier, and the daughter was afraid that if the anger between her and her mother were allowed to surface it could conceivably kill her mother. In such a situation the family is not ready for family therapy. Often family members need professional help and support on an individual basis before they are ready to face joint family sessions. It is possible that, in the case example cited, the mother and daughter could, after adequate preparation, have several joint sessions in which they could reach a better mutual understanding and a more satisfactory relationship.

Many adolescent drug abuse clients resist the idea of involving their parents and other family members in treatment. They want to be in control of what is talked about in therapy or counseling sessions, to tell their side of the story or to withhold information about their questionable behavior. They are often also afraid of confrontation with their parents. Thus, they need to be reassured that the therapist is not going to side with the parents against them. Parents are also afraid of what the adolescent might reveal in the family therapy sessions: a parent's questionable behavior, a family secret, or problems in the parents' marital relationship.

It is important to get the parents working together to reinforce the family's generational hierarchy. At the same time, it is necessary to find appropriate ways to join and support the adolescent. Each side should be helped to recognize what is legitimate in the other's position.

The therapist looks for possible ways that the family problems, the negative aspects of the family system to which the adolescent drug abuser is reacting, can be changed so that the more positive and functional tendencies of the adolescent can emerge and be facilitated. Also, the therapist looks for potential assets and strengths that can be developed and actualized in each family member, and facilitates the adolescent's developmental need for individuation and differentiation.

One of the family situations in which it is easiest to see how the parents have contributed to the development of the problem is where they have been poor role models, particularly if one of them has been a substance abuser himself or herself (most often an alcoholic father). This inevitably has caused a serious problem in the history of the family and in the childhood development of the adolescent.

One example of such a family, recently seen by the authors, was a split family in which the parents had been divorced for six years and the father was currently involved in cocaine abuse. The mother, 36 years of age, was living with the only child, a 13½-year-old daughter. The girl, Amy, was attractive, rather heavily made up with cosmetics, physically well developed, large for her age, giving the impression of being 15 or 16 years of age. She was quite popular in school. Some of the mother's complaints about the girl were: "Her behavior and attitude is getting worse, and she is failing in school. She rigged her school report card before she showed it to me. I had asked her in advance what grades I should expect to see, so that I would not be taken too much aback. She doesn't come home from school when she should. She lies to me all the time."

It appeared that Amy didn't have much self-restraint and was repeatedly asking her mother to buy things for her, to give her money, to permit her to go places and to do things. One day last week, Amy had telephoned her mother at work five times insisting that her mother agree to let her do something. The mother, who was busy at work, felt she couldn't take the pressure any more, "caved in," and agreed in order to get Amy off her back. Later, the mother was angry and reneged on a promise she had made to let Amy go skating on the weekend. "It's an impossible situation. I get angry at her every day. I'm 'lamming' off at her all the time. We never agree on anything or reach any conclusions."

The mother's inability to be consistent and firm with her daughter and to stand up to her was discussed. The mother admits that she "parentifies"

Amy, needs her to help make decisions about the mother's own life, and this gives up to Amy a lot of power and authority. The mother has always related to and used her older sister this way. It was pointed out that it will not be best for Amy in the long run to be conditioned to be so unrestrained, demanding, and aggressive.

During the preceding two sessions the daughter had been saying repeatedly, with intense feeling, that she hated her mother and wished she had a different mother. It appeared, when this was explored, that the girl was becoming preoccupied and somewhat obsessed with this idea. It would come to mind during school hours and would interfere with her concentrating on schoolwork. The therapist decided to use a paradoxical prescription and give the girl the assignment of scheduling two minutes every hour, including school hours, to think about how much she hated her mother, and then to take five minutes after school each day to write down how much she hated her mother. The girl readily accepted this assignment, and managed to follow the prescribed behavior during the subsequent week.

Amy had also been saying in an angry, surly, belligerent way that she could not tolerate living with her mother any more, that she wanted to go live with her father (who had much more money, a large house, and so on) and his new family. The mother said: "He splits, turns her against me. I told him that I rather she not see him. He has disappointed her once too often. I bear her pain. But she telephones him when she has an argument with me." The mother had told the therapist separately on the telephone that the father really doesn't want Amy to come and stay at his house for any length of time, but that he tends to misrepresent and to lead her to believe that he wants her. The mother also expressed that she took it as a personal insult to herself that Amy wanted to stay with her father.

The therapist took the position that it might be good for Amy to have the opportunity to learn from the actual experience how it would be to stay with, or live part-time with, her father's family rather than to fantasize about it and idealize it. The therapist encouraged the mother, who was afraid to let the girl go, to take a chance and let her go on a trial weekend to stay with her father. If she had used drugs before, she had not admitted it and the parents did not know about it.

On the girl's weekend at the home of the father's new family a crisis occurred: the girl left her father's house abruptly on Sunday afternoon and later arrived at her mother's house, and was "stoned" on drugs for the first time. Both parents had themselves used illicit drugs and the father was still using cocaine. Now Amy had, for the first time, seen her father and his second wife getting high together on cocaine. She had left his house and gone to some friends with whom she got stoned on drugs.

The parents each phoned the therapist immediately. The father had not seen the girl in her stoned state. His initial reaction was to be very angry at the mother for falsely accusing the girl of using drugs. Later in the day when he found out that the girl had lied to him over the phone and, in fact, had been stoned, he went over to the mother's house and struck the girl in the mouth. The next day at the end of the therapist's session with these family members, the girl dramatically threw her arms around her mother, and exclaimed, "Mommy, I love you." The mother was delighted, could hardly believe what was happening and was dancing in the hallway as she left the office. She called back to the therapist, "Did you see what she did?"

It was reasonable to assume that the father's hitting the girl may have had something to do with the dramatic turnabout in the girl's attitude toward the mother. The therapist's working with the family to lessen the impact of the girl's obsession with hating her mother might also have had an effect. It is conceivable that the therapist's authority involved in prescribing the hateful thoughts and feelings helped the mother to listen to such expressions without getting so angry and upset, and helped to release any guilt that the daughter might have experienced in connection with the hostile thoughts, and that somehow this process allowed whatever positive feelings the daughter had toward the mother to come through. In any event, such a sudden change may only have been temporary and superficial. This was suggested by the fact that the girl did not return home to her mother from school on the day of the next scheduled therapy session and missed the therapy session.

The adolescent girl had learned certain inappropriate ways to control the family situation in order to get what she felt she needed and wanted. The fact that both of her parents were emotionally immature, felt insecure in the role of parent, and related to each other to some extent as children, with sibling rivalry, laid some of the groundwork for the development of the adolescent girl's maladaptive behavior patterns. One got some impression of how the complex interplay of the motivations, needs, and problems of each family member and their relationship tendencies combined to make up the total family dysfunctional interaction system.

While the parents of the majority of adolescent drug abusers who come to treatment may not be users of illicit drugs themselves, as occurred in this particular family, or have alcohol problems, a number of the other characteristics observed in this family are seen in many of the families of adolescent drug abusers:

1. The family is split (the parents are divorced or separated).

2. The father has been abusive to the adolescent child.

3. The father has shown rejection of the adolescent.

4. The father displays impulsive and aggressive behavior.

5. The emotionally immature mother displays ambivalent feelings toward the adolescent (concerned about her, caring for her in some ways and trying to hold on to her, but resenting her and feeling inadequate as a mother and overburdened by the responsibility for her).

6. There is a lack of open, honest communication and trust between the mother and father, and between each parent and the adolescent child.

7. There is a lack of adequate understanding between the mother and child.

8. There is a breakdown of communication between the parents regarding the child, a lack of a unified approach to dealing with the child, and a lack of reasonable, consistent, and controlled discipline for the child.

As can be seen from the brief case report of family therapy above and the detailed case description to follow, the parents are likely to need a considerable amount of understanding, empathy, and support from the treatment team to help them with their difficult family situation. The following example of a family applying for treatment at a drug abuse clinic for their adolescent son is used to present a picture of the destructive impact of adolescent drug abuse on a family. It describes the personalities of the parents, their reactions to their son's drug abuse and delinquent behavior, and some of the family interrelationships. It also shows how the parents might have unwittingly contributed to the original development and to the maintenance or escalation of the adolescent member's drug abuse problem, and how their efforts to deal with it may be ineffective or counterproductive.

The following is a description of the scene at the drug abuse clinic when Bill Benson, an older adolescent polydrug abuser, arrived with his parents, who are both well educated and have provided what appears to be a stable home in an affluent suburban community.

Bill pushed open the clinic door and let it swing behind him as he entered. His father, who followed several steps behind, caught it just before it slammed and held it for his wife, Bill's mother. Bill took one of the available seats in the waiting area and picked up a magazine as his parents approached the receptionist. No one in the lobby would have been able to discern that there was any relationship between Bill and the couple that followed him into the clinic.

It was the established practice of this clinic to see adolescent drug abusers with their families, and this was to be the family's first step into treatment for Bill's drug use.

Bill was a handsome, 17-year-old high school senior. He was neatly dressed in the "preppie" style typical of the teenagers who lived in his suburban neighborhood, which suggested both his awareness of and allegiance to an upper-middle-class youth culture. As he leafed through a magazine, he appeared determined to maintain an air of sullen indifference—as if he wanted everyone who saw him to make no mistake about his feelings—he didn't like being there, but he was resigned to it.

The attitude of being "resigned" to going to treatment was the result of several catastrophic events of ten days past: his mother's discovery of his "stash" of coke, pot, and pills; his own panicked realization later that night that someone had found his stuff and taken it; then, his sense of terror at being caught which he overcame by adolescent bravado; and his outrage that his personal property was taken from his room.

In spite of the late hour, he had barged angrily into his parent's bedroom demanding to know what had happened to his drugs. His mother acknowledged that she had taken them and stated that he could not have them back. Usually a calm, reasonable woman, now as angry as he, she threatened to call the police if Bill didn't get out of the room. The amount of drugs she had found made it clear that he was doing more than using a little pot and coke. She knew he was selling the stuff. After finally getting Bill out of their bedroom that night, the Bensons discussed what future action to take. This was not an easy discussion for Nora and Sam Benson. On one hand, Nora intuitively understood that she and Sam had to come to an agreement and to present a united front to deal with Bill; on the other hand, Sam had great difficulty accepting that Bill was abusing drugs and refused to believe that Bill was selling them—even when Nora presented the incontestable evidence. It was terribly painful for Sam to admit that Bill was disturbed enough to be involved in selling drugs and that he, his father, hadn't had the slightest idea.

For years Sam had been very involved with his teaching post at a local university and with his computer consulting work. Like a lot of fathers he spent less time with his family than he intended. It was also true that, over the years, he had completely relied on his wife's role as house manager and disciplinarian. Nora's disciplinary function with their two daughters, one older and one younger than Bill, seemed effective and appropriate to Sam. Both girls were good students and appeared to be happy and well adjusted. In contrast, Nora had been struggling with Bill's adolescence for years, and for the first time Sam realized that he had experienced the majority of this struggle indirectly, through Nora's eyes and interpretations. He seriously wondered now if he hadn't abdicated too much responsibility as far as his son was concerned.

Sam Benson also had great difficulty with the type of high-pitched emotional scene that had just transpired in their bedroom. No one ever shouted at each other in his family when he was growing up. The confrontation between Bill and his wife upset him to the point that he was paralyzed. He seemed overwhelmed by a combination of what he was actually feeling and his anxiety about the need for some authority or action on his part, and his ignorance of what to do. Unable to sort any of this out in the midst of the battle, he did nothing.

After discussing the situation at length, Sam and Nora eventually agreed that they had to make it absolutely clear to Bill that he simply could not deal drugs out of their house. They were unprepared, however, for his retaliation.

Although Bill had stolen money from the house before, the following day he tore through his parents' bedroom leaving it in disarray and took, it appeared, anything he thought he could sell; the clock radio, souvenirs, and an assortment of jewelry, which incidentally had only sentimental value.

The upshot of this was that Mrs. Benson had the house locks changed while Bill was out that evening. Naturally, he couldn't get in when he returned and started to shout and pound on the door. Nora told him through the door that if he wanted in, he would first have to tell her where the things were that were stolen from her room. "No—let me in, and I'll get them," was his reply.

Once Bill finally realized that he would get inside only be revealing where he had hidden the objects, he surrendered. The scene at the locked front door, of course, did little to ease the mounting family tensions, which exploded the following day. Mrs. Benson was baking lemon squares when Bill decided to heat some frozen fish sticks. He wanted to put them in the oven immediately; she wanted him to wait until the cookies were done to prevent them from tasting like fish. Another heated battle of words ensued. "You'll just have to wait a few minutes—they're almost done," stated Nora firmly.

Bill was not about to accept this answer. He went about removing the fish sticks from the package and placing them on a baking sheet. Nora, in disbelief, stood in front of the oven and repeated that he would have to wait.

Mustering all his grandeur Bill responded icily, "You'll have to learn that I do what I want." With that Nora, now infuriated with his behavior, knocked the tray from his hand. He grabbed at her wrist in an angry gesture and she stumbled trying to regain her balance. Remembering his martial arts training, for the first time in her life Nora was physically afraid of her son.

With the tensions at an apex, Nora shouted that she was going to call the police. Bill then adopted a karate stance, and Nora ran from her home not knowing what he would do or just how out of control he was. By that time it was late afternoon, and realizing that her husband was on route home, she waited at a neighbor's to intercept him.

The Bensons returned to their home shortly thereafter to find Bill moving the upstairs TV, shouting that he was taking it to recoup his losses from the drugs Nora had confiscated. At that point Sam Benson called the local police.

Relaying the precipitating incidents to the police, the Bensons were told that there was enough evidence to hold him; and so 17-year-old Bill Benson spent the next ten days in the county detention center.

It should be said here, after the recounting of some of Bill's problem behavior related to drug abuse, that there were also positive aspects in Bill's adjustment.

In one particular area Sam and Bill had a very good relationship. Sam had taught Bill as much general computer programming and systems analysis as Bill could absorb—which was quite a lot for a high school student. Because of Bill's skill, Sam was able to employ him on various summer projects at the university, and Bill's performance on these projects was top-notch. He earned a good salary and the money was very important to him. Not only did he do the actual work very well, he was able to interact with other staff and apparently conducted himself in a mature, responsible manner. Sam could now see how Bill's good behavior on the job stood in contrast to his unacceptable behavior in other areas.

What he did not see, however, was that Bill used his adult role at work as one way to relate to his parents inappropriately as peers, rather than as parents. Bill was able to assume this adult role, and to break the generational boundaries, in part, because of Sam's and Nora's inability to agree on clear limits for Bill.

Bill's behavior served additional functions, possibly for both of his parents. Sam had a strong need to express the anger that his upbringing and values inhibited. Tacitly, and probably out of Sam's awareness, Bill was acting as Sam's emotional proxy in giving expression to these negative feelings with Nora.

Nora also had difficulty with the expression of strong or negative emotions. Growing up in a home with an explosive, sometimes violent, father, Nora reacted against the pain of these early experiences and developed values that did not allow her to convey similar negative feelings. For Nora, Bill's behavior provided a degree of excitement which she intuitively needed and which she was not in touch with in other areas of her life. Her characteristic nonreactiveness may at times have reinforced Bill's tendency for more and more extreme behavior—until finally a heated confrontation occurred between them. During these exchanges, Sam was typically either a silent observer or absent from the scene.

There was still no conversation between Bill and his parents as they waited in the reception area. Bill's parents would have been more upset with the recent events if they had not in a sense been seasoned by and somewhat resigned to his increasingly incorrigible behavior over the last few years. His mother was willing to go another step to see if they could help him, to get to Bill in some way, but not much more than that. It certainly wasn't as if she hadn't tried—as if she hadn't, from her point of view, beaten her brains out looking at Bill's problems from every possible angle, trying to effect a solution, or at least some change. Thus the events of the past two weeks were almost, but not quite, the final straw.

At this point, we shall leave Bill as he sat mentally reviewing the details of his probation from the county, which included mandatory drug treatment. His name was then called for the intake interview and the Bensons followed Bill into the office, sat down and began to participate in developing the psycho-social history interview.

Let us now begin to explore the treatment entry terrain from the perspective of the drug counselor or therapist. The step into drug treatment is for most adolescents and their families, a pivotal and highly charged event. It is usually the result of a situation that has deteriorated progressively, often unchecked, over a period of years. Each individual new adolescent client then brings into treatment the accumulated emotional weight of all past days and nights that led him or her to this place or juncture. Typically this includes enormous pain and sorrow, the memory of drug highs and lows, the binges, the acting-out, the fights and the remorse, the family crises, violent arguments, school problems, legal problems, embarrassment, and quite often, the overwhelming sense of failure and confusion.

During their first contact with a drug treatment program adolescents are most often described by therapists as "sullen" and "closed off." The idea of entering treatment, in most cases, did not originate with the youth. Most often he or she is referred by the schools, the juvenile courts, friends or desperate, frustrated parents.

The gloomy, resentful, and resistant attitude that these young drug users initially adopt toward treatment is often seen as one manifestation of adolescent bravado which for some is their primary psychological defense against their own underlying pain and fear. Just reaching and making some genuine emotional contact with these young clients is in itself a difficult task, even for skilled and experienced drug counselors or therapists.

Many young clients are very noncommunicative at intake. Consistent with the description of Bill the adjective "sullen" captures the adolescents' response style. Since this response is so typical, therapists must develop strategies for coping with the client's silence. Regarding this point, one older therapist explained his approach in this way. "I talk about the adolescent experience directly with the kid and some of my own adolescent experiences. There's no point in denying the reality of our helplessness feelings. When the youngster sees that the treatment situation is not one of judged and blamed, he begins to talk, and things begin to happen."

A younger, more streetwise therapist may ally him- or herself with the adolescent client in a variety of ways. The therapist may use humor, commiserate with the client about how "awful" it is to be taken to treatment when one doesn't want to go, or demonstrate his or her ability to speak the language of the adolescent. Once the therapist is established in the client's eyes as a non-enemy, he or she can usually be a powerful factor in helping the client to see that significant adult "others" are not enemies either.

The young client typically has great difficulty stating the problem, but most frequently, he or she may say: "I want to get my head together," or "I'm okay; my problem is that my parents are on my back." Commonly, however, the adolescent is denying a very real, serious, and acute problem.

The feelings and emotional state of the parents of a youth who is entering drug treatment are very telling for the treatment process, and therefore, must be explored, clarified, and understood. They themselves have most likely experienced a degree of emotional upheaval comparable to that of their child and have lived through the child's rebellion and antisocial and/or self-destructive acting-out behavior. Consequently, the emotional "baggage" and disturbed feelings that they carry to the first treatment session may be even heavier than those of their child, since they include the weight of their own problems as adults and often the feeling of having failed as a parents.

In describing the parents of adolescent clients at treatment entry, drug counselors report that the parents' feelings and attitudes are often muddled, confused, and in conflict with themselves. Also, conflict between the two parents is often apparent. They have been so emotionally exhausted by the events leading to treatment that they present a sense of hopelessness and willingness to give up. At the same time, they are described as overinvested emotionally in the problematic situation and as desperately seeking guidance and direction. From the therapist's viewpoint, the first task is to engage the adolescent client and the parents and attempt to establish some connection and rapport. Without such a connection (on a level of understanding, empathy, identification, or sympathy for the family) the therapist can have no real therapeutic effect. Different therapists approach the task differently. It seems natural that a young therapist would interrelate better with the adolescent client and that an older therapist would interrelate better with the parents. For this reason, if a program can afford it, it is often best to have a cotherapy team composed of an older and a younger therapist to work with the case, with the younger therapist providing the individual therapy to the adolescent client and the cotherapy team conducting family therapy sessions with the whole family. It also adds another useful dimension for the cotherapy team to be "heterosexual," and for the younger therapist who sees the adolescent client individually to be the same sex as the client. In some cases, the mother responds better to an older female counselor. The average drug treatment program, however, cannot afford to tailor the treatment team composition that is ideal for each case.

Almost all programs use the vehicle of the psychosocial history at the intake session for obtaining the necessary information, and as the first step in engaging the client and family in treatment. When this procedure includes meeting with the family members together in addition to interviewing them separately, it also allows the treatment team to obtain their first view of the nature of the family interaction and relationships.

A brief description of what the client and family will be asked during this treatment admission (intake) session follows:

The events and situations that led up to the application for treatment.

Basic demographic information about the client (age, sex, race, educational history, vocation history, hobbies and interests, living arrangements).

Reason(s) for applying for treatment.

Family background (parents' occupation, outline of structure of client's nuclear family, person(s) responsible for raising the client, siblings, birth order, a description of the quality of the client's family life, any alcohol or drug abuse history of other family members).

Information regarding the client's development and early childhood, particularly any disturbances/abnormalities in the client's birth, sleep patterns, unusual behavior, and so on.

Other notable features of the client's personal history (behavior problems, psychological problems, running away, physical or sexual abuse).

Medical history.

The history of the client's drug use and his or her perception of the effects of drug use: how it affected his or her life and functioning in school, at work, in the family, and so on.

Legal history, including the client's arrest record, details of his or her most recent brush with the law, and the client's probation/parole officer.

Previous treatment experience, if any.

In the history-taking session interactive family situations naturally emerge from the standard questions that are being asked. Some common parent-child interaction patterns noted by therapists are that a parent will identify the problem by reporting the child's bad behavior: "He's failing in school," "He breaks the rules," "He stays out all night and only comes home to shower and eat," "He's destroying the house," "She steals money," "He wrecks the cars," "She's acting out sexually."

In the face of such parent reports the adolescent will be on the defensive and will try to minimize the seriousness of the situation. Sometimes it appears that the parents, who have become tense, desperate, and angry, and worried for the future of their child, are overreacting.

While treatment philosophies, approaches and policies may vary from program to program it has become widely accepted that the family therapy approach has as good a chance as any other treatment approach to help solve the adolescent drug abuse problem.

References

Alexander, B.K. and Dibb, G.S. 1977. Interpersonal perception in addict families, *Family Process* 16: 17–28.

Brooke, J.S.; Lukoff, I.F.; and Whitman, M. 1980. Initiation into adolescent marijuana use. *Journal of General Psychology* 137: 133–142.

Cannon, S.R. 1976. *Social Functioning Patterns in Families of Offspring Receiving Treatment for Drug Abuse.* Roslyn Heights, New York: Libra Publications.

Friedman, A.S. 1983. High school drug abuse clients. *Clinical Research Notes,* July. Rockville, Maryland: National Institute on Drug Abuse.

Friedman, A.S.; Pomerance, E.; Sanders, R.; Santo, Y.; and Utada, A. 1980. The structure and problems of the families of adolescent drug abusers. *Contemporary Drug Problems* 9(3).

Hunt, D.G. 1974. Parental permissiveness as perceived by the offspring and the degree of marijuana usage among offspring. *Human Relations* 27: 267–285.

Jessor, R. 1975. Predicting time of onset of marijuana use: A developmental study of high school youth. In Lettieri, D., ed., *Predicting Adolescent Drug Abuse: A Review of the Issues, Methods and Correlates.* DHEW Publication No. (ADM)76-299. Washington, D.C.: U.S. Government Printing Office.

Jessor, R. and Jessor, S.L. 1977. *Problem Behavior and Psychosocial Development—A Longitudinal Study of Youth.* New York: Academic Press.

Kandel, D. 1982. Inter- and intragenerational influences on adolescent marijuana use. *Journal of the American Academy of Child Psychiatry* 21(4): 328–347.

Mead, D.E. and Campbell, S.S. 1972. Decision-making and interaction by families with and without a drug abusing child. *Family Process* 11: 487–498.

Mellinger, G.D.; Somers, R.H.; and Manheimer, D.I. 1975. Drug use research items pertaining to personality and interpersonal relations: A working paper for research investigators. In Lettieri, D.J., ed., *Predicting Adolescent Drug Abuse: A Review of the Issues, Methods and Correlates.* DHEW Pub. No. (ADM) 76-299. Washington, D.C.: U.S. Government Printing Office.

Streit, F.; Halsted, D.; and Pascale, P. 1974. Differences among youthful users and nonusers of drugs based on their perceptions of parental behavior. *International Journal of the Addictions* 9(5): 749–755.

5

The Parents' Predicament

Leslie H. Daroff
S.J. Marks
Alfred S. Friedman

Introduction: "Not My Child"

Our society tends to hold parents responsible for the behavior of their adolescent children. Some jurisdictions even punish parents by levying fines against them if their children are involved in drug abuse, are not attending school, or are refusing treatment. But in reality, many thousands of parents feel powerless to control their children's behavior or to cope with the myriad problems generated by their youngsters. The fact that their child is using drugs is, for most parents, very difficult and painful to accept. This pain of the parent adds to the emotional complexity of the problems associated with adolescent drug use.

To begin with, few parents are ready to believe that their own child is using drugs. They have a tendency to disbelieve or deny the symptoms of drug use in their children and to interpret even obvious indicators in other ways. Many parents attribute the abrupt changes in their child's behavior and personality to "adolescence." As a result, it is common to find that a youngster's drug problem has gotten quite serious before the parents take any action on their own or seek professional help. Most parents believe that they have raised their children with love, guidance, and support, so that the children should have developed the personal values and self-assurance needed to resist peer pressure to use drugs. A parent may believe tentatively that the teenager is using drugs but doesn't confront the teenager. The child may see the parent's reluctance to confront the problem even though the youngster may be inwardly yearning for help.

One of the frequent questions that parents ask is "How can I tell if my child is on drugs?" Parents are often looking for a simple guide to recognizing physical and/or behavioral signs. There are booklets providing this information, but, in spite of what has been said above, one should be careful not to jump to conclusions. For example, there are many reasons other than drugs why youngsters might have bleary eyes. It could possibly be because they stayed up late at night talking on the telephone to a boyfriend or girlfriend, or watched a late television show, or couldn't sleep because of personal concerns. The more important factor for parents to consider is the quality of their relationship with their children and whether or not open communication is possible. If the relationship is solid, it is probably unnecessary to play medical detective.

Generally, parents should be advised to communicate openly with a child when there is any evidence of drug use. They should express their concerns for the child's health and future, and encourage the youngster to get help from someone who has more knowledge about these matters. It is likely that the youngster will deny using drugs regardless of the evidence. Typical responses are: "It's not mine; I'm holding it for a friend of mine," "I tried it once and didn't like it."

When the evidence becomes too obvious to ignore, parents either find that they do not know what to do or else they take actions that escalate the tensions that already exist in the family. The first reaction of many parents to teenage drug use is panic. However, panic usually does not help the situation and can very well complicate it. The authors surveyed seventy-eight mothers of adolescent drug abusers to find out how they reacted when they first discovered that their children were using drugs. The mothers reported that they

Expressed concern for the effects of drug use on his/her life (89 percent)

Gave reasons against drug use (84 percent)

Withdrew privileges (55 percent)

Threatened to discipline or punish (54 percent)

Argued with (or yelled) at him/her (53 percent)

Punished him/her (46 percent)

Threatened to get rid of him/her (kick out of the house) (32 percent)

None reported that they did or said nothing.

Forty percent discovered the drug use when they found illicit drugs or drug paraphernalia in the adolescent's room. Only 11 percent found out by being notified by school personnel. Sixty-three percent of the mothers reported that their drug-abusing children "never" confided in them regarding their use of drugs, and another 28 percent reported that the children only confided in them "occasionally" or "seldom." Fifty-six percent of these mothers reported that they understood "nothing" or "little" about why their child was using drugs.

Other specific problem behaviors of the drug-abusing youngsters which were reported by the mothers were

He/she is difficult to talk to (78 percent)

His/her behavior warrants checking up on (71 percent)

He/she does what he/she pleases without consideration for me (69 percent)

He/she ignores house rules (68 percent)

He/she doesn't let me know where he/she is or what he/she is doing (67 percent)

He/she is distant and aloof (60 percent)

He/she doesn't respect me (59 percent)

His/her behavior frightens me (53 percent)

Findings of another research study (Glickman and Utada 1983) show a dramatic degree of misunderstanding, disagreement, and conflict between parents and their adolescent children who are seriously involved in drug abuse. The young drug abuse clients reported the following attitudes and reactions from at least one of their parents to them and their behavior, indicating a severe degree of family conflict:

Objects to my friends (77 percent)

Is disappointed in me (69 percent)

Complains too much (64 percent)

Doesn't trust me (63 percent)

In addition, at least half of the clients reported that their parents had negative perceptions of each of at least ten items of client behavior. Adolescent drug users have also been reported to perceive their parents as having less influence on them than their peers (Jessor 1975), and to perceive less shared authority and poorer communication in their families, compared to adolescents who do not use drugs (Cannon 1976).

Whether to take drugs is a choice that most children are going to have to make at some point in their lives. One of the most important elements in a family to counteract drug abuse is honesty. Parents should explore methods of fostering an atmosphere in which honesty is rewarded and communication with children is open. If a child honestly admits to using drugs, it should not prompt an extreme reaction from the parents or automatic punishment.

If parents create a situation in which honesty brings only emotional upheaval, then the children certainly are not going to be honest. This does *not* mean that parents must give permission to use drugs. They still must say, "You don't have my permission to do that." It is important that the adolescents know what parents' rules, limits, and expectations are. If children feel that they can come to parents from the beginning, not only with their questions but also with their mistakes, it can avoid later crises when the choices become limited (when the youngster gets suspended from school, or the parent receives a phone call that the youngster has been admitted to a hospital emergency room with an overdose).

The following suggestion can be offered to parents who suspect that their teenage youngsters are using illicit drugs: there should be open discussion and an open atmosphere in the family about the pros and cons of drug use and, particularly, marijuana use. If there is good, open communication and if the parents do not overreact, do not get too uptight and do not moralize or threaten too much, the results of communication will be more positive.

Parents who confront the situation in an honest, open manner, talking about their own helplessness, guilts, fears, and angers, are more likely to gain the youngster's trust and have some influence on his/her drug taking. At times, parents need to be persistent and tenacious in order to succeed in their attempts to resolve disagreements, resentments, and impasses which prevent understanding and communication with their children. Some parents attempt to discuss their concerns in a calm and rational manner (as indicated by the majority of mothers referred to above) but are met with an unreasonably hostile response from their offspring. It is sometimes very difficult for a parent to know how to react, or what to do. The advice that the National Institute on Drug Abuse (NIDA) has for parents who think that their children are abusing drugs is as follows:

> In a straightforward way, tell your child about your concern and the reasons for it: taking drugs is harmful to one's physical, mental, and social well-being. Tell your child that you are opposed to any drug use and you intend to enforce that position. WHAT YOU SHOULD TRY TO BE IS: *Understanding* ("I realize you're under a lot of pressure from friends to use drugs."); *Firm* ("As you parent I cannot allow you to engage in harmful activities."); *Self-examining* ("Are my own alcohol and drug consumption habits exerting a bad influence on my child?"). WHAT YOU SHOULD NOT BE IS: *Sarcastic* ("Don't think I don't know what you're doing."); *Accusatory* ("You're lying to me."); *Stigmatizing* ("You're a terrible person."); *Sympathy-seeking* ("Don't you see how much you're hurting me?"); *Self-blaming* ("It's all my fault."). Such statements tend to make the child defensive and likely to tune you out. (NIDA 1984a, p. 4–5)

Confronting a Painful Situation

A typical urgent phone call comes into a drug treatment clinic, from an anxious and confused mother. She has just been cleaning the child's room, and has come across "pills," "joints," a bag of "grass," or "liquor." Initially, she may simply want some advice—whether she should tell her husband, whether they should confront the child, whether they should ignore it, whether they should take the child somewhere for help or whether they should contact others (clergy, school personnel). The counselor should try to reduce the anxiety and let the parent know that this is a serious but not necessarily an emergency situation. One must be careful in trying to diagnose by telephone because the situation is often different from the view of it that the parent has. The parent should be encouraged to discuss the situation with the spouse, so that they can make a united effort. Frequently, mothers are afraid to inform their husbands. "Oh, no, I couldn't tell my husband; it would kill him," or "I could never tell my husband, he would throw our son out in the street, or beat him up," or "My husband and son would come to physical blows."

Making the initial decision to address the problem is particularly difficult because it forces parents into a myriad of painful feelings and self-realizations. They are likely to feel that they have failed as parents and lost control of their children; that their own weaknesses are reflected in their children's "bad behavior"; that the child they have known and loved has become a stranger. How and why did this happen? "What's the matter with me/us?" It is only natural for parents to resist and defend themselves against looking at such implications until the drug problem has escalated into a very serious situation.

In addition to painful self-reflection, love and concern can lead to overwhelming grief, disappointment, and despair, as well as concerns about the child's physical and mental state and his or her ability to function in the future. Other emotional responses that parents frequently have are anger, embarrassment, and outright hostility toward the youth. While anger with the child's lying and rule breaking surrounding drug use may be appropriate and expected, open hostility among family members is a condition which was probably years in the making.

With this backlog of feelings, when parents confront their child on the issue of his or her drug use the encounter is often a very charged, emotional event complete with angry words, accusations, and counter-accusations. Such a scene usually results in further deterioration in the communication between parent and child and in everyone's feeling worse than before. The frequency of this type of disturbing interaction may well be greater than was indicated by the 53 percent of the mothers surveyed above who "argued with (or yelled) at him/her."

Mixed, Ambivalent, and Contradictory Feelings of Parents toward Their Adolescent Children

Parents have both positive and negative feelings toward their adolescent children who are using drugs. They want to protect and take care of them in certain ways, and they love them and are concerned for their welfare. But they also can get angry and even feel hostile towards them at times. They may want to get rid of the burden and responsibility, especially when the drug abuse problem becomes acute or has been going on for a long time. Many parents feel that it is not appropriate to admit having such negative and hostile feelings toward their own child, or to admit that they sometimes feel like getting rid of the child and the problem. They cannot handle these feelings in an honest, appropriate, or constructive way, and talk only about their positive feelings and concerns for the child. But children are very sensitive to the negative feelings and can pick them up very quickly. Some parents do not handle such ambivalent feelings constructively because they are in conflict—wanting to hold onto the child forever and to keep the child dependent on them, but at the same time wanting to get rid of the problem. One such mother, a divorced single parent, gave her 16-year-old drug-abusing son a deadline to leave home and be out on his own when he graduated from high school. However, she could not tolerate the idea of her son's not graduating from high school, and she needed him in certain ways particularly because she was divorced. He worked hard after school, earned money for drugs, but failed his courses in school, although he was very bright and had made good grades in the past. At 19 years of age he was still at home, still in school and his mother was still battling with him daily over his drug use and still trying periodically to get him to move out.

Parental Guilt and Self-Blame

Most parents have expectations about their children's leading successful lives. If the children fail, the parents may feel that they haven't prepared them appropriately, or haven't been good parents. A parent may feel ashamed or humiliated when a child fails or gets into trouble for example, being a self-destructive drug abuser, or getting into trouble with the school authorities or the law. Some adolescent drug abusers may take some pleasure in humiliating their parents.

Parents who take the position that "it must be my fault because of my parenting" generally feel helpless to do anything about the situation. If they confess these feelings to their youngster, it may help them to relieve the guilt feelings, but it may not help the youngster to change his/her behavior and stop using drugs. It is best if parents keep an open mind and approach the problem objectively and non-defensively, trying to understand how they may have contributed to the problems that led to the youngster's becoming seriously involved with drugs.

Sometimes both drug-abusing adolescents and their parents feel guilty about the problem. However, built feelings and self-blame do not necessarily result in improvement. In the following case, both the mother and the drug-abusing adolescent daughter blamed themselves.

An Italian Catholic mother, who had worked hard all her married life and supported her three daughters after her husband had died, was ashamed of her 22-year-old daughter, who had been on PCP and other drugs since she was 12 years of age. The daughter had overdosed, made eight suicide attempts, and the last time almost succeeded. The daughter knew how ashamed her mother was that the neighborhood people knew about her drug use and that she had given birth to a child out of wedlock. Her mother had been quite satisfied to raise the grandchild for the past five years while her daughter continued to use drugs. The daughter had expressed to her therapist genuine feelings of guilt at having embarrassed her mother publicly and stated that her mother didn't deserve to be hurt this way. She had recently had an abortion when she became pregnant a second time and had not been able to bring herself to confess to her mother about the pregnancy and the abortion. The reason the daughter gave for her most recent suicide attempt was that because she felt guilty she could not tell her mother that she was going to have an abortion. At the same time, she seemed oblivious to the fact that her suicide attempt may have hurt and embarrassed her mother as much or more than the pregnancy and abortion. The mother said that she felt that she had failed as a parent to her daughter. Both mother and daughter felt ashamed and guilty. But having these feelings, while better than being indifferent, callous, or hostile toward each other, was not sufficient to improve the daughter's behavior or the relationship.

Some parents of adolescent drug abusers do not blame themselves or try to explore an understanding of the problem objectively. Many of these parents have been programmed all their lives to avoid blame. They tend to project the blame onto others—society, the school, the police, or their youngster. Having such guilt feelings would be too painful and uncomfortable, and they automatically defend themselves from experiencing such feelings.

It is not easy for the family to explore objectively how other family members might be involved, unwittingly, in the continuation of a youngster's drug abuse, nor to find ways as a family to improve the situation. Such an effort often requires the help of a professional third party, a family therapist who is experienced in working with such families.

You Are Not Alone

Because of the difficulties and suffering that they endure with adolescent drug problems and their need for support, many parents have banded together and developed organizations to help them deal with their uncertainties about the need to act and to find ways to assert their responsibility and authority. A publication entitled *Parents, Peers and Pot II: Parents in Action* (NIDA 1984b) encourages these parental and community efforts and describes approaches that parent groups can take. Parent groups in some communities set up appropriate uniform curfews and party rules so their children and their friends will follow the same parental guidelines. Some parent groups function on a political and community level to counter the dissemination of illegal drugs and drug paraphernalia. Other parent groups have assisted youth groups to organize and promote drug-free alternatives, programs, and activities for themselves. Parent peer groups also help to dispel the sense of isolation of parents who must cope with the drug abuse of their adolescent offspring. The sharing of common experiences, values, and rules for their children, and ways of enforcing the rules, creates a common bond; it strengthens each parent's confidence in coping with the problem, which otherwise might loom as too overwhelming. One organization, United Parents of America, Inc., promotes a school policy whereby parents will be called as soon as any drug or alcohol use is suspected, without fear or threat of legal suit.

> Parents working together can help each other. As a group, they can set rules for their children's behavior, make these rules clearly known, and be consistent in enforcing them. If you work with the parents of your children's friends in setting these rules, you will spend less time arguing about curfews, parties, chaperones, and other issues, and have more time to spend with your children in constructive or fun activities. (NIDA 1984b, p. 7)

We know that parents have had to bear the brunt of the problem, or at least a large share of the burden of the problem, of teenage drug abuse. Also, parents, no matter how good their intentions, often get caught up in the problem and become part of it. It may seem paradoxical, therefore, to say that the problem, in many cases, cannot be solved without the input of the parents and their resources and efforts. Parents in parent-organized communities no longer feel quite so powerless in regard to the drug use of their adolescent children.

Why Teenagers Use Drugs

A basic question that parents generally ask is, "Why do youngsters take drugs?" There are probably as many reasons why individuals take drugs as there are people who take them. The youngsters who use drugs heavily are usually using them for more reasons than just to go along with the group, or to rebel against parents. Drug abuse may serve a youngster's personal needs (pleasure, recreation, relief from tension or boredom, self-medication, or need for peer socializing).

To understand fully what adolescent drug use is all about and how to prevent or treat it, one must look at it in the full context of a teenager's life. Teenagers, probably more than any other age group, tend to have feelings of low self-esteem and inadequacy. As they struggle to achieve an identity, they frequently doubt whether they are going to make it in life. Upon experimenting with drugs, some youngsters are likely to find that they blur these negative feelings, at least temporarily. Many parents are unable to recognize or relate to the challenging and anxiety-laden aspects of modern adolescent development. They neither understand nor know how to deal with such adolescent behavior as rebellion, drug and alcohol use, sexual promiscuity, and school failure. Adolescents often distrust their parents and people who could be of help and turn to chemical solutions in an attempt to "feel better fast."

Psychoactive drugs take away depression, anxiety, or tension, or produce euphoria. Thus, some youngsters end up taking drugs to escape from uncomfortable or painful feelings. It is difficult for parents to identify with or understand why or how adolescents might be self-medicating. A typical response might be "What has my boy got to be depressed or anxious about? He doesn't have a mortgage to pay, he doesn't have car payments, he doesn't have to go to work or work at something he doesn't like." Problems of the adolescent are often minimized or discounted. If a sensitive youngster is disappointed in love, the frustration may be discounted and the full impact never really understood: "Oh, that's puppy love and you'll have a hundred other loves." Yet the adolescent might feel that the world is coming to an end. There are school pressures and the pressures to choose a career and make important decisions for their future lives. Like all human beings, adolescents have their pressures, their depressions, their anxieties, their losses, their fears; and it is sometimes difficult for others to know what toll these hardships may take.

A Generation Gap

It is generally recognized that there is a gap between the attitudes of adults and the attitudes of adolescents regarding the use of drugs. Nowlis (1969) concluded that there is some contradiction when so many adults react with moralism, anger, and punitiveness on hearing of youth drug abuse when it is adults "who are the main consumers of tranquilizers, pep pills, addictive sleeping pills, brain-damaging drugs like alcohol, and cancer-producing agents like cigarettes." Smoking cigarettes results in the death of more people than injecting heroin. It follows that parents who smoke cigarettes are not in the best position to be effective in warning their children of the harmfulness of drugs like marijuana. One survey showed that 25 percent of all women over the age of thirty were receiving prescriptions for amphetamines, barbiturates, or tranquilizers, with the proportion approaching 40 percent for women of higher-income families (Cohen 1971). Excluding alcohol, coffee, and cigarettes, Cohen estimated that "over 50 percent of the total American population over thirteen years of age has at least tried some powerful mind-altering drug via prescription or on the illicit market" (p. 16).

Friedman and Santo (1984) found that 99 percent of parents in PTA groups disapproved of use of marijuana by their children, compared to 47 percent of high school seniors who disapprove; 30 percent of the parents responded that there should be different standards for adults and young persons regarding the use of drugs and alcohol. Only 9 percent of the parents said that parents should refrain from use of alcohol if they disapprove of use of marijuana by their children. The reasons that the parent group gave for not wanting their child to smoke marijuana were, in order of frequency of response, as follows:

It is harmful to the mind (impairs mental functioning) (88 percent)

In interferes with performance of school work or with functioning in other important serious life tasks (87 percent)

In interferes with the development of good, mature personality (79 percent)

It impairs positive motivation, drive, or ambition (induces apathy) (78 percent)

The child could get arrested, get into trouble with the law or with school authorities (75 percent)

Modern-day parents should be familiar with what has been learned about drugs. Children will pay more attention if they know their parents are well informed, and it helps to counteract some of the less reliable information that they learn from their peers. What are some of the reliable scientific facts that parents can tell their youngsters about the dangers of using drugs like marijuana? For example, it is true that recent research has shown that there are more serious, long-term, harmful physical and mental effects from heavy use of marijuana than had been known earlier. It is known that impaired lung function, similar to that found in cigarette smokers, follows the extended use of marijuana. The research also suggests that there may be serious effects on the human reproductive system. More directly relevant for youngsters is the fact that acute marijuana intoxication interferes with mental functioning and may impair the learning and thinking processes. It is, thus, an impediment to classroom performance. In addition, marijuana use has effects on perception and motor coordination and therefore may affect driving performance, increasing the likelihood of automobile accidents.

Young people tend to believe that they cannot be seriously harmed by drugs. It is not easy to frighten them away from using drugs. It is therefore essential that parents have the facts, and not try to use "fire and brimstone" tactics, and do not threaten or moralize too much.

An argument that youngsters throw at parents is "Well, you yourselves drink and smoke." If the parent(s) use illicit drugs it becomes even more difficult to present an argument against their use. Parents who are social drinkers might emphasize that it takes a certain amount of development and maturity to be able to use alcohol in a responsible manner.

The Family Role in Adolescent Drug Abuse

In adolescence there is a search for family stability. When a family breakup occurs through divorce or when the parents are living together but emotionally divorced or there is an atmosphere of unremitting tension or quiet despair in the family, the teenager's anxiety intensifies and there is more likelihood of using drugs. Teens may miss the protection and warmth of the family and the support that they had during childhood. Involvement in drug use could be a signal that the youngster is having difficulty moving toward a more independent status.

There can be problems in the family relationships or in the child's perception of the parent-child relationship of which the parents are not aware. As a matter of fact, it has been found that approximately one half (49 percent) of adolescent clients who enter treatment for drug abuse report that "family problems" are one of the main reasons they apply for treatment. Included in the category of family problems are family crises in the areas of health, mental health, death, and so on; lack of family interest and support in schoolwork; chronic family disruptions; and runaways (Friedman et al. 1980).

Some adolescents exaggerate the seriousness and importance of family problems and minimize the seriousness of their own drug abuse problems. The parents of these youngsters tend to see the situation quite differently: the worst problem is their adolescent child's drug abuse, without which they claim the family would manage reasonably well.

However, serious involvement in drug use has been found to be influenced by family relationship factors and the quality of parent-adolescent relationships. The degree of severity of abuse is significantly related to such family factors as the religious background and educational level of the parents, the disruption and dissolution of family structures, certain family constellation factors, and the number and types of problems which the adolescent clients perceived to be present in their families (Friedman et al. 1980).

Newcomb and his colleagues (1983) concluded that parents, particularly the mother, are a powerful modeling influence for their children, either encouraging or discouraging drug use. When the mothers are cigarette smokers and/or moderate drinkers, teenage children are more likely to use a variety of drugs (Miller and Cisin 1983). Unconventional parents, excessively passive mothers, lack of perceived closeness to parents by adolescents, and drinking and drug use patterns of parents are all factors which have been found to be positively correlated with drug use (Kandel 1982; Brook et al. 1980; Jessor and Jessor 1977). These reported characteristics are, however, not true of all families in which adolescents use illicit drugs and they can also be found in some families where the adolescent members do not use illicit drugs.

Families of adolescent drug users differ significantly from families in which the adolescent offspring either do not use drugs or have used marijuana only experimentally. In contrast to experimental drug users or non-users, adolescents with serious drug problems come from families with the following characteristics:

There is more discrepancy between how the parents would ideally like their children to be and how they perceive them actually to be (Alexander and Dibb 1977).

Parents are perceived as having relatively less influence than peers. Both parents are perceived to be more approving of drug use (Jessor 1975).

Offspring perceive less love from both parents, particularly from fathers (Mellinger et al. 1975; Streit et al. 1974).

There is less shared authority and poorer communication in the family (Cannon 1976; Hunt 1974).

There is less spontaneous problem-solving in structured family interaction tasks (Mead and Campbell 1972).

High levels of perceived parental support and perceived positive parent-child relationships have been found to be related to low levels of drug use in adolescents in several studies (Blum 1972; Bethards 1973; Streit et al. 1974). Cooper and Olson (1977) noted that high school students who reported little or no drug use also reported that they perceived a high degree of parental supportiveness in their families and that they experienced high personal esteem; whereas low perceived parental support and low self-esteem were related to frequent drug usage.

In his family therapy work, Reilly (1978) found nine dysfunctional family interaction patterns to be characteristic of families with substance abuse members, which he postulated could maintain and exacerbate drug abuse. These characteristics are not unique or specific to substance abuse families, but tend to occur more regularly and in more extreme or intense form in these families.

Negative interaction (family members give negative messages when they communicate: criticism, put-downs, complaints, and nagging).

Inconsistent limit setting or structuring by parents.

A cry for help or attention by the substance abuser revealing drug use and related problems as a way of getting a particular response such as attention from parents.

Global or massive parental denial (they manage not to see what is going on). They fail to relate to either the evidence of substance abuse or to accidents and other signs which indicate that the problem is getting worse.

The use of drugs by offspring provides vicarious gratification which parents need either consciously or unconsciously.

Use of drugs and alcohol as self-medication or as a disinhibitor by the substance abusing member who needs this aid for expressing or acting out reactions or feelings such as destructiveness or violence.

Difficulty in expressing anger between parents and children (unexpressed rage). There is no appropriate continuum of expression, resulting in either no expression or violence.

Irrational parental expectations of the substance-abusing child, who is perceived in terms of the parents' feelings about a grandparent or other relative, and is not seen as a real person for him or herself.

"Incredible language." Family members make statements, such as promises about their behavior in the future, that are so unrealistic they cannot be believed.

Obviously, one way to try to solve family problems is to work directly with the family. It is not just the adolescent drug abuser, but the parents and other family members who need help. Aside from other problems that may exist in the family, the impact on the parents' lives resulting from their adolescent child's drug abuse is often devastating. The youngster's drug-related problems (difficulties at school, involvement with police, erratic and sometimes violent behavior) themselves create a family crisis.

Also, it obviously would help the situation if family members would try not to blame each other for problems. Each family member should try to adopt an objective and non-defensive stance, and to search their own attitudes and behavior for any possible way that they could be contributing to the maintenance of the adolescent's drug abuse.

What Is Real Help?

Several frantic phone calls came into the drug treatment clinic one day from the mother of an 18-year-old girl. The mother wanted to know what to do about her child who was not coming home at night. According to the mother, her daughter was apparently using and selling drugs, and behaving in such a way as to cause a tremendous amount of stress and anxiety for the family. The parents were bending over backwards in trying to be helpful, but they were fearful of the complications and concerned that they might be pushing the girl to suicide (the ultimate threat).

The therapist talked about some of the things the parents might do. While it would probably be inappropriate to confront their daughter in a threatening way, she could nevertheless be confronted in a supportive and loving way. The parents could let her know how concerned they were and also how painful and disruptive the experience was for them, not just because they cared about her but because they cared about their own lives and couldn't continue to live like that. If the daughter really wanted to live a disruptive lifestyle—she was over 18—there might be little the parents could do. They might have to accept that reality but point out to the daughter that she would have to set up her own residence because they could not approve of her behavior. The situation would still worry the parents, and would continue to be very painful, but her departure would cut down the level of stress in the home. It was important to be supportive but also firm (in terms of setting limits and by insisting that the daughter go into treatment), because she was showing that she needed help by the nature of her behavior.

Many young drug abusers manage to keep their drug problem secret. Those who let it become public knowledge, or at least known in the family, are often asking either for limits and control or for help, no matter how much they say they are not. This mother was urged to get everybody in for a family session and the girl was scheduled for individual counseling.

Another type of phone call that comes into a drug abuse treatment clinic is a call from a parent wanting help or advice on how to handle the problem of an adolescent who has gotten into trouble. He may have stolen something from the house, and one parent knows about it and is trying to protect the child from being restricted or punished by the other parent. Or he may have had a run-in with the law related to drugs and his parents are trying to keep it a secret from other relatives and to avoid the legal consequences of the offense. The parents may be trying to avoid restrictions that the school has placed on drug and alcohol users. The parents may have been repeatedly rescuing their youngster. When parents collude with a child to protect him or her from the consequences of his/her actions, they teach a lesson that isn't true. In the larger world, outside the family, there are consequences to human actions. For some adolescents, the parents' continuous rescuing only results in the youngster taking more chances and provoking a more serious problem. For these adolescents it appears that there is a tendency, albeit not conscious, to continue testing the relationship and the situation, until they miscalculate and end up either with a serious overdose or in court. Even though adolescents assert that they don't want limits put on their behavior, they feel safer in a milieu in which they know what the limits are and know the limits are enforced. There is a point at which the parents are going to have to face the inevitable and tell their youngster that past rescuing has not improved the situation and that they are going to have to let the youngster face the consequences of his/her actions. Of course, it is helpful if the parents get the youngster into counseling or treatment before they cut off the rescuing.

Many parents cannot emotionally tolerate seeing their children face any kind of pain or disappointment. They never teach them how to deal with loss. When a goldfish dies, rather than let the child mourn the goldfish, they take the dead one out and go to the store to replace the fish so the youngster doesn't have to experience the loss. A parent must be willing to admit that it's all right to have a depressed day, a happy day, an angry day, to feel sad, or to cry. People learn from what they experience.

Children learn how to fall down in the process of learning to walk. If they are held all the time, they do not learn balance. And if they are not permitted to walk on their own, the muscles atrophy and they never walk. Emotional strength needs to be exercised in the same way. If one is carried emotionally throughout life, then one never develops the ability to cope with difficulties.

We have seen literally hundreds of parents who continue to give money to their adolescents which they know is being spent to buy illicit drugs. They are afraid that if they stop giving money, their youngster will steal and get in trouble with the law. Also, it is often a way of holding on to their relationship with their youngster as they are afraid of losing the relationship.

Another question that parents ask: If our child has started smoking grass and drinking beer, isn't it better to let him continue on condition that he only use these substances in the house? These parents think that by allowing a youngster to use drugs in the home, he or she is less likely to use them on the street or in the school yard, and less likely to be picked up by the police, or to get into some other trouble. They accept the problem as a fait accompli, and are looking for a way to contain it. They are not thinking of the future implications of the message that although they disapprove, they are trying to make a compromise because they feel helpless. Their mixed feelings of disapproval and helplessness are conveyed to the child. Their chances of being obeyed are not enhanced.

Don't promise things or make threats that you can't keep. Don't buy your children's obedience. All you do by giving all the time is teach your children how to take. In substance-abusing families, we see that often language doesn't mean anything. Kids lie all the time and parents threaten all the time, but they often make ineffective threats. "If I catch you doing this again, I'm throwing you out of the house," or "I'm going to beat you up." Or, "I'm going to turn you over to the police." A threat doesn't mean anything, if you're not going to carry it through. And if the threat is carried out, it often only leads to more drug abuse on the part of the teenager. Something that is most difficult for parents to face and understand is that a child who is very seriously involved in drugs over a long period of time may be committing a kind of passive suicide.

Listening

Adolescents often feel that they are not heard, listened to, or adequately regarded by their parents. When that happens they feel rejected. Parents are often not aware that they have a tendency to shut children out. Michele Marks, the daughter of one of the authors of this chapter, put it this way: "Parents should listen to their children's problems but not just to give their advice. I like it when I can go to my parents and they share their experiences with me. It makes me feel closer to them. I'm sure many other kids would love for their parents to open up to them, not feel that their parents are above them. Kids can gain a lot from talking, not getting lectures, from their parents. A discussion or retelling of a parent's earlier experience when the parent was young can help their kid much more when it comes to living their lives."

Thirteen-year-old Connie is an example of how an unexpressed hidden fear of an adolescent can lead to disturbed and rebellious behavior. Her father was a fire-fighter, and her mother was not in very good health. Connie was afraid that her parents would die soon and therefore she could not talk to them about her problem and was upset and angry. She had no living relatives to go to if her parents were to die. She began hanging out more with a group after school and, like the others, used marijuana. She stayed out late some nights, and her school performance worsened. Connie's parents were making an effort to listen and understand what was making Connie's performance change. They discovered that she was using drugs, but they had not been able to elicit the underlying fear. Seeking help, the family went to a family therapist who was able to help the family understand what was really bothering Connie. When Connie was reassured, she began to return to her earlier, more cooperative behavior. Fortunately, Connie was reached early before her drug use became a serious problem.

Why is it that parents have difficulty listening to their adolescent children? Why is it that many adolescents feel they are not being heard or understood by the parent? Some parents have defenses or barriers that make it difficult for them to hear or understand certain attitudes or feelings. Some interrupt or block out the adolescent's expression of unacceptable attitudes.

Parents must not only understand the content of what the adolescent is expressing or trying to express, but also the feelings associated with the content. This often means encouraging the adolescent to say more about and explain further his or her feelings and attitudes relating to a particular issue at hand. To learn how to be a good listener, a parent must be able to adopt a non-judgmental attitude and a non-defensive stance. It does not mean that the parent has to agree with everything the adolescent is saying, or even to take it all as being factual or accurate. One can listen with sensitivity and empathy, accepting the child's right to his or her feelings, without accepting the child's behavior. Also, in ruling out a particular behavior the parent should be careful not to give the impression of rejecting the child.

Some teenagers are impatient, intolerant, and eager to act; they have no time for thoughtful consideration. They test and challenge. They frequently respond to parents and other authority figures with irritation, argument, and denial. They may also become moody and depressed—overly serious and with a dark outlook on life. The challenge for their parents and teachers, and other older people who deal with them, is to change the mood from anxious intensity, despair, and anger to a more positive and thoughtful climate.

Parents faced with such challenging situations should ask themselves, "Can we listen to our child's complaints and anger (especially when directed at us) with an open mind? Do we have the capacity to listen with understanding to ideas, activities, and values that are antagonistic to our own?" This is illustrated by the following brief excerpt from a family therapy session. The parents and the other children of this "blended" family (including two children from the mother's previous marriage and three children from the father's previous marriage) were admonishing Jeanne, a 13-year-old drug user, that she should make every effort to "adjust" to the situation, like everyone else:

Jeanne: "I hate you all." (To the stepmother and her two children.) "I don't want to be around you. I want to stay in my own house where I'm comfortable, I don't want to talk to you."

Therapist: "That's all right. At least you got it out."

Father: "Do you know how you are hurting us? Do you know how much pain you caused for your mother? You've got to adjust."

Therapist (to Father): "Let her express herself."

Jeanne: (Turns away from parents, the back of her head faces them and she talks to wall.)

Stepmother: "Turn around, if you want to talk."

Therapist: "That's okay, as long as she keeps talking. Let her talk away from you; make an attempt to listen."

By the end of the session the parents weren't just asking her to adjust, they were listening. Later that evening Jeanne hugged her stepmother: "I want you to know I don't just hate you." Once she was able to express her hatred, she could begin to give it up. She had been allowed to express her feelings. Her parents and her brother and sisters had accepted her statements, and no one had criticized her for them.

It is, of course, easier for the therapist to be patient with a rebellious, challenging adolescent since the therapist has to deal with this situation for only one hour a week. It is much harder for parents living with the child to respond with the objectivity and patience of a therapist. Expressions of adolescent disrespect and hatred can be tolerated in a therapy room, but are too difficult for many parents to deal with at home.

"I hate you; I have always hated you." Most parents consider such a statement from their child as inappropriate and may refuse to listen to it or punish the child for saying it. A red flag goes up when a child expresses disrespect, hostility, challenge, or hatred. Nevertheless, usually the best thing the parent can do in the situation is to listen to the negative expressions and try to understand more about why the child feels that way. There is likely to be fear, anxiety, and confusion behind the anger. Most parents can do this only after they have been helped to learn how to control their own feelings, since the tension of a rebellious and disturbed adolescent is wearing on the parent.

Parents can even take advantage of the child's hostile and provocative expression to improve the relationship. An appropriate response by a parent might be: "I didn't know that you hated me that much. Obviously, it upsets me a great deal and hurts me, and even makes me angry at you. But it's more important that we find out why you have been hating me and then to see whether there is something we can do to improve the situation between us."

This is a lot to ask of a parent: to accept hostility, deflect anger, foster positive feelings, and try to restore the teenager's trust. Parents are to be forgiven if they cannot hold to this objective, understanding model. Nevertheless, it can be a goal toward which parents strive.

Acceptance, Approval, and Disapproval

A genuinely compassionate attitude on the part of the parent creates a facilitating atmosphere. This does not mean that the parents should give unconditional approval to anything their child does. Adolescents tend to respond to the need for immediate results or gratification, while parents often look at the larger picture, and at what will be the best for the adolescent in the long run. It is generally best not to approach the behavior of adolescents from a judgmental or disapproving point of view, but only to point out what may work better for the adolescent's life.

It is sometimes helpful if the parent has a capacity for humor and the ability to tap into the liveliness and natural exuberance of the teenager. The adolescent who has learned to laugh at what angered, embittered, or frightened him or her, or caused shame or guilt, is likely to be showing improvement.

Adolescents may question how useful it is to confide in parents or to talk over such issues as whether to smoke marijuana. Times are different from when the parents were teenagers and social attitudes are different. Parents have not been in the same situations as their children and have not had to make the same decisions. A parent can say, "I did not have all the same experiences that you have been having lately, but I knew what it was to be disappointed or frustrated, or angry at my parents or unhappy or confused. Those are human conditions that we all share." Parents do not have to have the answers at all times, and it is sometimes better to empathize with feelings rather than acting and sounding as if one has the answers at all times.

It is important to communicate in order to keep the conversation or dialogue going, to remember when one was a teenager with frustrations, confusions, and impulsiveness, and to share what you felt and did during adolescence. However, it is not easy for some parents to share their adolescent experiences and problems in a frank, open way.

Differences between Firmness and Punishment

Can you stop your adolescent child from using drugs through punishment? Generally, the temporary withdrawal of privileges is more effective, as a disciplinary measure, than harsh types of punishment, especially with older adolescents. For young children who are misbehaving, temporary restraint is better than harsh retaliation, and most parents know this.

The older adolescent needs more explanation of the parent's actions. Firm and consistent limit setting, which is often sufficient for the younger adolescent, will be less often sufficient for the older one unless accompanied by reasonable discussion and explanation. Teenagers desire and need the respect of their parents. They are struggling themselves to become responsible men and women.

Almost everyone agrees that parents have to be in charge. Parents have to provide direction, give guidance, and sometimes must exercise discipline. There is less unanimity of opinion regarding the use of punishment. Some parents seem to know how to use punishment judiciously and constructively and other parents don't. In general, it is wise to think twice about imposing punishment and to be careful not to do it in the heat of anger. For example, if an adolescent has been refusing to behave as considered appropriate by the parent, or has been disrespectful or challenging, the parent might say, "I want you to go to your room and stay there for a while." In some families, as stated above, this may work reasonably well. The alleged "punishment" may actually serve more as a cooling-off mechanism for both parent and child than as an unpleasant experience or a threat to the teenager. It could possibly have the effect of teaching the teenager to avoid in the future the types of misbehavior that led to the punishment. In other cases, it might engage the teenager and the parent in an adversarial relationship or cut off communication. The teenager might become more angry because of having the punishment imposed. As a result, he/she might continue the misbehavior in the future but try to do it in a more covert way to lessen the likelihood of being caught. Or the teenager might retaliate against the parent in a different way.

There are some parents who appear to be successful in teaching their adolescents to maintain adequate self-control and acceptable behavior without resorting to punishment. While it is doubtful that adequate control of a 4- or 5-year-old can be achieved without exercising some restraint or punishment, procedures that make it possible to maintain adequate control of adolescents without punishment are to be desired. However, there are other risks or dangers which the parent must watch for in the no-punishment situation. Has the parent achieved this degree of control by inducing too much guilt or too much fear, thus severely constricting the child's spontaneity, or by putting too great an emotional burden on the child?

When there is anger, it may work better for some parents to say, "I'm aware that I am angry at you now and I don't think you and I can deal with this problem constructively at this time. I suggest that we put it aside for now but I would like to talk with you about the problem in an hour from now." After the cooling-off period, the parent will be better able to control any impulsive or emotional reactions and to understand the teenager's side of the situation. This break also gives the youngster time to reflect and consider his/her own motivations and actions. Sometimes an adolescent is unintentionally being rebellious and provocative in a search for secure and realistic boundaries, and actually wants this rebellious behavior controlled by the parent. If the parent can explain the limits, boundaries, and rules in a clear, firm, and consistent way, and feels reasonably confident of the usefulness and justice of his/her position, rather than feeling insecure or guilty about depriving the youngster, it is likely that it will make some positive impression on the teenager, even if it doesn't solve the problem immediately.

How to Be a Good Parent

There are plenty of readily available books on how to be a good parent. Reading one or two such books can be a worthwhile investment of a parent's time. However, such reading can be of limited value. The advice given is more appropriate for preventing the development of serious problems in parent-child relationships than for eliminating or solving the problems after they have already developed. Many parents feel that it is easy to give the advice, but not so easy to apply it effectively in a real-life situation. The advice often does not seem to fit the parent's unique family situation, or the actions and attitudes recommended by the book do not fit the particular parent's values or personality.

While recognizing the limited value of such advice, there is nevertheless some point to presenting here the following brief synopsis of one such approach to positive parenting. In his systematic approach to *Confident Parenting*, Silberman (1982) suggests that parents accept a view of their children's needs which balances the "executive" and "caring" roles of parents:

> The executive role involves all those parental tasks which directly let a child know that he or she is under the influence and direction of an adult who is *in charge.* When parents are doing their executive job, they meet children's need for advice, coaching, choices, direction, discipline, limits, religion, responsibility, role models, structure. . . . Children are reassured by having parents who make decisions about the directions their lives are taking and the rules by which they must live. . . . Children get valuable practice early in life on not getting their own way all the time and being confronted with demands for responsible behavior. . . .
>
> The caring role involves things parents express and do to let a child know that he or she is accepted, nurtured, supported, and loved. When parents are doing their caring job, they meet children's needs for acceptance, attention, communication, encouragement, friendship, fun, love, material things (food, money, clothes), patience, protection, respect, time, trust, understanding. . . . The degree to which parents have the power to

reinforce their children's behavior, both through rewards and penalties, depends upon children's feelings that they are valued. . . . When children feel continually rejected, they become immune to parental reinforcements. . . . Children cannot weather the frustration caused by their own limitations and failures without parental support. . . .

Parents need to perform both roles to have *influence* over their children's behavior. Often, parents see these two roles conflicting with each other. Therefore they tend to favor one over the other *or* jump back and forth between them, totally confusing the child. It is important *and* possible to blend the two roles into one approach to parenting. (pp. 6–8)

If the parent-child relationship has developed reasonably well, the adolescent should need a lesser degree of each of the executive and caring parental functions than he/she needed at an earlier age. But the adolescent's strivings and demands for autonomy and independence can be deceptive, and he or she still needs a fair amount of parental direction as well as nurturing and caring.

In his discussion of how parents should implement their executive role in an assertive and confident manner, Silberman presents the following table of parental responses ("authority styles") which is helpful in differentiating between "nonassertive, aggressive, and assertive stances toward children" (p. 39):

Nonassertive	Aggressive	Assertive
You:	You:	You:
are evasive	blow up in anger	persist
beg	get into power struggles	listen to children's point of view
act flustered	endlessly argue	
try to "make things do"	accuse	reveal honest feelings
are confusing, unclear	discredit children's thinking	give brief reasons
let yourself be treated unfairly	trick, tease, put down	politely refuse to do something
worry about being popular	give harsh punishments	empathize
	nag	carry out reasonable consequences
are afraid of upsetting children	withhold information about what you expect	make clear, direct requests
blame yourself		

Notes

Alexander, B.K. and Dibb, G.S. 1977. Interpersonal perception in addict families. *Family Process* 16: 17–18.

Beschner, G.M. and Friedman, A.S. 1985. Treatment of adolescent drug abusers. *Journal of the Addictions* 20 (6 and 7): 971–993.

Bethards, J. 1973. Parental support and the use of drugs. *Humbolt Journal of Social Relations* 1:26–28.

Blum, R.H. 1972. *Horatio Alger's Children.* San Francisco, California: Jossey-Bass.

Brook, J.S.; Lukoff, I.F.; and Whitman, M. 1980. Initiation into adolescent marijuana use. *Journal of General Psychology* 137: 133–142.

Cannon, S.R. 1976. *Social Functioning Patterns in Families of Offspring Receiving Treatment for Drug Abuse.* Roslyn Heights, New York: Libra Publications.

Cohen, A.Y. 1971. The journey beyond trips: Alternatives to drugs. *Journal of Psychedelic Drugs* 3: 16–21.

Cooper, D.N. and Olson, D.H. 1977. Perceived parental support and self esteem as related to adolescent drug use. Minneapolis: Multi-Resource Center.

Friedman, A.S.; Pomerance, E.; Sanders, R.; Santo, Y.; and Utada, A. 1980. The structure and problems of the families of adolescent drug users. *Contemporary Drug Problems* 9(3): 327–356.

Friedman, A.S. and Santo, Y. 1984. A comparison of attitudes of parents and high school senior students regarding cigarette, alcohol and drug use. *Journal of Drug Education* 14(1).

Glickman, N. and Utada, A. 1983. *Characteristics of Drug Users in Urban Public High Schools.* Rockville, Maryland: Project Report to National Institute on Drug Abuse, Grant No. H81 DA 01657.

Hunt, D.G. 1974. Parental permissiveness as perceived by the offspring and the degree of marijuana usage among offspring. *Human Relations* 27: 267–285.

Jessor, R. 1975. Predicting time of onset of marijuana use: A developmental study of high school youth. In Lettieri, D., ed., *Predicting Adolescent Drug Abuse: A Review of Issues, Methods and Correlates.* Washington, D.C.: DHEW Publication Number ADM–76–299, National Institute on Drug Abuse, U.S. Government Printing Office.

Jessor, R. and Jessor, S.L. 1977. *Problem Behavior and Psychosocial Development: A Longitudinal Study of Youth.* New York: Academic Press.

Kandel, D. 1974. Inter- and intragenerational influences of adolescent marihuana use. *Journal of Social Issues* 30 (2): 107–135.

———. 1982. Epidemiological and psychosocial perspectives on adolescent drug abuse. *Journal of the American Academy of Child Psychiatry* 21 (4): 328–347.

Mead, D.E. and Campbell, S.S. 1972. Decision-making and interaction by families with and without a drug abusing child. *Family Process* 11: 437–498.

Mellinger, D.E.; Somers, R.H.; and Manheimer, D.I. 1975. Drug use research items pertaining to personality and interpersonal relations: A working paper for research investigators. In Lettieri, D.J., ed., *Predicting Adolescent Drug Abuse: A Review of Issues, Methods and Correlates.* Washington, D.C.: DHEW Publication Number ADM–76–299, National Institute on Drug Abuse, U.S. Government Printing Office.

Miller, J.D. and Cisin, I. 1983. *Highlights from the National Survey on Drug Abuse: 1982.* Rockville, Maryland: National Institute on Drug Abuse, DHHS Publication Number ADM–83–1277, U.S. Government Printing Office.

National Institute on Drug Abuse. 1984a. *Parents: What You Can Do About Drug Abuse*. Washington, D.C.: NIDA, U.S. Government Printing Office, DHHS Publication Number ADM–1267.

———. 1984b. *Parents, Peers and Pot II: Parents in Action*. Washington, D.C.: NIDA, U.S. Government Printing Office.

Newcomb, M.; Hula, G.; and Bentler, P. 1983. Mothers' influence on the drug use of their children: Confirmatory tests of direct modeling and mediational theories. *Developmental Psychology* 19: 714–726.

Nowlis, H.H. 1969. *Drugs on the College Campus*. Garden City, New York: Anchor Books.

Reilly, D.M. 1978. Family factors in the etiology and treatment of youthful drug abuse. *Family Therapy* 2: 149–171.

Silberman, M.L. 1982. *Confident Parenting: Assertive Relationships with Children*. Ardmore, Pennsylvania: The ARC Program.

Silberman, M.L. and Wheelan, S.A. 1980. *How to Discipline without Feeling Guilty: Assertive Relationships with Children*. New York: Hawthorn Books.

Streit, F.; Halsted, D.; and Pascale, P. 1974. Differences among youthful users and nonusers of drugs based on their perceptions of parental behavior. *International Journal of the Addictions* 9(5): 749–755.

6

The Family Therapist's Use of Self

S.J. Marks

Editors' Note: *In this chapter, Jeff Marks has shared himself in his unusually open and sometimes terribly honest way. In allowing us to see the extreme authenticity of his commitment of his whole self to his patients and families, he has given us a rare gift.*

Selected Quotations That Are Cornerstones of My Philosophy of Life and My Psychotherapy

1. I believe that insight is a byproduct of change. You have to go past it to see what it is.—Carl Whitaker

2. Those who cannot remember the past are condemned to repeat it. —George Santayana

3. To express what one thinks and feels unafraid and unashamed is one of the great consolations of life.—Theodore Reik

4. I can stand anything but pain.—Oscar Levant

5. There is nothing that man fears more than the touch of the unknown. —Elias Canetti

6. *Negative capability*, that is when a man is capable of being in uncertainties, mysteries, doubts, without any irritable reaching after fact and reason. —John Keats

7. The last freedom that not even the concentration camp could take away—to decide how one wishes to think and feel about the conditions of one's life. . . .—Bruno Bettelheim

8. I can't go on. I'll go on.—Samuel Beckett

9. I want the poetry I read to make me happy, but unless it deals with the hell of our lives it leaves me cold.—James Wright

10. I can destroy the object and it will still survive.—D.W. Winnicott

11. Live or die, but don't poison everything.—Saul Bellow

12. What people do is what they want.—S.J. Marks

13. The difficulty is, I trick myself while trying to be honest.—R.C. Day

14. If you're afraid of loneliness, don't marry.—Anton Chekhov

15. The road to hell is paved with good intentions.—Old adage

16. Sometimes you have to take a long time to play like yourself.—Miles Davis

17. A lifetime burning in every moment.—T.S. Eliot

18. Every day's a great day to play baseball.—Ernie Banks

19. You only go around once; get all the gusto you can out of life.—Schlitz beer commercial

20. I have very little faith in rational thinking or the rational components of psychotherapy. So I think of healing as both the repair of the intuitive and the integration of the intuitive and the rational.—Carl Whitaker

21. To abolish hope is to bring thought back to the body.—Albert Camus

22. I am speaking now of the person of the analyst in so far as he represents and embodies a certain deep inner attitude which, in my opinion, is a decisive factor, and that is why I have often maintained that it is what the analyst *is* rather than what he *says* that matters.—Sacha Nacht

23. With the torches of chaos and doubt, the sage lights his way.—Chuang Tzu

24. Love is desire for another person's growth.—Erich Fromm

25. No amount of drilled-in rules or reflexes can prepare the swordsman for the infinity of different attacks which he may have to face, especially when confronted with more than one opponent. He is taught, therefore, never to make any specific preparation for attack nor to expect it from any particular direction. Otherwise, to meet an unusual attack he will have to retreat from one stance before being able to adopt another. He must be able to spring immediately from a relaxed center of rest to the direction required. This relaxed openness of sensitivity in every direction is precisely *Kuan*, or as it is more commonly called in Zen, *Mushin*, which is to say—"no mind," no strain of the mind to watch for a particular result.—D.T. Suzuki

26. A Chinese allegory tells how a monk sets off on a long pilgrimage to find the Buddha. He spends years and years on his quest and finally he comes to the country where the Buddha lives. He crosses a river; it is wide river, and he looks about him while the boatman rows him across. There is a corpse floating on the water and it is coming closer. The monk looks. The corpse is so close he can touch it. He recognizes the corpse, it is his own. The monk loses all self-control and wails. There he floats, dead. Nothing remains. Anything he has ever been, ever learned, ever owned, floats past him, still and without life, moved by

the slow current of the wide river. It is the first moment of his liberation.—Janwillem van de Wetering

27. It is a violence from within that protects us from a violence without. It is the imagination pressing back against the pressure of reality. It seems, in the last analysis, to have something to do with our self-preservation; and that, no doubt, is why the expression of it, the sound of its words, helps us to live our lives.—Wallace Stevens

28. I'm a fairly practical and handy person; I was brought up on a farm where we learned how to figure things out and fix them. During the first year or two that I was at Daitoku-ji Sodo, out back working in the garden, helping put in a little firewood, or firing up the bath, I noticed a number of times little improvements that could be made. Ultimately I ventured to suggest to the head monks some labor- and time-saving techniques. They were tolerant of me for a while. Finally, one day one of them took me aside and said, "We don't want to do things any better or any faster, because that's not the point—the point is that you live the whole life. If we speed up the work in the garden, you'll just have to spend that much more time sitting in the zendo, and your legs will hurt more." It's all one meditation. The importance is in the right balance, and not how to save time in one place or another. I've turned that insight over and over ever since.—Gary Snyder

29. Each of us is so ashamed of his own helplessness and ignorance that he considers it appropriate to communicate only what he thinks others will understand.—Czeslaw Milosz

30. What made me take this trip to Africa? There is no quick explanation. Things got worse and worse and worse and pretty soon they were too complicated.

    When I think of my condition at the age of fifty-five when I bought the ticket, all is grief. The facts begin to crowd me me and soon I get a pressure in the chest. A disorderly rush begins—my parents, my wives, my girls, my children, my farm, my animals, my habits, my money, my music lessons, my drunkenness, my prejudices, my brutality, my teeth, my face, my soul! I have to cry, "No, no, get back, curse you, let me alone!" But how can they let me alone? They belong to me. They are mine. And they pile into me from all sides. It turns into chaos.

    However, the world which I thought so mighty an oppressor has removed its wrath from me. But if I am to make sense to you people and explain why I went to Africa I must face up to the facts.—Saul Bellow

This is the beginning of a selective or partial description of my journey as a psychotherapist. I began thinking about writing this years ago, but I have found no certain way yet to say it. Another way of saying this is that I lacked conviction, lacked patience, lacked faith in my own technique, in my language, in myself. I want to state what I've needed to do to position myself to become an effective family therapist (especially with violent and drug-abuse families). I also want to talk about some of the attributes, the discipline, and the training of a family therapist.

I want to describe my use of self with difficult treatment families, including my efforts to retrieve and get in tune with the out-of-conscious feelings and reactions stirred up in me by a family during a session, and to use these as a tool to work with the family at times of impasse. I hope to share with you, the reader, some anecdotes and vignettes about this to give you some sense of me in process; I want to share with you some incidents in the treatment process—a sense of what I do and what I try to do with individuals and families. You'll look at what I present from many different levels, perhaps seeing quite different things from what I see. Your grounding and mine are part of the process; you see or hear from different angles and frames of reference.

Whenever, in the role of family therapist, I start on a journey with a new family, I have feelings of helplessness and uncertainty. What I'm going to present is Jeff Marks struggling, battling, contending with patients and families who are competent and successful in a variety of ways, and who, sometimes, make me feel dumb and inadequate and incompetent. But that's what intrigues and challenges me—my apprehensiveness. When treating drug and alcohol patients and their families, there's often a sense of hopelessness and incipient burnout in therapists; there's little sense you can do something to help or be of use to drug and alcohol patients. You hear about the cures and the perpetual optimistic predictions based on the idea of coping daily with sobriety ("Live one day at a time"), with drugs and alcohol as a disease; but my experience is that the rate of recidivism or relapse is high.

One of the key elements in terms of overcoming the tendency of patients to relapse is the development of oneself as a therapeutic instrument (that is, a responsive and human psychotherapist) with stick-to-itiveness or persistence or tenaciousness, to hold on to an issue and to explore it thoroughly, or to return to it again—someone who has the capacity to stay with the problems, come hell or high water, to do the job, to endure the difficulty, to endure the conflict, to endure the disappointment, and to continue with the task. Sometimes I address or confront a problem or a conflict head-on. I'm reminded of an example; a male patient whom I'd been working with for three years bruised his thumb while prying the fender of his car back from a tire after he'd had a slight accident—he's bumped his car against a fence in a parking lot while he was under the influence of drugs. Though he reported the incident in treatment, he refused to accept responsibility for the accident; it just "happened" to him. Subsequently, he neglected his wounded thumb, which became infected and gangrenous and had to be partly amputated (the tip of it). For the next year and a half in therapy, he attacked my interpretation of the accident—that he'd unconsciously set up damaging and castrating himself—calling me "rigid, pompous, and arrogant." But I weathered his insults and attacks, stuck with my interpretation, and continued to treat him. And he continued to come in to be treated. At that point, he was involved in another vehicular accident—one, however, where his car was struck by a trolley while legally stopped at a traffic light. Though he'd done nothing illegal, this accident triggered a new and different sense of viewing the incident in him—he began spontaneously to take a look at and explore his part in creating the situations of these accidents and how it functioned in his life (that is, his need to be a victim).

What I found through all of my training and treatment experience was that if you increase your sensitivity and investment enough, you can reach isolated people whose sense of self is blurred, confused, and distorted (sometimes by drug use); you can affect the family system (slowly, painfully, with many fits and starts and detours), and you can be the factor that brings change to their lives.

I'm pointing to the need to have a long training process. It's like being a top-flight gymnast or pianist—you have to put your time in to develop your responsiveness and incisiveness, to develop your sense of the possible, to develop your sense of what's going on with the difficult patient family and what's going on between them and you.

One of the things in embarking on this journey (in addition to investing oneself in a training program that will lead to learning the ground rules of psychotherapy and family therapy—to know how to do what is done) is to work hard on the issue of the use of yourself. This is done mostly by you, but it also requires intensive or close supervision. In my view, technique in family therapy comes from the therapists' use of self. Carl Whitaker is fond of quoting Barbara Betz: "The dynamics of the therapy are in the therapist."

The other thing that helps in this process, which I did, was to be involved in my own therapy. This is something I have done and still do, on occasion. I believe Rollo May did something marvelous for the profession when, in an interview that was published in a West Coast newspaper, he said he'd put himself in psychoanalysis as a patient at four different times in his life to learn about himself. I have the sense that the more I can understand myself and my family of origin the more I can be sensitive to my own confusions and subconscious processes. The more I can know myself the more I can develop myself, as that instrument, as the mutative factor in therapy. As a patient myself in therapy (I've been in psychoanalytic psychotherapy twice, in marital and family therapy on three occasions, and group therapy three times), I had some notion of what aspects of my therapists' characters and presences I responded to and what helped me to clarify my distortions and begin to face what in myself and what as a part of my family system was blocking my growth.

Other relevant experiences that I had were these: "live" supervision in group and family therapy, where I was observed working and received immediate feedback and review (and my performance anxiety was high); and case conferences and discussions where we would present in detail what we were doing in terms of our own feelings and countertransferences. These were stimulating in encouraging my thinking and in encouraging personal risk taking in exposing oneself and making oneself vulnerable.

Earlier, in 1962, when I was teaching English in Maryland, my brother gave me a subscription to the first two issues of the journal *Family Process*. When I sensed what family therapy was about, I remembered being twelve years old and hoping all of us in the family would get together in the living room—usually we were together in the breakfast room where "children were to be seen and not heard"—and to really talk to each other, to pour our hearts out, so to speak.

I have had a high investment in my interaction with psychotics, drug addicts, and other difficult-to-reach people for my parents were difficult-to-reach people and so am I. Eventually, I learned that this was a resonance to my need to be helpful (as distinguished from rescuing) to my family of origin.[1] Several years later, when I learned what family therapy actually was, I made this connection (association) to my fantasy of my family being together and talking about our real emotional issues and conflicts. It was a fantasy, a wish, because we never did get together and talk about our feelings and thoughts.

I began working with very difficult patients at Byberry (Philadelphia State Hospital)—people who were very withdrawn. I was trained by and observed Bob Martin, a psychologist who ran a group therapy training program there. Bob was forceful, clear, concise, and empathic. When Bob led a group, what I saw was a therapist who was intrusive, invasive, direct, demanding, and who entered into each person's world and asked for a personal response to their shared present reality sitting together. What I further saw was that these people began to talk and relate. He enabled them to make contact with him and each other and was able to bring a sense of usefulness or value in terms of the immediacy of their lives. What I learned was that you can reach isolated and shattered people in this way with aggression, clarity, and sensitivity.

Then, John Sonne came to Byberry, and I spent two years training with him and learning family therapy and the relation and function of the patient's florid symptomatic behavior to the family system and its dynamics. I want to mention John's incisiveness as a trainer—he has a thoughtful and thought-provoking mind.

After that, I became a student in the Family Institute of Philadelphia's three-year clinical training program in marital and family therapy, and after a year of supervision with Al Friedman, he offered me a position in a new drug abuse program he was starting at Philadelphia Psychiatric Center. (From Al, I learned about personal acceptance, a "let's talk about it" attitude he exemplified toward any issue.) There, at P.P.C., I met patients who felt they were lost causes, who trusted only themselves to doctor themselves—to prescribe and medicate themselves (yet they were at the same time certain, in their desperation, of their ability to assess their problems and treat themselves). But of course their actions to help themselves were also confused and destructive, and often their lives were at risk or draining away. Their ability to distance themselves from themselves and you was much better than your ability to connect with them—they could hold on to their symptomatology and die with it. (By the way, at that time, other clinicians in other drug and alcohol programs predicted to us that we would get only 5–10 percent of families into treatment. We regularly got between 70 and 80 percent of substance abuse families in.) I spent thirteen and a half years in that program, and during that time I spent two years (part-time) treating the families of juvenile delinquent substance abusers at the nonpublic De La Salle Vocational High School (part of the St. Gabriel's system) in Bensalem, Pennsylvania, as a therapy component to a research demonstration project.

In psychoanalysis, there's a whole theory about the unconscious, and as part of our learning experience, it's important to learn as much as you can. I believe we should have a personal therapy (individual and family) to sensitize ourselves to the reality that there is more in us than our conscious sense of ourselves, and further, I believe that some of what is there will, in all likelihood, be unpleasant or painful for us to face.

In my training process, I learned about letting your own consciousness float, about how to use your consciousness and use your free associativeness during the therapy process at times of impasse and blocks—to turn your imagination loose, to look at the conflict (the situation) from different vantage points, to see if there's a different way you could look at what's going on. And that's part of my point here, to encourage you to explore different ways to look at a situation (just as each family member expresses a different experience of the family situation). Learn to trust your feelings and intuitions even when you don't understand where they're coming from.

I've also tried to develop the art of becoming aware of out-of-conscious responses on my part through my capacity to free-associate in the course of the session, particularly when I'm feeling bored or stuck. I think one thing that I have is the capacity to be spaced-out by patients (and, at the same time, to enter them or be close to them at forbidden or terrifying or sad emotional places inside them). But when I get trapped, I try harder to pay attention to the family, and then I'm lost. At this point, my superego, my sense of responsibility, tells me to struggle and stay attentive and listen closely rather than simply accept how I am. So I've instructed my patients that if they pick up a sense of my drifting off to please ask or tell me about it and I'll try to understand with them what's happening in the current situation that has me spacing-out. An example of a time I got into this spaced-out state was the other night, when a fifty-five-year-old female patient in the third year of treatment who refuses at this time to take any initiative with her emotional life and who's physically deteriorating stopped me from closing my eyes, saying, "If you're going to sleep, I'm going to leave," which was the most assertive thing she'd said for many weeks. Then, she said, she had no energy to do anything in her life. She might have thought I was bored or uninterested or moving away from her and was rejecting her. Nevertheless, I thought she was telling me goodbye. Was I zeroing in to her subconscious? Was I merely rejecting her? Would she lose me as a therapist? Was she frightened of losing me? I was moving into the unknown. This raises more questions that it answers. What really was going on between us? Because she had a tendency to isolate herself and withdraw from human contact, I thought she was using my closing eyes to support her own tendency. My drowsiness roused her. I was not moving away from her; I was moving with her on an affect level. Now that I think about it, why did I think she was telling me goodbye (isolating herself and curling up to die)? Through the interaction that followed, she was reassured of my presence: I told her that I thought she was telling me goodbye, and I said I guessed I was joining her for a brief time. She asked me if I wanted to continue to see her. I said it was her decision and that I would be, as I have been, available to see her. She said she wanted to schedule an appointment for next week, to go on.

As I've become more seasoned as a therapist, I've developed more confidence in my use of my own feelings—to find to what extent I can trust them. Sometimes, when you become aware of feeling a little uncomfortable during a session, and you're not quite sure of what is happening to you, it's important to take a moment out and attend to yourself, to look inside, and explore why it's bothering you. I usually have a brief time delay (maybe five or ten seconds) when I can decide whether to make use of this or not. Then I rigorously monitor to what extent this was useful or valuable or to what extent it wasn't.

Treatment develops out of personal reactions and the responsiveness by the family therapist to the immediate family situation he or she faces. A twenty-eight-year-old recently divorced women who'd been a patient in our clinic previously (she'd come in for treatment with her husband—both were drug abusers with impulse-control problems, and there'd been a history of violence between them) applied for readmittance (she'd been in marital and group therapy for ten months; her family of origin had been seen once). Her former therapist was no longer working in the clinic; he had described her as a "difficult client," and, as I'd seen her previously in a group I was running and was somewhat familiar with her, I took the case. I asked her to bring her family (including her father, her mother, and a half-sister from her mother's first marriage who lived in New York) to a modified multiple-impact family therapy assessment interview. The family complied, and they were all (four) there on the next Saturday morning. We (four members of the clinic team, all experienced family therapists) saw them together as a family, then split them into generational dyads (the parents and the sisters), then as individuals, then had them meet together alone while we met together to talk about our impressions, evaluations, and suggestions openly and directly. The purpose of the interview was to gather information and to share an experience together in order to decide whether to accept them for treatment and how to go about it; we were much more hesitant (because of our previous failure with the index patient) to take this particular family in treatment than we usually were. Three aspects that characterized the family were: (1) the family members' evasiveness, deceptiveness, and misrepresentation; (2) limit and boundary setting was not adhered to in a firm way; and (3) the mother had a serious heart condition. After discussing treatment possibilities and the family's motivation with them, the team accepted the index patient and her family as patients in the clinic; the team prescribed a multimodal approach—family therapy and group therapy each, once a week. At the end of the session, I suddenly said the family would have to spend at least three years in treatment. I've never stipulated a minimum course of treatment before or since. Though it wasn't clear to me at the time why I said this, my hunch now is that some intuitive part of me was in touch or in tune with some part of the family's emotional system. Some part of me anticipated the mother's death and the importance of the family's processing their grief in treatment. Surprisingly, they agreed and treatment commenced. At two-and-a-half years, the mother died, and helping the family work through their grief reaction was an important phase of the therapy.

But I don't say that I know my unconscious. What I am saying is that I trust my responses as they come up within me, my spontaneous feelings and reactions to the patient's behaviors and statements, without understanding where they come from within me. This acceptance of my intuitive spontaneous reactions may appear to represent an excessive degree of self-acceptance and self-confidence, and an arrogance, in addition to an underlying optimism, but I have found that it works for me in the therapist role.

Let me digress. I was in with a family that was frightened, deceptive, and secretive; they were in the third year of treatment with many absences, hiatuses, and episodes of acting out by all members of the family (that is, they all used drugs). They were about to leave treatment again—the father said he wouldn't come back. I felt stuck, uneasy, and I looked at the daughter (who, when I thought about it later, I felt was the healthiest and clearest member of the family), and I said, "You're not telling me something I need to know about your family and maybe you're too frightened to tell me now, but one day you'll call and tell me what it is." I had a hunch and I said it. Once I had said it, I felt clearer, though still uncertain what it was about. I've never done exactly that before, and I've never done it since. Seven years later, after the sudden and unexpected death (by heart attack) of her husband in his thirties (her brother had suicided a couple of years earlier) and while being hospitalized at the Institute of the Pennsylvania Hospital for depression, the daughter called and told me what was being concealed: how her brother had bored a hole in his closet to his sisters' room as a protective maneuver to help keep his father from sexually molesting his sisters. I then felt together, not partly split off, unconfirmed; my hunch had been on target. That was her acknowledgment of my acknowledgment of my perception, except I didn't know where it came from. I didn't and still don't have a language or an explanation for it. It doesn't thrill me not to have an explanation. I was telling me something, but I don't know where it comes from (except that it's a human capability) to have that sense—I know enough to trust my doing that. When you live with some people who are close to the edge of life, you have to look for whatever leverage or coping you can in terms of working with them, and that was my opening, what I had.

One of the challenges, then, is learning to trust your feelings even when you don't adequately understand the relevance of the feelings to the current situation. My conscious plan or intention as a family therapist is to approach the family by looking in the treatment situation to get some sense for what might be useful interventions; but there are parts of myself I'm not aware of, and only by accepting, expressing, and exploring them in the session with myself and with the family (and out of the session with colleagues or supervisors) will I be able to know them fully and make them useful in our interchange. This resonance also acts as a model of exploration for the family. (Learning to trust your unconscious comes, of course, from exploring yourself in your own personal therapy.)

One of the things in working with difficult patients and their families is to try to understand why you choose to take a particular patient or family (though often in clinics or agencies, the therapist may have little choice— the clients may be assigned and you have to take them or refer them to a colleague in the clinic). We may do it out of rescue or saving fantasies (explorations by the therapist into who he or she is trying to rescue symbolically or transferentially from one's family of origin in the treatment family can be helpful in clarifying the therapist's muddy self). We may do it because we're hungry and need the money and we have to work and that's what we're there for. We may do it because they may tap into some special interest of ours. There may be all kinds of reasons. One of the things in first working with a patient or family is to find out why you choose to work with them.

I think you need to bring certain attributes to your work if you're going to treat families with difficult members or a difficult or ingrained family system. I'll just run over some.

I think you need to bring the capacity to be predictable or reliable, in the sense of being yourself and being alive—that you'll be fully and humanly available and that you'll be persistent and tenacious in returning as a therapist to the treatment situation (that you'll be there). Not that we are always the same way; in working over the years, I respond in different ways with different people at different times. At times, I just sit silently and listen (though family therapists are usually much more active than other therapists). Sometimes, however, passivity and patience can be useful. My capacity to be fresh and resonant to myself as a person, as a potential therapist, provides a nourishing ground (what D.W. Winnicott calls a <u>holding environment</u>) for the focusing on problems to take place.

Second, I think the therapist has to be scrupulously honest—you have to be honest with yourself. Also, with difficult patients, if they pick up a confused or blurred affect or a hidden or double message in you which you can feel is there, I think it's important to validate their perception. Otherwise, you'll be in collusion with the deception in the family system. I think the members of difficult families are people who have had their perceptions not validated (they've been lied to, deceived, and emotionally betrayed—for example, when a child picks up the negative side of the mother's ambivalence about the child, the child asks about it and the mother denies it: "You know we love you, honey"). The children have had no consensual validation, which often takes away their sense of self. The parents are generally people who don't want to know their children's points of view (they may be competitive with them), or they have another way of viewing things.

Often, in substance abuse families, the children will stay loyal to the parents by living out the denied negative side of the parents' message or testing it and enacting it. A seventeen-year-old female I'd been seeing provides an example of sticking to or holding on to a "don't-exist" message. She was born after her father had left her mother and had never seen him. Her mother had gone to her parish priest after she found she was pregnant (she had two other daughters) asking if she could receive absolution if she had an abortion. The priest said no. This young woman's earliest childhood memory is of being four years old on a farm in Ohio and her mother saying, "Why don't you go out on the highway and play in traffic?" So it's no surprise to hear that at seventeen she's jumping out of moving cars when she's upset and angry at the driver, breaking her arms, legs, and ribs, or that she's walking around the city high on drugs at 2:00 or 3:00 A.M. and not caring what happens to her. (Later, when I got her mother to come into family therapy a few times and the daughter insisted on her mother's being more affectionate with her, the mother responded, pointing at her cheek, "If you have to kiss me, kiss me here.") Years after that, the daughter is living with her mother, now taking care of her (they've reversed roles), and still hoping her mother will love and want her.

The third thing is you have to have the capacity to be nonthreatening. I think that often has to do with the therapist's not bringing in his unconscious residue. Also, if a therapist has established a caring or supportive atmosphere, then in spite of the therapist's being challenging or confrontive, or reaching into vulnerable and wounded areas, the family member(s) will probably not be too defensive or feel too threatened, and will respond.

One of the challenges and attributes we need to bring is the capacity to rekindle aliveness and morale in the patients. It's useful to have the capacity to work with creative metaphors. I think that capacity offers you the possibility to work at several levels. I think part of what I do when I'm stuck at an impasse is to look for different possible ways to approach this situation where we're (the family and I) stuck. I can use different levels, and often being able to do this opens up the possibility for different things to happen, other than the usual or predictable. You need to be flexible, to be able to resonate to yourself, and to be able to express the resonance of the interaction between you and the family. For example, it may be important and freeing in the therapeutic exchange for the therapist to express his vulnerability and say, "Right now, in this situation, I feel impotent and foolish."

Now I also think that you need to work with primitive affects. We see a lot of violent emotional reactions—it is part of understanding the intensity that love or hate and other strong basic emotions can produce. I think, sometimes, it's very difficult for some colleagues to be comfortable and work with situations where a patient or a family member is murderous toward you—really wants to kill you—then five minutes later is talking pleasantly to you. (See the Wallace Stevens quote at the beginning of the chapter.) I've had patients threaten me; I've had patients wrestle with me; I had one family member (not the IP) throw an ashtray at a wall near me; I've sat in a family session where a mother threatened to smash my female cotherapist in the face with a frying pan (for persistently asking for some factual information about one of the mother's dead parents). That's tremendously challenging to me—how do you handle that kind of situation? Not that that's happened that often, and certainly less frequently as I've become middle-aged and less provocative.

There are various ways to look at those threats and murderous feelings— they are intimate acts. Somebody's contemptuous but intimate. It depends on how it affects you. I think, oftentimes, it's a marvelous distancing technique. You've gotten too close.

I've only been physically attacked once. I was sitting in a family session, with a PCP-induced psychotic seventeen-year-old hospitalized male, his twenty-year-old sister, his mother, and the mother's man-friend. I had been listening for three or four minutes (about halfway into the session) to his mother talking, when he wound up and blind-sided me and broke one of my teeth. He stood up, as I did, and looked at me docilely, his arms at his sides. I told him to get out of my office and had an attendant take him back to his unit. (Later, when another therapist asked him why he'd hit me, he said, "He was looking funny at my sister.")

I'd like to tell you how I handled this situation afterward. The attending psychiatrist the next day wanted to band-aid the situation and have the patient apologize to me, and for me to say nothing except to accept his apology. I wanted the opportunity to tell the patient, in the presence of people who could restrain him if necessary, how angry I felt about what he'd done to me. The psychiatrist refused to permit my saying that, and I refused to have the patient simply apologize to me and me say nothing. The patient and I had no further contact at that time, and he was discharged a week or so later. Though I was not in supervision or therapy at that time, I had discussions with several of my former supervisors to explore how I'd invited (what I'd done to invite the attack) and not protected myself from his attack. I'd overlooked him—I hadn't asked his permission to contact his family and invite them into a family therapy session, and I had turned away from him (he was out of my vision) while I was listening to his mother. Subsequently, several months later, he was readmitted to P.P.C. for the same condition but not to our program. We met, by chance (I didn't know he'd been rehospitalized), in a hallway.

He recognized me first. "You're Marks aren't you? I hit you when I was here before, didn't I?" he said. "I felt bad about it; why don't you hit me now?" I said, "I don't want to hit you. I'm not here to hit patients. I'm not supposed to hurt them, and I'd be fired if I did that and I'm not going to jeopardize myself and my family. But I want you to know that I hate you for punching me and breaking my tooth. I don't hate you for anything else, but I hate you for that." "I understand," he said, and offered again to let me hit him. I said, "No," and we parted. For me, and I think for him too, the emotional wound between us about his hitting me was healed. It had been a challenge to watch myself struggle with the tremendous urge to slug him after he'd hit me during the family session. (Still, had I not restrained myself and pinned him to the floor, this would not have been an inappropriate response for me.) To feel myself struggle and see how difficult it was for me to understand that if you're going to work in this area you may need the capacity to shift when the patient shifts and still be able to work with these challenging, difficult family members.

Once you enter the treatment world of the substance abuser, and particularly those with tendencies to become violent, you really need to make a commitment to work it through, come hell or high water. (Of course it becomes more difficult with certain philosophies of treatment that some hospitals and agencies may have regarding avoiding violence or having it handled solely by aides, by medication, and by restraints and isolation rooms.) But from my standpoint, what I'm presenting to you, and the kind of work I think is effective, I think you need to make a decision to stay with this treatment situation, to really try to achieve a modulation and moderation of their primitive rage, their ambivalence, and their very intense primitive feeling states by directly addressing the hatred.

Another thing I think you need to do with difficult patients who might stir you to tap into your own out-of-conscious thoughts and associations is to deal with their despair and their resignation. The capacity that we have to tolerate despair is not great, and it is not easy to cope with it. But if you resonate with their despair, you yourself are quite capable of feeling it. If you're open to feeling it (it's an agonizing feeling); if you can tolerate it, then often you are much more in a position to be creative, or, from viewing things a different way, to offer some kind of experience or way out of that despair.

One Friday afternoon, an eighteen-year-old girl, whom I'd been seeing as a patient for a little less than a year and who'd made me a promise as a condition of her coming in for treatment that I not inform her mother and stepfather (her father had disappeared from her life when she was four) that she was in therapy, called and said she had to see me that day.[2] As I was completely scheduled until 8 o'clock that evening, I told her I could see her then. (At that time, the clinic staff would all have long since left.) She arrived on time and stood just outside my doorway and said, "Well, I'm going to kill myself this weekend and I've come to say goodbye to you." I said, "Why don't you come in and sit down and let's talk about it." So she came in and sat down, and we talked for about forty minutes. Then she said, "You know why I *really* came in, don't you?" And I said, "No, why did you really come in?" And she replied, "So you could talk me out of it." I asked, "Have I talked you out of it?" And she said, "No." I said, "Well, I've said everything I can think of right now and, if we continued further, I'd only be repeating myself, so why don't we end." I went on to say I would honor our agreement of my not contacting her parents; nor would I call upstairs to the hospital staff and try to have her hospitalized against her will; nor would I call the police. I said she'd have to choose whether to live or die, and that I thought she knew very little about life (that there was more life out there than she had yet experienced). I said I'd probably be very anxious over the weekend because I liked her and didn't want her to die, and that if I heard she'd died I'd be very saddened. Then we stopped the session. I lived in Center City Philadelphia at that time, and she lived in South Philly; she was going to Center City, she said, and asked if I'd give her a lift there. I said okay. We drove downtown along the Schuylkill River in silence; I dropped her off at Rittenhouse Square (a Center City park) where she said she wanted to go. We said goodbye, she went into the square, and I drove off. (Editor's note: For those who want to know, this woman did not commit suicide. The therapist's point, however, was the stance he took in this situation, unrelated to whether she took her life or not.)

Implicit in much of what I have been saying is that you need to have an understanding of the countertransference that develops in you. Each one of us is quite likely as a therapist to develop unconscious responses to patients and family members. If we didn't, I think we'd be less capable of being effective. We have the same capacity for unconscious responses that our patients have. How can we possibly access or how can we define and identify our unconscious responses? (We don't make a decision to access our unconscious. There is no direct access to the unconscious. It's not that simple and automatic.)

We work at understanding ourselves (it's an investigative framework, part of our mental coatrack, so to speak, so that when things pop up out of our unconscious, in a session or at some other place in our lives, we have a place to hang it on). And that's an important aspect in sensitizing ourselves to our capacity for countertransference.

Let me give you an example from a supervisory session. Earlier this week, a supervisee-therapist said he was furious with a father who, in a family session when confronted by his six-year-old daughter ("Daddy, I smelled liquor on your breath"), denied it; later that week, he phoned his therapist saying he needed a detoxification treatment, and adding that he'd been drinking for two months. The supervisee-therapist said, "He [the father] was cheating me" (through lying and not meeting the therapist's expectations). With the supervisor's encouragement, the supervisee-therapist began to talk about and resonate to his previous marital situation, then to a childhood situation, and finally to his relations with his parents—all situations where he'd felt "messed with" and felt cheated. Eventually, his anger cooled, and he saw the sadness of the father trying to deceive the daughter; and, since the father saw the therapist as being helpful, he turned to the therapist for additional help and is continuing treatment. In my view, the key dynamic issues in the family have to do with the father's lying and his attempt, albeit later in the week, to become honest and direct; the key treatment issue has to do with the therapist's countertransference, and that it was resolved and that the therapy could move on.

I also track how I am with patients and families to see if I'm in any way different, to see how I'm changing. It's important for me to have a sense of whether I'm being different, and may appear to be inconsistent or unpredictable to the family I'm working with.

Further, I listen to what a patient says about me and about our interaction very carefully, to see if I can pick up a trend, something that will lead to a new resonance to myself.

I also often work with cotherapists, and ask them to track and be honest with me (if they question or disagree with something that I have said or done in a session). And, of course, it's hard to track subtle nuances and details, but that's what we train ourselves to do—to note and resonate to the clues (like Columbo, the television detective, coming to the scene of a killing, noting the tiny details that give him pause or catch his curiosity).

It's enormously useful for me not only to get another's perception, but also sometimes (though not always) to have the receptivity in myself to hear and be thoughtful and reflective about things I find unpleasant, distasteful, loathsome, or disgusting about myself.

As Harold Searles says about access to the unconscious and countertransference,

> Our own personal analysis, if we had one, can be effective in giving us more ready access rather than removing our capacity for primitive jealousy, rage, fear, and symbiotic dependency. . . . So listen carefully to what the patient says; try not to be defensive; look for those aspects of reality in their perceptions in their transference. . . . If the patient is to develop a better integrated and more comprehensive relatedness and reality, he must experience a therapeutic symbiosis in which the therapist participated at the feeling level.[3]

I'd like to end with a quote from the beginning of Walter Kempler's essay, "Experiential Psychotherapy with Families":

> Upon these two commandments hang all the law—upon which experiential psychotherapy within families stands: attention to the current interaction as the pivotal point for all awareness and interventions; involvement of the total therapist-person who brings overtly and richly his full personal impact on the families with whom he works (not merely a bag of tricks called therapeutic skills). While many therapists espouse such fundamentals, in actual practice there is a tendency to hedge on this bi-principled commitment.[4]

Finally, images remind us of our incompleteness in the world. A comment, attributed to the poet Robert Frost, is that wisdom is the ability to act, when it is necessary, on the basis of incomplete information.

In treating families, there is always something important we don't know about. Can we come to enjoy some mysteries in doing therapy and in life and not fall prey to factualism or endless explanation?

Notes

1. One of the roles in families that gets assigned and adopted is that of the healer or rescuer. The therapist as rescuer is symbolically rescuing or saving him- or herself from problems in the family, or is rescuing a parent from a bad or conflicted marital situation. One has a feeling of satisfaction and importance in rescuing.

2. In Pennsylvania, a seventeen-year-old substance-abuser can ask for and receive psychotherapy without the therapist notifying the parents if the adolescent client requests it. In this case, the patient was brought in for treatment by her high school counselor, a young woman.

3. From "Jealousy involving an internal object." In Harold F. Searles, *My Work with Borderline Patients* (Northvale, N.J.: Jason Aronson, Inc.): 139.

4. *Family Process*, vol. 7 (Baltimore, Md.: Waverly Press, 1968), pp. 88–99

7

The Interactions of the Person of the Family Therapist with the Family in Treatment

Samuel Granick

At one point or another, the family therapist (as is the case with all psychotherapists) is confronted with the basic issue of how his or her person interacts with and affects the people being treated. Of great concern, of course, is the question of whether the personality characteristics, patterns of behavior, ways of showing feelings and expressing ideas, attitudes, and values are helpful or hurtful to the clients. The purpose of the discussion here is to consider the major conditions and problems confronted by the family therapist which require reactions that are in accord with professional limits and yet allow for valid expression of his or her personal qualities. Moreover, consideration will be directed toward showing how the interactions of the person of the therapist with the family may facilitate maturation and effective handling of life experiences on the part of all concerned.

Most of what we believe we know about the qualities and characteristics of the "good" therapist is derived from clinical experience rather than from scientific research. Despite the multiplicity of clinical orientations of both individual and group types of psychotherapy, however, there seems to be a surprising extent of agreement as to what the desirable qualities of an effective psychotherapist should be. In one form or another, most writers on the subject accept the following elements as being characteristic of the effective psychotherapist:

1. Dependable
2. Reliable
3. Empathic
4. Supportive
5. Patient
6. Perceptive
7. Communicative
8. Warm

9. Competent
10. Genuine or authentic

These qualities are expected to stimulate trust in clients toward the therapist (thereby facilitating honest mutual communication and release of the growth potential in the individual and the family), to motivate willingness to face and deal with problems realistically, and thus to use the therapy to achieve a constructive and satisfying pattern of living.

Additional traits could be listed as characterizing the effective psycho-therapist, such as the ability to be a mature model for the clients and the willingness to disclose appropriate aspects of his or her own life. All of the elements noted, however, require a considerable degree of caution and sensitivity on the part of the psychotherapist, so that their manifestations in the therapy sessions will be appropriate to the needs of the clients or the family being dealt with, and will not be largely a reflection of the ego needs of the therapist. This is not to suggest that the personal gratifications of the therapist cannot be an integral part of psychotherapeutic practices. It must be clear, however, that whatever is done is to be primarily oriented toward the therapeutic welfare of the client.

For the individual who is learning and practicing family therapy it is not enough to have a list of qualities, attitudes, and ways of behaving that define the effective psychotherapist. These elements should also be made actual and placed in the perspective of clinical practice. Guidelines should be made available that can help him or her integrate them into regular professional conduct and behavioral interaction with families in therapy. Accordingly, the discussion to follow will center on what appear to be the most usual and significant types of experiences confronting the psychotherapist who is attempting to help family members face and deal effectively with the problems and dysfunctions within their family systems. The areas covered will not, of course, be exhaustive, since the possible variety of experiences is legion. It is anticipated, however, that enough direction and specificity in handling situations can be provided to enable the psychotherapist to proceed with perspective, realism, and some self-confidence.

Some Characteristics of an Effective Relationship

Being Available

The most elementary investment of the self by the therapist in conducting family therapy is the fact of being available to a family and being interested in being helpful with their problems. This calls for a sense of personal commitment to the welfare of this family. The therapist must sense internally that he or she will set aside the time and energy required for working on the behalf of the family members. Should the family require some attention other than what is provided during the scheduled sessions, there should be a readiness on the therapist's part to do this. Should an emergency arise, he or she must be willing to try to deal with it. Generally, the therapist is expected to have a positive orientation toward the family and to perceive it sympathetically, as well as realistically. He or she must also be confident that he or she has the skill, experience, knowledge, and understanding that are appropriate for dealing constructively with the problems presented by the family. For the therapist in training, and indeed, even for the experienced therapist, opportunities for supervision and consultation should be available and used as needed.

It should, therefore, be evident that one must be careful not to overload one's time commitments to a point where one feels too overburdened and, consequently, unable to be available for contact with clients other than in the scheduled therapy periods. Such feelings may also result in an unintentional communication to the families during treatment that the therapist does not have the time and energy to be sufficiently in touch with their concerns, or that they represent an unwanted burden to him or her. Rapport with the therapist and motivation for therapy may thereby be severely compromised.

Sharing Information and Reactions

The essence of an effective relationship between the therapist and family in treatment is the quality of comfort and confidence that can be developed toward meaningful communication. Toward this end a spirit of honesty and an orientation toward openness of expression and sharing of information and reactions should be encouraged and conveyed from the start. As the therapy procedure is being structured with the family, this can be presented in the nature of a contract. The therapist can indicate that one aspect of his or her role is to be frank and open in providing information, as well as in sharing opinions, feelings, impressions, and attitudes with the family members about what they are doing and how the sessions are proceeding. The point may also be stressed that the family members should adopt the same orientation in communicating with the therapist, as well as with each other. Some family members may then protest that they do not want to be pressed or forced to say all they may have in mind. It can then be explained that a commitment to openness and truth telling does not mean that anyone is required to tell everything and to withhold nothing. It does mean, however, that what is said should be the truth, and that if one wishes to withhold anything, it should be understood that one is not ready at that time to share what is felt and thought—that one will do so when one is ready and willing.

Providing Support

It is wise for the therapist to convey to the entire family that he or she is concerned about each person's welfare, as well as the integrity of the family. Praise should be offered, when it is appropriate, for their courage and determination to try to deal with their problems realistically and intelligently. As occasion and circumstances permit, support should be provided to each individual who is attempting to express ideas, feelings, and information, and for the efforts being made to deal constructively with problems. The therapist should also show pleasure and pride in the family members and in the family as a whole as they try to make constructive use of the therapy.

Stroking, soothing, comforting, reassuring, protecting, and being compassionate—these and related supportive interventions should be used by the therapist as often as seems realistically helpful. Such behaviors on the part of the therapist can be very helpful in enabling the family members develop a positive working relationship with the therapist during the early sessions. They can be helped thereby to perceive family therapy as a safe haven for them, but they must also be enabled to recognize that the therapist will not solve their problems for them or save them from their dysfunctional or irresponsible ways of dealing with their experiences. The therapist must be cautious about promoting within the family the idea that he or she will be like a protective, all-powerful parent for them. What needs to be made clear is that the therapist is interested in their welfare and is a caring, compassionate person, but that he or she is also trying not to become enmeshed in their problems. When he or she perceives that any of the family members is hurting or that the family is in a disturbed state, supportiveness, stroking, compassion, and the like can be provided, along with encouragement to believe and feel that there is hope for them and that effort should be expended in dealing constructively with their situation.

Empathic Reactions

Reacting with empathy to family members is widely regarded as one of the most important aspects of the psychotherapeutic process. It reflects the extent to which the therapist is sensitive to and aware of people's feelings, both those that are outwardly expressed or hinted at and those that are experienced inwardly but are not openly evident. Often such feelings may not be clearly at the level of awareness of the individual himself. The family therapist must try to sense how each family member feels so as to enable these feelings to be appropriately communicated and thus produce increased mutual understanding and honest sharing of thoughts and emotions within the family.

The personal maturity and skill of the therapist are most clearly manifested by his or her ability to perceive what is occurring within the emotional make-up of the family members and how these reactions are affecting the functioning of the family. Of particular significance is the therapist's delicacy in stimulating and facilitating each person's willingness to reveal these feelings in ways that are benign, constructive, and oriented toward the welfare of the family.

It seems generally preferable for a client to reveal his insights, attitudes, and feelings to the other family members than for the therapist to provide this information and interpretations. At times, of course, it is desirable and constructive for the therapist to disclose or show what he or she has uncovered or concluded from observing and listening to the interactions among the family members. As a rule, however, it seems more constructive and helpful for the therapist to facilitate each client's recognition and sharing of these matters through gentle questioning, dialogue, and the encouragement of spontaneous expression.

A significant aspect of the therapist's empathic reactions to the family is evident in the ways in which the family members are enabled to gain an understanding and sense of the nature of their family system of operations. In this instance also it is safest and potentially most constructive when this is brought about through questioning, discussion, sharing of observations, tentatively suggesting possibilities, and making available means through which the family can observe and analyze itself (such as audio and/or video recordings, role playing, and group problem solving, each of which is then evaluated by the family). Once this is achieved, the therapist can lead the family members into clarifying how they feel about the system and its effects on them. As a next step the therapist may encourage the family to consider ways and means of relieving and/or changing the dysfunctional elements of the family system along positive and realistic lines.

Empathic sensitivity on the part of the therapist is also important in instances in which the family members try to deal with such negative emotions as hostility, jealousy, competitiveness, irritability, depression, and anxiety. Often these feelings are suppressed by family members and even covered up or defended against through denial or through counterexpressions of positive feelings. Thus, for example, a brother may indicate that he is not envious of his sister's successes in her school work, and add that in fact he is very happy and proud about them for her. But at another point in the discussion he may criticize her for being too conscientious and not developing herself socially. The therapist can raise questions at such times regarding the possibility that he may be experiencing emotions that are too disturbing to reveal or to allow himself to think about. Reassurance should be offered about the fact that it is natural, normal, and psychologically healthy to experience one's emotions, whatever they may be, and that such awareness can be useful in enabling one to find outlets for them that are constructive, reasonable, and realistic. This may encourage the youngster to be more open with his feelings at that point or later and eventually to be more honest in dealing with the other family members.

The therapist's empathic sensitivity or awareness may be particularly helpful to the process of family therapy when family members can be enabled or encouraged to express their feelings about him or her and about the therapy itself. Often clients are disinclined to reveal such emotions toward the therapist and reactions to what is going on, such as annoyance, boredom, anger, and fear. They tend to deny such feelings or hide them through silence, distractibility, absence from sessions, and changing the subject at hand. In actuality this may be an excellent opportunity for the therapist to stimulate much openness and honesty of expression of opinions, and the sharing of feelings within the family. It can be remarked by the therapist that experiencing varied emotions, both positive and negative, about the therapist and the therapy is usual and expected, and that revealing them would be welcome as well as very desirable for the benefit of all concerned. Moreover, the therapist can point out that he or she has feelings and impressions about them which are to be expressed and given consideration. Thus, for example, he or she can point out their defensive posture regarding the revelation of their emotions and express sadness and regrets about the lost opportunities for them to get to know and understand each other better.

In general, the therapist's empathic reactions toward the family members can be a very powerful stimulant to them toward therapeutic progress. When they are enabled to recognize that their feelings are sensed, understood, and dealt with sympathetically and constructively, rapport is likely to be more fully established, and communication can become more meaningful, frank, and oriented toward positive interaction within the family. It may reduce or even eliminate defensiveness and open the way to realistic and functional revisions of the family system.

The Effective Therapist

The Therapist's Emotional Reactions

As the therapist observes and experiences the family and its members, their effects on him or her are likely to be varied and complex. For these reactions to be kept hidden from the family in treatment would, in effect, be to act in a way that is the opposite of the way in which the family members are being encouraged to behave. It is likely that the degree of suppression of emotions that this would demand would result in the therapist's experiencing and showing much tension, stiffness of manner, and anxiety. Developing an effective rapport with the family members would then be difficult, if not impossible, since the therapist's manner would tend to be cold, aloof, unsympathetic, and artificial. It would also become apparent to the family members that the therapist is not being open and honest with them, which would probably lead to their loss of faith in the likelihood of the therapy's being helpful to them.

The therapist, accordingly, is faced with the challenge to share his or her reactions, impressions, thoughts, and emotions with the family members, but yet to do so in ways that are constructive and beneficial to them. It is crucial that what is communicated is not done mainly to relieve the therapist's tensions or to represent the acting out of his or her own needs and impulses. Basically, one must be reasonably certain that what is done is not motivated by the drive for ego gratification by the therapist or to enhance his or her status.

It seems desirable for the therapist to set the stage early in his or her contact with the family to encourage an atmosphere of freedom to exchange communication regarding attitudes, impressions, ideas, and feelings. Agreements can be made about this which include mutual reassurance that the orientation of these interchanges is to be sympathetic, constructive, and in the interest of being therapeutic toward the problems at hand. Within the framework of such an understanding it should be possible for the therapist to be authentic and frank in sharing feelings, impressions, concerns, and ideas.

For the family members their orientation can be presented as a challenge to face and deal with feedback that may sometimes be unfavorable in their eyes, and that they might prefer to deny or overlook. This offers the therapist the opportunity to encourage sympathetically the family to endure the pain of confronting unpleasant realities and to try to work conscientiously to resolve their problems constructively. At the same time the therapist can reveal any admiration and warmth he or she may be experiencing for them because of their willingness to engage in this process, despite its difficulties and discomforts. In addition, he or she can point out that being part of this struggle with them is a professional fulfillment that is personally pleasing and represents the basis for working in the area of family therapy.

As family therapy proceeds and the therapist invests increasingly greater amounts of interest and effort in the process, it is likely that he or she will experience varied emotional reactions in response to how the family is dealing with the experience. It is easy, of course, to share one's pleasure and pride with the family when the therapy proceeds well and favorable progress is evident. The situation is more complex and problematic for the therapist, however, when such feelings are experienced as disappointment, insecurity, uncertainty, fear, and anger in response to disturbing or destructive things the family members may be saying or doing or when the family is dealing with the therapy in an unfavorable or distorted fashion.

It seems wise at such times to show oneself as having "normal" human responsiveness to conditions that are out of line with reasonable expectations, and to situations that are difficult to understand or deal with and which may be threatening to any of the participants (including the therapist). Examples of such situations are threats or possibilities of violence, indications of illegal behavior, and indications of suicidal thoughts or gestures. To try to maintain a cool detachment would be virtually impossible and probably counterproductive. On the other hand, to respond with panic, rejection of the family, hostility, or other forms of defensiveness is likely also to lead to unfavorable results. An approach that is realistic and directed toward dealing with the situation at hand from a problem-solving perspective would seem to be both professionally valid and potentially constructive.

Accordingly, much of the tension and anxiety in the atmosphere is likely to be defused or dissipated if the therapist openly acknowledges his or her emotions and concerns, but at the same time stresses the importance and value of dealing with the circumstances intelligently, realistically, and as a set of problems to be faced. The fact that the therapist's emotional reactions are centered around concerns for the welfare of the family, and that efforts are being made by all during and away from the family therapy sessions to deal with the problems, should help to foster a team spirit and sense of united effort in dealing constructively with the difficulties. This kind of heightened emotional interaction in the therapy session can often go a long way toward reducing communication barriers and speeding up movement toward personal growth and the expenditure of effort in the direction of improved family functioning. It can also help the therapist to integrate his or her family therapy skills, as well as to develop and act on the conviction that freedom honestly to express and share ideas and opinions is likely to facilitate the therapeutic process, provided the basic orientation of concern for the welfare of the family can be maintained throughout.

The Therapist's Personal History

A rather delicate but important aspect of use of self in family therapy is the matter of sharing with the family one's own experiences, background, and understanding of self. This can serve often as a form of useful and productive modeling for the family, but it can also distract the family from its own problems or lead to resentment on the part of some or all of the family members. The therapist must be aware whether he or she is merely ventilating for his or her own needs or actually providing the family with a learning experience. Accordingly, it seems important to approach this cautiously, indicating to the family that a personal experience or anecdote or reaction is being shared which the therapist hopes can be useful to them in understanding themselves or in finding direction for their own behavior.

The therapist should also try to elicit reactions from the family about what he or she tells them about him- or herself so as to have a basis for evaluating the effects of what has been discussed. Associated with this feature of the communication between the therapist and the family is the matter of sharing with them his or her feelings about how effectively they are using the family therapy sessions, and what he or she estimates is the family's potential for helping itself through the family therapy. Sharing his or her hopes and wishes for them can be encouraging and stimulating to the family, but the therapist must also be cautious about making this sound like a demand, since this may in turn lead to increased resistance and resentment on their part. Open discussion and exploration of these issues is extremely important for maintaining an orientation of honesty and reality testing within the family therapy process.

Role Modeling by the Therapist

Role modeling for the family and its members is a two-edged sword and must therefore be handled cautiously. On the one hand, the therapist can provide a concrete demonstration that can guide the family and its members to improved functioning. It is possible, on the other hand, for the therapist to present him- or herself as a paragon, which could then discourage the family and also be taken by them as criticism. The therapist must be careful to avoid projecting an image of superiority and virtue which the family could not hope or even want to emulate. If the therapist can present his or her modeling in a spirit of tentativeness and experimentation rather than as something that is polished and final, the family may be able to perceive and react to it as something from which they can try to learn and imitate, and finally develop behaviors that are their own and for which they can feel responsible. These issues should be discussed openly with the family as they present themselves so that the modeling and the behaviors that follow will be perceived realistically.

Normally the therapy experience offers the therapist opportunities to show the family how to listen to what others are saying, watch what they are doing, and respond realistically, sympathetically, and constructively. The differences between arguing and dialoguing can be demonstrated repeatedly, thus showing the family members how to communicate with each other and resolve conflicts and misunderstandings effectively and with mutual satisfaction. In this regard the therapist can also demonstrate respect for each individual's rights, privacy, and value as a human being, something that is too often disregarded and violated in family functioning. The therapist, in the conduct of the therapy, can, moreover, model being a team player and thus encourage the family members to perceive themselves as a mutually sharing and cooperating unit instead of the narcissistic, competing orientation that generally characterizes the behavior of members of a dysfunctional family.

Dealing with Resistance

The need to resist the acceptance of insights and interpretations presented by the therapist and to deny realities or potential short- or long-term consequences of behaviors or attitudes is a common and frequently used defensive maneuver on the part of individuals and groups. It is associated with the resistance to change of attitudes, beliefs, orientation, and behavior which is likely to show up in families as they confront their dysfunctional problems. Often one observes that individuals and families wish or hope to be free of the pain and disturbances their problems bring about without having to introduce changes into their systems or patterns of functioning or ways of orienting themselves and viewing their environment and circumstances.

This resistance to change or to new ideas or attitudes or perceptions represents, in actuality, part of the normal urge toward homeostasis or stability, and the related fear of destabilization that change is almost certain to bring about. Yet such destabilization is a virtual necessity in order for the dysfunctional system of operation to be reorganized in the direction of more balanced, effective, and satisfying ways of functioning. For both the individual and the family this is in the nature of an approach-avoidance conflict. Thus, the closer they approach change, the greater the resultant tension and anxiety that the abandonment of old, known, and practiced adaptive patterns may generate. Consequently, resistance to change may be stimulated and a return to the old ways of dealing with life experiences. On the other hand, the return to these dysfunctional ways tends then to rekindle the unhappiness and disturbance that brought them to treatment in the first place, leading to increased cooperation with the therapy for the time being, until once again the approach to change makes that hard to tolerate.

Accordingly, as therapy encourages a family and its members to move toward destabilizing their dysfunctional system and toward exploring and experimenting with new, more effective ways of functioning, the therapist can help the situation considerably by providing encouragement, support, positive feedback, and other forms of aid aimed at reducing the fear and anxiety stimulated by change. This can enable the family members to persevere in their efforts at readjusting to the point of consolidating their gains and reinforcing their new ways until these are firmly integrated. At such times it would be a miscalculation for the therapist to give in to the temptation to be confrontive or to give the impression to the family of being critical of them for showing resistance and denial. The therapist could be more helpful to the family by showing an understanding of and sympathy for the pain and anxiety being experienced. It is likely to be therapeutic also for the therapist to combine this with encouragement to the family to examine their denying and resistive reactions in order to gain some insights into their motivations. This in turn may enable the family members themselves to confront the defensive maneuvers. It would provide the therapist with the opportunity to show his or her further support for and personal pride in and admiration for the courage shown by the family members to face up to their pain, discomfort, and problems.

Confrontation is, of course, an important intervention procedure in helping families deal with their resistances and defenses, but it is best to avoid this approach during the early phases of family therapy. Confronting resistance and denial could actually reinforce such defenses rather than reduce or relieve them because the family members might be led to perceive or interpret such actions as competitive or adversarial on the therapist's part, and they might act accordingly. It might also be counterproductive to be confrontive with a family when the members show much anxiety about the stability of the relationships and when the family organization seems either fairly chaotic or very rigid. In either case, the response to the therapist's intervention along such lines might be to tighten resistances and/or to terminate therapy entirely.

This is not to suggest that confrontation as a therapeutic procedure, or persistence in encouraging family members to face and move away from their defensive resistance and denial, should not be employed in family therapy. On the contrary, this is a valuable and potentially effective intervention that can be a normal or standard element in the therapist's array of procedures. Caution, however, is required so that the therapist can be reasonably confident that the use of confrontation will achieve the desired results. Thus, it seems best to restrain the tendency to confront until the therapeutic contract is firmly established and the relationship of the therapist with the family is quite secure. In addition, the therapist should have reason to be confident that the family will be able to perceive the confrontation as a friendly challenge rather than as a devaluative criticism.

Confronting and Provoking

When the therapist considers it desirable and appropriate to be confrontive and provocative, the effective application can be very productive in enabling the family members to become seriously engaged in the therapeutic process. As has been noted, this intervention procedure must be applied with caution. It should probably be structured as part of the therapeutic contract so that the family members may expect it sooner or later to occur. When it is finally attempted, however, the therapist should be quite confident that the family members clearly perceive him or her as sympathetic to their welfare and oriented to helping them resolve their difficulties. Under such circumstances the confrontation and provocation are not likely to be regarded as an attack, but rather as a stimulus or challenge to change the family's ways of functioning in a more positive direction.

The therapist tends to assume a very active posture when this type of intervention procedure is introduced. It demands good self-control on his or her part, along with confidence and definiteness about what is being attempted. This is not an area in which fumbling and exploration should be allowed, since strong emotional reactions in the family members may be generated which require skilled, firm management by the therapist. Accordingly, it is highly recommended that the relatively inexperienced family therapist have some training in this area before attempting it on his or her own. Working with a cotherapist, who can help in the management of the therapy session is also advisable, even for the experienced therapist, when confrontation and provocation are to be attempted.

A relatively mild but effective and often dramatic way to use confrontation and provocation with a family is to introduce these elements via a psychodramatic exercise. Playing out specific roles and problem situations within the family is one such procedure. Role reversals can facilitate the production of confrontation and provocation on the part of family members— particularly when the role of the target person is taken by the therapist, and the family members are encouraged to be frank and direct in their remarks and reactions.

It is important for the therapist to be aware that these types of activity in the therapy sessions can produce a good deal of impulsiveness and acting out that may be injurious or unduly unpleasant and disturbing. Thus, ground rules should be worked out and agreed upon which set limits to what is done. For example, violence or efforts to hurt or threaten anyone physically should be ruled out. It should also be agreed that the procedure or what is occurring will be stopped when any of the participants request it. In addition, the therapist should indicate to the family members that he or she will be willing to talk or meet with them should they find themselves upset over what has occurred some time after the therapy session, because delayed reactions are not unusual in such situations.

At times the therapist can choose to be very direct with one or all of the family members. One possibility is when the therapist remarks to the family with some feeling and intensity, after they have been defensively asserting that they are close, open, and honestly communicative with each other, that they are actually deluding themselves. Contradicting them in this fashion is likely to provoke heated denials on their part and even criticism of the therapist for not understanding or being helpful to them. It is vital, however, that the therapist persist and be able then to respond in a factual way to support those assertions. He or she may then encourage the family members to look more deeply into what is going on in the family and how the problems that brought them to therapy came about and are being perpetuated. As the initial sense of shock and emotionality subsides thereafter, one or another of the family members may start the process of increased frankness and more valid characterization of communication in the family. This can lead to significant therapeutic progress.

There are, of course, many other ways in which confrontation and provocation can be introduced into family therapy sessions. Part of one's training in family therapy should include supervised practice in these procedures, including evaluation and clarification of the therapist's own reactions to this intervention technique. It is important that the therapist feel comfortable and confident when engaged in such situations. If the therapist is unable to achieve such a psychological state, it seems best not to use this approach. Should he or she nevertheless desire or consider it important to engage in this procedure, it is recommended that it be done with an experienced cotherapist participating.

Probing and Not Probing

Probing for essential facts, attitudes, motives, and patterns of family interaction is an aspect of diagnosis and analysis of the family system with its dysfunctional elements. It may be expected to be helpful and therapeutic to the family as ventilation and relief of tension, as well as for achieving insights into their problems and in orienting them toward the effective use of the therapy. For the family therapist it is, of course, useful in setting the goals for treatment and for planning intervention procedures.

Normally, probing by the family therapist is expected and well accepted by family members. Some difficulties, however, are likely to be manifested when one or more of the participants objects to coming for therapy, indicating that he or she is present only under duress and resents the entire procedure. Varied resistances may then be shown, along with efforts to sabotage the therapist's efforts. At times siblings or a child and a parent may join forces to try to inhibit the participation of the other members, or to prevent information from being communicated.

This calls for considerable sensitivity, patience, and flexibility on the part of the therapist, but firmness in dealing with these family members must be exercised so as to prevent them from dominating the session and making it chaotic. As was mentioned earlier, resistances challenge the therapist to be perceptive and inventive to enable the family members to overcome inhibiting fears and anxieties that the attempt to deal with the problems tends to generate. The therapist's display of warmth, caring, and sympathetic understanding of the feelings and concerns being experienced by the family members can then go a long way toward cementing a favorable working relationship with them. Thus, as the probing proceeds, it must be adapted to the tolerance level of the clients and to what they are ready to reveal and deal with at the time. It can be helpful to remark at times to the family that not everything needs to be revealed and discussed at once. Many things can be taken up later when all are more comfortable with the procedures and the situation.

Normally, when the family senses the professional quality of the therapist's behavior and management of the sessions, confidence in his or her judgment will be established. This should open the way toward increased in-depth probing and consequent sharing of information, attitudes, and feelings, both with the therapist and among family members. Snags in the process, however, are likely to occur when highly personal, tender issues and facts are close to the surface or implied by what is said or done during the session. The therapist must be alert to the vulnerabilities of individuals in the family and/or the family as a whole so that what is revealed does not lead to disorganizing reactions and possible refusal on the part of some or all of the family members to continue with the therapy.

Accordingly, recognizing when it may be counterproductive to probe is an important aspect of working with family therapy. Generally it is desirable for the therapist to convey a sense of confidence and patience in interacting with the family so that the participants may understand that they are not under pressure to reveal or discuss what they prefer for the present to conceal. They should be reassured that they can choose their own time to share such matters and that whatever they do tell or show will be held in strict confidence.

Often, of course, highly personal, emotionally disturbing matters are evident to the therapist on the basis of what may be implied by communications and behaviors of the family members during the sessions. It may then be tempting to probe and externalize these issues so as to deal realistically with them. Caution, however, is called for to time such probing to the revealed readiness of the family as a whole to tolerate the tension and emotional arousal that may result. Reassurances, appreciation, and sympathy from the therapist may lessen the pain and fear of the family members so that the material that does come through can be directed toward the resolution of family conflicts and dysfunctional elements in the family system. Such highly emotional moments may often represent turning points for the family in their commitment to the therapy, and to communication with each other that is open and frank, and handled in a sympathetic, constructive fashion. Should the therapist perceive evidence that suggests that the family is not ready for such open revelations and for being able to deal realistically with the conflicts or problems, delaying the probing to a more opportune time is highly desirable.

Interpretation and Timing

Interpreting a person's behavior and thoughts is a common practice but one that often leads to much misunderstanding and conflict between people. For the therapist this is an important skill and a reflection of sensitivity to the motivation, covert thoughts, and feelings of clients. It is closely linked with the empathic awareness that he or she may be expected to have and share with the family in treatment, as discussed earlier. When applied appropriately and well timed, it can go a long way toward enabling the family members to achieve crucial insights, relate with intimacy and conscientiousness to the therapy, and work realistically and seriously toward constructive functional changes.

When not appropriately timed, on the other hand, particularly when interpretations are offered early in the therapy, resentment and resistance may result. An interpretation may be perceived by family members as a confrontation or as a kind of accusation or criticism. Even if it is an accurate appraisal of what is occurring below the level of awareness, the clients may not be insightful enough to recognize it or emotionally secure enough to accept it. There is considerable danger that such a state of affairs may result in a family's refusing to continue with therapy.

It seems safest and most practical, therefore, for the therapist to be sure that a firm therapeutic relationship has been established before interpretations are attempted. Even then, this type of intervention should be approached with caution and tentativeness. For an interpretation to have the best chance of being effective in enabling the family members to achieve insights into the underlying motivations for their behavior, and for orienting toward using such insights constructively, the family should be ready to understand and accept its validity.

It would, accordingly, seem wise to let interpretations flow from the content and process of the therapy sessions. Well-placed questions by the therapist can generally lead the family members toward recognizing their own inner struggles, motives, and emotional reactions. When asked for the implications of what is occurring, they are likely to achieve at least part of the interpretation. This may then be used by the therapist to elicit more complete insights and/or to suggest what those might be. Such an approach thus times the interpretation to the readiness of the family to deal with it and to accept responsibility for it.

The Therapist's Self and Family Therapy

In summary, what characteristics of the therapist and his or her behavior appear to be conducive to the effective administration and management of family therapy? An important practical issue is the willingness of the family therapist to organize his or her daily work program so as to reserve adequate time and energy for the needs of the families being served. The therapist must be oriented toward being helpful to people and reflecting an attitude of optimism about people's ability to mature and to solve problems of living constructively, no matter how difficult and complex those problems may seem to be. An element that is often very helpful to families struggling with a dysfunctional system of dealing with their experiences is for the therapist to demonstrate a quality of hopefulness about people's capacities for change and problem solving. This should be accompanied by indications of determination and conscientiousness on his or her part to persevere with the family for as long as its members are willing and able to make use of therapy.

Another necessary, though not sufficient, element related to effectiveness as a family therapist would seem to be a personal commitment to the family therapy approach to mental health problems and faith in its potential usefulness. In this regard one must adopt an orientation or philosophy of family therapy with which one is comfortable and which one is able to apply with conviction and professional integrity. Clinical reports and some research suggest that virtually all defined schools or procedures of family therapy work adequately in the hands of well-trained and experienced psychotherapists. The same applies to what may be considered to be an "eclectic" approach, which combines the elements of several viewpoints and models, and which is generally a unique mixture that fits the individual therapist's inclinations.

Related to the above elements is the therapist's basic feelings about people generally and about families experiencing difficulties in particular. Unless he or she can demonstrate a genuine respect for the family members and stimulate in them the feeling that he or she cares and even likes them, it is not likely that an effective working relationship can be established with the family. The ability to sympathize with the family's suffering and struggles to maintain its integrity should be communicated, along with empathic understanding of the problems and emotions being experienced. A readiness to be warmly supportive must be shown by the therapist. He or she should also be ready to try to help the family members achieve a balanced perspective in their perception of their family's circumstances. As the negative, painful aspects and problems of the family system are revealed, attention should also be given to the positive, productive elements that are manifest, thus helping them to recognize that they have resources that can be useful to them in their efforts to resolve their difficulties.

It is critical that a family therapist be a patient and willing listener to what the family members convey, both in their verbal and nonverbal communications. Equally important is the effective family therapist's ability to communicate with the family members in a clear and concise fashion. He or she should be able to reflect a grasp of the problems with which the family members are struggling and to verbalize them in terms that are well understood by all concerned. It is also desirable that the family therapist clarify for the family various appropriate concepts of the psychology of the individual and family functioning, thus further establishing a common language frame that may facilitate communication.

It is highly desirable, furthermore, that the family therapist demonstrate his or her positive regard for each family member's individuality. This may be achieved by such matters as supporting each person's need for privacy, right to self-expression, and drive to discover and achieve his or her social, vocational, cultural, and intellectual goals. At the same time, however, emphasis should be given to the crucial importance to all of the family requirements, and the need for teamwork for their fulfillment. These elements may set the stage for engaging all the participants in the family therapy process. The desired open and frank communication may then be stimulated, leading to the sharing of ideas, perceptions, feelings, and impressions.

A valuable quality for the family therapist is a pleasant and active sense of humor. This becomes particularly useful when much nervous tension and a depressive mood pervade the therapy sessions. A sensitive introduction of humor may then be helpful to all concerned and can lead to friendly and sympathetic communication among the family members. It is also important that the family therapist exercise imagination and flexibility in introducing interventions, and to be alert to their potential effectiveness in facilitating the family therapy process.

Pervading the total picture is the self-directedness of the family therapist and his or her maturity and professional orientation in interacting with the family in a genuine and honest fashion. This calls for recognizing his or her own emotional reactions to the family and its members, and the ability to share these in a constructive fashion with them. Extremely important is the care that the therapist must exercise not to become enmeshed in the family's problems or in confusing them with his or her own personal and family problems and concerns.

The issue of gratification from one's work is a very sensitive and delicate element for the family therapist because a distinction needs to be drawn between what the therapist hopes to achieve and what the family in therapy chooses or is able to accomplish. Accordingly, the therapist's satisfaction must be derived primarily from the opportunity to practice his or her profession and the effectiveness with which he or she applies the intervention skills that are appropriate to the situation at hand. Much gratification may also be experienced from the privilege of being permitted to enter the family's privacy and to exercise a constructive role in enabling the family members to clarify their problems and find effective ways to deal with then. The therapist cannot expect that the family will benefit from the therapy in ways that he or she expects or desires. His or her pleasure must come from having the opportunity to exercise influence and show the way. At times, of course, the family does follow the lead of the therapist. He or she may then be proud of the family for their achievements, but this must be viewed as the free choice of the family rather than as the accomplishment of the therapist. To perceive this as the basis for one's professional fulfillment and gratification is to flirt with the likelihood of enmeshment in the family's system and with the consequent distortion of the therapy process.

Readings

1. Boszormeny-Nagy, Ivan, and Barbara R. Krasner. 1986 *Between Give and Take*. New York: Brunner/Mazel.

2. Kneil, John R., and David P. Kniskern, eds. 1982. *From Psyche to System: The Evolving Therapy of Carl Whitaker*. New York: Guilford Press.

3. Kramer, Jeannette R. 1985. *Family Interfaces: Transgenerational Patterns*. New York: Brunner/Mazel.

4. Minuchin, Salvador, and H. Charles Fishman. 1981. *Family Therapy Techniques*. Cambridge: Harvard University Press.

8

Families of Adolescent Drug Abusers Are "Rigid": Are These Families Either "Disengaged" or "Enmeshed," or Both?

Alfred S. Friedman
Arlene Utada
Margaret R. Morrissey

The Olson's Circumplex Model (FACES) instrument of family functioning was administered to ninety-six adolescent drug-abuse clients and their parents. The majority of these families categorized themselves as disengaged" (rather than "enmeshed") on the cohesion dimension, and as "rigid" (rather than "chaotic") on the adaptability dimension. These findings were unexpected as they were substantially different from published findings on families with other types of problems. Family therapists, utilizing Olson's Clinical Rating Scale for the Circumplex Model, characterized significantly more of these same families as "enmeshed," rather than "disengaged." Possible explanations for the difference between the therapists' perceptions and the families' self-perceptions are discussed in this chapter.

The main purpose of this chapter is to report how family therapists perceive families of adolescent drug abusers in regard to the dimensions of "cohesion" and "adaptability" of the Olson Circumplex Model[29], compared to how these same families are perceived by the family members (mothers, fathers, and the adolescent drug-abuse clients). A secondary purpose is to characterize and classify families of adolescent drug abusers in accordance with the Olson Circumplex model and to compare them with the classifications that have been reported for families that have adolescent offspring with types of problems other than drug abuse.

Comparison of Therapists' Perceptions with Family Perceptions

The "insider's perspective" of the family (derived from self-reports of the family members about their family functioning) has been found usually to differ from and conflict with the outsider's perspective," as derived from behavioral and observational assessment.[25] Two recent journal articles[1,12] compared the Olson Circumplex model with the Beavers-Timberlawn model of Family Competence[2,20] and reported that there was "a surprising lack of association between measures of these two prominent family assessment models" when they were applied to a sample of families of delinquent adolescents[12]. The specific relevance of those articles to our report derives from the fact that the Beavers-Timberlawn instrument utilizes ratings of expert outside observers of the families, while FACES utilizes self-report by the family members in a questionnaire format. In our study, instead of comparing the results on a group of families obtained from two different instruments with different conceptualizations, we compared the results obtained from two instruments that were developed from the same model and conceptualization: the *FACES-II Family Adaptability and Cohesion Scales*[28] and the *Clinical Rating Scale for the Circumplex Model*[26], both of which are based on the Olson Circumplex Model.

Green and his colleagues[12] have noted that although "Olson and Beavers concur that adaptability and cohesion represent the salient dimensions of family life, thereby suggesting that both models may be addressing the same constructs," they differed in regard to linear versus curvilinear assumptions about family health and adjustments. The

> Beavers Model portrays family life as existing on an infinite linear continuum of competence and emphasizes thereby the limitless potential for growth. . . . Indeed, for the Circumplex Model, optimal family functioning is achieved when families reach a balance, or midpoint, between the dysfunctional extremes of both adaptability and cohesion. For adaptability, these extremes consist of chaos (too much change) at one end of the curvilinear continuum and rigidity (too little change) at the other end. Similarly, for cohesion, family health or balance exists between the extreme conditions of enmeshment (overly close) and disengagement (not close enough).[12]

Olson[27], when noting that families in his "enmeshed" group, who scored abnormally high in the "cohesion" dimension, had reported high levels of family satisfaction, suggested that this was due to their inability to admit dissatisfaction—thus attempting to adhere to his curvilinear model. The position of Beavers[1], however, is that

> *cohesion* defined operationally in a self-report instrument may, probably will, have little or nothing in common with clinical or observational definitions. It leads to confusion compounded to assume that families scoring high on a self-report labeled cohesion are "enmeshed" and "pseudomutual." These concepts have gained respect and currency by being

derived from clinical work; they have clinical meaning and significance.(p. 402; Beavers' emphasis)

Given these varying statements, we planned a study to compare family therapists' perceptions of families with the family members' self-reports on the same two dimensions.

It is quite possible that family "cohesion," or cohesiveness, as measured in the FACES-II, is a different concept than the concept of "enmeshment" in a family, as referred to by family therapists and clinicians. A key problem in the interpretation of the scores yielded by the FACES-II comes about when working with certain kinds of families. For example, in a split family in which alliances have not permitted the formation of a triadic image, there might be a close (cohesive) relationship between the mother and the adolescent son, but there might not be a close or cohesive relationship between the father and that son. On the FACES-II, the members of such a family might report the family, as a whole, to be "disengaged" or "separated." For example, the family might agree with the FACES-II item, "family members pair up rather than do things as a total family," and this response would subtract from the FACES-II cohesion scores. A family therapist, on the other hand, may be struck by the intense, close dyadic relation between mother and son, and consider the family to have excessive diffusion and blurring of the generational boundaries, and to be enmeshed.

It is a central concept of the structural model of family therapy[23] that pathology (family dysfunction, symptoms) is expected to occur when the family is too enmeshed, lacking subsystem differentiation, or disengaged (that is, lacking in sufficient sub-system connection). The idea that too much cohesion, togetherness, or "we-ness" in a family is not good, or is too much of a good thing, is related to the concepts of pseudomutuality[37], undifferentiated ego mass[4], binding[35], or enmeshment[23] in families, which interfere with the individuation and the development of autonomy in younger family members. This appears to be the basis for treating the "cohesion" dimension in FACES-II as a curvilinear, rather than a linear, variable or characteristic. A problem with this concept is that it is not the *quantity* or the frequency of the family doing things together or deciding issues together that should be in question, but, rather, the type and *quality* of each interaction that occurs—which, incidentally, is partly determined by the underlying emotional and psychodynamic tendencies and needs of each family member. The clues to "enmeshment" are probably more subtle, *and* more extreme or unusual forms of behavior than those represented by the specific items of FACES-II. If any item by itself does not describe a family behavior or a family pattern that is in itself dysfunctional or pathological, it should not matter how many such items the family reports to be characteristic of the family, or how frequently family members engage in such behaviors; and an extremely high total "cohesion" score will not, in our view, represent pathology or dysfunction. This is the reason why other investigators[1,12,22], in addition to ourselves, are questioning the curvilinear Circumplex Model of FACES-II.

In many families, tendencies toward projective identification, overprotectiveness, intrusiveness, and so on, are often cloaked or covered by, or combined with healthier forms of closeness, cohesiveness, intimacy, and love, and they may be difficult to distinguish. Certainly, many families, particularly parents, do not make the distinction well, nor do many items on family self-rating scales make such distinctions well. It may take several meetings with a family in order for a skilled clinician to make such distinctions.

Nearly all of the items that load positively on the cohesion factor of the FACES-II probably sound healthy to most respondents. This is supported by the fact that family members tend to achieve high scores when asked to respond to the items according to the instructions: "*Ideally,* how would you like your family to be?" The items, for the most part, sound healthy to clinicians as well. No one item by itself sounds clearly pathological. For example, there is no item in FACES-II that reflects or captures the quality of diffusiveness or vagueness of the ego boundaries between family members, which is one of the key measures of excessive family closeness or enmeshment used in the Beavers-Timberlawn Family Evaluation Scale[20]. Illustrative of this point is the following: A friend encounters an adolescent daughter and her mother and compliments the daughter on an achievement or on having done something well, and the mother promptly interjects, "Yes, we do things well in our family." The quality of this mother's way of relating would not be easy to capture in a short item on a self-report scale. If these clinical speculations of ours and of Beavers's[2,20] are on target, we would not expect to find much relationship in this study between our family therapists' ratings of family "cohesion" and the families' self-ratings of "cohesion," at least at the "enmeshment" (extreme high) end of the scale.

Families of Adolescent Drug Abusers

The concepts of "disengagement" (a lack of subsystem connection) and "enmeshment" (a lack of subsystem differentiation), as representing symptoms of family pathology or dysfunction, may be expected to apply to families of adolescent drug abusers as well as to families with other types of problems. The finding of lack of "closeness"[17] and the finding of "low perceived parental support"[9] in families of adolescent drug abusers could suggest a low degree of cohesion and of emotional bonding in these families. On the other hand, some of the clinical observations in the literature about these families could be taken to suggest that there is a lack of clear intergenerational boundaries, and that some of the families tend to be excessively cohesive or enmeshed.

Findings from at least one research study[5] can be interpreted to support the above clinical observations, and also to be consistent with the curvilinear concept of the Olson Circumplex Model. That is, in those families in which there is a greater degree of parental control, a high premium on achieving, high expectation, and structured, shared parent/child activity, there is a lower likelihood of substance abuse. If any of these attitudes are overdone, then the converse may be true. These parental over-concerned attitudes and excessive but ineffective demands may then lead to or perpetuate substance abuse.

There have also been numerous relevant observations over the years that male heroin addicts are overinvolved with their mothers[7,21,36]. Noone and Reddig[24] reported that while drug abusers and addicts have "mock separations" from their families of origin, the majority maintain close ties. Stanton et al.[34] found that 66 percent of a sample of male heroin addicts who were 28 years of age on the average either lived with their parents or saw their mothers daily. All of these subjects, veterans, had previously been separated from home and in the military service for at least several months. Stanton concluded from a review of the literature that there is evidence that a majority of drug addicts maintain close families ties up to age 30 and, in many cases, beyond. The prototypic drug-abuser family is one in which one parent is intensely involved with the abuser, while the other is more punitive, distant, and/or absent. Further, the abusing offspring may serve a function for the parents, often as a channel for their communication. Consequently, the onset of adolescence, with its threat of losing the adolescent to outsiders, elicits parental panic. The initiation of drug abuse behavior during the adolescence of the future heroin addict is seen as "related to an intense fear of separation experienced by the parents in response to the addict's beginning attempts at individuation." The drug-abuse behavior permits the addict "to simultaneously be both close and distant, 'in' and 'out,' competent and incompetent, relative to his family of origin. This is *pseudoindividuation*"[33]; Stanton's emphasis). It may be reasonable to assume that a more-than-average fear or resistance on the part of the parents regarding the separation of the adolescent from the family will be associated with a tendency to maintain a close connection and possibly a type of enmeshment, and that such families would be considered basically enmeshed, rather than disengaged, in spite of the adolescent's "in" and "out" pattern, because his efforts to individuate are unsuccessful.

In a study of mothers of heroin addicts, Kaufman and Kaufman[19] found, by means of subjective observations by experienced clinicians of a series of videotaped family sessions, that 88 percent of the mothers were "enmeshed" with the addict-patient and only 3 percent were classified as "disengaged." Of the fathers, 43 percent were found to be "disengaged" and 41 percent "enmeshed" in their relationships with heroin-addict offspring. There were also ethnic differences that complicated the findings: "In the majority of Italian and Jewish families . . . the entire family, including the father, was quite enmeshed. Puerto Rican and Protestant fathers were quite "disengaged"[18]. Some of the other difficulties encountered in the effort to characterize families as being either disengaged or enmeshed included: (*a*) a father who was earlier in an enmeshed or balanced relationship with a child may become disaffected or disillusioned and adopt a disengaged stance after the child has become seriously involved in drug abuse, and (*b*) a family member who was ostensibly disengaged, but in reality quite enmeshed, may become upset and involved when a change that threatens this member's position starts to occur in the family.

Other conclusions regarding the family patterns from Kaufman's[19] study are not inconsistent with those from other studies of family patterns of heroin addicts[24,33,34]:

> The addict provides a displaced battlefield so that implicit and explicit parental strife can continue to be denied. . . . The addict forms cross-generational alliances which separate parents from each other. . . . Generational boundaries are diffuse—there is frequent competition between parents. Frequently the crisis created by the drug-dependent member is the only way the family gets together and attempts some problem solving, or is the only opportunity for a "dead" family to experience emotions. (pp. 44–45)

As for characterizing the family as a whole, these descriptions do not appear to suggest a family that is very cohesive but, rather, a family that is split by dyadic alliances, a family that has not succeeded in developing a triadic family image, that is, both parents in a unified position in relation to the adolescent offspring. Fishman, Stanton, and Rosman[10] recommended that in conducting therapy with adolescent drug abuse families "importance is attached to getting parents to work together, reinforcing the family's generational hierarchy . . . to achieve an intact, in-the-home hierarchy that remains in place at the end of therapy". Such recommendations suggest that the families before treatment are not cohesive and are not working together well as a unit.

In regard to the "adaptability" dimension, the literature seems to suggest that these families are not very flexible or adaptable to changing needs and conditions, and that they might be found at one of the two extreme ends of the continuum on this dimension ("rigid" or "chaotic")—and thus "unbalanced." There appears to be little in the literature, however, to suggest which of the two extremes of the adaptability dimension would be more characteristic of these families.

Procedures

Data Collection Instrument

FACES-II was selected as the instrument for this study because (*a*) FACES-III, the recent revision of this instrument, was not available at the time this study was started; (*b*) it is a short instrument and relatively easy to administer; (*c*) it was standardized on a large sample (*n* = 1,000 families), although not representative of the national general population, or with adequate empirical reliability (Cronbach Alpha − .90) and statistically independent dimensions (factors); (*d*) there have been several studies that show that it discriminates between different clinical types of families; and (*e*) it yields an actual-ideal discrepancy score that measures the level of satisfaction of each member with the family, and indicates the direction of change desired.

Two central dimensions of family behavior are conceptualized and integrated in the Circumplex Model and constitute the conceptual basis for the use of the FACES-II[28]:

> *Family cohesion* assesses the degree to which family members are separated from or connected to their family. Family cohesion is defined as: *the emotional bonding that family members have toward one another.* Within the Circumplex Model, specific concepts used to diagnose and measure the cohesion dimension are: emotional bonding, boundaries, coalitions, time, space, friends, decision-making, interests and recreation.
>
> *Family adaptability* has to do with the extent to which the family system is flexible and able to change. Family adaptability is defined as: *the ability of a marital or family system to change its power structure, role relationships, and relationship rules in response to situational and developmental stress.* Specific concepts used to diagnose and measure the adaptability dimension are: family power (assertiveness, control, discipline), negotiation style, role relationships and relationship rules.
>
> Within the Circumplex Model, there are four levels of family cohesion ranging from extreme low cohesion (disengaged) to extreme high cohesion (enmeshed). The two moderate or balanced levels of cohesion have been labeled separated and connected. There are also four levels of family adaptability ranging from extreme low adaptability (rigid) to extreme high adaptability (chaotic). The two moderate or balanced levels of adaptability have been labeled flexible and structured.
>
> For each dimension, the *balanced levels* (moderate) are hypothesized to be most viable for healthy family functioning and the extreme areas are generally seen as more problematic for couples and families over time.

Sixteen distinct types of marital and family systems are identified by combining the four levels of the cohesion and four levels of the adaptability dimensions. Four of these 16 are moderate (*balanced types*) on both the cohesion and adaptability dimensions. Eight types are extreme on one dimension and moderate on the other (*mid-range types*) and four types are extreme on both dimensions (*extreme types*). (18, pp. 5–6)

Comparing Families' FACES-II Self-Ratings to Therapists' Ratings of the Families

The procedure used for obtaining ratings by the therapists of the families on the "cohesion" and "adaptability" dimensions was the following:

1. The definitions and concepts of these dimensions as provided in FACES-II—Family Adaptability and Cohesion Evaluation Scales[28] and the Clinical Rating Scale for the Circumplex Model[26]—were made available to the family therapists for their study (see tables 8–1 and 8–2).

2. Two training sessions consisting of presentations and group discussions of the definitions and concepts were conducted for and with the family therapists.

3. The family therapists were required to determine, after the third family therapy session, the degree of "cohesion" and the degree of "adaptability" for each family by (*a*) completing the Clinical Rating Scale (CRS) of the Circumplex Model on the family and (*b*) locating the appropriate place (point) on the FACES circumplex grid.

The instructions for the use of the CRS[26] include: (*a*) "to encourage the family to dialogue with each other regarding how they handle these general issues, i.e., time, space, discipline, etc.," and (*b*) to ask "the family to describe what a typical week is like and how they handle their daily routines, decision making, and conflict." "After the family interview(s), the therapist selects the value on the eight-point scale that is most relevant for the family as a unit" for each of the concepts that constitute the two dimensions. The concepts that are included in the "cohesion" dimension are "emotional bonding," "parent-child coalitions," "marital relationship," "family involvement," and "internal boundaries." The concepts that are included in the "adaptability" dimension are: "leadership-control," "discipline," "negotiation," "roles," and "rules." For example, the therapist's observation that there are "frequent role changes" and "rules inconsistently enforced" (see table 8–2) would result in a very high rating of "8" on the "rules" concept, which would tend to classify the family on the "chaotic" level of the adaptability dimension. A global rating is made for each of the two dimensions, based on the sum of the ratings of the five concepts, and it then

Table 8–1
Family Change (Adaptability)

Couple or Family Score:	Rigid (Very Low) 1 2	Structured (Low to Moderate) 3 4	Flexible (Moderate to High) 5 6	Chaotic (Very High) 7 8
Leadership (control)	Authoritarian leadership Parent(s) highly controlling	Primarily authoritarian but some equalitarian leadership	Equalitarian leadership with fluid changes	Limited and/or erratic leadership Parental control unsuccessful Rebuffed
Discipline (for families only)	Autocratic, "law & order" Strict, rigid consequences Not lenient	Somewhat democratic Predictable consequences Seldom lenient	Usually democratic Negotiated consequences Somewhat lenient	Laissez-faire and ineffective Inconsistent consequences Very lenient
Negotiation	Limited negotiations Decisions imposed by parents	Structured negotiations Decisions mainly made by parents	Flexible negotiations Agreed upon decisions	Endless negotiations Impulsive decisions
Roles	Limited repertoire; strictly defined roles	Roles stable, but may be shared	Role sharing and making Fluid changes of roles	Lack of role clarity, role shifts, and role reversals
Rules	Unchanging rules Rules strictly enforced	Few rule changes Rules firmly enforced	Some rule changes Rules flexibly enforced	Frequent rule changes Rules inconsistently enforced
Global adaptability rating (1–8)				

Table 8–2
Family Cohesion

	Couple/Family Score:	Disengaged (Very Low)	
		1	2
Emotional bonding		Extreme emotional separateness. Lack of family loyalty	
Family involvement		Very low involvement or interaction between members	
		Infrequent affective responsiveness between members	
Marital relationship		Extreme emotional separateness	
Parent-child coalitions		Lack of parent-child closeness	
Internal boundaries		Personal separateness predominant	
Time (physical & emotional)		Time apart from family maximized. Rarely time together	
Space (physical & emotional)		Separate space needed and preferred	
Decision making		Independent decision making	
External boundaries		Mainly focused outside the family	
Friends		Individual friends seen alone	
Interests		Disparate interests	
Recreation		Mainly separate recreation	
Global cohesion rating (1–8)			

Table 8-2 continues

Separated (Low to Moderate)		Connected (Moderate to High)		Enmeshed (Very High)	
3	4	5	6	7	8
Emotional separateness Occasional family loyalty		Emotional closeness Loyalty to family expected		Extreme emotional closeness. Loyalty to family is demanded	
Involvement acceptable but personal distance preferred		Involvement emphasized but personal distance allowed		Very high symbiotic involvement, members very dependent on each other	
Some affective responsiveness is demonstrated		Affective interactions encouraged and preferred		Affective dependency is demonstrated	
Emotional separateness		Emotional closeness		Extreme emotional reactivity	
Clear subsystem boundaries, some p/c closeness		Clear subsystem boundaries with parent-child closeness		Parent-child coalition Lack of generational boundaries	
Some personal separateness encouraged		Need for separateness respected but less valued		Lack of personal separateness	
Time alone important Some time together		Time together important Time alone permitted		Time together maximized Little time alone permitted	
Separate space preferred; sharing of family space		Sharing family space. Private space respected		Little private space permitted	
Individual decision making but joint possible		Joint decisions preferred but not necessary		Decisions subject to wishes of entire group	
More focused outside than inside family		More focused inside than outside family		Mainly focused inside the family	
Individual friendships seldom shared with family		Individual friendships shared with family		Family friends preferred with limited individual friends	
Separate interests		Joint interests preferred		Joint interests mandated	
More separate than shared recreation		More shared than individual recreation			

becomes possible to classify the family at one of the four levels of cohesion (disengaged, separated, connected, or enmeshed) and one of the four levels of adaptability (rigid, structured, flexible, and chaotic).

Thus, the therapists' ratings of the families of drug abusers (recorded by placement of each family at a specific point on the circumplex grid) were based on their clinical impressions of the family behavior, interaction and dynamics, as organized and classified by the *CRS* and were not based on the specific items on FACES-II. The therapists were actually categorizing families according to clinical concepts or labels (for example, as being "enmeshed") at least as much as they were rating families on the degree of "cohesion," and as being "chaotic" or "rigid" rather than as high or low on adaptability. The fact that the "cohesion" dimension on the *CRS* includes the "internal boundaries" concept (with a scale point defined as "diffuse and weak personal boundaries") indicates that the therapist's rating of the family on the cohesion dimension cannot be considered to be directly comparable to the family's self-rating on the FACES-II instrument; there are no items on the FACES-II that refer to "internal" or intrapsychic states.

Other problem situations in families that complicate the rating task of the therapist are (a) "split" families that consist of one or two close dyadic alliances, referred to earlier in this article, and (b) the fact that in some mother-father-child (adolescent) triangles there is a constantly shifting emotional process in which one dyad (mother-child) is closer together at one point in time whereas the father is the outsider, and another dyad (mother-father) is closer together at another time and the child is the outsider.

The Therapists

Six family therapists participated in the study. All had, as a part of their earlier training in family therapy, graduated from the three-year course of the Clinical School of Marital and Family Therapy of the Family Institute of Philadelphia, which is accredited as a postgraduate school by American Association of Marital and Family Therapy. This is an eclectic training program that teaches six different models or "schools" of family therapy, including the most prominent and most widely practiced models. The number of years of experience that these six therapists had in conducting family therapy ranged from four to seventeen years.

Results

Comparison of Some Perceptions by the Family Members

The perceptions of the families of drug abusers, as perceived by three different family members, were compared to each other (see Table 3).

Fathers, as well as mothers described the families as having both greater cohesion and greater adaptability, to a statistically significant degree, than did the adolescent clients. These findings held for both the perceptions of the "now," or actual degrees of cohesion and adaptability, as well as for the descriptions by the family members of their "ideal" degrees of cohesion and adaptability. The only minor exception to the foregoing generalization is that there was only a trend toward significance between adolescents' and fathers' descriptions of their ideal degrees of adaptability.

Although there were some statistically significant positive correlations across families between the mothers' perceptions and the adolescents' perceptions, and between the fathers' perceptions and the adolescents' perceptions, the positive correlations between the mothers and the fathers were greater ($r = .50$, $r = .53$, respectively) than were the positive correlations between either the mothers and adolescents ($r = .39$, $r = .34$, respectively), or the positive correlations between the fathers and adolescents ($r = .26$, $r = .33$, respectively).

As for the family members' perceptions of ideal family relationships ("How you'd like your family to be"), both the mothers and fathers reported a significantly greater degree of cohesion as their ideal, compared to the young clients. There were no significant differences between the mothers' and fathers' ideal perceptions on either the cohesion or adaptability dimensions.

The correlational findings reported in table 8–3 were obviously based on considering the cohesion and adaptability scales to be linear scales rather than curvilinear or bipolar scales. Thus, extreme high scores on the cohesion scale may, in these results, be considered to indicate a high degree of cohesiveness in the family and to be a positive family trait, rather than to indicate a pathological state of "enmeshment," as suggested in the Olson Circumplex Model.

Comparison of Families' Self-Ratings to Therapists' Ratings of the Families

Because the therapists were not instructed to rate the families at the beginning of the study, therapists' ratings on the families are available on only the last 37 of the 96 families. The scores assigned by the therapists to the families were found to be significantly *higher* on both the cohesion and adaptability dimensions than were the scores from each of the three family members, as determined by their responses to the thirty items of FACES-II (see table 8–4). The therapists differed from the adolescent clients to a greater degree in their categorizations of the families than they did from either of the parents; the young clients rated their families somewhat lower in both cohesion and adaptability than did either of their parents.

Table 8–3
Comparisons of Perceptions of Pairs of Family Members on Faces-II Scales of Cohesion and Adaptability

	Clients (n = 96)		Mothers (n = 96)		Mothers (n = 52)		Fathers (n = 52)		Clients (n = 52)	
	Mean	SD	Mean	SD	Mean	SD	Mean	SD	Mean	SD
Cohesion (now)	46.8	11.1	51.0	10.8	51.0	10.5	50.9	9.7	46.4	11.3
Adaptability (now)	36.4	9.3	39.9	7.2	39.8	7.2	40.8	7.1	36.5	9.8
Cohesion (ideal)	53.9	10.6	66.4	7.0	65.8	6.0	67.1	5.6	53.0	10.8
Adaptability (ideal)	49.0	9.4	52.7	5.6	51.8	5.8	51.9	5.1	49.2	10.0

t-Tests

	Client vs Mother (n = 96)		Client vs. Father (n = 52)		Mother vs. Father (n = 52)	
	t	P	t	P	t	P
Cohesion (now)	4.1	.000	3.0	.005	.04	.967
Adaptability (now)	4.1	.000	3.0	.004	.90	.370
Cohesion (ideal)	10.1	.000	7.8	.000	1.26	.214
Adaptability (ideal)	3.0	.004	1.6	.109	.10	.925

Correlations

	Client and Mother (n = 96)		Client and Father (n = 52)		Mother and Father (n = 52)	
	r	P	r	P	r	P
Cohesion (now)	.39	.000	.26	.066	.50	.000
Adaptability (now)	.34	.002	.33	.016	.53	.000
Cohesion (ideal)	.06	.626	.15	.311	.27	.056
Adaptability (ideal)	-.16	.148	-.01	.937	.06	.684

Table 8–4
Comparison of Clients', Mothers', and Fathers' Perceptions of the Family with the Therapists on Faces-II Scales of Cohesion and Adaptability
(*n* = 96 *two-parent families*)

	Clients (n = 35)		Therapist (n = 35)		t Value	P Value	Correlations Pearson r	P
	Mean	SD	Mean	SD				
Cohesion (now)	43.0	11.5	67.1	9.0	11.6	.000	.31	.071
Adaptability (now)	33.6	8.9	51.1	7.6	9.3	.000	.11	.548
	Mother (n = 35)		Therapist (n = 35)					
Cohesion (now)	49.9	9.2	67.0	9.0	7.8	.000	−.03	.863
Adaptability (now)	39.7	6.6	50.0	7.5	6.9	.000	.21	.223
	Father (n = 22)		Therapist (n = 22)					
Cohesion (now)	50.1	9.2	67.4	9.5	6.1	.000	−.01	.962
Adaptability (now)	41.3	6.4	48.4	8.1	4.1	.000	.40	.068

The correlation between the therapists' ratings and the ratings of the family members, although statistically significant, was generally low. The highest correlation on the "adaptability" dimension was between the therapists' ratings and the fathers' scores (r = +.40); and the highest correlation on "cohesion" was between the therapists' ratings and the clients' scores (r = +.31). The lowest correlations were between the therapists' and the mothers' ratings on cohesion (r = −.03) and the therapists' and fathers' ratings on cohesion (r = −.01).

The classification of the families is indicated by the distribution of the scores and ratings across the four quadrants of the circumplex grid. By this method of classifying, it was found that the largest significant difference between the family members and the therapists was in regard to locating the families in the low adaptability–low cohesion quadrant: clients, 83 percent; mothers, 94 percent; fathers, 82 percent; compared to only 19 percent for therapists (chi-squares = 82.0, 114.4, and 79.4, respectively). Conversely, the therapists located a significantly greater percentage of families in the diagonally opposite quadrant, defined by high (above the mean) adaptability as well as by high-cohesion scores: 46 percent for therapists compared to 9 percent, 3 percent, and 0 percent clients, mothers, and fathers, respectively (chi-squares = 34.4, 50.0, and 59.7, respectively). Most noteworthy however, is the marked tendency of parents to classify the families as low on both cohesion and adaptability (94 and 82 percent for mothers and fathers, respectively.) (All of the six above-listed chi-square values are significant at the .01 level or better.)

As can be seen in table 8–5, there were highly significant differences between the percentages of family members who classified the families in the extreme "rigid-disengaged" category and the percentage of the families that were so classified according to the therapists' judgments. Dramatically high percentages of clients, mothers, and fathers classified their families as being quite low (poor) on both the cohesion and adaptability dimensions (43 percent, 61 percent, and 53 percent, respectively) regardless of whether all 96 two-parent families were considered or whether only the 37 families were considered, for which therapists' ratings were also available (57 percent, 69 percent, and 64 percent, respectively).

Discussion

The marked tendency of the families to describe themselves as "disengaged" rather than as "enmeshed," in FACES terms, is in sharp contrast to the marked tendency of our family therapists to characterize the same families as being "enmeshed." One possible explanation for this difference is that the six family therapists may have followed their earlier, usual clinical concepts (diffuse ego boundaries, fusion in family relationships, etc.) as indicators of "enmeshment." They utilized the Olson CRC, which included the concept of "internal boundaries," and they were not familiar with the items of the FACES-II instrument used by the family members of their self-ratings. The therapists' characterizations of most of the families as being "enmeshed" is consistent with the clinical impressions reported in the literature on families of drug abusers, referred to earlier in this paper, namely, (a) the parents' fear of separation impedes the adolescent's individuation process, or results in pseudoindividuation[10]; (b) "the addict forms cross-generational alliances which separate parents from each other [and] [g]enerational boundaries are diffuse"[19]; and (c) our own clinical impressions of families with a close parent-child dyadic alliance that splits off the other parent so that the family does not develop adequate triadic images and relationships. Also, Minuchin[23] stated that dyadic groupings have difficulty functioning in the families that he considered to be enmeshed: "Dyadic transactions rarely occur; integration is either triadic or group . . . , which promotes a sense of vagueness and confusion in all family members". Certainly, such families do not fit very well the FACES cohesion items in which the whole family is described as working together well and cohesively as a unit.

Another way to explain or rationalize the marked difference between the therapists' characterizations and the families' self-ratings ("enmeshed" versus "disengaged") is to assume that they refer to two different levels of the family experience. The items of FACES-II, which the family rates, refer to

Table 8–5
Family Profile: Faces-II: Rating on Cohesion Scale for Two-Parent Families[a]

Adaptability	Cohesion			
	Disengaged Parents (56.9 or below) *Adolescent* (47.9 or below)	*Separated Parents* (57.0–65.0) *Adolescent* (48.0–56.0)	*Connected Parents* (65.1–73.0) *Adolescent* (56.1–64.0)	*Enmeshed Parents* (73.1 and above) *Adolescent* (64.1 and above)

Chaotic:
Parents 56.1 or above
Adolescent 52.1 or above

Flexible:
Parents 50.1–56.0
Adolescent 45.1–52.0

Structured:
Parents 44.0–50.0
Adolescent 38.0–45.0

Rigid:
Parents 43.9 or below
Adolescent 37.9 or below

All Other

	Client	*Mother*	*Father*	*Therapist*
	57% (n = 96)	39% (n = 96)	47% (n = 56)	92% (n = 37)
	43% (n = 37)	31% (n = 37)	36% (n = 37)	92% (n = 37)

Rigid-Disengaged

	Client	*Mother*	*Father*	*Therapist*
	43% (n = 96)	61% (n = 96)	53% (n = 52)	8% (n = 37)
	57% (n = 37)	69% (n = 37)	64% (n = 37)	8% (n = 37)

chi-square values

Client vs. Therapist: χ^2 = 54.7, ($p \leq .01$)
Mother vs. Therapist: χ^2 = 78.6, ($p \leq .01$)
Father vs. Therapist: χ^2 = 68.1, ($p \leq .01$)

[a]Statistics for present study, using the Olson et al, form for rating cohesion, from Olson, D.J., J. Portner, and R. Bell, 1982. FACES-II (University of Minnesota: Department of Family and Social Science).

the overt behavior of the family, but the therapists' judgments may be based more on subtle cues to the nature of the underlying "psychodynamics" of the family's emotional relationships, and to the implied feelings between family members that are not clearly and openly expressed. Thus, for example, members of a family who are emotionally tied to or overidentify with each other, who engage in projective identification, are overdependent on each other, and are unable to individuate adequately, may still not work well together as a family unit (for example, in making family decisions). Another possibility is that although members of a family may stay at home more, not relate to others outside of the family, and do many things together as a family, they may still relate to each other only on an emotionally superficial level; thus, they may not be judged by a therapist to be emotionally close, intimate, or "cohesive."

One may expect therapists, as compared to family members, to be more qualified to assess, or at least to be more perceptive about the pathological aspects or implications of specific family behaviors or interactions. Therapists would probably claim that the families are not aware of and lack insight into the fact that they are so emotionally enmeshed, and that they confuse their own feelings and attitudes with those of the other members. Perhaps it is not possible, at this stage of research, to explain adequately, why the therapists tend to perceive many of these families as being "enmeshed" while family members tend to describe their families as being "disengaged."

Low or Poor Adaptability ("Rigidity") in Families of Drug Abusers

What are the possible explanations for family members' (particularly mothers') descriptions of the families as being low on the adaptability dimension, and overly structured or "rigid," while therapists tend to perceive these families as being structured or "chaotic"? It may be that the therapists were more attuned to the inconsistency in the parents' efforts to apply rules (discipline) while negotiating with their adolescent, drug-using offspring, and in performing their roles in parent-child relationships. The therapists were more likely to see these parental efforts as being inconsistent and "chaotic" than as being "flexible."

Inspection of the FACES items that determine the adaptability score indicates that many of these items refer to freedom of expression by the children, egalitarian leadership, rules flexibility enforced, reasonable discussion, sharing responsibilities, compromising differences, trying new solutions to problems, and fairness of discipline. It is not unexpected that the drug-abuse adolescents tend to perceive the family leadership as authoritarian and autocratic, and the parents as controlling, rigid, enforcing rules strictly, and imposing unilateral decisions. Such perceptions of the family yield low scores on the adaptability dimension and classify the family as "rigid." It is more unexpected that the parents also tended to describe their families the same way.

It is worth noting that one of the findings of a study by Brook et al.[5] appears to fit with our findings of low scores on the adaptability dimension in that "parents in drug-free families engage in a number of shared activities with their offspring". Also, it is sometimes believed that parents who have traditional and conservative social orientations are more likely, than are "permissive" or "liberal" parents, to perceive an emphasis on parental authority and strict enforcement of rules as appropriate for parent-child relationships. According to this way of thinking, the parents in our families of drug-abusers, with their "rigid," authoritarian response and the low adaptability scores, may be expected to have traditional and conservative social orientations. On the other hand, parents of college students who use marihuana have been described in the literature[3,13–16,22] as tending to be permissive, laissez-faire, providing few rules and little structure, being less traditional or religious, and, in some cases, even smoking pot themselves. It may be that this latter descriptive picture is more likely to apply to middle-class or affluent families, whereas the families in our sample are predominantly working class or lower middle class, with relatively uneducated parents, few of whose offspring will go to college.

A partial test of the hypothesis of a positive relationship between adaptability dimension scores and family SES scores was available. The clients' adaptability scores were correlated with the scores derived from a measure of family SES, but this correlation was found to be nonsignificant. This was, however, probably not an adequate test of the hypothesis because of the restricted range of SES variables in the study samples of families. For example, only 18 percent of the fathers in this sample had completed college, compared to 34 percent in Olson's national, Lutheran-normative sample (n = 1,112). The foregoing references to possible associations between socioeconomic status, educational background, religious commitment, social conformity, and so on, to the adaptability dimension in parent-child relationships, remain hypothetical as far as our data are concerned, and they await clarification through further research efforts.

Comparison of Drug-Abuse Family Sample with Olson's National, Lutheran Family Sample

The two FACES-II scales are considered to be linear scales for the purpose of our *t*-test comparison. All three members of the drug-abuser families (mothers, fathers, and adolescent clients) perceived their families to have significantly less cohesion and significantly less adaptability than did members of the normative family sample. But because our sample of families differs significantly from the national standardization sample of families on some of the key demographic and background variables, it is not feasible to associate the "deviant" self-descriptions on cohesion and adaptability made by families in our study to the presence of drug abuse in these families.

The most striking and dramatic difference found between the drug-abuser and control families was in the proportion of families in each group who were classified as being *both* "rigid" and "disengaged." As shown in table 8–5, 57 percent of parents and 43 percent of adolescents in families of drug abusers described their families as being both "rigid" and "disengaged," compared to only 8 percent of parents and 7 percent of adolescents in the normal control families. The extremely significant differences are indicated by the chi-square values of 54.7 ($p \leq .01$) and 34.6 ($p \leq .01$), respectively.

The two kinds of families did differ significantly, but not as dramatically, on the proportion of families described as "enmeshed" by the family members. Of particular interest here is that only 1 percent of the parents and 5 percent of the adolescents in the drug-abuser families describe their families as being "enmeshed," compared to 15 percent of the normal control parents (chi-square = 13.3), and 20 percent of the normal control adolescents (chi-square = 10.3). This finding appears to be consistent with the heavy weighting of the drug-abuser families in the direction of being "rigid" and "disengaged," that is, in the diagonally opposite direction on the grid from the "enmeshed-chaotic position.

Comparison of Drug-Abuser Family Sample with Samples of Families with Other Types of Problems

Based on our review of the literature, the findings derived from administration of the FACES instrument to samples of various types of families are as follows:

30 percent of Olson's "clinic sample" were both "disengaged" and "chaotic"[30]

29 percent were "disengaged" and 23 percent were "chaotic" in Olson's sample of families of runaway children[30]

64 percent of families of neurotic patients and 56 percent of families of schizophrenic patients were found among the "extreme" types[8]

49 percent of families of sex offenders were found among the "extreme" types[6]

more "high-risk" than "low-risk" families were found to be "chaotic" and "enmeshed"[11]

59 percent of Rodick's[31] sample of families of adolescent delinquents were found to be both "chaotic" and "enmeshed"

30 percent of Green et al.'s[12] sample of families of delinquent children and adolescents were found to be "chaotic," and 43 percent were "disengaged"

In none of the above studies is it reported that any significant or high percentage of problem families were found to be "rigid." These samples of families with other types of problems are sometimes referred to as having a tendency to be both "disengaged" and "chaotic," but not as both "rigid" and "disengaged." Is this latter pattern unique to families of adolescent drug abusers? In Rodick's[31] study, 59 percent of the families of delinquents were reported to be "chaotically enmeshed," which is about as different from the predominant "rigid-disengaged" pattern of our sample of families as can be yielded by measurement with the FACES instrument. Because many of the adolescents in our sample are delinquent as well as drug abusers, are the patterns of functioning in their families so very different from the patterns in families with other types of delinquent offspring?

More detailed information is available on Green's sample of families with delinquent adolescents, which makes it possible to report tests of significant differences between that sample and our sample of drug-abuser families. A disclaimer must be stated, however, about the reporting of such differences. Any differences that are found in the cohesion and adaptability scores could conceivably be related more to differences between the two groups on demographic and other background variables than to the differences in the type of presenting problem (delinquency versus drug abuse).

Compared to the three members of each of our drug-abuser families, a significantly lower percentage of the corresponding members of Green's court-referred delinquency families classified themselves as being "rigid": (*a*) for mothers, 8 percent versus 69 percent (chi-square = 95.5); (*b*) for fathers, 7 percent versus 62 percent (chi-square = 53.9); and (*c*) for adolescents, 13 percent versus 59 percent (chi-square = 59.4). Similarly, fewer mothers and fathers in the delinquent families classified their families as "disengaged": (*a*) for mothers, 24 percent versus 71 percent (chi-square = 30.7); and (*b*) for fathers, 24 percent versus 64 percent (chi-square = 24.2). (All of the chi-square values were significant at the .01 level or better.) The comparison of the two groups of adolescents was not statistically significant, but it indicated a trend in the same direction (chi-square = 3.3). Again, by this comparison, as well as by the earlier comparison with Olson's normative families, the families of adolescent drug abusers are found to describe themselves as being extremely "disengaged" and extremely "rigid." At the same time, significantly fewer parents (but not adolescents) in the drug-abuser families classify their families as being "enmeshed." These same parents also less often classified their families as being "balanced" or normal, according to Olson's curvilinear model.

The contention of Beavers[1] and Green[12] that the FACES dimensions are linear rather than curvilinear variables, as opposed to Olson's idea[27] that high scores in the cohesion dimension represent either "enmeshment" or "pseudomutuality" (a superficial, false, or exaggerated picture of family unity) rather than a genuinely healthy family system, is an important issue for the conceptualization and use of FACES-II. This issue, however, has little impact on the findings of our study because few (less than 5 percent) of our drug-abuser families represent themselves on the FACES-II as being either very cohesive (or "enmeshed"), or as being very adaptable (or "chaotic"). Thus, we assume that they are representing themselves fairly accurately, according to their perceptions of their family situations. There is no apparent advantage for them to claim that they are in a "disengaged" or "separated" state if they honestly believe that they are cohesive, and in either a "connected" or "enmeshed" state. Similarly, there is no advantage to their representing themselves as being low in adaptability, or "rigid," if they believe that they really are more "flexible." Whereas one may speculate that adolescents would tend to perceive their parents as being more "rigid" than they actually are, one would not speculate that the parents are likely to have this tendency. In fact, our data indicate that a higher percentage of parents, than of adolescents, rated the family as being "rigid" and low in adaptability. The families, to be sure, were describing themselves at a time of crisis, when they were feeling relatively hopeless about their situation (the severe drug abuse of the adolescent client and other family problems), at a time when the family was unable to work together to solve their problems, and the family was falling apart or splitting apart. One could speculate that this may have influenced their responses to the FACES-II items in the direction of being classified as "disengaged" rather than "cohesive." But, then, why did samples of families with other types of severe problems not respond in the same direction? It cannot be denied that the responses to FACES-II are a valid reflection of the family's perception of itself at that particular time.

This study is limited to families of clients who enter into treatment, and it provides no information on families of substance abusers who do not enter treatment. It is possible, even perhaps probable, that families of substance abusers who enter treatment are more dysfunctional and pathological than families of substance abusers who do not enter treatment. One may also postulate that families who become involved in and participate in family therapy are at least as likely to be "enmeshed" (versus being "disengaged") as are families who do not participate in family therapy.

References

1. Beavers, W.R., R.B. Hampson, and Y.F. Hulgus. Commentary to Green, R.G., Kolevzon, M.S., and Vosler, N.R. *Family Process 24*:398–405, 1985.

2. Beavers, W.R., and M.N. Voeller. Family models: Comparing and contrasting the Olson Circumplex Model with the Beavers Systems Model. *Family Process 22:* 85–98, 1983.

3. Blum, R.H., et al. *Horatio Alger's Children*. San Francisco: Jossey-Bass, 1972.

4. Bowen, M. The family as a unit of study and treatment (Workshop 1959): Family psychotherapy. *American Journal of Orthopsychiatry 31:* 40–60, 1961.

5. Brook, J.S., I.F. Lukoff, and M. Whiteman. Family socialization and adolescent personality and their association with adolescent use of marijuana. *Journal of Genetic Psychology 133:*261–71, 1978.

6. Carnes, P. *Counseling Sexual Abusers*. Minneapolis, Minn.: CompCare Publications, 1985.

7. Chein, I., D. Gerard, and E. Rosenfeld. *The Road to H*. New York: Basic Books, 1974.

8. Clarke, J. The family types of schizophrenics, neurotics and "normals." Unpublished doctoral dissertation, Department of Family Social Science, University of Minnesota, 1984.

9. Cooper, D.M., and D.H. Olson. Perceived parent support and self-esteem as related to adolescent drug use. Minneapolis, Minn.: Multi-Resource Center, 1977.

10. Fishman, H.C., M.D. Stanton, and B.L. Rosman. Treating families of adolescent drug abusers. In M.D. Stanton, T.C. Todd, and Associates, eds., *The Family Therapy of Drug Abuse and Addiction*. New York: Guilford Press, 1982.

11. Garbarino, J., J. Sebes, and C. Schellinbach. Family at risk for destructive parent-child relations in adolescents. *Child Development 55*:174–83, 1985.

12. Green, R.G., M.S. Kolevzon, and N.R. Vosler. The Beavers-Timberlawn model of family competence and the circumplex model of family adaptability and cohesion: Separate, but equal? *Family Process 24*:385–98, 1985.

13. Groves, W.E. Patterns of college student drug use and lifestyles. In E. Josephson and E.E. Carroll, eds., *Drug Use: Epidemiological and Sociological Approaches*. Washington, D.C.: Hemisphere Publishing, 1974.

14. Jessor, R., S. Jessor, and J. Finney. A social psychology of marijuana use: Longitudinal studies of high school and college youth. *Journal of Personality and Social Psychology 24*:1–15, 1973.

15. Johnston, J.D. Drug use during and after high school: Results of a national longitudinal study. *American Journal of Public Health 64*(suppl.):29–37, 1974.

16. Josephson, E. Adolescent marijuana use, 1971–72: Findings from two national surveys. *Addictive Diseases 1*:55–72, 1974.

17. Kandel, D. Inter- and intragenerational influences on adolescent marihuana use. *Journal of Social Issues 30*:107–35, 1974.

18. Kaufman, E. Myth and reality in the family patterns and treatment of substance abusers. *American Journal of Drug and Alcohol Abuse 7*:257–79, 1980.

19. Kaufman, E. and P.N. Kaufmann. From a psychodynamic orientation to a

structural family approach in the treatment of drug dependency. In E. Kaufman and P. Kaufmann, eds., *Family Therapy of Drug and Alcohol Abuse*. New York: Gardner Press, 1979.

20. Lewis, J.M. W.R. Beavers, J.T. Gossett, and V.A. Phillips. *No Single Thread: Psychological Health in Family Systems*. New York: Brunner/Mazel, 1976.

21. Mason, P. The mother of the addict. *Psychiatric Quarterly 32:*189–99, 1958.

22. Miller, I.W., N.B. Epstein, D.S. Bishop, and G.I. Keitner. The McMaster Family Assessment Device: Reliability and validity. *Journal of Marriage and Family Therapy 11:*345–56, 1985.

23. Minuchin, S. *Families and Family Therapy*. Cambridge: Harvard University Press, 1974.

24. Noone, R.J., and R.L. Reddig. Case studies in the family treatment of drug abuse. *Family Process 15:*325–32, 1976.

25. Olson, D.H. Circumplex Model and family functioning. In C. Ramsey, ed., *Handbook in Family Medicine*. New York: Guilford Press, in press.

26. Olson, D.H., and E.A. Killorin. *Clinical Rating Scale (CRS) for the Circumplex Model*, Department of Family Social Science, University of Minnesota, 1985.

27. Olson, D.H., H.I. McCubbin, H. Barnes, A. Larsen, M. Muxen, and M. Wilson. *Families: What Makes Them Work*. Beverly Hills: Sage Publications, 1983.

28. Olson, D.H., J. Portner, and R. Bell. *FACES-II*. Department of Family Social Science, University of Minnesota, 1982.

29. Olson, D.H., C.S. Russell, and D.H. Sprenkle. Circumplex Model of Marital and Family Systems: VI. Theoretical update. *Family Process 22:*69–83, 1983.

30. Olson, D.H., J. Portner, Y. Lavee. *FACES-III*. Department of Family Social Science, University of Minnesota, 1985.

31. Rodick, A., S.W. Henggler, and W. Hanson. An evaluation of Family Adaptability and Cohesive Evaluation Scales (FACES) and the Circumplex Model. *Journal of Abnormal Child Psychology 14:*77–87, 1986.

32. Segal, B. Reasons for marijuana use and personality: A canonical analysis. *Journal of Alcohol and Drug Education 22:*64–7, 1977.

33. Stanton, M.D., T.C. Todd, and Associates. *The Family Therapy of Drug Abuse and Addiction*. New York: Guilford Press, 1982.

34. Stanton, M.D., T.C. Todd, D.B. Heard, S. Kirschner, J.I. Kleiman, D.T. Mowatt, P. Riley, S.M. Scott, and J.M. Van Deusen. Heroin addiction as a family phenomenon: A new conceptual model. *American Journal of Drug and Alcohol Abuse 5:*125–50, 1978.

35. Stierlin, H. *Separating Parents and Adolescents: A Perspective on Running Away, Schizophrenia, and Waywardness*. New York: Quadrangle, 1974.

36. Vaillant, G.E. A 12-year follow-up of New York narcotic addicts: Some social and psychiatric characteristics. *Archives of General Psychiatry 15:*599–609, 1966.

37. Wynne, L.C. Rychkoff, I.M., Day, J., and Hirsch, S.I. Pseudo-mutuality in the family relations of schizophrenics. *Psychiatry 21:*205–22, 1958.

9

What Mothers Know about Their Adolescents' Alcohol/Drug Use and Problems, and How Mothers React to Finding Out about It

Alfred S. Friedman
Nita W. Glickman
Margaret R. Morrissey

Data was collected from 189 adolescent clients, ages thirteen to twenty-one, and separately from their mothers, in a structured interview format, at time of application for outpatient drug treatment. Based on the assumption that the adolescents know more about their own substance use than their mothers, and do not exaggerate their substance use in their reporting, the results indicate that the mothers' information is not very complete or accurate. The adolescents reported significantly more use of alcohol, but significantly less problem with alcohol use, a finding consistent with the usual assumption that heavy alcohol users deny their problem. In regard to the reports on the mothers' reactions upon finding out about the substance use, the best degree of agreement was on whether the adolescent was punished, and the least degree of agreement was on whether the mother expressed concern about the harmful effects of drugs on the adolescent's life.

Our society tends to hold parents responsible for the behavior of their adolescent children. But the experience of professionals in drug treatment programs indicates that many thousands of parents feel powerless to control the drug use and the related problems generated by their youngsters. The fact that their child is using drugs is, for most parents, very difficult and painful to accept. This pain of the parent adds to the emotional complexity of the problems associated with adolescent drug use.

To begin with, few parents are ready to believe that their own child is using drugs. They have a tendency to disbelieve or deny the symptoms of drug use in their children and to interpret even obvious indicators in other

The work of this research project was conducted with the support of Grant Number 5 R18 DAO3184 by the National Institute on Drug Abuse, entitled "Assessment of Family Therapy for Adolescent Drug Abuse."

ways, such as that it is only a brief atypical phase, or a temporary experimentation to go along with a friend's interest in trying a drug. A parent may believe tentatively that a teenager is using drugs but hopes the problem will go away and doesn't confront the teenager.

When the evidence becomes too obvious to ignore, parents either find that they do not know what to do or else they take actions that escalate the tensions that already exist in the family. The first reaction of many parents to teenage drug use is panic. However, panic usually does not help the situation and can very well complicate it.

It has been reported that approximately one-half of adolescent clients who enter treatment for drug abuse report that "family problems" are one of the main reasons they apply for treatment.[1] Based on our observation of adolescent drug clients and their parents, reported before the start of the current study, we stated "Some adolescents exaggerate the seriousness and importance of family problems and minimize the seriousness of their own drug abuse problems. The parents of these youngsters tend to see the situation quite differently: the worst problem is their adolescent child's drug abuse, without which they claim the family would manage reasonably well."[2]

This is a report on what mothers actually know about the drug use of their adolescent children, and about the problems related to the drug use, and on the mothers' reactions to finding out about the drug use.[3]

The Study Sample

The data for this study were collected from 189 clients and from their mothers at the time of application for treatment for drug abuse in several outpatient drug-treatment programs.

The demographic characteristics of the client-subject sample are shown in table 9–1. The age range was thirteen years to twenty-one years, inclusive, with a mean of 18.0 years and a standard deviation of 2.0 years. The sex distribution was 66 percent male and thirty-four percent female. The race distribution was eighty-seven percent white, eleven percent black and three percent other.

The data on the prevalence rates of use, the number of times used during the preceding month, and the age of first use, for fourteen different substances, are presented in table 9–2, for this sample. It can be seen that this is a relatively heavy-drug-using sample, with a high degree of severity of abuse, on the average. For example, 68 percent reported amphetamine use, 45 percent reported cocaine use, 34 percent reported hallucinogen use, and 32 percent reported PCP use, during the year preceding application for treatment. However, the frequency of use that was reported for the preceding application for treatment, was not very high for any of the substances other

Table 9–1
Demographic Characteristics of the Adolescent Client-Subject Sample
(N = 186)

	Percentage	*Mean*	*S.D.*
1. Age		18.0	2.0
13–14 years	3		
15–16 years	16		
17–18 years	46		
19–21 years	29		
22–23 years	6		
2. Sex			
Male	66		
Female	34		
3. Race			
White	87		
Black	11		
Other	3		
4. Religion			
Catholic	63		
Protestant	22		
Other	8		
None	7		
5. Education (school grade completed)		9.3	1.5
Less than 8th grade	8		
8th grade	22		
9th grade	24		
10th grade	26		
11th grade	11		
12th grade	9		
6. Parents' education			
Mother		12.4	2.0
Father		12.6	2.7
7. Parents' marital status			
Natural parents married, living together	51		
Natural parents separated or divorced	43		
One natural parent deceased	6		

than alcohol, marijuana and amphetamines. It is reasonable to assume from these data that, as a group, these subjects did not tend to deny or under-report their substance use in any gross way. It may also be reasonable to assume that with such heavy multi-drug use by their adolescent children, the mothers should not only have been aware of the use, but also had some idea regarding the degree of severity of the problem.

Procedures

The client and his/her mother were interviewed and examined separately. This usually occurred within one week after the client's admission to the

Table 9–2
Client Self-report of Substance Use of Client-Subject Sample
(N = 189) (prevalence rates, frequencies, and age of first use)

Drug	Used Past Yr. Percentage	Used Past Three Months Percentage	No. Times Used Past Month X̄	(S.D.)	Age of First Use X̄	(S.D.)
Alcohol	95	89	8.2	(13.7)	12.6	(2.1)
Marijuana	95	89	25.2	(32.2)	12.6	(2.3)
Inhalants	9	5	0.6	(4.2)	14.0	(2.0)
Amphetamines	68	51	6.9	(20.4)	14.7	(1.6)
Barbiturates	23	13	1.0	(5.4)	14.3	(1.7)
Tranquilizers	42	22	1.1	(4.7)	14.8	(1.4)
Sedatives	26	12	0.7	(4.3)	14.6	(1.6)
PCP	32	15	0.6	(3.1)	15.0	(1.3)
Hallucinogens	34	21	0.6	(3.6)	14.6	(1.4)
Cocaine	45	28	1.3	(7.0)	15.4	(1.6)
Heroin	6	3	0.5	(3.6)	14.7	(1.2)
Other opiates	22	10	0.4	(2.2)	15.1	(2.0)
Other drugs	5	2	0.2	(2.0)	13.9	(2.4)
Nonprescription	11	5	0.1	(0.9)	14.6	(1.6)

	X̄	(S.D.)
Of Five Friends, How many are using:		
.... Alcohol	3.9	(1.6)
.... Marijuana	3.7	(1.6)
.... Other drugs	2.5	(2.1)

treatment program. In most instances the mother had been involved in the treatment intake process. Thus, she may have heard and learned more about the client's drug use and drug-related problems than she knew before the admission to treatment. To this degree the data obtained from the mother are not totally independent, or may be considered to be somewhat contaminated. These data, accordingly, can be expected to give the impression that the mother may have known somewhat more about the client's drug use and drug-related problems than she actually did know before the application for treatment.

A structured interview format, based on prepared interview questionnaire forms, was utilized. A number of the same questions were asked, independently, of both the client and his/her mother. The results to be reported are based primarily on correlating the scores derived from the mothers' responses to the same items, and performing t-tests to determine any significant differences between the clients' responses and the mothers' responses.

Drug Severity Index

This summary score of drug use was calculated for each client-subject by the following method: A severity weight was assigned to each type of drug used, according to the "risk level" of each drug as suggested by the White House Paper on Drug Abuse (1975). Opiates, sedatives, amphetamines, tranquilizers, hallucinogens, PCP, cocaine, and inhalants were assigned a score of 3; and marijuana, hashish, alcohol, and over-the-counter drugs were scored a 1. For measuring frequency of use, a nine-point code was developed (e.g., once per week = 4; three or more times per day = 9). The index score was derived according to the following formula: The sum, for all types of drugs used during the preceding three months' period, of the multiples of the risk level score times the frequency of use score.

There are, obviously, some limitations and some problems related to the use of this index score, as there might be to any single summary score utilized to represent a whole behavior pattern as complex as drug use/abuse can be. For example, in the DSI scoring formula, smoking marijuana three times daily is equated with using heroin once every two weeks, in the sense that each of these drug-using behaviors is scored for nine points. But there are many different and more serious implications to using heroin than there are to using marijuana, and the two behaviors cannot really be equated.

Results

Initially the mothers were asked, in an open-ended question, to name the "drugs" that the adolescent used. The list of drugs to be considered, was not present. Seventy-nine percent spontaneously named marijuana. When the mothers were asked directly whether the adolescent used alcohol during the preceding three months' period, seventy-nine percent reported some alcohol use, compared to ninety percent for drug use (substances other than alcohol). In regard to the frequency of use of alcohol, forty-seven percent reported at least weekly use, and seven percent reported daily use (see table 9–3). In regard to frequency of use of "drugs," eighty percent reported at least weekly use, and forty percent reported daily use. According to the adolescent's self-reports sixty-two percent used alcohol at least weekly, and seven percent used alcohol daily; and seventy-six percent used marijuana at least weekly, and forty-two percent used marijuana daily. The largest difference between the mothers' and the adolescents' reports is in regard to use of alcohol at least once per week (sixty-two percent reported by adolescents versus forty-seven percent reported by mothers'), which is a statistically significant difference (chi-square = 4.31). Both the mothers and the adolescents reported that there was more frequent use of drugs (other substances) than of alcohol, to a significant degree.

The correlations between the client's affirmation of use of each type of substance and the mothers' reporting of her knowledge of the clients' use of the same substance are presented in table 9–4. If the usual assumption is made that the clients report their substance use fairly accurately—or at least

Table 9–3
Reports of Adolescents' Frequency of Use of Substances during
Preceding Three Months' Period
(in percentages)

	No Use	Less Than Weekly	Weekly	Daily
Mothers' reports:				
Alcohol	8	45	40	7
Drugs (Other				
Substances	5	15	40	40
			(chi square = 38.03)	
Adolescents' self-reports:				
Alcohol	11	27	55	7
Marijuana	11	13	34	42
			(chi square = 22.26)	
Comparison of mothers'				
with adolescents'				
reports on alcohol use:				
Mothers' report	8	45	40	7
Adolescents' report	11	27	55	7
			(chi square = 39.73)	

Table 9–4
Correlations and *t*-Values between Clients'
Self-Reports and Mothers' Reports on Whether
or Not Specific Substances Were Used during
the Preceding Three Months' Period

	Correlation (Relationship)	t-Value (Difference)
Marijuana	.44[a]	3.47[a]
Inhalants	−.03	1.96[a]
Amphetamines	.34[a]	4.28[a]
Barbiturates	.16[a]	4.40[a]
Tranquilizers	.12	4.78[a]
Sedatives	.17[a]	2.91[a]
PCP	.24[a]	2.84[a]
Hallucinogens	.37[a]	4.99[a]
Cocaine	.23[a]	5.71[a]
Heroin	.28[a]	1.64[a]
Other opiates	−.05	3.20[a]
Other drugs	−.01	0.45
Nonprescription	.16[a]	2.13[a]

[a]Indicates a statistically significant relationship (for correlations) or a statistically significant difference (for *t*-values) at the .05 level of confidence, or better. (More clients than mothers reported use for every type of substance.)

that they do not often report using types of drugs that they have not been using—it then appears from the table that the mothers, by comparison, do not tend to have very complete or accurate information about their adolescent offsprings' substance use.

The substances about which there occurs least agreement (i.e., negative correlations) in regard to whether the adolescent uses the particular substance at all, are: inhalants, "other opiates," and "other drugs." If consideration of these three types of substances are put aside, because of their relatively low prevalence rates, the other substances for which there appears to be a relatively high degree of disagreement (and less adequate knowledge by the mother) are: tranquilizers ($r = .12$), barbiturates ($r = .16$), non-prescription drugs ($r = .16$), and sedatives ($r = .17$). While the mothers tend somewhat less often to know whether or not any of these four types of drugs is being used, they at the same time tend to underestimate to a greater degree than for any of these four substances the frequency of use of cocaine ($t = 5.71$).

The mothers reported that sixty-three percent of their adolescents who had used any alcohol during the preceding three months had a problem with alcohol, while thirty-seven percent of those did not have a problem. Of the adolescents for whom the mothers reported no alcohol use during the preceding three months, the mothers said that eighty-six percent had no problem, but fourteen percent did have a problem (chi-square $= 26.2$).

Shown in table 9–5 is a correlation matrix which includes five variables derived from the mothers' reports and ratings of the adolescents' alcohol use and alcohol problem, and five variables derived from the adolescents' self-reports and ratings on alcohol use problem, and harm to self from alcohol use. Three of the ten variables in the matrix are dichotomous variables, and thus point bi-serial correlations (rather than Pearson r correlations) were performed when each of these was correlated with an ordinal or interval variable.

The highest correlation (bi-serial $r = .54$) between any two mothers' variables is the correlation between mother's report that the adolescent used alcohol during the preceding three months' period and the mother's rating of the degree of the alcohol problem. The corresponding correlation derived from the adolescent clients' data ($r = .31$), although statistically significant, is considerably lower than the correlation derived from the mother's data. Thus, the adolescents appear to be somewhat less consistent, or less reasonable in this reporting, than do the mothers.

Seventy-five percent of the clients who reported some alcohol use during the preceding three months' period said that they had no problem with alcohol. Only thirty-seven percent of the mothers who reported that their adolescents used alcohol stated that there was no problem related to this alcohol use. Thus, significantly more alcohol-using adolescents reported that there was no problem with this use (chi-square $= 14.7$).

Table 9-5
Correlation Matrix of Variables Related to Alcohol Use

	M-PRB-ALC	M-U-ALC-3	M-FRQ-ALC-3	M-FRQ-DNK	M-CON-FID	C-ALC-PROB	C-FRQ-ALC-3	ALC-NUM-1	C-ALC-HRM	C-ALC-PSYC
1. (M-PRB-ALC)	—	.36	.54	.43	.11	.24	.29	.25	.11	.15[a]
2. (M-U-ALC-3)		—	.54	.26	.03	.19	.38	.23	.01	-.09
3. (M-FRQ-ALC-3)			—	.45	.08	.30	.45	.35	.06	.06
4. (M-FRQ-DNK)				—	.10	.19	.20	.20	.01	.17
5. (M-CONFID)					—	.23	.06	.14	.01	.03
6. (C-ALC-PROB)						—	.31	.39	.21	.30
7. (C-FRQ-ALC-3)							—	.42	.18	.15
8. (ALC-NUM-1)								—	.13	.22
9. (C-ALC-HRM)									—	.56
10. (C-ALC-PSCH)										—

Note: **Legend** (explanation of acronyms):

Mother's Reports:
1. (M-PRB-ALC)   Four-point rating scale of degree of problem with alcohol
2. (M-U-ALC-3)   Whether or not client used alcohol during preceding three months
3. (M-FRQ-ALC-3)   Four-point rating scale of frequency of use of alcohol
4. (M-FRQ-DNK)   Number of times observed to be "drunk" during the preceding three months
5. (M-CONFID)   Four-point rating scale of frequency of adolescent's confiding in mother about alcohol problem

Client's Reports:
6. (C-ALC-PROB)   Four-point rating scale of degree of problem with alcohol
7. (C-FRQ-ALC-3)   Four-point rating scale of frequency of use of alcohol
8. (ALC-NUM-1)   Number of times used alcohol during preceding month
9. (C-ALC-HRM)   My use of alcohol causes me physical harm
10. (C-ALC-PSCH)   My use of alcohol causes me psychological harm

[a]For the N of 189, a correlation of .15 is significant at the .05 level of confidence, and a correlation of .23 is significant at the .01 level of confidence.

Although the adolescents reported significantly more frequent use of alcohol than the mothers reported on the adolescents (see table 9–3), the adolescents rated themselves as having a significantly lesser degree of problem with alcohol use, compared to the mothers' ratings of the degree of the problem. These findings fit the usual assumption that alcohol users tend to deny their problem.

While the mothers' estimates of the degree of the problem their adolescents had with alcohol use were related to a significant degree to the adolescents' own estimates of the degree of the problem ("r" = .24), the degree of agreement between these two estimates is nevertheless not very good (see table 9–5).

The second highest correlation in the matrix ("r" = .45) is between mother's ratings of frequency of use of alcohol, and adolescents' ratings of frequency of use of alcohol. Thus, while mothers have a fair degree of knowledge of the adolescents' alcohol use, it is nevertheless not a very impressive degree. In general, the correlations in the matrix tend to be relatively low, even when significant. As expected, the intercorrelations between the four variables derived from mothers' reporting (omitting M-CONFID) with the five variables derived from adolescents' reporting (shown in upper right quadrant of the matrix in table 9–5), tend to be lower and less often significant, than the other intercorrelations in the matrix.

The correlations of mothers' ratings of the degree of problem the adolescents have with alcohol use with the adolescents' reports on whether there was physical or psychological harm to themselves from alcohol use, are quite low (bi-serial "r" = .11 and "r" = .15, respectively). Mothers apparently tend to be lacking in awareness of the adolescent's thought or feelings on this issue. Also, mothers may have tended to rate the degree of the problem more on the basis of the problem caused to the family by the adolescent's drinking, than on the basis of the harm caused to the adolescent.

There was a somewhat better degree of agreement than there was in regard to alcohol use, between the mothers' estimates and the clients' estimates ("r" = .32) on the degree of the problem that the clients had with drugs (i.e., all substances other than alcohol, considered together). Also, there was a similar degree of significant relationship ("r" = .33) between the mothers' estimates on the degree to which the adolescents had a problem related to drug use, and the "drug severity index" scores (a formula based on the adolescents' self-reports on frequency of use of all illicit substances during the preceding three months' period). The correlation obtained between these adolescent summary drug use scores and the mothers' ratings of the frequency of use of drugs was .30. The correlation between the mothers' ratings of the degree to which the adolescents' drug use made the family situation worse, and the adolescents' ratings of the degree to which their drug use added to the family problems was .36. Thus, in general, the order or size of the correlations obtained between the adolescents' reports and the mothers' reports in regard to drug use (other substance use) is not too different from the correlations obtained in regard to alcohol use.

The second part of the results to be reported here relate to the mothers' reactions and behavior upon finding out about the adolescent's substance use. The comparison of the adolescents' reports with the mothers' own reports, on the mothers' reactions and behavior are presented in table 9–6. The generally low levels of the correlations suggest that the agreement on the perception and memory of the mothers' reactions tended to be quite poor. Aside from the question of whether the mother did or said nothing, the least amount of agreement occurred in regard to whether the mother expressed concern about the effects of drugs on the client's life ("r" = .06). The best degree of agreement that was attained ("r" = .32) was in regard to whether or not the adolescent was actually punished. Since punishment involves an action or an event and is not just a verbal expression, it is understandable that the perception and memory for punishments would be more accurate than for some of the other types of reaction.

Significantly more mothers than adolescents (eighty-three percent to sixty-three percent) reported that the mothers "Gave reasons against drug use," but significantly less mothers than adolescents (fifty-eight percent to seventy-six percent) reported that the mothers expressed anger. It is also interesting that more mothers than adolescents reported that the mothers threatened punishment (fifty-one percent to forty-three percent) and that the mothers actually punished (forty-nine percent to forty-four percent), although these differences are not statistically significant. (This suggests either that the adolescents do not tend to exaggerate the negative aspects of the mothers' behavior, or that they do not view punishment as negative behavior. Also,

Table 9–6
Relationships (Correlations) between and Differences (*t*-Values) between Mothers' and Adolescent Clients' Reports on Mothers' Reactions When They First Found out about Clients' Drug Use

	Percentage Mothers	*Reporting Adolescents*	*Correlation*	*t-Value*
Did or said nothing	3	4	.03	0.90
Gave reasons against drug use	83	63	.16	4.65[a]
Expressed concern about effects of drug use on client's life	85	81	.06	1.02
Threatened punishment	51	43	.27	1.71
Expressed anger	58	76	.21	4.14[a]
Punished client	49	44	.32	0.88
Withdrew privileges	52	52	.20	0.0
Threatened to throw client out of the house	29	28	.26	0.0

[a]Indicates a statistically significant relationship, or difference, at the .05 level of confidence, or better.

this is somewhat encouraging regarding the question of the reliability of the adolescent clients' reporting on their mothers' behavior.)

Discussion

It is also not very surprising that a high percentage of adolescent clients (eighty-nine percent) reported use of alcohol at the same time that relatively few of them (only twenty-five percent) reported that they believed they had a problem with alcohol. This kind of denial is already legendary and to be expected.

Although the adolescents reported significantly more frequent use of alcohol than the mothers reported regarding the adolescents' frequency of use of alcohol (see table 9–3), the adolescents nevertheless rated themselves as having a significantly lesser degree of problem with alcohol use, compared to the mothers' ratings of the degree of the problem. These findings fit the usual assumption that heavy alcohol users tend to deny that they have a problem. Thus, the adolescents appear to be somewhat less consistent, or less reasonable in this reporting, than do the mothers. On the other hand, the mothers do not appear to be very consistent themselves in their reporting, since more mothers reported that their adolescent had at least a "mild" degree of problems with alcohol, than reported that their adolescents used alcohol within the most recent three months' period.

Based on the assumption that the adolescents' reports are more accurate and complete than the mothers', the findings indicate that the substances about which the mothers have the least adequate or complete knowledge regarding whether or not they are being used, are tranquilizers, barbiturates, sedatives, non-prescription drugs, inhalants, "other" opiates, and "other drugs."

Given the relatively low level of the correlations between the adolescents' and the mothers' perceptions and memory of how the mother reacted when she discovered the adolescent's drug use (albeit that several of the correlations did attain statistical significance), it can concluded that, in general, there is not very good understanding between the mothers and the adolescent, or not very good consensus between their perceptions and/or memory of how the mothers reacted when they first discovered that their adolescents were using drugs.

In our earlier study of PTA parents' attitudes towards hypothetical marijuana use by their children, we found that eighty-three percent of the parents reported that the "most important" way for parents to react was to "discuss with them the harmful effects of use and express personal concern about the harmful effects."[4] Only ten percent reported that "forbidding its use and threatening punishment if it occurs," was most important. (The majority of these parents had reported that their youngsters were not engaged, at least as yet, in drug use.) Since these earlier findings regarding parents' hypothetical reactions are so widely different from the way the mothers in our current study reacted in the real situation, when they discovered their child's drug use, it raises a question about the objectivity and accuracy of the opinions or predictions of the earlier group of parents, regarding how they would react in the actual situation. Possibly some of the difference can be explained by postulating that parents whose adolescent children need to apply for treatment react differently than the PTA parents would react if they discovered that their children were actually using drugs. Also, some of the parents in the current study were reacting to the use of other drugs in addition to the use of marijuana.

From the results of the data analysis it appears that the mothers do not have very complete or accurate knowledge of their adolescents' substance use. This should be no big surprise since many adolescents withhold this information from their parents.

Disclaimers

There are legitimate questions regarding the validity, objectivity, and usefulness of the clients' self-report of drug use at time of admission to treatment. Obviously, it would have improved the validity of the measure if some objective test of drug use (e.g., a urine test) had been employed in addition to client self-report. This is a limitation of this study, but it is a limitation which this study has in common with the majority of research studies conducted on adolescent substance abusers (particularly in drug-free outpatient treatment settings, as distinct from methadone clinics and hospital settings).

The degree to which the findings of a study can be applied to or generalized to the population at large is limited by the special characteristics of the study sample. The findings reported here should not be generalized to all mother-adolescent dyads. For example, the findings of this study may not be applicable to young adolescents and their mothers, since the majority of the study sample was seventeen years of age or older. It is conceivable that mothers of younger adolescents in the thirteen to fifteen age range, might tend to know more about the behavior of their youngsters than do mothers of older adolescents. Also, the findings reported here are limited to adolescents who apply for drug treatment in outpatient programs. It is possible that for drug-using adolescents who do not come to treatment there is better communication between them and their mothers. Their mothers would accordingly have more information about their drug use.

Notes

1. Y. Santo, The methodology of the national youth polydrug study (NYPS), in G.M. Beschner and A.S. Friedman, eds., *Youth Drug Abuse: Problems, Issues and Treatment* Lexington, Mass.: Lexington Books, 1979, p. 144.

2. L.H. Daroff, S.J. Marks, and A.S. Friedman, Adolescent drug abuse: The Parents' predicament, in G.M. Beschner and A.S. Friedman, eds., *Teen Drug Use* Lexington, Mass.: Lexington Books, 1985, p. 196.

3. A Medline search of the literature revealed very little on information obtained from mothers that was relevant to our topic.

4. A.S. Friedman and Y. Santo, A comparison of attitudes of parents and high school senior students regarding cigarette, alcohol and drug use, *Journal of Drug Education 14:*1, 1984.

10

The Functional Family Therapy Model

James Alexander
Holly B. Waldon
Alice M. Newberry
Norman Liddle

Editors' Note: *The exposition of the "functional" family therapy (FFT) that is presented in this chapter was included in a chapter by the same authors entitled "Family Approaches in Treating Delinquents" in* Families in Trouble, *edited by* K.S. Chilman, F.N. Cox, *and* E.W. Nunnally *(Beverly Hills, Calif.: Sage, 1988). Since this family therapy model was originally developed primarily for the purpose of treating juvenile delinquency rather than adolescent drug abuse or other types of individual behavior or family behavior problems, the chapter includes a number of examples of families that had an adolescent who was adjudicated as "delinquent."*

FFT is the model of family therapy that is featured more than others because the editors of this book selected it for use in a systematic demonstration of the effects of family therapy on adolescent drug abuse. The experience and the results of the demonstration are presented in a number of other chapters of this book. The FFT model was selected for the following two reasons: (1) it has been shown in several controlled research studies, reviewed in this chapter, to be effective in reducing adolescent delinquent behavior, which is known to be associated with adolescent substance abuse behavior (Elliott, Huizinga, and Ageton 1985); and (2) the authors were closer to completing a manual for systematic training of therapists in this family therapy model than were the proponents of any other such model.

The Functional Family Therapy (FFT) model is a family-based approach, developed for treating juvenile delinquency, that integrates behavioral, systems and cognitive intervention strategies. In an early demonstration of effectiveness using random assignment, this model produced reductions in recidivism of 21 percent to 47 percent, depending on the comparison group, at a one-year follow-up interval (Alexander and Parsons 1973). No treatment

Reprinted from Elliott, D.S., Huizinga, D. and Ageton, S. 1985. *Explaining Delinquency and Drug Use.* (Beverly Hills, CA: SAGE Publications, Inc), with permission.

produced a 48 percent recidivism, two comparison treatments produced 46 percent and 73 percent, whereas FFT experienced only a 26 percent recidivism. A later evaluation at three-year follow-up demonstrated a significant reduction in sibling referrals of 20 percent to 43 percent (Klein et al. 1976).

The effectiveness of FFT also has been demonstrated with probationers (repeat offenders of moderate severity) and with youth at high risk for foster placement (Barton et al. 1985). Moreover, the model has also been replicated at a different site with totally different treatment staff, producing recidivism rates of only 10 percent for the treated group and a 70 percent recidivism rate for controls (Gordon et al. 1985). Based on such outcomes, FFT often is cited as an important family-based program with demonstrated effectiveness for delinquents (e.g., Todd and Stanton 1983).

The purpose of this chapter is to describe the elements and philosophy of this model, highlighting the model's particular strengths. These strengths include a strong research base: the inclusion of all three major components identified in Garrett's (1985) and Gendreau and Ross's (1980) reviews (a family focus, the use of cognitive techniques, and the use of specific behavior change techniques with consequences for behavior); a dialectical flavor of both generality and specificity that includes a multivariate and multilevel focus; and a careful specification of the different phases of intervention.

The outcome data reviewed above reflect the research base for the model. A considerable amount of additional research has focused on the process of family therapy, including the effects of therapist gender (Mas et al. 1985; Warburton et al. 1980), the effects of therapist characteristics (Alexander et al. 1976), and changes in family behavior (Parsons and Alexander 1973). Recent research also has focused on some of the mechanisms of change in family therapy (Barton and Alexander 1979; Mas 1986; Morris et al., in press; Waldron 1987). This research is described below as it applies to the therapy context.

The dialectical flavor of FFT derives from the inclusion of general principles that apply across most if not all families, coupled with goals and techniques that are individualized for each family. An effective model must have sufficient flexibility of techniques so as to be applicable across a variety of treatment contexts and populations. At the same time it must have sufficient conceptual integrity so that therapists and program developers can understand how general principles relate and can be uniquely tailored to each individual context. FFT postulates that all therapeutic contexts involve certain general features. At the same time FFT emphasizes the individualization of treatment goals and techniques for each case and the unique context in which it exists. This individualization requires a wide range of clinical maneuvers that can be applied differentially to individual contexts, a wider range of maneuvers than what is generally described in other treatment programs.

Moreover, programs must be able to be adapted to the unique circumstances of each family. For example, many families of delinquents are economically deprived, but some are in fact wealthy. Many parents of delinquents have neglected their children, but others have been overprotective. And many delinquents appear to have learning problems, but others are clearly quick learners. FFT has the relatively broad multivariate and multilevel focus necessary for effectively working with the diverse delinquent population.

FFT also emphasizes that family therapy does not occur in a vacuum, nor can it by itself modify all the (at times seemingly myriad) factors that influence delinquent behavior. If family approaches fail to look outside the family, they fail to recognize that the "treatment unit" they are dealing with is part of a larger and very influential context. So while FFT treats the family as an interdependent unit, at the same time it formally considers extrafamilial factors in both assessment and treatment planning. For example, a learning-disabled adolescent's verbal aggression in school may in part result from the adolescent's frustration with an inappropriate classroom placement. The poor school placement may compound the conflict in the family when the adolescent's parents pressure him or her for better grades. Integrating a focus on schoolwork with family therapy may preclude school problems from "undoing" progress made in the therapy session. Similarly, collaborating with the adolescent's juvenile court probation officer may allow the therapist and the probation officer to develop a court treatment plan that is consistent with family therapy.

Finally, along with the family focus and the extrafamily focus, FFT integrates an individual focus. The values, needs, and behaviors of each individual family member are assessed in addition to more global family patterns. Further, as a therapeutic goal the needs of all family members must be respected and incorporated into family change. So-called family cure must not be accomplished at the expense of any single member.

In conceptually integrating individuals, intrafamily relationships, and extrafamily factors, FFT considers the bidirectional effects each of these levels has on one another (Alexander, Mas, and Waldron, in press). This consideration creates complexity for the therapist but at the same time provides the therapist with a wide range of possible avenues to change.

Phases of Intervention: A Schematic for Change

FFT and a more recently developed framework (AIM—Analysis of Intervention Model), which describes therapy process at a general level, have identified five phases in the process of family therapy. Each of these phases must be addressed if the intervention process is to work effectively (Alexander, Barton, Waldron, and Mas 1983). Within each phase goals are described that often require unique therapist skills and techniques. The five phases of intervention articulated by the FFT and AIM Models are introduction/impression, assessment/understanding, induction/therapy, behavior change education, and generalization/termination. These phases are conceptually separate, but in practice therapists may switch between one phase and another on a frequent basis, to the point that some phases may appear to be occurring simultaneously. However, the tasks of some phases must be completed before the therapist can proceed to tasks of later stages. For example, a considerable amount of assessment must be accomplished to identify the targets of change before long-term change techniques can be initiated safely (Barton and Alexander, 1981).

The Introduction/Impression Phase

This phase concerns the clients' expectations that are created prior to therapeutic interaction, up to and including the clients' initial responses to the superficial stimulus qualities of the therapist as well as the service delivery system as a whole. For example, Mas and colleagues (1985) and Warburton and colleagues (1980) have demonstrated that therapist gender alone is a context for markedly different patterns of communication behavior among participants beginning early in the first session of family therapy. With younger female therapists (versus male therapists), fathers seem to be more defensive and less accepting of the therapist as "credible." Delinquents of both sexes also talk significantly less when the therapist is female versus male. These different patterns appear to demand different therapeutic strategies for male-versus-female family therapy trainees. For example, younger female therapists may need to move more quickly to the induction phase, which addresses resistance more directly. The application of therapeutic strategies is likely to be less effective if female therapy models ignore the differential impact of superficial therapist characteristics (e.g., attire) during the early moments of intervention (Alexander et al. 1983). Of course, therapist gender is but one of many variables that may influence client expectations.

The therapists' major goal in the introduction/impression phase of intervention is to create positive expectations for change in the family, taking into account the family's reactions to the therapist, agency, and referral process. Although the families' positive expectations must be maintained throughout the therapy process, this acquainting phase can be seen as relatively transitory because it ends at the point when therapists begin to engage in the processes of assessment, therapy, and education. Nevertheless, since this phase sets the stage for subsequent activities, it can either facilitate or inhibit the subsequent intervention process.

For family members' expectations to be productive, the therapist must present an image of one who can help to move the family from its fixed, dysfunctional patterns of behavior to more positive patterns. More simply, family members must perceive the therapist as someone who can help them solve their problems and reduce their pain. To do so, the family therapist must appear credible as a helper to the family. Even the best therapist encounters resistance in moving a family toward its desired goals during subsequent phases of treatment if at the outset the family finds the therapist unconvincing as a change agent. For example, a 16-year-old minority gang member from a lower-class background may wonder how a middle-aged, well-to-do white therapist in a three-piece suit could empathize with or understand him. Similarly, the father of a delinquent youth might have trouble accepting an unmarried young female therapist in jeans as a credible change agent because "she couldn't possibly know what it's like to be the parent of an adolescent."

The Assessment Phase

Assessment occurs throughout the intervention process but receives greatest emphasis during and between the first few sessions. During these sessions one of the therapist's goals is to identify the affective, behavioral, and cognitive expectations of each family member. In addition, the therapist must understand what family processes must be changed and what family variables, including reactions to the therapist, will enhance and/or impede beneficial change. This helps the therapist to understand actual and potential sources of resistance and to plan the unique set of changes that must be accomplished in each family. The therapist's own reactions, the clients' behaviors, and formal assessment devices such as questionnaires can be sources of information that yield both subjective and objective information about the behavior, affect, and cognitions of clients.

From this information the therapist can devise a unique assessment picture for each family that takes into account the characteristics and needs of each individual as well as the fit between these individual characteristics at the relationship level. For example, the family therapist may observe a situation in which the daughter of a single-parent father is constantly getting into trouble with the law. This behavior pulls the father into contact with his daughter and away from his girlfriend. The FFT therapist would involve all three persons, finding ways for the daughter to maintain a relationship with the father that do not involve pathological behaviors while helping the father develop skills so that he can, if he chooses, keep his relationship with his girlfriend intact.

The therapist skills necessary during this phase to elicit and interpret relevant information and identify the targets for change are intelligence, perceptiveness, and the use of a clear conceptual model. This model can help the therapist distinguish between those aspects of delinquent families that must be changed (e.g., coercive family processes—see Patterson and Reid 1970) and those aspects that can be allowed to remain unchanged without interfering with long-term beneficial outcomes. For example, FFT considers it unnecessary to change either the presence or absence of certain basic values (e.g., political and religious) and basic functions of interpersonal behavior (e.g., interpersonal distance-closeness needs). In fact, FFT argues that techniques that attempt to change interpersonal functions elicit considerable resistance and are inappropriate for use in a short-term intervention program (Barton and Alexander 1981).

Assessing Functions

The FFT concept of a person's interpersonal function is unique to this model. People develop characteristic interpersonal ways to regulate their relationships, and the concept of function helps the therapist understand how each of the members of a particular family accomplishes this end. Stated simply, a function is the interpersonal interdependency one person attempts to create with another. Because people may have markedly different capacities, learned behaviors, and behavioral contexts, different people can have different ways to attain their desired interdependency. Regardless of how functions are achieved, relationships between any two individuals can be reduced to three basic interpersonal states: closeness (high interdependency), distance (low interdependency), or a mixture that is an in-between amount of each (midpointing).

Although the functional states of contact/closeness and distance/independence are often seen as opposite ends of a continuum, it is more accurate to consider each as a separate dimension. The magnitude of each dimension can vary from little to large amounts. For example, a teenager can create considerable distance (e.g., by running away to another state), can create considerable contact (e.g., by becoming depressed and overtly begging for nurturance), and can send strong messages of both (e.g., by alternating messages of anger with messages of dependency). When family therapists are observing a set of problematic interactions, the result of these interpersonal payoffs and interactions from a relational standpoint must be addressed: that is, what was their function in regulating relationships within this family? By asking this question, therapists can often achieve an insight into families' behaviors when the family members are unable to tell them.

For example, a mother's arguments with her teenage daughter may pull the father out of his usual isolated behavior and into a disciplining role along with the mother. In such a situation, one function of the argument is to force the father into involvement. However, if in a different situation the same argument forces the father out of the house, then in this case one function of the argument is to create distance for the father.

Therefore, to understand families, therapists must look beyond the apparent problem and refocus on all relationships and the interpersonal impact of repetitive, problematic, behavioral sequences. In this process therapists often must go beyond the motives people verbalize and focus on the interpersonal results—the function of the behavior. Therapists must understand both the context and functions of problematic behavior to understand why family members contribute to interactions that on the surface seem to create misery for all of them (Barton and Alexander 1981).

A problem that can arise for both therapists and family members is to think of these functions as good or bad. Our society typically stereotypes closeness or intimacy as desirable in relationships and distance as undesirable. However, "smothering" represents closeness but in the nonadaptive form of enmeshment. Furthermore, rather than being necessarily "bad," maintaining distance from other people may facilitate the development of independent thinking and a sense of autonomy and competence. Thus, both types of functions are legitimate. The ways people attain them may be problematic, however, and may need to be changed. For example, the adolescent who attains contact by constantly being "in trouble" should not be labeled "bad" because of the function of closeness that is created. The behavior used to create the contact is unacceptable, but not the function per se. Thus, in FFT the therapist modifies the family system so that some alternative behavior such as seeking advice in a friendly manner can serve to create contact/closeness.

Some members in family systems may behave in ways that produce neither closeness nor distance but contain elements of both functions. This "midpointing" function also can be expressed in either adaptive or maladaptive ways. For example, a drug-abusing adolescent may at times use his addiction as a way of escaping from his family and at other times use it as a way of bringing them closer ("You need to help me pay this fine"). There also can be nonpathological expressions of midpointing, such as the teenager who remains active in her family's affairs but also has a part-time job after school and a boyfriend with whom she spends time. Both of these contexts create a balance of contact and distance, albeit in very different ways.

An important factor to be considered is that functions are unique to each relationship. A teenage girl simultaneously may create the functions of distancing from her father, midpointing with her mother, and closeness with her boyfriend. In addition, while certain behaviors more commonly produce certain functions (e.g., running away produces distance), a particular behavior must never be assumed to create a specific function. For example, an adolescent's running away, which may create distance for the adolescent in some families, characteristically may produce an end result of contact/closeness in other families. Thus, an entire behavioral sequence must be examined and the final result determined so that an accurate functional assessment can be inferred for each family member.

As a result, for each family a unique assessment picture must be drawn that takes into account the characteristics and needs of each individual. Then the picture must identify the configurations, that is, "fit" between these individual characteristics at the relationship level. For example, a total blended family picture may involve a mother's functions of closeness with her new husband while she is simultaneously midpointing with her daughter and young son. The daughter in turn may attempt to create closeness with her boyfriend, midpointing with her brother and stepfather, and distance from her mother. The stepfather may be developing closeness with his new wife and distancing with the children, and the son may attempt to achieve closeness with his parents and distance from his sister. All these functions must be ascertained and taken into consideration when long-term change is initiated.

The Induction/Therapy Phase

This phase specifically targets the motivational and attributional realities of disturbed families. Family members typically enter therapy with strong ideas about what the problems are and who is "to blame." In delinquent families these blaming attributions often center around the traits or dispositions of the referred adolescent. This adolescent is frequently seen as "the problem": "If only he [she] was not so 'lazy' [or 'irresponsible'], everything would be fine." The recipient of the negative attributions in turn tends to meet the expectations of the family by behaving defensively and being uncooperative (Alexander and Parsons 1982). Upon referral for delinquent behavior, then, other family members tend to view therapy as a way to "fix" the member who is seen as causing the problem. Often, however, therapy is not expected to work, as the family has given up on finding a solution.

Explaining problems in terms of personality is quite common. Attribution theorists see people as having a need to explain and predict the events around them, particularly those involving other people (Heider 1958). When problems begin to arise, a cause is searched for, usually in terms of a trait attributed to one or more family members (Jones and Davis 1965). Once this label has been applied, it serves to explain and predict future behavior, which in turn reinforces the label. The family develops patterns of interaction that maintain the dysfunctional behaviors (Brem and Smith 1986; Minuchin 1974; Snyder and Swann 1978; Watzlawick et al. 1967).

The primary goal of the induction/therapy phase is to change this situation by creating a context or climate in which families are willing and motivated to change. During this phase, therapists set the stage for long-term change by changing the meaning of family members' behavior with particular emphasis on decreasing negative attributions. If family members can be helped to consider their behavior as being motivated and maintained by variables other than individual malevolence (i.e., "they don't know how to show their affection," "expressing anger is really demonstrating concern"), they are much more motivated to change and more likely to see it as possible. This and focusing on relationships are the therapist's two major strategies for effecting cognitive changes in families.

Surprisingly, to do this the therapist first must "confuse" the family by disrupting the negative attributions family members have about each other and requiring them to search for new explanations of family behavior (Morris et al., in press). There are many maneuvers that allow the therapist to accomplish these goals, but these strategies cannot be applied in a cookbook fashion (Alexander and Newberry, in press). Instead, the therapist must respond contingently to different members so that each member within a family feels that the therapist hears, cares for, and empathizes with her or him. Further, because the therapist is interacting with a specific family and, indeed, with a number of specific individuals, the therapist's behavior must fit the value system, learning history, and the intellectual abilities of each family member. Techniques must be plausible and appropriate for each individual as well as the family members taken together. Thus, while the therapist needs interpersonal skill and sensitivity in any phase of intervention, these characteristics are essential for success in the induction/therapy phase.

A number of cognitive techniques are used heavily in the induction phase (Alexander and Parsons 1982). *Relabeling* changes the meaning and value of a negative behavior by describing positive antonym properties of the behavior, and/or by suggesting positive motives for the behavior, and/or by portraying family members as victims rather than perpetrators (Barton and Alexander 1981). For example, a delinquent may be described as someone who is struggling to become independent and is confused about her identity (Morris et al., in press). A relabel gives family members new information about behaviors and is most effective if it ascribes benign or benevolent motives. *Nonblaming* lowers defensiveness and allows for the possibility of changing without being forced to admit fault for previous difficulties. If family members can see others in the family as victims, then the maladaptive patterns of hostility are diminished.

Another useful technique is *overtly discussing* what would happen if the symptom were removed. For example, to help family members consider other relationship issues, a therapist may ask what a marriage would be like if the adolescent was not a constant problem. The therapist may also attempt *changing the impact or context of the symptom* by exaggerating the symptom. If the parents of a young fire setter are instructed to monitor the child as he lights matches, the interactions around his fire setting are dramatically changed (Minuchin 1974). The symptom has lost its meaning, and the typical sequence of parental behaviors after fire setting is changed (Alexander and Parsons 1982). *Shifting the focus* from one problem or person to another is sometimes useful in demonstrating the relational impact of symptoms. The therapist can move to issues in the family by changing the emphasis from the identified patient.

Focusing on the relationship also "takes the heat off" the identified patient, which may allow him or her to be less defensive and willing to change with the rest of the family. In disturbed families, individuals don't usually see their behavior as contributing to their current difficulties in a contingent or interdependent fashion. Rather, they view their own behavior as a necessary reaction to the misbehavior of other members (Barton and Alexander 1981). Part of the therapist's job is to point out the interactions between family members so that they become aware of how they affect each other and how the relationships affects their behavior. For example, Sam is a straight-A student who gets lots of praise from his mom, a single parent. Sam's little brother, George, age 13, recently started stealing and using drugs. Their therapist can shift the focus from George's "problem" by helping the family to understand George's need for attention and feelings of inadequacy when compared to Sam.

The therapist can begin to make this shift by using yet other techniques, those of *asking relational questions and identifying sequences*. The therapist can guide the family away from discussions of the adolescent's misbehavior by asking about relationships and about the roles people play in the family. This can help families to see how their behaviors are contingent on one another. When families tend to become involved in rapid chains of interaction, identifying these sequences helps to slow the interaction. If Mom is complaining about Debbie's misbehavior, for example, the therapist may ask how Grandma, who lives with the family, fits in. What was she doing during the last argument? In contrast, asking questions about the "problem person" may encourage blaming.

Two other techniques the therapist can use are *making nonblaming process comments* on the apparent impact various behaviors and feelings have on other family members and *showing how feelings, behaviors, and thoughts interrelate*. These comments help family members to see themselves as having unhappy relationships in which everyone is suffering instead of having a bad person in the family. For example, in Debbie's family Grandma may dread coming home from work because both Mom and Debbie will want her immediate support. The therapist can point out how one person's behavior is interpreted by another and how that person then feels. This technique diminishes the need to prove that someone else is the cause of the problem. For example, Mom may be thinking that Debbie does not need her anymore when Debbie tries to assert her independence. Further, Grandma interprets both their behaviors as a demand for her to take sides.

Making interpretations goes beyond the obvious and makes inferences about long-term motivations and the impact of behaviors. The therapist uses knowledge about her family, inferences, and guesswork to make interpretations about behavior. These can be very powerful in changing people's understanding of their family's history. For example, Roger has been caught stealing several times. During court-referred therapy, the therapist learns that Roger's dad left home early in life after a family battle. His mom was 15 years old when she married Roger's dad. The therapist may suggest that neither parent had any experience in the normal exiting of a teenager from the home. Thus, Roger knows no other way to "grow up" and leave his family than to get in trouble.

Finally, *stopping and starting interactions* is also an option for the therapist. Stopping an interaction that is a customary pattern for the family helps them experience a change, albeit brief, in the usual outcome. Coupled with relabeling, the therapist may reduce the blaming that takes place between family members. As the family interacts in a less blaming fashion, they may in turn change their perspective on the behaviors being discussed. The therapist may also ask the family to try a new positive interaction, which again can foster positive attributions and an increased motivation for change. For example, Susan is an adolescent with cerebral palsy. She has been violating her curfew by coming home after dark, alone, in her wheelchair. By the time she enters the door, her mother is so distraught that a battle begins at once. The therapist may concentrate on Susan's need for independence and point out that the family can discuss safer ways to reach this goal. The therapist then can help Susan and her mother discuss a plan for Susan to go to a city museum alone during the daytime. They could negotiate on issues of safety and let Susan demonstrate her ability to cope more independently.

While engaging in these various techniques, the therapist must take care to avoid forming a coalition with one family member at the expense of another. For example, a parent often tries to enlist a therapist, particularly a therapist of the same sex, to be on his or her side. If not dealt with carefully, this process can alienate a teenager and/or the other parent in the family. The therapist can sometimes overtly comment on how he or she fits into the family system as a way of defusing these coalition attempts and reducing the defensivenss of the other family members.

The Behavior Change/Education Phase

The major goal of this phase is to produce long-term behavior change in the family. During the previously described induction/therapy phase, techniques are used to change the meaning of behavior, the attributions family members have about one another, and family members' motivations. Although such changes are important prerequisites to long-term change, by themselves those changes may not be maintained unless interaction patterns are changed in a carefully planned way. Behavior change education is designed to implement these latter changes and involves the application of behavior-change techniques such as communication training, contracting, modeling, and the manipulation of environmental events. Which of the activities or techniques are used and how they are applied in changing interaction patterns depends on the configuration of individual characteristics and relationship patterns previously identified in assessment.

A successful induction/therapy phase can create positive motivation and even attempts at change on the part of the family. To avoid false starts and perhaps disillusionment, therapists must take control early in the behavior-change phase. During this time the goal is not so much to develop "final" positive interactions but to initiate new and positive interactions so the family can experience that such interactions are possible (Alexander and Parsons 1982).

Interactions during this phase are highly structured and usually involve some degree of communication training and technical aids. Sessions are also held as closely together as possible, again to minimize the family's opportunity to relapse into maladaptive interacting between sessions. By maximizing the success experience of families, the therapist can decrease resistance and continue the positive momentum established through increased family motivation in the induction phase. If initial behavior-change attempts are unsuccessful during this phase, high-degree structure and a short time frame make it easier to target exactly what went wrong. When change attempts do go awry, the problem may be therapy technology or may be therapist skill (Warburton and Alexander 1985). That is, an inappropriate behavior-change strategy may have been presented or the therapist may not have been sufficiently clear, directive, and otherwise informative for family members to be able to carry out the behavior.

However, even technically correct and well-developed behavior-change strategies will fail, that is, meet resistance, if they are inconsistent with one or more of the family members' interpersonal functions. Therapists must match the correct intervention techniques in a way that protects each family member's functions. Resistance arises if the therapist begins to elicit changes from one family member without simultaneously making certain the changes allow others to maintain the functions they previously held. For example, consider a truant adolescent whose behavior provides a context for her father's contact/closeness function with her mother who otherwise is distant from him. That is, the daughter's acting out allows the father to call the mother and talk to her about the problem, whereas the mother stays very busy in her job when the "kids don't need me." While a contingency contract with the daughter may reduce the daughter's truancy, such an intervention alone, which decreases the delinquent behavior, may not allow for maintaining the father's interdependency (closeness function) with his wife. If this is the case, the father may resist or "undermine" change. Hence, the intervention must be tailored not only to address the target behavior but to do so while not interrupting other family members' functions (Barton and Alexander 1981).

Thus, during the education phase, noncompliance (or resistance, in "traditional" terms) may occur if the tasks of earlier phases such as assessment have not been completely and effectively accomplished. When resistance occurs, therapists must change their conceptual "set" and "recycle" back to the assessment/understanding and induction/therapy phases to identify and modify the family parameters that are producing the resistance, before again proceeding with the treatment/education phase (Warburton and Alexander 1985).

The Generalization/Termination Phase

The goals of the generalization/termination phase are to maintain the changes previously initiated while producing independence from the therapist. The therapist in this phase attempts to disengage from the family and provide temporal and setting generalizability. To accomplish this, the therapist must ensure that not only have the referral problems been terminated but also that family members have been able to develop adaptive interaction patterns and problem-solving styles. Additionally, these interaction processes and problem-solving styles must be spontaneous and operate independently of the therapist's constant monitoring and prompting.

If this spontaneity and independence are not evident, specific educational techniques that ensure generalization must be applied. Such techniques begin with the therapist taking a less active role in intrafamily process. As family members experience short-term changes, they are helped to consider alternative ways to continue positive change. However, rather than dictating highly structured interactions that are designed to last only a few days, the therapist asks family members if they can develop techniques that might work for them on their own and at the same time extends the interval between sessions.

During this time, therapists also consider and sometimes deal directly with relevant extrafamily influences such as school personnel, employees, and so on. In doing so, FFT specifically can help families interact more effectively with extrafamilial influences not only by enhancing adaptive intrafamilial processes but also by anticipating extrafamilial stresses and helping family members develop more effective interactive styles to deal with them. On occasion FFT therapists even deal directly with extrafamilial influences such as legal and educational systems on behalf of the family, particularly during the later stages of therapy when a family is about to complete therapy (Alexander et al. 1983). During sessions family members are helped by exploring, and often role playing, solutions to future difficulties with other family members and extrafamily influences. For example, the therapist may role play the principal while the delinquent practices positive assertive behaviors in order to be allowed back into school. Parents in turn are helped to learn how to facilitate such behaviors.

Summary

At this point it is important to restate that the skills and techniques presented here cannot be discussed in strict behavioral terms independent of the family members' reactions. Each phase of family therapy represents a context for therapist-family interaction, and the meaning and impact of the therapist's behavior in each phase is a function of all participants. That is, therapist goals and behaviors cannot be defined in terms of their intent and form alone because their meaning and impact depends on family members. For example, a female therapist's behavior that might be perceived as "warm" when directed at a teenage daughter may be perceived quite differently (e.g., seductive) if the very same behavior is directed at the father. And to add further complexity, that behavior that the daughter perceives as warm may be seen by Mom as "coddling" or "siding with" the daughter.

This contextual and interactive nature of family therapy requires that therapists (and family therapy researchers) must consider two different kinds of "reality." One reality is that perceived by the therapist based on his or her theory, experience, intuition, and various sources of information. The other reality (actually, set of realities) represents how each family member perceives events. The therapist's and family members' realities exist in a parallel fashion, and while they may overlap, these realities are not necessarily integrated at a given point. In the induction phase, the therapist must focus on reality as the family experiences it and may choose to withhold even accurate interpretations if these interpretations will be experienced as blaming by family members (Haley 1963).

In the assessment phase the therapist's focus is on reality as the therapist experiences it and is based on the therapist's conceptual model. Then in behavior change/education both realities must be considered: Change techniques must produce the changes identified by the therapist, but at the same time the changes must make sense to the family. Thus, during behavior change/education a true partnership emerges where all participants work toward an overtly and consensually defined goal. This partnership continues throughout the rest of treatment as family members, using their own energy and motivation, become increasingly skilled at solving their own problems. Therapists and family members alike enjoy the fact that, in a sense, therapists become increasingly "useless" to the point of successful termination.

Notes

Alexander, J.F., C. Barton, R.S. Shiavo, and V.B. Parsons. 1976. Behavioral intervention with families of delinquents: Therapist characteristics and outcome. *Journal of Consulting and Clinical Psychology* 44(4):656–64.

Alexander, J.F., C. Barton, H. Waldron, and C.H. Mas. 1983. Beyond the technology of family therapy: The anatomy of intervention model. In K.D. Craig and R.J. McMahon (eds.), *Advances in Clinical Behavior Therapy* (New York: Brunner/Mazel):48–73.

Alexander, J.F., C.H. Mas, and H. Waldron. In press. Behavioral and systems family therapies—or—Auld Lang Syne: Shall old perspectives be forgot? In R.D. Peters and R.S. McMahon (eds.), *Marriages and Families: Behavioral Systems Aproaches* (New York: Brunner/Mazel).

Alexander J.F., and A.M. Newberry. In press. Interviewing in functional Family Therapy. In E. Lipchik (ed.) *Interviewing in Family Therapy* (Rockville, M.D.: Aspen).

Alexander J.F., and B.V. Parsons. 1973. Short term behavioral intervention with delinquent families: Impact on family process and recidivism. *Journal of Abnormal Psychology* 81 (3):219–25.

Alexander, J.F., and B.V. Parsons. 1982. *Functional Family Therapy: Principles and Procedures.* (Monterey, CA: Brooks/Cole).

American Humane Association. 1985. Highlights of official child neglect and abuse reporting—1984 (Denver: American Humane Association).

Barton, C., and J.F. Alexander. August 1979. *Delinquent and normal family interactions in competitive and cooperative conditions.* Paper presented at the annual convention of the American Psychological Association, New York.

Barton, C., and J.F. Alexander. 1981. Functional family therapy. In A.S. Gurman and D.P. Kniskern (eds.), *Handbook of Family Therapy* (New York: Brunner/Mazel).

Barton, C., J.F. Alexander, H. Waldron, C.W. Turner, and J. Warburton. 1985. Generalizing treatment effects of functional family therapy: Three replications. *American Journal of Family Therapy* 13 (3)13–26.

Brem, S.S., and T.W. Smith. 1986. Social psychological approaches to psychotherapy and behavior change. In S.L. Garfield and A.E. Bergin (eds.), *Handbook of Psychotherapy and Behavior Change*, 3rd ed. (New York: Wiley):69–115.

Garrett, C.J. 1985. Effects of residential treatment of adjudicated delinquents: A meta-analysis. *Journal of Research in Crime and Delinquency* 22 (4):287–308.

Gendreau, P., and R.R. Ross. 1980. Effective correctional treatment: Bibliography for cynics. In R.R. Ross and P. Gendreau (eds.), *Effective Correctional Treatment*. (Toronto: Butterworths).

Gordon, D.A., K.E. Gustafson, and J. Arbuthnot. March 1985. Cost effectiveness analysis of a family therapy program with juvenile delinquents. Paper presented at the Banff International Conference on Behavior Modification, Banff, Alberta, Canada.

Haley, J. 1963. *Strategies of Psychotherapy*. (New York: Grune & Stratton).

Heider, F. 1958. *The Psychology of Interpersonal Relations*. (New York: Wiley).

Jones, E.E., and K.E. Davis. 1965. From acts to dispositions: The attribution process in person perception. In L. Berkowitz (ed.), *Advances in Experimental Social Psychology* 2 (New York: Academic Press):219–66.

Klein, N.C., J.F. Alexander, and B.V. Parsons. 1976. Impact of family systems intervention on recidivism and sibling delinquency: A model of primary prevention and program evaluation. *Journal of Consulting and Clinical Psychology* 45(3)469–74.

Mas, C.H. 1986. *Attribution Styles and Communication Patterns in Families of Juvenile Delinquents*. Doctoral Dissertation, University of Utah at Salt Lake City.

Mas, C.H., J.F. Alexander, and C. Barton. 1985. Modes of expression in family therapy: A process study of roles and gender. *Journal of Marital and Family Therapy* 11(4):411–5.

Minuchin, S. 1974. *Families and Family Therapy*. (Cambridge, Mass.: Harvard University Press).

Morris, S.B., J.F. Alexander, and H. Wardron. In press. Functional family therapy: Issues in clinical practice. In I.R.H. Falloon (ed.), *Handbook of Behavioral Family Therapy* (New York: Guilford).

Parsons, B.V., and J.F. Alexander. 1973. Short term family intervention: A therapy outcome study. *Journal of Consulting and Clinical Psychology* 41 (2):195–201.

Patterson, G.R., and J.B. Reid. 1970. Reciprocity and coercion: Two facets of social systems. In C. Neuringer and G.L. Michael, (eds.), *Behavior Modification in Clinical Psychology*. (New York: Appleton–Century–Crofts).

Snyder, M., and W.B. Swann, Jr. 1978. Hypothesis testing processes in social interaction. *Journal of Personality and Social Psychology* 36:1201–12.

Todd, T.C., and M.D. Stanton. 1983. Research on marital and family therapy: Answers, issues, and recommendations for the future. In B.B. Wolman and G. Stricker (eds.), *Handbook of Family and Marital Therapy*. (New York: Plenum Press).

Waldron, H. 1987. *Modifying Blaming Attributions in Families with a Delinquent Member*. Doctoral dissertation, University of Utah at Salt Lake City.

Warburton, J.R., and J.F. Alexander. 1985. The family therapist: What does one do? In L. L'Abate (ed.), *The Handbook of Family Psychology and Therapy* (Homewood, Ill.: Dorsey).

Warburton, J.R., J.F. Alexander, and C. Barton. August 1980. *Sex of client and sex of therapist: Variables in family process study.* Paper presented at the annual convention of the American Psychological Association, Montreal, Canada.

Watzlawick, P., J.H. Beavin, and D.D. Jackson. 1967. *Pragmatics of Human Communication* (New York: Norton).

11

Family Therapy versus Parent Groups: Effects on Adolescent Drug Abusers

Alfred S. Friedman

The families of adolescent drug-abuse clients who were admitted to six outpatient drug-free (OPDF) treatment programs were randomly assigned to either a family therapy method or a parent group method. It was later found that in ninety-three percent of the family therapy families, one or both parents participated (N = 85); but that in only sixty-seven percent of the families assigned to a parent group did one or both parents participate (N = 50). This is considered to be an important practical advantage for family therapy.

At follow-up evaluation fifteen months later (after a six-months' course of treatment and a nine months' follow-up period) the clients and their mothers in both groups reported significant improvement on numerous outcome criteria, including reduction in substance use. There was no significant difference between the two groups in degree of improvement.

Family therapy versus Parent Groups: Effects on Adolescent Drug Abusers

Because adolescence is the phase of the life cycle during which the use of illicit drugs is usually initiated, and because adolescents usually are intensely involved in their relationships with their parents, it is natural to think of involving the family in the treatment of the adolescent drug abuser. The plan of the study reported here was to compare the outcomes, for adolescent drug abusers, of a particular family therapy method, functional family therapy, and a parent group method. Apparently no study has been reported on adolescent drug abuse in which random assignment was used to compare a family therapy method with some other treatment method. There has, however, been at least one report (Garrigan and Bambrick 1977) of a relatively small study (*N* = 28) that, without random assignment, compared the outcome of a family therapy method with the effects of a "parent group discussion and seminar method." In this study, conducted in a school for middle-class emotionally disturbed boys, cases assigned to a brief course of Zuk's "go-between" method of family therapy showed more improvement than cases assigned to the parent group method.

The Two Treatment Methods

The Family Therapy Method

There were two reasons for adopting the "functional" method as the method of family therapy to be employed in this demonstration project: (1) the authors of the method had shown its effectiveness in a research-controlled evaluation study, with a client population similar to the one in this proposed study (adolescent delinquents instead of adolescent drug abusers); and (2) the authors were close to completion of a systematic manual for training therapists in their family therapy model.

Developed by James F. Alexander and C. Barton (1976), the functional family therapy method was originally derived from efforts to integrate aspects of two models of human behavior: systems theory and transactional behaviorism. It assumes that behavior occurs in circular and reciprocal ways, and that the relationship context, rather than the individual focus, creates the major meaning of the behavior. It uses some of the same behavioral techniques used by the strategic method (such as tasks and directions, and problem solving), but not "paradoxical intervention." Other techniques used in the functional family therapy method are: (1) the positive relabeling and reattribution of family function processes and transactional patterns; (2) improving family communication by working to make it clearer, consistent and open, and less defensive; and (3) creating a safe atmosphere for self-disclosure, fostering self-esteem, instilling hope, encouraging responsibility, fostering trust, and providing feedback so that one can learn to see oneself as others see one. This method also requires the use by the therapist of certain positive relationship-building skills, such as integrating affect and behavior, nonblaming, nonconfronting, demonstrating interpersonal warmth and acceptance, alleviating tension with humor, and use of self and self-disclosure.

Six part-time family therapists conducted the functional family therapy in six different "drug-free" outpatient drug treatment programs. They received their instruction in the functional approach in a two-day workshop and in a continuing bi-weekly seminar on the method with case reviews and critiques. These six therapists had four to seventeen years of experience in conducting family therapy. The degree to which the therapists adhered to the standardized treatment model as described in the training manual was measured as follows. Tapes of twenty family therapy sessions (of twelve different families) were randomly selected, and a monitoring procedure was used in which twenty-minute segments of each of the sessions were scored by two independent raters for degree of adherence to the manual. In all, 346 therapist interventions were rated; and only 10 of these, or 3 percent, were considered to be inconsistent with the functional method as described in the manual. Most of these questionable interventions consisted of comments by the therapist regarding the negative behavior of a family member—for example, when the therapist said to a parent, "What you are saying is pushing your son away from you."

The Parent Group Method

This program of twenty-four weekly sessions was based on a "package" developed by this author which combined ideas, elements, and procedures borrowed from: (1) the Parent Effectiveness Training (PET) method (Gordon 1977); (2) the Parent Communication Project of Canada's Addiction Research Foundation (Shain, Suurvali, and Kilty 1980); and (3) the Parent Assertiveness Training program (Silberman and Wheelan 1980). PET derives philosophically from the Rogerian principles of unconditional positive regard and active listening and has as a basic premise the idea that "everybody wins" (rather than one family member winning at the expense of another). Power is negotiated and shared by both the parent and the child, unlike the authoritarian model, in which the parent has all the power, or the permissiveness model, in which either the child gets too much power or most of the power is dissipated. Parents learn and practice "active listening" and nonblaming skills, constructive confrontation, "I" messages, and the "no-lose" method of resolving conflicts.

A report of the results of a series of the parent communication course stated that (1) "the courses appeared effective in producing at least short-term positive changes in both the skill levels of the parents and in how their children perceived the quality of family life," and (2) that "the exercise of these skills was shown to be associated with abstinence from the use of alcohol among the younger children in the sample" (Shain, Riddell, and Kilty 1977). This plan, which detailed the material to be presented and the procedures to be conducted for each of the twenty-four parent group sessions, and included two films on substance use problems, was developed in consultation with Heather Lee Kilty of the Addictions Research Foundation and Melvin L. Silverman of Temple University, who conducted training workshops with the project's three parent group leaders.

The Two Treatment Groups

It was necessary that individual drug counseling be made available for those adolescent clients whose parents were randomly assigned to parent groups (that is, the clients were not included in family therapy). There was no significant difference between the two groups of clients in the number of individual sessions they attended. In 93 percent of the families assigned to family therapy, either the mother alone or both parents started in treatment; but in only 67 percent of those assigned to a parent group did the mother alone or both parents start in treatment. (The reasons for this significant difference, and the implications of it, will be discussed.)

Follow-up Evaluation

This evaluation was planned to be conducted at fifteen months after the initiation of treatment. For those families who completed the twenty-four week course of family therapy or parent group intervention, this evaluation occurred approximately nine months after the end of treatment. For the drop-out families, or early terminators, there was a longer period between termination of treatment and the follow-up evaluation.

Of the 169 families who started in treatment, 135, or 80 percent, were retrieved for follow-up evaluation fifteen months later. There were 85 family therapy clients and 50 parent group clients in the follow-up evaluation.

Subjects

The client study sample was predominantly male, white, and Catholic (see table 11–1). The age range was 14–21, with a mean age of 17.9 years (S.D. = 1.84). The mean number of years of education completed (9.3 years; S.D. = 1.44) is significantly below the norm for a sample that has a mean age of 17.9 years. The parent group clients were significantly younger and had significantly less education than the family therapy clients, in spite of the random assignment procedure. This is partially explained by a selective bias that occurred, after the random assignment, in the parent group subsample: a disproportionate number of parents of the relatively older clients in this subsample did not show for any of the parent sessions. (The mean age of the twenty-five clients whose parents did not show was 18.0 years, compared to a mean age of 17.2 years for the fifty clients whose parents did participate: p = .06). It could be that the parents were less likely to feel responsible to participate in the groups if the client was over eighteen years of age; that is, was able to vote, had graduated from high school, and should; therefore, have been less dependent on parents.

Only fifty-four percent of the clients were living with both parents. Slightly less than half (forty-four percent) of the clients admitted to having sold drugs, and forty percent reported having been arrested at least once for some sort of offense. As can be seen in table 11–2, of the prevalence rates for use of substances during the three-month period before treatment, the

Table 11–1
Comparison of Two Treatment Groups at Admission on Demographic, Family Background, and Other Key Behavior and Attitude Variables Potentially Relevant to Treatment Outcome

Intake Variable	Percentages		Significant (Trend) Differences Between Groups Parent Group vs. Family Therapy "P" Value
	Parent Group (N = 50) %	Family Therapy (N = 85) %	
Sex:			
Male	60	61	—c
Female	40	39	
Race:			
White	86	92	—
Nonwhite	14	8	
Religion:			
Catholic	62	68	—
Non-Catholic	38	32	
Parents separated	6	9	—
Parents divorced	40	33	—
Parents living together	52	49	—
Client lives at parents' home	90	92	—
Client's Perception:			
Home is not a pleasant place to live	30	34	—
Parents argue or fight a lot	14	14	—
Parents don't like each other	4	12	.09b
Ever Arrested	26	40	.09b

Intake Variable	Means ($\overline{X}$) and Standard Deviations				Significant (Trend) Differences Between Groups Parent Group vs. Family Therapy "P" Value
	Parent Group (N = 50)		Family Therapy (N = 85)		
	$\overline{X}$	S.D.	$\overline{X}$	S.D.	
Age	17.2	1.5	18.2	2.0	.01a
Grade	8.8	1.3	9.6	1.5	.01a
Mother's education	12.5	2.0	12.5	2.0	—
Father's education	12.9	2.9	12.8	2.7	—
Occupation of head of household	6.1	1.8	6.0	2.0	—
Parents have problems with alcohol/drugs	0.3	0.6	0.5	0.8	.10b
Number of Arrests for:					
Drug use	.04	0.2	0.3	1.2	.06b
Drug sales	.04	0.2	.02	0.2	—
Amount of time spent in jail	.14	0.5	.26	0.7	—
Drug Severity Index	25.3	24.2	26.5	26.1	—
How strong an effort client will make to stop drug use	2.0	1.2	2.1	1.1	—
Client wants parents to participate in treatment sessions	1.7	0.8	2.0	0.9	.05a
Client wants parents to participate in parent groups	2.5	0.7	2.5	0.7	—

aThe difference between the two groups is significant at the .05 level of confidence or better (P ≤ .05).
bThere is a trend toward a significant difference (P ≤ .10).
cThere is no significant difference or trend.

Table 11–2
Substance Use of Client Subject Sample
(N = 169) (prevalence rates, frequencies, and age of first use)

Drug	Used Past Year Percentage	Used Past Three Months Percentage	No. of Times Used Past Month		Age of First Use	
			X	(S.D.)	X	(S.D.)
Alcohol	95	88	8.6	(14.1)	12.7	(1.9)
Marijuana	94	87	25.7	(31.6)	12.6	(2.3)
Inhalants	8	7	0.8	(4.6)	14.1	(2.2)
Amphetamines	69	52	7.1	(20.7)	14.6	(1.5)
Barbiturates	20	15	1.1	(5.9)	14.3	(1.7)
Tranquilizers	36	23	1.0	(4.5)	14.8	(1.3)
Sedatives	24	14	0.9	(4.7)	14.7	(1.5)
PCP	30	15	0.7	(3.4)	15.0	(1.4)
Hallucinogens	34	22	0.8	(4.0)	14.5	(1.4)
Cocaine	41	28	1.4	(7.7)	15.4	(1.5)
Heroin	5	5	0.7	(4.0)	15.0	(1.1)
Other opiates	18	11	0.4	(2.3)	14.9	(1.9)
Other drugs	3	2	0.2	(2.3)	13.5	(2.4)
Nonprescription	10	6	0.1	(1.0)	14.9	(1.5)

	X	(S.D.)
Of Five Friends, How many are using:		
.... Alcohol	3.9	(1.7)
.... Marijuana	3.7	(1.6)
.... Other drugs	2.4	(2.1)

eight substances that had the highest prevalence rates were: alcohol, eighty-eight percent; marijuana, eighty-seven percent; amphetamines, fifty-two percent; cocaine, twenty-eight percent; tranquilizers, percent; hallucinogens, twenty-two percent; PCP, fifteen percent; and barbiturates, fifteen percent. The mean frequency of use of marijuana during the month before treatment was approximately three times as great as the mean frequency of use of alcohol; 25.7 times versus 8.6 times. (According to the client-subjects' reports, an average of 3.7 of the five friends whom each subject knew best were using marijuana.) It is clear that the degree of severity of substance abuse within this study sample was generally high, and that at least the majority of the sample could be considered to have a major drug abuse problem.

Assessment Procedures (Instruments)

The Client Interview Form

The Client Interview Form is a 193-item comprehensive, structured interview schedule that collects extensive information on the client's background, personal history, behavior, relationships, and attitudes. In addition the following instruments were administered: (1) the Rosenberg Self-Esteem Scale (11 items); (2) the Brief Symptom Inventory (BSI) (DeRogatis, Rickels, and Rock 1976) (53 items); (3) the Family Role Task Scale (Friedman and Friedman 1973) (25 items); and (5) the Parent-Adolescent Communication Form (Olson et al. 1982) (20 items).

The Parent Assessment Battery

The Parent Interview Form, a structured interview administered to the mother of the client, includes forty-eight items that parallel those on the client Interview Form described above. This form also elicits detailed information on family history membership and structure, demographics, socioeconomic status, living arrangements, how and why the client entered treatment, the mother's knowledge of the client's drug use and problems related to drug use, and the client's other emotional and behavioral problems.

The parent's forms for ratings the client include: (1) the Family Role Task Behavior Scale (twenty-five items); (2) the Parent-Child Relationship Problems (thirty-five items); and (3) the Emotional/Psychological Problems Inventory (thirty-five items). These three forms included many of the same items and variables that were included on the parallel client self-report forms, but the items were worded to refer to the other person (that is, the client) rather than to the self.

Drug Severity Index (DSI)

In addition to the frequency of use of each type of substance, a summary score (Drug Severity Index), based on the sum of the multiples of the frequencies of use, multiplied by the "risk levels" of each of the various substances, was used as a key criterion outcome variable. The risk levels, as suggested by the White House Paper on Drug Abuse (1975), were as follows: "Opiates, sedatives, amphetamines, tranquilizers, hallucinogens/PCP, cocaine and inhalants were assigned a score of 3; and marijuana, hashish, alcohol, and over-the-counter drugs were scored a 1."

Results

Satisfaction with the Type of Family Treatment

At follow-up, 69 percent of the family therapy clients, compared with 63 percent of the parent group clients, reported that they had been either "somewhat satisfied" or "very satisfied" with the type of family treatment (either parent group or family therapy) that their families had received. Also, 56 percent of the family therapy clients, compared with 52 percent of the parent group clients, reported at follow-up that the particular type of family treatment had helped them either "a fair amount" or "a lot." Neither of the differences between the reports of the two groups of clients were statistically significant.

At follow-up, 78 percent of the family therapy mothers and 85 percent of the parent group mothers reported that they had been either "somewhat satisfied" or "very satisfied" with the family type of treatment. When the satisfaction ratings of the mothers from both groups combined are compared with the ratings of the clients, the mothers are shown to report significantly greater satisfaction with the type of family therapy received. Also, significantly more mothers (80 percent) reported satisfaction for themselves with the type of family treatment they received, compared with the percentage of mothers (50 percent) who reported that they believed that the clients were satisfied with the type of family treatment provided to the family (chi-square = 16.5).

Improvement at Follow-up

Twenty-five variables from the clients' data and forty variables from the mothers' data were selected as appropriate outcome criteria (measures of change or improvement). A significant degree of improvement, from pretreatment to follow-up, at the .05 level of confidence was found by paired t-test, for fifty-eight of the criteria for the family therapy group, and for fifty-six of the sixty-five criteria for the parent group. This very impressive improvement cannot, however, be ascribed solely to the effectiveness of these two family treatment methods, since clients in both groups participated in some individual counseling sessions. (In spite of this complication it is still feasible to compare the outcomes of the family therapy and parent group methods with each other, as is done below, because there was no significant difference between the two groups of clients on either the number of individual sessions or the number of peer group sessions in which they participated.) Some of the other criteria on which both groups showed significant improvement in client behavior were: (1) reduction in substance use by more than 50 percent of the mean value of the Drug Severity Index scores; and (2) improvement in the total scores derived from the following inventories: (*a*) the Parent-Adolescent Communication Inventory (the total mother score and the total father score); (*b*) the Family Role Task Behavior Scale (total positive behavior score and total negative behavior score); and (*c*) the Brief Symptom Inventory (BSI).

Selection of Outcome Criteria

Since some of the twenty-five variables were selected from the client data as outcome criteria were intercorrelated with each other to a fairly high degree, a factor analysis was performed, for data reduction purposes, using the intake (pretreatment) scores on these twenty-five variables. The "lead item" (that is, the item or variable with the highest loading) on each of four of the factors was selected to be used as an outcome criterion (or change score): (1) "How well you get along with mother"; (2) "Client Negative Self-Image Score"; (3) "Number of client's positive role behavior in the family"; and (4) "Degree of conflict within the family." However, for one of the remaining factors, the Drug Severity Index was selected rather than the "Number of Hours High or Stoned," because the former is a more comprehensive, summary measure that takes into account the frequency of use and the risk level of all illicit substances, and since the reduction of drug use/abuse is obviously the main purpose of drug treatment. Also, in the other remaining factor, the Parent-Adolescent Communication (PAC) score on adolescent-father communication, based on a twenty-item questionnaire, was selected, in lieu of the single item, "How Difficult Is It to Talk to Father?" because the former is probably a more reliable measure.

A similar varimax rotation factor analysis yielded nine factors from the forty variables that had been selected from the mothers' data as outcome criteria. For eight of the factors the lead variable was selected as an outcome criterion; for the remaining factor the variable with the second-highest loading was selected because it was a total score derived from an eighteen-item checklist: "The number of the client's negative or problem behaviors." The other eight outcome criteria from the mothers' data were:

1. How often have family relationships been tense?

2. Client's delinquency (stealing, and so forth); client has problems with the law

3. How frequently has the client been using drugs during the past three months?

4. Number of mother's negative types of reactions to client checklist (nineteen items)

5. To what degree do you approve of his or her behavior/attitude during the past months?

6. How frequently has the client been using alcohol during the past three months?

7. Client has problems in school (academic)

8. Is client in conflict with parent(s)?

Data Analysis Procedure for Multiple Regression Analysis

The method of analysis used for determining whether either of the treatments showed a significantly greater degree of change or improvement on any of the outcome criteria was multiple regression analysis. For each of the regression equations to be constructed, classes of independent variables were entered as follows. First, entered in step number one as control variables (covariates) were those variables on which the two treatment groups to be compared differed significantly or showed a trend toward a significant difference (that is, $p < .10$) in status at admission. A list of thirty-nine variables had been selected which were measures of those characteristics of the clients and the families that seemed most likely to affect the response to treatment (for example, demographic characteristics, family structure and living arrangement variables, family problems, client's legal status, client's attitudes towards and motivation for treatment, and problems directly related to substance use—see table 11–1). Entered as step two were the characteristics of the clients or families at pretreatment which correlated to a significant degree with the amount of change in the dependent variable from pretreatment to follow-up (the "change score"). Entered as step three was the value (score) obtained by each subject in the two treatment groups at pretreatment on the outcome criterion variable. Entered as step four was the dichotomous variable designating the assignment of the subject to either of the two treatment groups being compared (that is, family therapy versus parent group) as the key independent predictor variable in the regression equation. The dependent variable in each equation was the value (score) obtained by the subject at follow-up evaluation on the particular outcome criterion variable being analyzed.

For the fifteen multiple regression analyses performed (six based on the factor scores from the client data, and nine on the factor scores from the mother data) none showed a significant difference between the two groups in outcome (change or improvement). There was one that showed a trend toward a significant difference ($p = .09$). This was on the mothers' variable, "Having academic problems in school" (grades, and so on), and the trend was in favor of greater reduction in such problems for the family therapy group (see table 11–3).

Discussion

The most likely explanations for the relatively large percentage of families that did not participate in the parent group treatment appear to us to be: (*a*) some parents, although they had already signed the consent form agreeing to be assigned to either family therapy or a parent group, did not feel ready

Table 11–3

Multiple Regression Equation Indicating a "Trend" for Mothers in Family Therapy Group to Be Less Likely to Report at Follow-up That Client Has Academic School Problems

Characteristic	"F" Value	Level of Significance	Amount of Variance in Outcome Accounted for "R² Change"
Step 1:			
Age	2.59	.113	.014
Sex	.05	.832	.000
Client's education	.20	.653	.006
Father's education	.36	.552	.015
Mother's education	.64	.428	.000
Head of household's occupation	3.01	.087	.024
Both natural parents married/living together	1.40	.242	.000
Mother and/or father remarried	1.03	.313	.000
Mother and father have drug/alcohol problems	.38	.541	.013
Client ever in treatment before	.10	.832	.000
Client ever been arrested	.22	.637	.003
Number of times arrested for drug use	.42	.521	.000
Involved in selling drugs (if never arrested for it)	.02	.904	.002
Client's feelings about involving parents in treatment	.27	.605	.003
Mother treats "me" (client) like a child	3.27	.075	.046
Step 2:			
Parents divorced	5.05	.028	.020
Number of times arrested for drug sales	2.56	.114	.029
Amount client feels his drug/alcohol use contributes to family problems	3.94	.051	.039
Step 3:			
Mother reports client has academic school problems	8.00	.006	.060
Step 4:			
Assignment to Treatment (Family therapy vs. parent group)	2.91	.093	.030

to expose or share their own family problems with other families. Several parents actually stated that they felt they were being "punished" by having to attend a group, while their adolescents, who had the drug problems and were to blame, were not required to attend any family sessions; (*b*) some families apparently preferred family therapy, or had had it recommended to them, and they may have hoped to be randomly assigned to family therapy; and (*c*) given the small number of adolescent clients admitted per month to some of the participating clinics, it sometimes required three to six weeks to get mothers from five different families who agreed to meet at the same time, on the same evening, to form a new parent group. It may be that after that amount of time, some of the mothers lost their motivation for participating in the treatment, after the critical moment or the precipitating event that led them to apply for help had passed and their desire for help had diminished.

It may also be a fair assumption that those parents who did attend and participate in the parent groups, after an initial delay of three or more weeks, were on the average more motivated to participate and to try to improve the family situation than were those who did not attend. If this were so, it might then follow that the parents in the final parent group subsample would have been more highly selected than the parents in the final family therapy subsample, and this could then partially explain the finding that the outcome for the parent group clients was as good as the outcome for the family therapy clients.

The families that participated in the parent group sessions were found on admission to have scored significantly higher on the intellectual-cultural orientation factor of the Moos Family Environment Scale than the families assigned to a parent group who did not participate. The definition provided for this factor is: "The extent to which the family is concerned about political, social, intellectual and cultural activities (Moos 1974)." This may provide a clue to understanding why some parents were more likely than others to participate in parent group discussions.

There are legitimate questions regarding the validity, objectivity, and usefulness of the clients' self-report of drug use at the time of admission to treatment. It might possibly have improved the validity of the measure if some objective test of drug use (such as a urine test) had been employed in addition to clients' self-report. This is a limitation of this study, but it is a limitation that this study has in common with the majority of research studies conducted on adolescent substance abusers (particularly in drug-free outpatient treatment settings, as distinct from methadone clinics and hospital settings). Self-reports have generally been accepted as fairly reliable indicators of drug use behavior (Radosevich et al. 1980; Whitehead and Smart 1972). This author's brief survey of research reports on adolescent substance use in one of the leading research journals in this field showed that all of such research studies published during a one-year period relied solely on self-report for their measures of substance use. There are those who may be more skeptical than is warranted regarding self-report. After all, these subjects have come to a drug treatment program and have all admitted that they use illicit drugs. Some of them may try to deny early in treatment that their drug use is a problem to them. It is of course possible that some of them at time of follow-up evaluation want to deny that they are still using illicit drugs or to minimize the degree of their use. A test-retest reliability check that was conducted recently by this author with a small sample (N = 18) in one of the clinics that participated in the study showed these following

following results: Pearson "r" = .71 for a summary score of drug use, and Pearson "r" = .86 for a summary score of alcohol use.

The findings of the study reported in this chapter can with some degree of confidence be applied to treatment in outpatient drug-free clinics or programs, since the data were collected from a number of such programs. It might be less appropriate to generalize these findings to other types of treatment settings, such as inpatient programs and nonhospital residential programs.

Conclusion

In several outpatient drug-free (OPDF) settings and programs, a parent group procedure has been shown to be as effective as the functional family therapy approach in reducing substance use and in achieving other types of improvement in the behavior and attitudes of adolescent drug abusers at follow-up evaluation, fifteen months after the start of treatment. Considerable improvement was reported at follow-up for both groups, according to both the clients' reports and the mothers' reports.

For the sixty-five outcome criteria measured, fifty-eight significant positive changes, from pretreatment to follow-up, were reported between the clients and the mothers of the family therapy group, compared with fifty-six significant positive changes from the parent group clients and mothers. The types of improvement reported by both groups included: (1) a reduction in clients' substance use and abuse by more than 50 percent in each of the two groups, according to the mean value of the clients' Drug Severity Index scores, and according to the mothers' estimates of the clients' frequency of substance use; (2) a decrease in client psychic symptomatology, on the Brief Symptom Inventory (BSI); (3) a decrease in client negative family role task behavior and an increase in positive behavior with the family; and (4) an improvement in client communication with mother and father, on the Parent-Adolescent Communication Inventory. This is very impressive improvement. The degree to which the family therapy and parent group methods of treatment contributed to this impressive improvement is, however, obscured by the fact that the clients also participated in some individual counseling sessions. It may be reasonable to assume that the improvements that occurred in the mother-client relationship were related in large measure to the two family types of treatment.

There was no significant difference found between the two groups in the degrees of improvement reported on the fifteen outcome criteria on which the two groups were compared. The mothers who participated in either of the two family types of treatment expressed significantly more satisfaction with this treatment than did the clients, their adolescent offspring.

Providing parent group sessions is obviously less costly in staff time (per case or per family) than providing family therapy sessions and is therefore more cost-effective. But a parent group takes longer to organize and start and is more difficult to organize than is family therapy. It is not likely, for most outpatient programs, that providing the parent group modality would achieve the participation of as high a proportion of the families as would providing the family therapy modality. This limitation of the parent group modality could, however, probably be overcome if a clinic were to require the participation of at least one of the parents in a parent group as a condition of accepting the adolescent client for treatment and did not offer family therapy as an alternative.

It might in fact not be an unreasonable requirement to expect parents of adolescents to participate in the treatment process, including those parents of adolescents who would like to rationalize that it is solely the treatment program's responsibility to eliminate the adolescent's drug use and his or her other problem behavior. Many OPDF programs apparently are not ready to adopt such a policy, either because they need to accept all cases referred to them in order to maintain their census, or they don't have the staff qualified to work with parent groups.

Notes

Alexander, J., and C. Barton. 1976. Behavioral systems therapy and delinquent families. In D.H. Olson, ed., *Treating Relationships*. Lake Mills, Iowa: Graphic.

DeRogatis, L.R., K. Rickels, and A. Rock. 1976. The SCL-90 and the MMPI: A step in the validation of a new self-report scale. *British Journal of Psychiatry* 128:280–89.

Friedman, C.J., and A.S. Friedman. 1973. Drugs and delinquency. In Michael R. Sonnereich, ed., *Drug Use in America: Problem in Perspective* (Washington, D.C.: Superintendent of Documents, U.S. Government Printing Office) 398–487.

Garrigan, J.J., and A.F. Bambrick. 1977. Family therapy for disturbed children: Some experimental results in special education. *Journal of Marriage and Family Counseling* 3:83–93.

Gordon, T. 1977. Parent effectiveness training: A preventive program and its delivery system. In G.W. Albee and J.M. Joffe, eds., *Primary Prevention of Psychopathology*, Hanover, N.H.: University Press of New England.

Moos, R.H. 1974. *Family Environment Scale—Form R*. Palo Alto, Calif.: Consulting Psychologists Press.

Olson, D.H., H.I. McCubbin, H. Barnes, A. Larsen, M. Maxen, M. Wilson. 1982. Family inventories. *Family Social Science*, (St. Paul, MN.: University of Minnesota).

Radosevich, M., L. Lanza-Kaduce, R. Akers, M. Krohn. 1980. The sociology of adolescent drug and drinking behavior: A review of the state of the field. *Developmental Behavior* 1:145–69.

Shain, M., W. Riddell, and H.L. Kilty. 1977. *Influence, Choice and Drugs—Towards a Systematic Approach to the Prevention of Substance Abuse.* Toronto: Addiction Research Foundation.

Shain, M., H. Suurvali, and H.L. Kilty. 1980. *The Parent Communication Project: A Longitudinal Study of the Effects of Parenting Skills on Children's Use of Alcohol.* Toronto: Addiction Research Foundation.

Silberman, L., and A. Wheelan. 1980. *How to Discipline without Feeling Guilty: Assertive Relationships with Children.* (Toronto and Vancouver: Clarke, Irwin and Company, Ltd).

Whitehead, P.C., and R.G. Smart. 1972. Validity and reliability of self-reported drug use. *Canadian Journal of Criminology* 14:1–8.

White House Paper on Drug Abuse. *A Report to the President from the Domestic Council Drug Abuse Task Force.* Washington, D.C.: U.S. Government Printing Office: 1975.

12

Is Father Participation Crucial for the Success of Family Therapy?

Alfred S. Friedman
Lynn A. Tomko

T his chapter presents a report on the relationship to treatment outcome or success of the degree of participation (that is, the number of sessions attended) by the father of the family in the family therapy process; and of retention in treatment (that is, the number of family sessions conducted). These relationships have been studied and are reported here for the eighty-five families who participated in the systematic comparison of family therapy with a parent group method, which has been reported in chapter 11 of this book.

It might be reasonable to expect that if the father participates in the family therapy that is provided by a drug treatment program there would be a greater chance that the adolescent client would reduce or discontinue the substance abuse. Family therapists generally assume that, at least for two-parent families, the involvement of both parents, rather than only the mother, in the family therapy sessions improves the chances of obtaining positive change in the family, and in such dysfunctional behavior as substance abuse. It has been observed frequently by family therapists that many adolescents tend to form cross-generational alliances with one parent which separate the parents from each other, and that the therapy process is handicapped if both parents are not available to work on and repair this split in the family.

Apparently, however, there has been very little evidence, if any, derived from systemic studies either to support or to dispute such an assumption. (Our computer literature search did not yield a single reference to a research study on this question.) The study reported is intended to be only a preliminary exploration of this question; it raises some more specific questions regarding the relationship of the father's participation to the outcome of family therapy, and these questions will be seen to require more detailed research study.

There is some evidence available to indicate that drug and alcohol use tends to be greater for adolescents in single-parent families, which usually are homes from which the father is absent (Friedman et al. 1980). There is also some clinical evidence that adolescent substance users are less likely to report and to discuss their substance use, and any problems related to substance use, with their fathers than they are to discuss such matters with their peers, or even with their mothers. These findings suggest the following possibilities, among others: (1) the father is an important figure for the transmission of values; (2) the presence of a father in the home serves as a stabilizing influence; and/or (3) the presence of a father is a deterrent to such behaviors as illicit substance use.

Retention in Treatment

Treatment tenure has been shown to be the most consistent predictor of successful outcome for residential therapeutic community programs (DeLeon and Jainchill 1986). Sells and Simpson (1979) reported for the adolescent subsample of the DARP study that time in treatment and completion of treatment were positive prognostic indicators of outcome. In a study of drug-free programs in Pennsylvania (Rush 1979), retention, or time spent in treatment, was found to be positively related to, and to be the best predictor of, improvement on "productivity" (combining education, training, and employment) for adolescents in therapeutic communities. However, for adolescent clients in outpatient drug-free programs, the time in treatment was, conversely, negatively related to the productivity outcome criterion. Rush noted, "Probably some of the juveniles who have the best potential to become more productive in education and employment do not need to stay in treatment very long to achieve these particular goals."

Using retention as the independent variable predicting to treatment outcome may be quite appropriate for residential programs because the treatment is provided to each client every day in such programs (DeLeon 1984). The measure of retention in the current study is simply the number of family sessions conducted with each family. Neither the retention measure nor the measure of the amount of treatment that is used in this study adequately controls for the degree of motivation and readiness of the client for treatment or for other variables that could conceivably relate significantly to outcome, including how the clients perceive themselves (DeLeon and Jainchill 1986).

Subjects

The client study sample (N = 85) was predominantly male, white and Catholic (see table 11–1). The age range was 14–21 years, with a mean age of 18.2 years (S.D. = 2.0). The mean number of years of education was 9.6 (S.D. = 1.5). Forty percent reported having been arrested at least once, and 51 percent admitted to having been involved in selling drugs. In addition to use of marijuana by the great majority of subjects during the three-month period preceding admission, the following percentages reported use of other drugs during that period: amphetamines, 55 percent; cocaine, 32 percent; hallucinogens, 25 percent; PCP, 17 percent; barbiturates, sedatives, or tranquilizers, 28 percent; heroin or other opiates, 14 percent. At least the majority of the sample could be considered to have a major drug problem.

The family therapy method that was conducted and the assessment procedures that were administered are both described in chapter 11 of this book. The follow-up evaluation occurred nine to twelve months after the termination of treatment for most subjects.

The Drug Severity Index (DSI), a global, or summary, score of substance use, was considered to be the primary criterion variable for measuring treatment outcome. In addition to the frequency of use of each type of substance, this summary score was based on the sum of the multiples of the frequencies of use mutliplied by the "risk level" for each of the various substances. The risk levels, as suggested by the White House Paper on Drug Abuse, were as follows: opiates, sedatives, amphetamines, tranquilizers, hallucinogens/PCP, cocaine, and inhalants were assigned a score of 3; and marijuana, hashish, alcohol, and over-the-counter drugs were scored a 1.

Data Analysis

Twenty-six additional variables were selected as outcome criteria to determine the changes in client status and behavior that occurred from pretreatment to follow-up. It is not implied here that all the statistically significant changes that will be reported are solely the effects of the family therapy. How much of the improvement to be reported in this study was due to the treatment per se and how much was due to other factors (maturation, changes in life situations, and so forth) is not clear, because the study did not have a no-treatment control group. The statement made by Harford (1978), based on the findings of his five-year follow-up study of drug clients, is relevant to this point: "It seems probable that most of the major causes for improvements are independent of any benefits derived from treatment . . . No-treatment comparison groups are indispensable for controlling maturation and history."

It is reasonable, however, to assume that some of the improvement was due to the effects of treatment because drug-using adolescents are in a life phase in which they are usually increasing rather than decreasing their drug use.

It is intended to report here the relationships between the degree of change that occurred on each outcome criterion and (1) the number of family sessions that the family attended, (2) the number of sessions that the father participated in, and (3) the ratio of the number of father participation sessions to the total number of family sessions, for each family.

Twenty-seven outcome criterion variables have been selected as more than sufficient for our new analyses, to determine the relationship between retention in treatment and outcome, and between degree of father participation and outcome.

The results from the data analysis were obtained by the following correlational procedure: (1) for each of the twenty-seven outcome criterion variables a "change score" was developed by subtracting the score obtained on this variable at follow-up from the score obtained at pretreatment assessment; (2) the change scores obtained for each outcome criterion variable were then correlated in turn with each of the three predictor variables: (*a*) the number of family therapy sessions conducted with the family, (*b*) the number of these sessions that were attended by the father, and (*c*) the percentage of the sessions conducted that were attended by the father (that is, the ratio of *b* above to *a* above).

Results and Discussion

As is shown in table 12–1, relatively few significant correlations (p < .05) were found for any of the three predictor variables. There were several additional associations that showed a trend toward significance (p < .10), and these are also indicated in table 12–1.

Retention

It is consistent with the finding reported by Rush (1979), cited earlier in this chapter, in regard to increased productivity of the outpatient adolescent clients, that the current study found for the intact families that there was a trend toward less decrease in substance use in relation to having participated in more family sessions. A possible explanation (if it is not only a rationalization) is that in those instances in which the adolescent client decreased the degree of substance use more, or more quickly, the family did not feel the need to continue participating in more family sessions. (It was determined that those clients whose families participated in more family sessions also tended to participate in more individual counseling and peer group sessions. Accordingly, the finding of less decrease in substance use associated with more family sessions did not appear to be related to a greater effectiveness of either of the other two modalities for reducing substance use.)

The association of less improvement in negative self-image and less decrease in the number of different types of client problems outside the family, with more family sessions can conceivably be understood (or rationalized) the same way as presented above for the association of less

Table 12–1
The Relationships of the Number of Sessions (Retention), the Numbers of Sessions Attended by the Father, and the Percentage of the Sessions Father Attended, to Each of Twenty-seven Change Scores (Outcome Criterion Variables)
(The "probability" of significance of the correlations) (N = 85)

	"P" Values		
	Number of Family Sessions	*Number of Sessions Father Attended*	*% of Sessions Father Attended*
Client report:			
1. Drug Severity Index Score			
2. Self-image (negative item score)	− .02[a]	− .03[a]	
3. Number of other family problems			
4. How much conflict is there in your family?			
5. How well do you get along with mother?			
6. How well do you think your parents understand you in general?	− .08[a]	− .08[a]	
7. Parent-adolescent communication—total mother score			
8. Parent-adolescent communication—total father score			
9. Client family role—total positive score			
10. Client family role—total negative score			
11. Psychic symptoms (BSI total score)			− .06[a]
12. Parent-adolescent communication—negative, mother	+ .09		
13. Parent-adolescent communication—positive, mother			
Mother's report:			
1. How frequently has the client been using drugs during the past three months? (3 = daily, 0 = no use)			
2. How much do you feel client's use of drugs has made the family situation *worse* than it would have been otherwise?			
3. How often has she or he confided in you about his or her drug/alcohol use?			
4. Client has problems in school (academic)			
5. Number of types of client's problems outside the family	− .09[a]		
6. To what degree do you approve of his or her behavior/attitude during the past month? (0 = none, 3 = a lot)		+ .08	− .01[ab]
7. How well does she or he get along with mother? (0 = not well, 3 = very well)			
8. Number of client's positive family role task behaviors (checklist)			
9. Number of client's negative family role task behaviors (checklist)	+ .04[b]		
10. Number of client's problems in the family			

Table 12–1

(Continued)

	"P" Values		
	Number of Family Sessions	Number of Sessions Father Attended	% of Sessions Father Attended
11. Number of mother's negative types of reactions to client (19-item checklist)	+ .01[b]		
12. How often have family relationships been peaceful and relaxed? (0 = never, 3 = usually)			
13. How often have family relationships been tense? (0 = never, 3 = usually)			
14. How often has there been arguing in the family?			

[a]A negative correlation indicates that there was a greater degree of the problem reported (deterioration rather than improvement) at follow-up, compared with pretreatment.

[b]A correlation of >.22 is significant at the .05 level of confidence for an *N* of 85.

decrease in substance use with more family sessions. Significant positive associations, on the other hand, were found between more family sessions and the mothers' reports of decrease in clients' negative behaviors in the family, as well as in the mothers' own negative reactions to the clients' behavior. There was also a trend for the clients to report a decrease in negative communications with the mother, in those families that participated in more sessions. These mixed findings are somewhat puzzling, and they suggest that the relationship of number of family sessions conducted to outcome is a complicated one; there are no doubt multiple factors to be considered in determining the number of family sessions the family participates in, as well as in determining the various outcomes of the therapy.

The third and last column of "p" values in table 12–1, indicates that for the correlations of the change scores with the percentage of the family sessions conducted that were attended by the father, there were four negative correlations (indicating less improvement when there was relatively more participation by the father) and only one positive correlation. The clients reported less decrease in psychic symptoms (measured by the Brief Symptom Inventory) and less decrease in conflict in the family. The mothers reported less approval of client behavior and attitude, and less increase in the clients' confiding in the mothers. The one positive association with relatively greater participation by the father was the mothers' reports of more decrease in tension within the family. It is possible to speculate and to rationalize this apparent contradiction: how the father's presence in the sessions would have the effect of reducing the tension in the family generally, but would not have the effect of increasing the adolescent's tendency to confide in his or her mother and would not increase the mother's approval of the client's behavior and attitude. If the mother and client attended sessions alone, with father or siblings absent, this treatment situation could induce more confiding, more work on improving communication within this dyad; and this sharing could conceivably result in the mother's becoming more approving (less critical) of the client's behavior and attitude.

Results of Separate Analysis for Subsample of Two-Parent "Intact" Families

Would the findings be the same or different if the same analysis were performed for only those families in which the adolescent client was living at home with both biological parents (N = 41)? It appeared possible that the father's participation in the family therapy process would be more important or essential if the father were living in the same home, rather than in a family in which (a) the parents were separated or divorced, and the client had little or no contact with the father; (b) father was deceased; or (c) there was a stepfather or a paramour of the mother's living in the home. The results from performing the same data analysis procedure with this select subsample of forty-one families, as was performed for the total sample of eighty-five families, are presented in table 12–2. Again, it was found that the attendance of the father (the percentage of the total number of family sessions conducted in which the father participated) had a significant correlational relationship to the outcome for only a few of the twenty-seven outcome criteria (change scores).

Conclusion

The findings of this study do not support the principle widely accepted by family therapists that the father's participation is important, if not essential, for the success or effectiveness of family therapy. In some of the families, when the father does not participate, this may represent either his lack of interest or motivation, his resistance or defensiveness, his lack of willingness to try to change, or his lack of understanding of how family therapy can help. But in other families, when the parents make a judgment that the fathers' participation in the sessions is not essential for getting help and for making progress by means of family therapy (and/or the father may not be readily available because of his work schedule), the parents' judgment may not be far off the mark.

Table 12-2

The Relationships of the Number of Sessions (Retention), the Numbers of Sessions Attended by the Father, and the Percentage of the Sessions Father Attended, to Each of Twenty-seven Change Scores (Outcome Criterion Variables)

(The "probability" of significance of the correlations) (N = 41)

	"P" Values		
	Number of Family Sessions	*Number of Sessions Father Attended*	*% of Sessions Father Attended*
Client report:			
1. Drug Severity Index Score	−.06[a]	−.07[a]	
2. Self-image (negative item score)	−.09[a]		
3. Number of other family problems			
4. How much conflict is there in your family?			−.07[a]
5. How well do you get along with mother?			
6. How well do you think your parents understand you in general?			
7. Parent-adolescent communication—total mother score			
8. Parent-adolescent communication—total father score			
9. Client family role—total positive score			
10. Client family role—total negative score			
11. Psychic symptoms (BSI total score)			
12. Parent-adolescent communication—negative, mother			
13. Parent-adolescent communication—positive, mother			
Mother's report:			
1. How frequently has the client been using drugs during the past three months? (3 = daily, 0 = no use)			
2. How much do you feel client's use of drugs has made the family situation *worse* than it would have been otherwise?			
3. How often has she or he confided in you about his or her drug/alcohol use?	+.08		−.08[a]
4. Client has problems in school (academic)			
5. Number of types of client's problems outside the family			
6. To what degree do you approve of his or her behavior/attitude during the past month? (0 = none, 3 = a lot)	+.03[b]		
7. How well does she or he get along with mother? (0 = not well, 3 = very well)			
8. Number of client's positive family role task behaviors (checklist)			
9. Number of client's negative family role task behaviors (checklist)			
10. Number of client's problems in the family			
11. Number of mother's negative types of reactions to client (19-item checklist)			

Table 12–2
(*Continued*)

	"P" Values		
	Number of Family Sessions	Number of Sessions Father Attended	% of Sessions Father Attended
12. How often have family relationships been peaceful and relaxed? (0 = never, 3 = usually)			
13. How often have family relationships been tense? (0 = never, 3 = usually)			
14. How often has there been arguing in the family?		+.05[b]	

[a]A negative correlation indicates that there was a greater degree of the problem reported (deterioration rather than improvement) at follow-up, compared with pretreatment.
[b]A correlation of >.30 is significant at the .05 level of confidence for an *N* of 41.

References

DeLeon, G. 1984. The Therapeutic Community: Study of Effectiveness. *Treatment Research Monograph Series,* Department of Health and Human Services Publication (ADM) 84-1286, Rockville, MD: National Institute on Drug Abuse. Washington, D.C.: U.S. Government Printing Office.

DeLeon, G., and N. Jainchill. 1986. Circumstance, motivation, readiness and suitability as correlates of treatment tenure. *Journal of Psychoactive Drugs* 18(3):203–8.

Friedman, A.S., E, Pomerance, R. Sanders, Y. Santo, A. Utada. 1980. The structure and problems of the families of adolescent drug abusers. *Contemporary Drug Problems* 3(9).

Harford, R.F. 1978. Some likely alternative explanations for improvements during drug abuse treatment are maturation, statistical regression, history, criterion contamination. In Arnold J. Shecter (ed.), *Proceedings of the Fifth National Drug Abuse Conference,* Seattle, Wash. April 3–8. (New York: Plenum Press) 1981.

Rush, T.V. 1979. Predicting treatment outcome for juvenile and young-adult clients in the Pennsylvania substance-abuse system. In *Youth Drug Abuse: Problems, Issues and Treatment.* G.M. Beschner and A.S. Friedman, eds., Lexington, Mass.: Lexington Books.

Sells, S.B., and D.D. Simpson. 1979. Evaluation of treatment outcome for youths in the Drug Abuse Reporting Program (DARP): A follow-up study. In *Youth Drug Abuse: Problems, Issues and Treatment.* G.M. Beschner and A.S. Friedman, eds., Lexington, Mass.: Lexington Books.

II
Case Book: The Family Therapy Experience with Eight Families of Adolescent Substance Abusers

Editors' note: *This section of the book is composed of eight chapters that include descriptions of eight families and detailed process reports of the family therapy that was conducted with each of these families in which the identified patient was an adolescent who had recently applied for (or been brought to) treatment in an outpatient drug treatment program. Verbatim transcripts of whole sessions or parts of sessions are included in the reports on three of the families, and explanatory comments by the therapist and/or a colleague are provided with the transcripts. Two of these families (See chapters 17 and 18) were included in the sample of eighty-five families who received family therapy as a part of the systematic demonstration research study that compared the effects of the functional family therapy method with the effects of a parent group method (see chapter 11). The other families were treated by a variety of approaches including psychodynamic, structural, and eclectic approaches.*

The family therapy process reported in chapter 13 by Lillian Frankel was conducted according to the structural family therapy model. Frankel has reported the therapy process for the Miller family in detail, session by session, and has made very clear and explicit how she used structural principles in her conceptualization of the family system and of the family problems and has explained the rationale for the interventions she made. Accordingly we, the editors of this book, thought it would provide an opportunity for several acknowledged family therapy experts to react to this case report and to comment on how they might have treated this family similarly or differently.

Chapter 15 presents a detailed description of the treatment of two black families by a black family therapist. The therapist's awareness of the cultural and ethnic aspects of the community to which the families belonged is of particular interest and value in this presentation. Noteworthy in this respect are the implications these elements had for the conduct of the family therapy.

Chapter 16 presents the family therapy process that S. J. Marks conducted with the family of a patient he had worked with over a period of twelve years. It also includes a complete verbatim transcript of one family session, with comments by the author-therapist and a colleague on each intervention made by the therapist. Included are sections on the author-therapist's observations about each family member and about the family as a whole. In addition, Marks speaks of reflections on himself and on his experience with this family ("Notes to an Afterward"). The family therapy approach exemplified in chapter 16 is the therapist's own particular combination, including experiential, psychodynamic and existential aspects and the therapist's emphasis on "use of self" (see chapter 6).

13

Structural Family Therapy for Adolescent Substance Abusers and Their Families

Lillian Frankel

The preceding chapters provided an overview of family issues in relation to adolescent drug abuse and various models of family therapy. In this chapter, one model commonly used in drug treatment programs has been selected—structural family therapy developed by Salvador Minuchin (1974)—to show how adolescent substance abusers can be treated in the context of their families. The key concepts and strategies of this model are discussed and related to adolescent substance abuse. Starting with the initial meeting with the family, we move through the various procedures in family assessment and planning, therapist roles and behaviors, task assignments, and other stages of intervention inherent in structural family therapy.

Although this chapter can be viewed as a mini–training manual, it does not presume to teach the reader to become a therapist. Even if one read all the material listed in the references, learning how to become a family therapist would require a considerable amount of experience in working with real families. Some of the concepts presented in this chapter, however, will help make that experience somewhat easier and more meaningful.

Why Family Therapy?

The family is a sensitive organism made up of interdependent members. The system contains within itself subgroups. For example, the parents make up a subgroup or marital dyad. The children and grandparents compose other subgroups. Whatever a member or subgroup does may be felt by every other member in the family system. It can be likened to the ripple effect in a pond, or as the English poet John Donne wrote, "No man is an island entire of itself; every man is a piece of the continent . . ."

Many adolescent substance abusers use drugs, in part, as medication to ease the pain of what is going on in their families and to escape from family interaction and its pressures. At the same time they may be acting out their hostility against their families. When such youngsters tend to spend a lot of time with peers who have similar drug use behavior patterns, they are generally estranged from the family (Friedman et al. 1980).

The importance of working with the whole family and of trying to make a change in the family system is well demonstrated by the following cycle of family interactions (Vasquez et al. 1979):

> In one such cycle, the interplay between an abusing parent and an abused child includes the following dyadic patterns: (1) marital tension and threat of open marital conflict surfaces; (2) the father leaves or withdraws; (3) feeling abandoned, the mother drinks; (4) seeing parental withdrawal, child A soils pants or spills milk; (5) child B (well sibling) points accusatory finger at child A, bringing child A's transgression to the mother's attention; (6) drunken mother endorses child B as praiseworthy, turning her out-of-control wrath and frustration (due to anger at father) on child A; (7) child A protests and the mother abuses child A; (8) child C (rescuer), seeking to protect child A, calls in father; (9) father rides in as hero after the fact of the abuse, chastizes mother as another "child out of control," nurtures mother and children and makes peace, thereby equilibriating the situation until it is exacerbated again by mother-father conflicts.

All families operate by the same principles. They all have rules and roles and feelings of self-worth that determine the health of the family environment and the ways of handling crises in the family system. In a dysfunctional family a child may learn to alleviate stress through drug or alcohol abuse. In a healthier family a child may try to lessen pain through family discussion or more or less involvement in school work or play. All families try to solve their problems and lessen stress in the only ways they know. The functioning family, of course, uses workable and effective methods. The dysfunctioning family tries to solve its problems in ways that not only fail to eliminate the problem, but tend to create others as well. Thus, we must look at and assess the ways that they try to overcome their problems.

A well functioning family has appropriate mechanisms for coping, for adapting to demands placed upon it by its members, significant others, and by society and its institutions. The family is flexible and has the resiliency to withstand the cyclical pressures of normal living such as adolescence, marriage, childbirth, unemployment, graduations, children leaving home, illness, and death.

Family roles are clear in a healthy family and can be enacted without confusion. Furthermore, our changing society with its many alternate lifestyles often requires an openness and willingness to vary from traditionally accepted roles. If mother works late at her job, then father can get the meals. The family acts, relates, and communicates in ways known to each member, and rules are open to discussion and change without upsetting the family balance. A basic concept of normal family operation is good communication. Respect, trust, and openness to disagreement are inherent in this process.

The dysfunctional family shows either a rigidity (embedded in the status quo) and a greater than average resistance to change or much inconsistency, lack of structure, or chaos, together with resistance to change. There may be a lack of mutual sharing, a lack of effective communication, and the consequent hostility that begets more hostility and its attending problems. This kind of family cannot view itself objectively; it needs to blame: to blame each other and/or societal authorities. But especially to blame the adolescent child who is "into misbehaving" and causing the family problems.

In troubled families, roles are not clear. For example, a mother may feel she is a failure because her daughter is using drugs. She concludes that a competent mother would not have a chemically dependent daughter. This mother may have felt earlier that she was not able to care for her family in the traditional way, and a child may have taken on the role of nurturer and caretaker and thus become "parentified." Either the mother abdicated the role and the void had to be filled by someone else, or she selected a child to fill the role in her place.

In a dysfunctional family, messages are often unspoken or unclear. Communication is either closed, vague, indirect, or rife with double messages; for example, a mother may tell her son she wants him to stop drinking and then buy him a six-pack of beer. Rules are often unspoken. For example, in families that consider females inferior to the males, no one needs to voice the notion. It is there in the family interactions and expectations. These rules are deeply embedded in the family's emotional environment and to discuss them would tend to upset the tight balance that keeps the family in a vise. Products of these unspoken rules (that have not been processed and accepted by all members) may be feelings of failure, rejection, anger, and depression and acting out behavior such as chemical addiction.

Because of societal as well as internal pressures that impact on the unyielding family, something has to give. To keep the family from breaking apart and to maintain the homeostasis, some member of the family will begin to reflect this turmoil by developing antisocial behavior, emotional problems, learning disabilities, or such. All the family attention and energy will then be directed against that member, who becomes the family scapegoat. Consequently substance abuse problems are more than an individual's abuse of drugs or alcohol. They involve the family and all its behavior, e.g., family roles, rules, communication, feelings of self-worth, and relationships with extended family, friends, neighbors, and significant others. It follows from this formulation that the responsibility for change should be placed on all the family members, namely, the family itself.

When lines of communication, rules, and roles are not clear, when relationships become excessively enmeshed or confused, when there are feelings of failure or low self-esteem, then the family can be in trouble. Virginia Satir (1964) states quite simply:

> . . . by observing and learning to understand communication in a family we can discover the rules that govern each individual's behavior. . . . First, each member of the family should be able to report congruently, completely, and obviously on what he sees and hears, feels and thinks, about himself and others, in the presence of others. Second, each person should be addressed and related to in terms of his uniqueness, so that decisions are made in terms of exploration and negotiation rather than in terms of power. Third, differentness must be acknowledged and used for growth.

When these changes are achieved, communication within the family will lead to appropriate outcomes:

> . . . decisions and behavior which fit the age, ability, and role of the individuals, which fit the role contracts and the context involved, and which further the common goals of the family.

The characteristics of dysfunctional, problem families that may be found in families of adolescent drug abusers (some of which have already been reviewed above), may include: denial of problems (belief that if only the client "kicked the habit" all would be well); lack of good communication; excessive closeness (enmeshment) or lack of closeness (distancing, isolation); overfunctioning or underfunctioning of a parent or parents; lack of warmth; and power struggles.

Family therapy focuses upon family interaction and communication in an attempt to change old patterns. Changes in the family's emotional environment go hand-in-hand with changes in the repetitive patterns of relating. These changes are initiated through various interventions discussed elsewhere in this chapter. Throughout this process the therapist is active, like a traffic cop directing action. The therapist's strategy is to "join"* with the family to create a new therapeutic system, leading toward the goals that the family want to reach.

During the family therapy process, an understanding of the total family picture and the importance of the symptom (substance abuse) for maintaining the homeostasis of the family system gradually emerges. As a result, we become more understanding and tolerant of the family members who resist change and who may be scapegoating the adolescent drug abuser, and we look for creative ways to help those members to change.

One must keep in mind that adolescence is a time of weaning, when the

---

*See definitions of terminology used in family therapy at end of chapter.

child begins to separate from the family and strive toward independence and self-assertion. However, the separation for substance abusers is not only an integral aspect of the adolescent's psychosocial development, as with normal youngsters, but it is a separation fraught with dependency-counter dependency conflict and hostility and rage. It is also a departure from the family system, its morals and values.

Sometimes it may be inadvisable to use family treatment with the substance abusing adolescent. Many clinical observers have reported that families of adolescent drug abusers are disrupted by poor parental relationships and other types of family dysfunction (Stanton 1979; Friedman et al. 1980). Often, parents of adolescent substance abusers have been found to be alcoholics or drug abusers themselves. Research findings show a direct correlation between marijuana use by teenagers and their parent's use of drugs (Smart and Fejer 1979).

In some cases the parents are so heavily involved in unhealthy ways with their teenagers that the youngsters need to be separated from the oppressive environment in order to establish their own boundaries, to find their own identities. In other cases the parents may be so abusive that the adolescent needs to be physically removed from the home environment, or the emotional pathology may be so severe that it would impede any attempts at treatment. In situations like these, the youngster would be treated separately, and hopefully the parents would be seen in their own sessions until the family was ready to work together in therapy.

Various Schools of Family Therapy

Systematic evaluation studies required to compare the effectiveness of structural family therapy with the effectiveness of other types (models) of family therapy for adolescent drug abuse have not yet been conducted. While the structural model is probably the most popular, other models or "schools" of family therapy that are just as valid and appropriate for our purposes include: Strategic Communication (Haley 1976); Functional (Alexander and Parsons 1982); Multi-generational (Bowenian) (Bowen 1978); Symbolic-Experiential (Kempler 1971; Kniskern and Neill 1981); Conjoint (Satir 1964); and Psychodynamic (Ackerman 1970). By reviewing these various models, their conceptual bases, and their methods, therapists can determine which one best fits their personal style, training background, client population, and setting in which they work.

For example, the structural approach encourages the therapist to become a family "insider" and join the family, while the Bowen approach cautions the therapist to remain an "outsider" and not become too important to the family. One school may recommend an intervention that is diametrically opposite to that recommended by another school for the same family situation. Reviews of family therapy models relevant for treatment of the adolescent drug abuser are available in the literature, e.g., Beels and Ferber 1972, Kaufman and Kaufman 1979, National Institute on Drug Abuse 1980, Gurman and Kniskern 1981.

To present in this chapter all the various schools of family therapy and the detailed methods and rationale of each school would be overwhelming and probably confusing for the beginning family therapist. Accordingly, we have chosen a more realistic and practical approach and are limiting the presentation to one model, structural family therapy.

Structural Family Therapy

Minuchin (1974), who has been most instrumental in developing structural family therapy, describes it as

> a body of theory and techniques that approaches the individual in his or her social context. It is based on three assumptions: (1) that the context of an individual's behavior affects inner processes; (2) that changes in context produce changes in the individual; and (3) that the therapist's behavior is significant in any movement toward change in the family structure.

This family therapy model is being practiced with increasing frequency in adolescent substance abuse treatment facilities throughout the country. There are several reasons for its popularity. One is that the therapy is brief, sometimes limited to twelve sessions. Considerable progress can be made in many families within this period.

In most cases families of substance abusers do not stay in therapy over a long period. They find the experience painful and like their substance-abusing children want a quick cure. Many of these families feel the pain of failure and its accompanying guilt; but they are not ready to face the failure and guilt and to work them through. Thus, to effect changes in these families, a modality that is short and goal-oriented seems to be most effective. Some families, however, need and want more than twelve sessions, and the duration of the course of treatment should be determined by the particular family situation.

Another practical consideration in choice of therapy is the limited resources of many adolescent substance abuse programs in both funding and staffing, making investment in a short-term treatment plan more feasible. If a goal is reached and the therapist and the family wish to work on other problems, after a brief respite of one or two months to allow the therapeutic gains to consolidate, the family may return to renegotiate further treatment on a time-limited basis of about another twelve sessions.

The Family Comes to the Agency

Having described some of the principles underlying family therapy with drug dependent adolescents, we now turn more specifically to the process. The remainder of this chapter is oriented to the beginning family therapist: it presents techniques for the therapist and also principles governing the therapist's role.

Typically a family comes to the agency seeking help for one of its members, a drug-dependent adolescent, who is perceived as the problem in the family. The usual request is: "Help my child get off drugs. He is destroying the family. He is causing the family to fall apart. Cure him."

It may not be easy to get the family into treatment. Even when a parent, usually the mother, brings an adolescent in for treatment, she may not be ready to accept treatment for herself or for other family members. The perceptions of most families is that the young client needs a therapist, and not that the whole family needs a therapist. You need to consider the family situation realistically. This kind of family is likely to resist treatment even if it has been referred for family therapy by a court, a parole and probation department, a hospital, a school, a mental health clinic, or a social agency. Don't be too disappointed if the family doesn't follow through. Often it takes a great deal of reaching out on your part to get the family to come to the agency prepared to become involved in treatment. (Some principles and methods for engaging resistant families in treatment are presented in Stanton and Todd 1981.)

You may have to see the adolescent client on an individual basis until you can get the rest of the family to come in for treatment. In the meantime, try to elicit the client's help. You may even offer to make home visits, if this is in line with agency policy and acceptable to the family. Remember that the families of drug dependent adolescents may have little trust, along with their low self-esteem. They live with a feeling of isolation and expect rejection. Therefore, establishing a positive relationship with them will be difficult, but it is generally possible to make some connection. As a last resort, you may have to ask the referring agency to help the family accept treatment. However, a family that is coerced into coming may arrive with great hostility that may take a number of sessions to dispel.

Sometimes it is easier. When a member, or members, of a family walk in or phone for an appointment, talk with them at that time, if at all possible. If not, set an appointment as soon as possible, since it is important to act quickly while the client and family show some motivation toward treatment. Remember that this client may be ambivalent toward coming and can easily find many reasons for avoiding treatment. If you place the family on a waiting list, you may lose it, since experience has shown a high percentage of attrition in a waiting list. Make it clear that you expect the entire family to participate in the treatment.

Adolescents may want to come to therapy alone, especially if they feel they are the family members with the problems or do not want to reveal all their activities to the family. Your client may not want to involve the family and may resist by protesting that he/she has caused them enough trouble. Or the client may not want the family to know he/she is seeking help and may insist upon being old enough to be independent. Often the adolescent claims that the family does not care enough and would refuse to come even if the therapist were to request it. In such situations try to convince the adolescent that family therapy is the indicated process, and that it may take considerably less time than individual therapy. You may give the client one or two specific examples of problems that he has with his parents and demonstrate by role play exactly how you can help him work through these problems with his parents.

With adolescent drug abusers, it is often useful to alternate individual sessions with family sessions. Adolescents frequently need some sessions apart from their families, to discuss issues and problems that they are not ready to share with parents. Concurrent counseling and family therapy, when conducted by the same therapist, requires special skill to avoid collusion with the client in keeping secrets from the parents or misleading them.

It may be helpful to have the client's permission to invite the family in for treatment, to convey to them that it can be of help to you in your work with the client. In asking the client for permission you are also telling him/her you are respecting his/her confidences. Empathize with the family over the pain it must be feeling and the difficulties it faces in connection with the client's drug use and related disturbing behavior in the home. The family may respond and come in, albeit reluctantly. The family may then become your client, and you are ready to proceed with the first therapy session.

The Initial Family Session

If you have not been a family therapist very long, the fist session is usually a tense time for you as well as for the family. Be prepared for resistance, anger, outbursts, long silences, affected cheerfulness, and other reactions and emotions. This does not always happen—in some initial sessions family members relate to you in a friendly and productive manner. In short, be prepared for anything.

In the beginning, family members see their role in treatment as providing information to the therapist about the client, and receiving reports from the therapist about the client's problems and progress in becoming drug free. The therapist, however, views the family in another light, seeing the youngster as the symptom bearer of a disturbed or disorganized family. For some reason, syntonic or in harmony with his needs, this person has taken it upon himself, or somehow got selected, to absorb some of the problems of the family and as a "symptom bearer" of the family's conflicts, possibly to help the family keep its homeostasis or balance.

The problem stems in part from the parents and the parents' relationship. Thus the focus is not on the individual, but on the family itself with its myriad interactional patterns and ecological systems. If the identified patient were to be treated on an individual basis, he/she would still remain in the same family environment that caused the symptoms. So the family needs to change.

Structural family therapists divide the first interview into four stages; the *social stage*, the *problem stage*, the *goal-setting stage*, and the *interaction stage* (Haley 1976). The therapy process does not and should not necessarily proceed in any rigidly structured sequence or in predetermined stages or phases. The plan presented here is to provide the beginning family therapist with a map, a guide, a structure to keep in mind. The initial session can be more free flowing than might be suggested by this outline. For example, the goals of therapy might not be discussed in a first session or may even be postponed until the family understands enough to adequately determine the goals.

According to Minuchin, the chief concern of the therapist at the initial meeting is to set up a therapeutic unit (Minuchin 1974). You begin to map the family structure. That is, observe the family, broaden the focus from the identified patient to the entire family, and develop the therapeutic contact. The specific how-to-do-it suggestions that follow are intended to provide structure, as an aid to the beginning family therapist, and to allay the initial anxiety and feelings of unsureness that most beginning family therapists experience. None of the suggestions is to be taken as absolutes or to be followed routinely by the therapist. Good therapy cannot be done by the numbers. Be yourself, feel free to follow your own intuition and judgment, and be open to perceiving and experiencing the family as it is, as it presents itself. Every family, and every first family session, is unique. Nevertheless the suggestions offered below can be helpful and will apply to many family situations.

Social Stage

Prepare the group room. Check the ventilation and temperature. Make sure it is not too hot or cold—the family, as well as yourself, should be comfortable and family members should not have this excuse for leaving the session. Have enough chairs, arranged so that people can see each other.

When your family comes in, allow members to sit wherever they please. Wait for them to be seated before you sit down so that you do not interfere with their choice. However, if you feel more comfortable using your usual chair in your office, that is sufficient reason to continue to do so. Seat selection is significant since it helps you observe family alliances. Sometimes peripheral members sit off by themselves. Later on, you will find out why the family seated themselves as they did. It is best not to ask them to explain it immediately, as they will feel put on the spot.

Introduce yourself. Get the name of each member and greet each one personally, waiting for some kind of reply from each one. Your manner of greeting shows the family you were anticipating and awaiting them. You are the host, and this gives the family a feeling of security and shows your sincere concern over the problem and your interest in the family. Many families are put at ease if you introduce yourself by your first name and suggest the use of first names rather than formal titles.

Bear in mind that these people are anxious. They have come to discuss a family problem with a stranger. The family rule may be that "We solve our own problems. We do not go to outsiders." In most cases you are dealing with a family that is humiliated over having to bring its problems to a stranger regardless of his/her expertise. They are defensive and frightened, although they may try to hide these emotions under an overlay of cheerfulness.

Whatever the mood, assess it and try to match it. In other words, if the family seems to be jovial or concerned, attempt to blend into the emotional environment it is setting. This technique will be useful as you endeavor to enter the family system. This is discussed in detail in a later section of this chapter.

Engage in a few minutes of casual conversation in order to get acquainted, to give the family an opportunity to react to you and the situation. Be alert to the possibility that some members may try to engage you in a lengthy conversation, and you may be lured into a coalition with that member. To avoid this, politely turn to another family member and invite him/her to share in the getting acquainted process. Go from one person to another until all members have had a chance to introduce themselves and say something about themselves. Give the family a chance to feel more at ease before you proceed to ask about the presenting problem.

The Problem Stage

When you feel it is time to address the problem that brought the family in, you may need to use strategy in asking the opening question, "What brings you here?" (Of course, some family member may have already taken the initiative and started talking about their reasons for coming.) You can address this question to no one in particular, or if one member of the family, possibly the father, is deferred to or is important in the hierarchal structure of the family, you may ask him. You have choices. You may even choose to address him first if you feel he is a peripheral member and not well respected. This may be a way of bolstering his position in the family and also motivating him towards more participation.

One possible strategy is to save the identified patient for the end, as you go around the room eliciting impressions of the presenting problem. This takes the focus off this adolescent and makes it more evident that this is a family problem. It is more effective than immediately asking the client the nature of the problem. If you were to do so, you would be perpetuating what the family has been doing, namely singling out the client and labeling him/her as the patient.

Once each member has had a chance to tell you about the problem, encourage the members to discuss the problem with each other. Through this process you are helping to activate the family communication and interaction. It is natural that the family members will talk to you, rather than to each other, in the first session. If you find them addressing you exclusively, or looking at you while talking to someone else, you might gently suggest that they talk directly to each other. For example, if Fred turns to you to tell you about his sister's drug problem, let him do it briefly; but then suggest that he discuss it further directly with his sister.

While you are gathering information you should also be constantly alert to the way the family interacts, both verbally and nonverbally. Who sits next to whom? Who talks to whom? Who is ignored? Who argues with whom? As you watch for alliances and coalitions, patterns of communication, verbal and nonverbal, you are in the process of joining empathically the family system. You need to become part of the family in certain ways in order to understand and help it, while at the same time retaining your autonomy and your separate role and identity as the therapist. If you become too immersed in the family (swallowed up, as it were) you will lose your objectivity and your critical judgment, and you will not be able to help them any more than they can help themselves. The trick is to keep one foot in and the other foot out, at the same time.

Be sensitive to the pace of the family. How quickly do the members move, speak, or respond? Proceed at the family's pace. For example, if the members speak slowly and deliberately, do likewise. If you speak rapidly, try to slow down to fit the family's pattern. If this family tells anecdotes, tell some of your own. In order to fit into this family so that you can help restructure behavior, you need to be syntonic or in harmony with it. Feel free to tie into the family pattern so that you can be accepted by the family. As Salvador Minuchin (1974) says,

Change is seen as occurring through the process of the therapist's affiliation with the family and the restructuring of the family in a carefully planned way, so as to transform dysfunctional transactional patterns. If she/he has been able to affiliate with a family and feels the pressures of the family system, she/he does not need to guard against spontaneous responses, for those responses will probably be syntonic with that system.

As you listen to what family members, in their dyadic interaction, are saying about the problem (namely, that it revolves around the identified patient) do not share with the family that you see the problem in a different light. You may see the problem as having started originally within the marital dyad or as being a family problem; but if you want to keep this family in therapy you will not too quickly challenge its perception of the presenting problem. They say the problem is that an adolescent daughter is on drugs and that is why they are coming in. The quickest way to lose this family is for you to challenge this or too quickly change the focus.

Goal-Setting Stage

What changes does the family want? Notice that the family wants all the changes to be made by the identified patient. It probably does not see itself as a dysfunctioning family. A family in discussing desired changes may come up with the following list:

> Our daughter should get off drugs; she should get a job or go to school, learn a trade; she should take more responsibility in the home; she should stop going out with those "creeps"; she should get a good husband to provide for her; etc.

While both parents usually want, or at least believe that they want, the treatment to help their youngster to stop using drugs, they do not necessarily agree on other goals of treatment. One parent may want the adolescent to move out of their home and take all the drug problems elsewhere, since the situation has become intolerable, while the other parent may want to hold onto and protect the youngster and to continue to hope desparately that the problems can be worked out.

Young clients are often not quite so ready to state spontaneously in the presence of the family their goals and wishes regarding family therapy. But with solicitation and encouragement from the therapist they do get expressed. These goals, not likely to be very clearly thought out or formulated, are likely as not to be a wish that the therapist get their parents "off my back" regarding complaints about drug use and friends; that their parents start to understand, and to accept, why they are not able to stop using drugs; and that their parents continue to supply money for drugs. This latter is usually implied and not directly demanded.

Around this time (or at a later session) the identified patients may disclose some of their fears. Adolescent clients may be afraid to give up the support obtained from drugs and friends. They may be shy and uncomfortable with people when drug free and afraid of losing the few friends they manage to have. They may have no self-confidence and talk of the anxiety upon entering a room filled with lots of people. They cannot understand squares, they are so dull. There is much more excitement being around one's friends, but then again it is so difficult finding ways to support oneself. They are tired of being used by people, especially those who pretend to be interested and are not.

At the same time the clients may express some fairly unrealistic goals, such as their intention to move out of the parent's home or to get a job within a few weeks (a type of job that they have little real chance of obtaining). Or a girl may insist that her boyfriend will start supporting her, although he is not working and needs money for drugs himself. These goals may or may not be believed by the clients themselves, at the moment. It may be just conning, or it may be expressing what the parents want to hear and believe, or some other combination of motivations.

You are not beginning to witness some of the pain, frustration, and conflict that is being experienced by this family. The parents may have goals that they are trying to express and are hoping you will help them. The family members are giving you information through their verbal and nonverbal communication, through their manner of relating, and through their silences. You may express an agreement to work on some of the desires for change or goals that family members express. To this extent, such agreements may be considered to be shared goals or to constitute a tentative contract for treatment.

Interaction Stage

During the interactional stage you concentrate on observing and understanding the family patterns. You need to be aware of the systems that are operating to plan strategies to enable you eventually to restructure the interaction. One way to improve the communication and interaction patterns is to help the family define the boundaries between the subsystems and maintain the autonomy of its subsystems, as well as the integrity of the entire family system.

One method is to encourage two members (a dyad) to continue to discuss a problem between them, as they see it, and to keep other members from interrupting. Tell them you want to give this dyad more of an opportunity to work on their problem and that the others will have their turn to comment or to participate later. Getting people together in appropriate dyadic and triadic negotiations is a method of boundary setting. It is your task as therapist to become the boundary maker. To accomplish this role you need to join each subsystem and then listen carefully as you help them to communicate. You join by imparting to each subsystem that you respect its opinions and you believe in its ability to change.

Subsystems are parts of the family, like mother and father (the parental subsystem), or husband and wife (the spouse subsystem), or brother and sister (the sibling subsystem), or grandparents, etc. Each subsystem has its own rules about its manner of relating. For example, saying to grandmother, "You can't tell me what to do. You're not my mother," or a mother telling her daughter, "You take care of Billy. He's your son. I've raised my family already," expresses family rules of behavior and establishes boundaries.

Boundaries should be clear, with responsibilities and lines of authority clearly defined. In a dysfunctioning family, boundaries often are diffused. In the above example when the mother tells her daughter to take care of Billy she is expressing a clearly defined family rule, but if she were to have said the following, "Take care of Billy. He's your son. I've raised my family already," and then turns to Billy saying, "Hey Billy, come here. Let me tie your shoe laces," she would be diffusing the boundaries.

Another example of diffusion between the parental marriage subsystem and the sibling subsystem (children) is a child taking over the mother role and affiliating with the father in the executive or parental subsystem when the mother is the substance abuser and has regressed to the dependent role of the child in the family. It would probably be more difficult to establish, or reestablish, the appropriate generational boundaries in such a family than in a family in which the adolescent offspring is a substance abuser.

Joining

Structural family therapy is a therapy of intervention, a therapy that seeks to change the current family organization so it can function on a healthier level. Thus you, the therapist, in pursuit of your goal of bringing about a change, join the family system, and you work within that framework. The joining process begins in the very first interview and continues throughout your entire experience with the family. The three main types of joining operations are maintenance, tracking, and mimesis (Minuchin 1974).

Maintenance: As you become involved in the family systems you support them, even if you do not agree with them. For example, you may respect the leadership position of a member who may be autocratic and overbearing, qualities you may not be comfortable with. Yet you suggest to this person that he/she try to bring into the next session a reluctant family member. You may support an adolescent subgroup by finding something positive to say to it. You may compliment the adolescents on some articles of clothing they are wearing. In other words, you are maintaining the family system while you prepare to restructure patterns.

Tracking: You encourage the family members to communicate with each other and with you. You are unobtrusive, asking questions only in an attempt to fully understand the problem and to gain information useful to you in leading the family into areas it may not as yet have selected for discussion.

Mimesis: In the social phase we discussed mimesis or adapting to the family's style. If the members resort to humor, appreciate it and possibly tell an anecdote of your own. This can be very helpful in gaining family acceptance. Try to make use of common experiences. Sometimes mimesis occurs without your awareness. If a mother rolls a ball to keep a small child quiet and the ball rolls to you, you may find yourself rolling it back to the child without thinking anything of it. Mimetic operations are often spontaneous and helpful in strengthening your bond with individuals in the family.

Throughout the entire session you are involved in the process of joining. You are joining the family system through your interventions and by making sure that everyone is participating in discussions. Reach out to those sitting on the sidelines. Change your seat. Move around and enter the group. Ask for ideas and suggestions from subgroups. For example, you may address a sibling subgroup, "Your parents have a lot to say about the way things are going at home. It looks as if they want to see some changes. What do you have to say about it? Do you agree?" During this first session you need to hook all the members into the therapeutic system or you may have trouble getting some of them to return.

The family should shift around, too, in the seating arrangement. If father is off to one side while mother and grandmother are sitting close together, have grandmother change seats with father so that he is brought into the family even though you have the impression that these parents hardly ever talk to each other at home. This will break up the enmeshment between mother and grandmother for the moment and will demonstrate boundaries around the material dyad.

Observe the manner of interaction. How are people relating? Is father timid? Is he afraid of mother's wrath, or vice versa? Is he afraid the family will divulge the fact that he's an alcoholic? It will take skill on your part to keep from getting triangled into some of the discussions. A member may turn to you and ask what you think or ask for corroboration or ask you to settle an argument. Do not let yourself get involved; suggest that they need to work it out themselves. But do so in a helpful way, suggesting that perhaps they need to consider other aspects of the problem.

It may also happen that in the heat of discussion, the identified patient, upon hearing him/herself being labeled the cause of the family trouble, may try to disrupt the session by changing the subject, screaming, or stalking out of the room. You need to get this member back into the session. Someone should go out to get him/her. If the youngster has run out of the building and can't be found or pursuaded to return that hour, then the family should be told that it is important that he/she return the next session in order to handle the drug problem and all its ramifications.

During the interview be sure to bolster the dwindling ego of the chemically dependent adolescent. As stated earlier, you need to be mindful of the low self-image of both client and family. Try to find positive things to say and state them in ways that sounds credible, otherwise this defensive family unaccustomed to positive reinforcement will suspect you of trying to manipulate it into continuing therapy. You can say things such as, "What you say makes sense," or you can mention instances of past success such as, "When you gave up smoking, you showed determination and will power." Keep in mind that this family may be ambivalent about coming to therapy, and that some of its members will be looking for a convenient excuse for not returning.

Not all, but many, families of chemically dependent adolescents are resistant. If it were their choice they would not come in for treatment partly out of shame, partly out of low self-esteem and a feeling of hopelessness, and partly because the turmoil in their lives has become a habit—often a habit frought with a kind of excitement. Some families are unconsciously reluctant to give this up.

Toward the end of the session you might convey that it will require a sustained effort on the part of everyone to make changes and to alleviate the symptoms the family diagnoses as drug addition. Demonstrate to the family how you will guide the effort. You will have to show that you have empathy and that you realize the difficulties, but do not present yourself as the supreme authority. You *are* an authority, but you are also a caring person who is not infallible.

Restructuring techniques have the effect of inducing new stresses in the family, but this is sometimes necessary for achieving change. There is risk, as well as opportunity, inherent in making changes, and the therapist will need to provide support to counteract the new family stress and anxiety, at the same time encouraging the change.

Contract

You need to make a plan or contract with the family, a plan that ties in with its goals and what it wants to achieve. It is your job to help the family see its goals realistically. In the first session, you may set a time frame for the therapy. For example, you may set a period of 12 weeks, once a week, 1 to 1½ hours a session. There may be some individual sessions with individuals or subgroups, as the need arises. Rules of the therapy contract should be elicited from the family with your guidance. Some of the rules may be: Everyone must come each week. Everyone must participate and say something. No one may threaten. Members should feel free to say what they want without fear of recriminations at home. Members should try not to interrupt each other.

The contract should be based on the goals of the therapy and should be flexible enough to change as therapy goes on. Goals should be clearly stated and understood by the family. This will make it easier for the family to carry out some of the therapeutic tasks that you will assign.

When everyone agrees upon the goals, a family member can write them down, making one copy for the family and one for you. Suggest that members of the family look at the contract periodically. The contract keeps the family focused on the goals and can help prevent their attention from being diverted to less important issues.

Also in the first session tasks for the family to do at home are introduced. Task setting is an essential aspect of structural family therapy. It actualizes (makes real) and tends to consolidate the changes worked on during the session. This technique allows the family to keep the session with it all week. It is as if the therapist has gone home with the family. Suggest tasks that are possible and not too difficult to perform, as it is important, especially in the beginning stages of therapy, for the family to experience some success.

More often than not the family will not adequately implement the homework tasks. Their ingrained habits and resistances will get in the way. Even so, all is not lost, since the review of the problem during the next session will serve to enlighten the family regarding the bases for their resistance to change.

Thus tasks can serve as therapeutic probes. If they are not carried out, the flexibility or rigidity of the family is revealed. If they are carried out, in many cases the family, feeling a sense of accomplishment, returns with a closer involvement with you.

The first session is usually longer than subsequent ones, since there are several tasks to perform and you will need to touch base with each family member. Sometimes, however, a beginning therapist might take less time because he/she is anxious and works too quickly, not recognizing all the nuances and subtleties that are taking place. Keep to the time you have set with the family. This can be a helpful limit-setting device for a family that does not function according to time limits and arrives late or feels that things can be put off for tomorrow.

The Treatment Process

To clarify and possibly simplify the dynamics of structural family therapy and to apply some of the concepts reviewed previously, it may be helpful to consider one particular family and take it through the treatment processes.

The Miller Family

Although the Miller family is rather complicated, it is not atypical of many four-generational families that come into a drug treatment agency. This family was referred to the drug abuse clinic by the police when Sharon, the seventeen-year-old daughter, an unmarried mother, was caught shoplifting. She was also known in the area as a substance abuser. The mother, Betty, is a fifty-year-old diabetic who has not worked since she got married twenty-five years ago to Dick, a fifty-three-year-old alcoholic used car salesman. The family also includes two younger boys, John aged 16 and Fred aged twelve, and Sharon's two-year-old son Billy.

Father. Dick Miller seems to be uninvolved with his family, but active in his extra-familial system, the men at work. He blames his wife for the children's problems. He is short tempered, alcoholic, and hostile toward his wife's parents. At one time, he says, his relationship with his wife was good. "She did all the things you'd expect a woman to do, but then she became too thick with her mother," and she grew away from him. He has a strong denial system and is reluctant to discuss his drinking, seeing it as no problem.

Mother. Betty Miller is a medium-sized woman with her hair always in pink curlers. She tends toward obesity despite her physician's warnings. She doesn't watch her diet, but often goes on "junk-food" binges. Betty has a close relationship with Sharon, her chemically dependent daughter, and with her own mother, Mrs. Nelson. Betty feels her daughter is sick and relates to her on that basis, just as her own mother relates to her over her diabetes. She is fearful of her husband's temper, her daughter's outbursts, and her son John's anger. She has a close relationship with her parents and enjoys spending time with them. This is easily done since they live across the street. Betty has taken over the care of her grandson, albeit reluctantly. This frees Sharon to run around with the friends who are not allowed to come into the house. The Miller spouse system is frought with unnegotiated conflicts around father's alcoholism. Betty also uses strong denial as a defense mechanism. She does not want to discuss Dick's drinking because he gets "too nasty." When she does try to deal with Dick's drinking, she selects a time to complain when he is intoxicated and at his worst. This enrages him beyond control. Therefore, she prefers to ignore his alcohol problem. She also refuses to go to Alanon, rationalizing that it would be a fruitless task.

Sharon. The identified patient often complains to her grandmother about the family. Sharon is hostile toward and afraid of her father and is used by her mother, who triangles her into situations where she sides with mother against father. This is common in dysfunctioning families when the conflict is between the spouses. Thus Sharon forms an alliance with her mother against father when Sharon should not be involved at all. In a way Fred also finds himself in that position.

Sharon is ambivalent in her relationship with Billy. Often she considers him an encumbrance. Other times she dresses him up and takes him with her when she visits her friends. She had refused to give him up for adoption when this was proposed to her by her father.

Sharon left school in tenth grade, associated with a group of school dropouts who turned her on to drugs and alcohol. She was an attractive, shy, and insecure girl who was pleased to be accepted by this particular group. Soon she was into drugs, shoplifting, and later on, some prostitution. Her job history was sporadic. When she was still living at home, she ran away three times and each time was brought back by the juvenile authorities. Finally, upon turning fifteen she moved in with Tony, a drug dealer in trouble with the law.

After six months Sharon left Tony. Sick with hepatitis and pregnant, she called her mother, begging her to allow her to return home. She stayed with her grandparents until her mother could coerce father into allowing her to return to the family. Mother used her diabetic condition as a weapon in her argument with her husband. She told him she would stop taking her insulin injections if he refused to let Sharon come back. Sharon returned to the home, and this served a family purpose. Now all energy could be focused upon her again. Soon mother stopped bothering father about his drinking and socializing with the men at the used car lot. John's problems escalated, and he began to further distance himself from the family.

John. The sixteen-year-old son, a high school junior, is cutting classes and threatening to quit school. According to his mother, he drinks too much on weekends. John says he drinks no more than the other teenagers in his age group, about six bottles of beer in one evening. His mother worries, especially since John drives a motorcycle. He relates negatively to his parents and siblings. He crosses generational lines by being closer to his grandparents than his parents. He strives for autonomy and is underachieving at school. Before Sharon returned home, John was functioning on a more productive level. When Sharon shows signs of giving up her symptoms, he begins to develop his own brand of symptomatology, or behavior problem. John can be viewed as a potential symptom bearer for this family.

Fred. For some reason the pre-adolescent son seems to be the strongest member in the family. He has a close relationship with Sharon, his mother, and his grandparents. He often has disputes with his father over failure to do some of the tasks around the house. He is clever enough to stay away from his father when Mr. Miller comes home intoxicated or angry. Fred serves as the "switchboard" in the family: father commands him, "Tell your mother to clean up this kitchen," or mother says, "Tell your father that Sharon and I will need the car tonight," etc. Although Fred has learned to cope with his family situation, he seems unhappy over the lack of closeness with his older brother John. If given the opportunity, he runs errands for John and even takes over some of John's household tasks, such as mowing the lawn.

Billy. Billy does not know his father and seems unaware of his real position in the family. He calls his grandmother Mom. He calls his mother Sharon, and seems to relate to her as his sibling. His grandfather has little contact with him, does not play with him, and treats him more like an unwanted pet animal in the house.

Billy will play with Fred, but like Fred, seems enamored of John and would like to receive more attention from him, especially since John has begun to ride a motorcycle. His great-grandparents across the street provide some warmth and caring in their relationship with Billy.

Grandparents. This subgroup is very strong and plays an important role in the family. Mr. Miller resents their intrusion and has very little contact with them. Grandmother is a controlling woman, tightly enmeshed with her only child Betty, and she has no intentions of letting go. Sharon is also tied in with them, and the three generations of women are tightly locked together.

Mr. Nelson, her seventy-eight-year-old husband, is a very passive, uninvolved person who is peripheral as is Mr. Miller. However, these men have different personalities. Whereas Mr. Nelson is a rather sweet, docile person, willing to delegate all family intervention to his wife, Mr. Miller is an explosive person, resenting his position in the family. It would also seem that Mrs. Nelson, the matriarch of the entire family system, has more involvement with the female members of the family and in a way tries to render husbands, both hers and Betty's impotent.

The grandparents wanted to come to the first session, because they would like to establish and have confirmed that they are in charge of the Miller family. They see their daughter Betty as a depressed woman who cannot take care of her family or her diabetic condition. They see Sharon as a "spoiled kid" who is on drugs because her mother let her run around with a "bad crowd." They also blame the family situation on the father, citing his isolation from the family and his drinking problem.

Mapping

Family structuralists find it helpful to think in terms of a visual map and use it in planning therapeutic goals. It is an objective way of viewing the family relationship system. The following are examples of how it can be used with the Miller family.

Mother and Sharon are tightly enmeshed. Father is left out. Your goal is to bring mother and father together and for Sharon to be in her own subsystem. You will need to strengthen the boundaries around mother and father and put the generational boundaries in order.

$$\frac{M\ S}{F} \quad \text{SHOULD BE CHANGED TO} \quad \frac{M\ F}{S}$$

Another example is the restructuring of the subsystem involving Billy and Sharon. Billy is tied in with Mrs. Miller

$$\frac{B\ M}{F} \quad \text{SHOULD BE CHANGED TO} \quad \frac{M}{S\ B}$$

Another plan is the strengthening of the spouse system and weakening the bond between Mrs. Miller and her mother Mrs. Nelson. It would look like this:

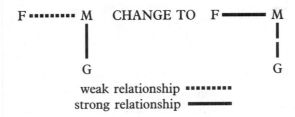

weak relationship ┄┄┄┄┄
strong relationship ━━━━━

You are also part of the mapping process. For example, you may find yourself allying with father in regard to a specific issue to enhance his credibility with the family. When you support his efforts to overcome his drinking as we will show later, the map may look like this:

$$\text{Therapist} \quad \blacksquare\!\!\blacksquare\!\!\blacksquare \quad \frac{\text{FM}}{\text{Children}}$$

The map is a visual blueprint that may help reduce your confusion during the session and is helpful in planning therapeutic goals. Often, especially when you are inexperienced, you may find yourself getting triangled into a situation. You can map this so that you can see how either one or both individuals try to elicit your support in an argument. Cut them off. Don't get involved.

$$S \underset{\text{Therapist}}{\diagdown\diagup} F \quad - - - \quad \text{cut off}$$

Figure 13–1 shows the family seating arrangement. Mother and Sharon were sitting close together. Grandparents were sitting on the other side of Mrs. Miller. Billy was off to a side playing with a toy at Freddy's feet. John sat at one end of the room, and Mr. Miller had pulled his chair away from his father-in-law and seemed isolated over on the side.

So, as early as the very first session you can attempt to carry out your restructuring maneuvers. As you strive for realignment you suggest that Sharon give her seat to father. He may balk at this, calling it "foolishness," but with good natured cajoling, chances are he will respond. Now the parents are sitting next to each other, and Sharon is not sitting where her father should have been. Have Billy move his toys over to Sharon, so he can be aligned with his mother.

Ask grandmother to change places with her husband. Ask Mr. and Mrs. Miller to face each other and plan an activity they might be able to do together during the week. It might be as innocuous as watching a television program together. Since their relationship at this point is so strained, it would be difficult to give them a task such as going out to dinner away from the children. Anything they can do together without getting into an argument would be a worthwhile activity. Encourage them to help select the task.

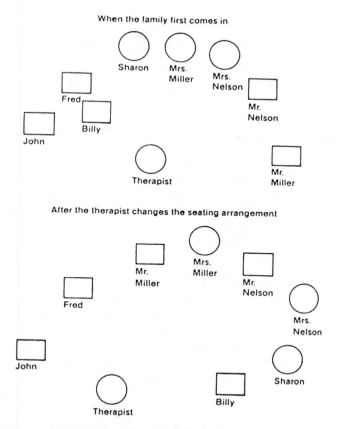

Figure 13–1. Seating Arrangement During First Session

Therapeutic Goals

Some appropriate goals for the therapy that could be established by you and the family are:

1. Help Sharon give up her symptom.
2. Increase and improve interaction in the spouse system.
3. Mr. Miller must attend to his alcoholism problem.
4. Disengage Mrs. Miller from her parental subsystem.
5. Strengthen the boundary around Sharon and Billy.
6. Disengage Sharon from enmeshment with mother.

7. Build positive relationships in the sibling subsystem.
8. Help Sharon toward individuation and independence.
9. Improve interaction between father and children.
10. Disengage grandparents from enmeshment with Miller family.

Although one of the goals is to loosen the hold the grandparents have upon the family, it is important to take into consideration ethnic and cultural backgrounds. In some cultures grandparents are a vital part of the family system. Among Italian, Spanish, Latin American, oriental, and many other groups, grandparents are highly respected and their involvement with the family is a basic component of the structure. Thus, one must exercise tact in handling grandparents. Often it is helpful to involve them in the therapeutic enterprise (cotherapists); in that way they may become more amenable to helping free their children from their enmeshment.

In this complicated family the numerous goals you want to achieve will benefit the family themselves, but will also help accomplish the primary goal—getting Sharon off drugs. One important goal is to strengthen the marital dyad, which probably cannot be accomplished until Mr. Miller stops drinking. Thus his alcoholism must be faced. Mr. Miller, typical of abusers, serves as the mood setter in the family, with the family reacting to him and afraid to deal with his illness. Separate marital sessions to work on Mr. Miller's alcohol problem will not be needed unless he seems more likely to discuss it if the children are not present. (Separate marital sessions are indicated if there are problems in the parents' sexual relationship.) In helping Mr. Miller go to an alcohol clinic and A.A., and Mrs. Miller attend a group such as Alanon, or in working to improve the marital sexual relationship, you are at the same time working toward restructuring the family.

This procedure is often not as easy as it may seem. Confronting a person like Mr. Miller may bring forth angry outbursts as he resists changing his way of life. He may protest that he's being singled out and attacked although he came to the clinic originally to help Sharon. You will have to agree with him that Sharon's substance abuse was indeed the presenting problem and you need his support in this, but you might explain to him how it would help Sharon and the whole family if he could do something positive about his alcoholism.

To strengthen the mother-child relationship between Sharon and her son Billy, Sharon may need some additional sessions with a psychotherapist, who may observe that she does not know how to play with him, or to relate to him in a motherly fashion, and who will be a role model for her and will give her tasks that will strengthen her role as a mother. It is probably better to have a different therapist perform this function, if possible to arrange.

This would avoid splitting your relationship with the family and adding to the transference problems.

Also you may need to refer Sharon to other agencies and resources such as vocational rehabilitation, courses or workshops in single-parent groups, etc. To break her involvement with her mother, it might be effective strategy to have Mr. Miller take charge with your supervision and guidance. This would also help strengthen the boundary around him and Sharon.

Intervention Techniques

Role Play

Therapy sessions often involve the family in more activity than sitting around and talking. You will be actively and creatively devising role play situations whereby the members engage in various interactions. Get the members to enact certain issues that are important in their lives. Have them reenact arguments that occurred during the preceding week at home. The children in the family might pretend that they are the parents, or the parents the children, in order to facilitate the subgroups hearing and understanding of each other. In the Miller family, if father and mother reverse their roles they may get a sense of each others' pain and feelings of worthlessness. The children can get Sharon's insecurity and anger.

Alter–Ego Technique

A sometimes effective device is to have you, the therapist, sit next to an individual in the family and as members address him/her, to speak for that person. You can say things about his/her feelings, his/her perceptions in relationship to the family. You can say things he/she would not dare to disclose, or you may stir things up within him/her so that this member is motivated to take over the task and communicate more freely with the family. This technique requires a great deal of sensitivity and skill. You may not want to use it in your beginning work with families, but be aware of its usefulness as you continue your family practice.

Improving Communication

To work toward improving communication, have two members of the family sit facing each other, and while looking at each other, describe what they would like from each other. Fred might say to John, "I wish you would take me with you sometimes when you visit your friends," or "I wish you would just toss a ball or a frisbee with me sometimes."

Get the group to practice speaking openly and honestly, even if critically, without fear of retaliation. Urge the family to practice this at home and to give you some feedback as to the success or failure.

Positive Reframing

Positive reframing helps an individual look at situations in a more positive light by ascribing a positive underlying meaning and motivation to the individual's behavior and communication. Also implied in the concept of reframing is the belief that people have the resources required to make the desired positive changes in attitudes. For example, when Mrs. Miller says to Fred, who stays in the house a great deal, "You should go out and play ball with the other kids," you can rephrase what she is saying by saying to her, "It is really important to you that Fred have friends and enjoy himself with them." Or when Mr. Miller complains, "Sharon is out running around with that lousy bunch of hoodlums half the week," you may respond with, "You would be happier if Sharon were doing something worthwhile."

This method reinforces the positive aspect of the individual's perspective. Have the family devise statements in the session using this technique. The family can continue this as a game when it is at home. Thus, it may become incorporated into its attitudinal system. To get the family started you may provide an example, such as instead of thinking of a bottle as being half empty, try thinking of it as half full.

Another intervention technique is to consider with the family what it will do when the identified patient is "cured." What will the family talk about? What will it do with all the time and energy that had previously been consumed through involvement with that family member? By doing this, you challenge the family to look at itself. In a sense you are telling the family a number of things—they may have a problem with being successful, and once Sharon is "well," mother and father may have to deal with their own problems, although for many reasons they would prefer to focus on Sharon or John. When the parents are faced with each other and Sharon is no longer the scapegoat, the realization that they may have to look at and work on their own relationship produces fear and tension. At this time the couple may need your attention and support.

It often happens that as the identified patient improves, the marital dyad begins to have problems. Deep-seated covert problems emerge, and the parents are in conflict with each other. They begin to talk more openly of father's alcoholism and mother's use of her diabetic condition to manipulate and threaten, and underlying all of this is the long-term anger the spouses have had toward each other. Often the couple talks of separation or divorce. At this time you need to watch the patient, to make sure that she does not regress to her former symptom-bearing state to rescue her parents and to keep the family together. For Sharon that would be drug taking; for John, drinking and truancy. This is an example of the concept of the family addiction cycle, reported earlier by Stanton et al. (1982).

As you help the marital dyad work on its relationship, you reinforce Sharon's newfound stability by offering her more visits and by involving her in support systems that will help her maintain her new identity. There is also concern around John, also a symptom bearer. He needs to be helped in individuating from the family. In a way, one can look at his distancing himself from the family as an attempt to stay out of the enmeshment in the dysfunctional family system (to avoid involvement in the parents' relationship problems).

More should be said about the role of the therapist in the sessions. As therapy continues and you see that you are successful in effecting some new interactional patterns, begin to extricate yourself from the family system by becoming less active. Support the family in its ability to mobilize itself towards the desired changes by validating, confirming and supporting its transactions. When you reassure the family that it can accomplish its goals by itself, the family becomes less dependent upon you as a therapist. If the contract called for 12 sessions, keep to that. However, as you get closer to the end, if you and the family feel more time is needed, you may renegotiate the contract and add more sessions.

When the goals have been accomplished, the parents have a more satisfactory marital relationship, and the identified patient is drug free and beginning to function independently, has a job or is going to school, it is time for termination. Arrange with the family for follow-up sessions, possibly once a month for several months, according to what appears to be needed. This plan will help maintain the gains made in therapy. It acts as an aftercare reinforcement and as a precautionary measure if you consider that the old patterns of interaction may resurface.

Summary of the Miller Family Therapy

We shall now undertake a more detailed look at each therapy session with the Miller family and attempt to recapitulate briefly some of the family dynamics and show the highlights of the process of the work with this family. The following summaries may serve to give you some idea of the sequence of events and interactions as well as some of the strategies employed by the therapist.

Session 1. The family came in for the first session. The group consisted of Mr. and Mrs. Miller, Sharon, John, Fred, Billy, and the grandparents, Mr. and Mrs. Nelson. They were greeted, there was some general conversation as the therapist got acquainted with the family. The therapist observed and experienced the family's patterns of interaction and joined the family system by blending into the style and pace of the family. The therapist empathized with the members who were experiencing pain and frustration as they discussed the problem and moved to the goal-setting and interactional (enactment) stages.

The therapist followed the communication paths and tried from the beginning to work out strategies for restructuring. The therapist supported Sharon in her rage against father's manner of ignoring her. Then the therapist moved to support the father when he described his feelings as being an "outsider," because "she [Mrs. M.] cares only for her parents."

The therapist asked Sharon to change seats with father, to move father next to his wife. Sharon was told to call Billy over to her. Grandmother, who was sitting next to Mrs. M., was told to sit next to her husband. When Mrs. M. turned to the therapist to explain the situation, she was advised to turn toward her husband, to look at him, and tell him what she wanted to say. There was an attempt at beginning communications between a couple that hardly had anything to say to each other. They were given the task of continuing to talk to each other at home. John, who is never at home, was asked to see that they did their homework.

The grandparents were told by the therapist that she recognized their concern and their importance to the family. Thus, the therapist was trying to tighten the boundaries around this subgroup in a tactful way. She asked the grandparents if they could be called upon in future sessions to offer their help. They agreed and were told that they did not have to come to the next session.

Since it was important that Sharon get off drugs as soon as possible, she was told to make an appointment with the drug counselor. After the contract was made, the family left.

Session 2. The Millers were back without the grandparents. The feedback regarding the homework was that John checked on his parents from time to time about talking to each other until father told him to stop bugging him; but when John went out of the house, Mr. M. would manage to say a few words, usually starting as a complaint, but then it would change to something about "the guys at work." After a few days communication was a little bit better.

Sharon reported that she had met with the drug counselor who wanted her to go through a detoxification process at the hospital. She was frightened because her friends had told her of the withdrawal symptoms, of possible diarrhea, vomiting, flulike joint pains, etc. In order to disengage Sharon from her enmeshment with mother, and to strengthen her bond with father, the therapist put father in charge. He was to drive Sharon to the hospital and take her home. The therapist made herself available to the family in case of crisis. This method of putting the father in charge is an example of a principle presented earlier by Stanton et al. (1982) in which the rationale for putting the distant or the disengaged parent in charge of the identified patient was discussed.

Session 3. Sharon was there without Billy or the grandparents. Mr. M. talked more freely to Sharon. Mrs. M. complained that her role as a mother had been usurped by the husband and accused the therapist of being in a coalition against her. Therapist then supported Mrs. M. by empathizing with her feelings, but told her that she needed to think of herself, and that the work around Sharon's detoxification from drugs was too much for her to do, both physically and emotionally. Mr. M. helped the therapist by adding, "She would have gone to pieces having to take care of Sharon." The therapist told Mr. M. to sit next to his wife, look at her and tell her that. (The therapist could have explored with Mrs. M. why she felt threatened in her mother role, but chose instead to avoid this issue and to use a "structural" maneuver as a shortcut.)

Sharon protested that the family was too involved with her, and she wished they'd stop treating her "like a kid." "I'm seventeen and a mother," she said.

The family was told to continue efforts at improving communication at home and for Sharon to start thinking about and making plans for herself and Billy.

Session 4. Sharon talked again of her drug-free condition. Mrs. Miller accused her husband of doing more drinking than before, and they began to argue. John supported his mother in her accusations. It began to appear that John was getting into the spot that Sharon was in the process of vacating, namely a tighter relationship with mother. Around this time, Mr. M. threatened to leave therapy. He wanted the therapist to know that they came in originally for Sharon to "kick the habit." "Okay," he says. "We can work out our own problems now. I always said that once Sharon got off drugs, everything would be all right." The therapist saw this as an avoidance tactic, as Mr. M.—threatened by the family's confronting him on his drinking problem—tried to blame the drug addiction for all the family problems and thus to free the family from further work toward restructuring family interaction. The therapist needed to support Sharon so she would not regress to her former role as symptom bearer, even though John showed evidence of becoming a good successor. The therapist was constantly trying to reframe Sharon as a strong and self-sufficient individual. On the other hand, the therapist had to use skill in keeping the marriage from collapsing and to help Mr. Miller recognize that the alcohol problem must be dealt with. The therapist scheduled a separate marital session with the parents. This was partly for the purpose of reestablishing the generational boundaries and for strengthening the marital relationship.

Session with marital dyad. In this session Mr. M.'s alcoholism was addressed. He used much denial, saying he could stop it any time he wanted to. He talked of his wife's involvement with her mother. "They have no use for me," he said. "I knew it all from the very beginning. It was all right for a little while, but then we had to move across the street from them, and from then on, for fifteen years, everything went downhill."

He finally said he'd go to A.A. just to show both Mrs. M. and the therapist that he wants to help the family stay together. He would let the people at A.A. tell him that he doesn't need to come, because they'll see he doesn't have a problem, and doesn't belong there! But he then said he would go only if Mrs. M. went to Alanon. This was a good suggestion, because with this maneuver, Mrs. M. was thrown into an activity she did without her mother, and thus, it loosened her bond to her mother and tightened her relationship with her husband.

Session 5. At this family session the Miller family reported that Mr. M. went to A.A. Mrs. M. had not yet gone to Alanon, but she had met a woman who would take her to the next meeting. Mr. M. insisted he still did not need to go to A.A., denying his problem, but said he'd go for a while and "check it out." Mr. M. revealed the fact that his mother-in-law had been coming around more than ever, "snooping around" to find out what's going on. Mrs. M., resenting this statement, got into an argument with him saying her mother had done more for the family than he ever had. Sharon got into the conflict yelling, "Just when I'm doing better you all start fighting. I thought you were all acting nuts because of me. I didn't do drugs for two weeks, and you're getting into all kinds of fights." Father threatened to leave, and then Sharon said she would leave home. Mother rushed to Sharon to assure here that if anyone left the home, it would be Mr. M. The therapist told Sharon to be quiet and allow her parents to handle this particular issue themselves.

Session 6. Although the therapist tried to avoid it, Sharon did go out with her friends and took some drugs. She showed lots of remorse and shame. She said she felt she let everyone down, especially the therapist. She talked about a compulsion to take drugs, and her father admitted that in drinking he also had this compulsion. This similarity between alcohol and drug addiction seemed to tighten the bond between Sharon and Mr. M. Sharon promised not to slip again, but she had promised before. Fred disclosed that last week John had been staying away from home more than ever.

The family cyclic pattern was evident in this sequence of behavior: the adolescent improved, the father threatened to leave, John's problems escalated; but when Sharon's behavior regressed the parents could find a way to stay together. (All the reasons for why this happens are not yet clear). The therapist continued to try to restructure the family pattern.

Session 7. The grandmother, Mrs. Nelson, had been asked to come to this session. It was evident that she was a dominant force in this family. She sat as in the first session with Sharon and Mrs. M. on either side of her. She was asked to change seats with Mr. M. When she talked, she addressed the therapist and explained what members were saying. She needed to be told to allow them to explain their statements themselves. She also tended to interrupt. When Mr. M. talked she looked to one side and smiled as if she didn't believe what he was saying. Her nonverbal method of communication was readily picked up and adopted by Mrs. M.

When Mr. M. touched upon his reasons for isolating himself from his in-laws, the therapist told him to turn to Mrs. Nelson and tell her. Mrs. Nelson was asked to look back at Mr. M. The family laughed at this maneuver, as these two reluctantly complied.

Mr. M., in the safe haven of the agency, disclosed many of the things he had not been able to say to Mrs. Nelson. He told her she was always meddling in his family's affairs and she had undercut his role. When Mrs. M. rushed in to talk for her mother, the therapist blocked her. Mrs. Nelson could not understand his anger, defending her actions by saying she had always been very helpful to the family. Wasn't she always there when her daughter was sick? Didn't she take care of the children when her daughter was in the hospital? She got angry and threatened never to enter their house again.

This threat severed any embryonic bond that was developing between the marital couple, as Mrs. M. went into an alliance with Mrs. Nelson saying that if Mr. M. kept her mother away, she'd rather have him leave. The therapist got into an alliance with Mrs. Nelson who protested *she* wasn't going to be instrumental in breaking up the marriage. Therapist wondered if they could work out some way whereby all could remain living where they were, learning to get along with each other, etc. Both Mrs. M. and her mother decided to visit each other four times a week instead of seeing each other every day.

Session 8. At this session, the entire family was present with grandmother. Therapist had thanked grandmother for her help and cooperation and made a point of inviting her to this session. Omitting her after the outburst at the previous session would constitute a rejection and a banishment from the family. Grandfather had not been asked to come since he was not well and also considered the entire family therapy experience "foolish."

The family had abided by the task assignment that mother and grandmother cut down the frequency of their visits in each others' homes. Grandmother rationalized by saying she was able to get more work done. Mrs. M. agreed that it also gave her more time. When she mentioned that she used to go grocery shopping with her mother just about every day, the therapist asked if Mr. M. could take her once or twice a week. Mr. M. agreed to do so.

Session 9. Grandmother was not present at this meeting. Mr. and Mrs. M. reported that they had been going to the A.A. meetings, and Mrs. M. had started going to Alanon and had met an old friend there. She was now beginning to associate with other women and giving up her isolation and total enmeshment with her mother. Sharon talked of job hunting and the need to have her own apartment. She was encouraged to pursue some job and housing leads. She wondered if she would be able to carry out these plans because of Billy.

Session 10. As Sharon began to move toward independence the reality of having to care for Billy became overwhelming. She told the therapist and family of her insecurity as a mother. She even blamed them for doing so much for Billy and not allowing her to take responsibility. She was reminded by the family that she could not blame them for shirking her duties. Therapist wondered if there were alternatives until Sharon got settled. She had been accepted by a halfway house that would not take Billy. If she were to wait until she could find and afford an apartment, it might take much longer, and one of the goals was for Sharon to move away from the nuclear family. Since Sharon had no job skills and was still very young, plans would need to be made for her to obtain public assistance.

Mrs. M. disclosed plans she had made with her mother to take Billy into her home and take care of him until Sharon was in a position to resume custody of him. This was based on the notion grandmother had that Mr. M. did not like Billy, and with Sharon out of the house, would not want Billy there. Whereupon, in a dramatic surprise move, Mr. M. voiced his opposition to that plan. Billy was theirs, he said. He was the son of his daughter, and he should remain with them while Sharon was in the halfway house. He stretched his arm toward Billy who came over to him and sat on his lap. This act so overwhelmed the therapist and the family that there were no homework tasks that week.

Session 11. The entire family was present at this session. Billy played with a little car near Mr. M. and Fred. The therapist said that she noticed an easier relationship between Mr. M. and Freddy. Fred thought it was because Mr. M. wasn't as angry as he used to be when he was drinking, so everyone was more relaxed, and so was he. The therapist was able to observe that a change in the structure in one section of the family brought about changes in other relationships. Sharon said she was glad that her father expressed his love for Billy. It made her feel much better, and she walked over to him and kissed him.

This display of emotion gave Fred courage to say that one thing he had hoped would happen but didn't was that John would be friendlier to him and more like the big brothers of other kids he knew. John said he'd often thought of taking Fred with him, but Fred was a tattler and John couldn't trust him. He was afraid he'd tell stories about him at home. Mrs. M.

jumped to Fred's defense, but the therapist cautioned her to let Fred and John straighten this out. John said he'd give Fred another chance and would take him along sometimes. The boys looked at each other and laughed self-consciously.

Session 12. This was the final session. Sharon was ready to move out. Billy seemed to like the idea of staying on with his grandparents. Fred had gone for a car ride with John and met one of his girlfriends. The parents will continue with A.A., and Mr. M. has stopped drinking. There were still many arguments, and the therapist told them to consider marital counseling. They said they would think it over and contact the agency when they decide. The family and therapist planned to have three follow-up sessions, once a month.

Three months later. After three months Sharon still lived in the halfway house. She was still drug-free and was getting involved with new friends. She looked back at her experiences with her substance-abusing friends as a thing of the past. Sharon worked as a waitress and hoped to go to school with the help of the Vocational Rehabilitation Agency.

Mrs. M. had abandoned the plan to see her mother only four days a week and was back to daily visits. Strangely enough however, Mr. M. did not complain about it. (Possibly, having been supported by the therapy to assert himself and to express his resentment of his mother-in-law's domination of his family, he no longer felt so threatened by his wife's excessively close relationship to her mother). The Millers still hadn't decided about marital counseling and said they'd learned enough in the sessions "for Sharon" that they thought they could do it themselves. They were still taking care of Billy, and with Sharon out of the house, found it less of a chore.

Six months later. The therapist phoned the Millers. She was told that John's school grades had improved. His relationship with Freddy was much friendlier. The Millers still argued, and sometimes Mr. M. drank, but not as often as before. The grandmother was as powerful as ever, and Mrs. M. wanted the therapist to know that now Mr. M. crosses the street to her parents' house and sometimes even sits on the porch with them!

The Miller family record may sound like a success story. Perhaps it has a happier ending than most. Yet one cannot overlook the hard work on the part of the therapist and a motivated family. And because of some important changes, both attitudinal and structural, the prognosis for this family is good. The older children, by this time, have left the home and hopefully will not repeat the dysfunctional patterns of their nuclear family.

We hope this chapter has given you an idea of some of the principles of the structural type of family therapy and a glimpse into the application of structural methods to the family treatment of a substance-abusing adolescent and her family.

Various Kinds of Families

The Miller family presented in this chapter is an involved family with a configuration of a two-parent family with four generational subsystems: grandparents, parents, children, and grandchild. However, there are many other kinds of families that come to an agency for treatment such as: (1) an adolescent with only one parent; (2) an adolescent in a foster home; (3) an adolescent in a group home; and (4) an adolescent in a halfway home.

There are numerous other combinations or constellations, but the basic concepts of structural family therapy and its strategies can still be employed to a greater or lesser extent. You may need to bring in significant others who are not living with the client at the time. You may find yourself more involved, in such a case, and will need to take an active part in exploring network strategies. You may have to help the client find support systems in the community. However, at all times be on guard against being manipulated, by your client or by your own excessive need to rescue, to arrange things that the client can arrange for himself/herself. Encourage him/her to get out into the community in an effort to learn to relate to others besides you, the therapist, and try to help this client to broaden the base of social contacts in a drug-free world.

A Review of Your Role As a Therapist

What are the essential aspects of your role as an effective therapist? You listen carefully, but your role is an active one. You are always on the alert, observing, listening, and planning strategies for effective interventions that may bring about a change in the family interaction. Consider yourself a change agent entering this experience with a conviction that you are helping a family that is in pain, a family that blames a member for its problems, and is unaware of its role in creating or maintaining the family problems or in scapegoating. You see each family as unique, with its own history, value systems, predispositions, aspirations, and conflicts.

Like a stage director you work with the family. You may arrange seating patterns. You may ask a family to reenact an argument that took place at home, or in role play you assign parts to be played. To be an effective director you need to win the confidence and acceptance of the family, otherwise the members will not follow your direction and instructions, and you will lose them. You "join" the family at the empathy level, but you also stand aside and look at it objectively. You are in and out of the family system so you can see it in all its dimensions, and as the family improves, you gradually withdraw from the active guiding role so it can begin to work independent of your guidance, and you prepare that family for termination of the treatment relationship.

The following guidelines may be of help in summarizing your role.

1. Respect the hierarchal structure in the family.
2. Listen to what is being said and not said.
3. Don't interrupt.
4. Watch nonverbal behavior closely, as a basis for understanding family relationships and for intervening.
5. Give equal attention to each member.
6. Do not minimize problems to the family.
7. Empathize with the family issues.
8. Be nonjudgmental so family feels free to discuss problems without fear of censure.
9. Establish communication patterns early in therapy.
10. Be aware of your own biases (and countertransference tendencies).
11. Be flexible enough to shift your approach if you find that it is not working.
12. Do not give advice, only suggestions as they fit the plan of operation.
13. Do not allow yourself to be triangled or manipulated. *You* are the leader.
14. Evaluate each individual in terms of depression, self-pity, self-esteem, tendency to project blame, etc.
15. When you sense the family feels it has failed, attempt to bring up past successful experiences as reinforcement.
16. Become a role model to the family.
17. Allow the family to see you as a person who can make mistakes and own up to them. Allow them to see you as a person with feelings.
18. Try to have a purpose and reason for all your actions or lack of action. (This might be too much to expect of a beginning therapist.)
19. Do not copy another therapist's style. Be yourself. Act in a manner that is comfortable to you and fits your personality.
20. Your role is to provide options for the family to select and pursue. You plant a seed for positive growth that will enable the therapeutic process to bring about a change.

Terminology Used in Family Therapy

Alliance—When two or more members of a family share either an interest, an attitude, or a set of values.

Alter-ego—To assume another's ego and talk for her/him.

Boundary—Invisible lines drawn in a family group that govern the way family subsystems work; the rules that determine who participates and how in any particular kind of family behavior.

Coalition—Members of a family joined in action against another family member.

Conjoint family therapy—Therapist meets with entire family regularly for therapy sessions and focuses on interaction patterns.

Contract—Agreement made between therapist and family.

Directives—Therapist-given directions, either directly or implicitly through nonverbal communications.

Double binds—Contradictory messages that tend to confuse, such as messages to both perform an act and not do it.

Dyad—Two members of a family who are involved in a relationship with one another.

Dynamics—The underlying tendencies, motivations, and psychological determinants of family interaction patterns and family conflicts.

Family life cycles—Critical stages of the human and family life span such as birth, starting school, graduation, unemployment, marriage, divorce, and death.

Family myths—Beliefs or attitudes held by principal members of the family, constructed by family about itself, and usually transmitted from one generation to the next.

Family network—All significant members of the family system, including extended family, friends, and significant others.

Family system—Overall structure and pattern of operation of the family: rules, roles, values, beliefs, expectations, needs, desires, emotional patterns, etc.

Genogram—Diagram of the family geneology.

Homeostatis—An established family equilibrium to ensure a relatively stable family environment.

Identified patient—The symptom bearer of the family illness.

Intervention—An action, statement or strategy used by the therapist to reach therapeutic goals.

Joining—Therapist entering into the family system to work effectively within the family. Therapist observes, validates, confirms, and supports the family's behavior.

Maintenance—Supporting the family system; an aspect of joining.

Mapping—Using symbols to map family structure and planned changes. A blueprint for action.

Mimesis—Technique where therapist adapts the family's style of behavior to strengthen the therapist's alliance with the family.

Nuclear family—Current family as opposed to family of origin.

Positive reframing—Restate sentences to create a positive effect.

Role—Individual's function in the family.

Rules—Spoken and unspoken behavior patterns.

Scapegoat—Family member who takes it upon him/herself, or is designated by the family, to become the identified patient in the dysfunctioning family.

Subsystem—Part of the family, such as the parents, the siblings, or the grandparents.

Structure—Arrangement of family members with regard to power and control. Made up of subsystems with coalitions, alliances, and various patterns of interaction.

Symbiotic—A mutually reinforcing relationship between two persons who are dependent upon each other.

Syntonic—In harmony with.

Tracking—As aspect of the joining process: questions are asked to gather more information.

Transactional patterns—Patterns of relationships and interaction between two or more family members that are repeated and become part of the family system.

Triad—Three members of a family who are involved in a relationship with one another.

Triangulation—Process by which the therapist or another third person is manipulated to become involved in a problem between two family members.

Notes

Ackerman, N.W. 1970. *Family Therapy in Transition* (Boston, Mass.: Little-Brown).

Alexander, J., and B.V. Parsons. 1982. *Functional Family Therapy* (Monterey, Calif.: Brooks Cole).

Beels, C., and A. Ferber. 1972. What family therapists do. In Ferber, A., M. Mendelshohn, and A. Napier (eds.), *The Book of Family Therapy* (Boston, Mass.: Houghton Mifflin).

Bowen, M. 1978. *Family Therapy in Clinical Practice* (New York: Aronson).

Friedman, A.S., E. Pomerance, R. Sanders, Y. Santo, and A. Utada. 1980. The Structure and problems of the families of adolescent drug abusers. *Contemporary Drug Problems* 9 (3): 327–56.

Gurman, A., and D. Kniskern (eds.). 1981. *Handbook of Family Therapy* (New York: Brunner/Mazel).

Haley, J. 1976. *Problem Solving Therapy* (San Francisco, Calif.: Jossey-Bass).

Haley, J. 1980. *Leaving Home* (New York: McGraw-Hill).

Kaufman, E., and P. Kaufman. 1979. *Family Therapy of Drug and Alcohol Abuse* (New York: Gradner Press).

Kempler, W. 1971. Experimental psychotherapy with families. *Family Process* 7 (1): 88–99.

Kniskern, D.P., and J.R. Neill. 1981. From *Psyche System: The Evolving Theory of Carl Whitaker* (New York: Guilford Press).

Minuchin, S. 1974. *Families and Family Therapy* (Cambridge, Mass.: Harvard University Press).

National Institute on Drug Abuse. 1980. *Family Therapy: A Summary of Selected Literature*. Services Research Monograph Series. DHEW pub. no. (ADM) 80-944 (Rockville, Md.: U.S. Government Printing Office, The Institute).

Satir, V. 1964. *Conjoint Family Therapy: Agenda to Theory and Practice* (Palo Alto, Calif.: Science and Behavior Books).

Smart, R.G., and D. Fejer. 1979. Drug use among adolescents and their parents: Closing the generation gap in mood modification. *Abnormal Psychology* 2: 153–60.

Stanton, M.D., and T.C. Todd. 1981. Engaging resistant families. *Family Process* 20: 261–93.

Stanton, M.D., T.C. Todd. 1979. Structural family therapy with heroin addicts. In Kaufman, E., and P. Kaufman (eds.), *The Family Therapy of Drug and Alcohol Abusers* (New York: Gardner Press).

Stanton, M.D., T.C. Todd, and associates. 1982. *The Family Therapy of Drug Abuse and Addiction* (New York: Guilford Press).

Vasquez, J., E. Bermann, B. Wolper, and M. Liepman. 1979. *A systems approach to child abuse and substance abuse*. Paper presented at the Fourth Annual Conference on Child Abuse and Neglect, Los Angeles.

14

Three Responses to Frankel's Report on Structural Family Therapy and the "Miller" Case

M. Duncan Stanton
Dennis M. O'Reilly
Ross V. Speck

The editors of this book considered the case report in chapter 13 to be a good example of adherence to the structural model in the treatment of a family of an adolescent drug abuser. Accordingly, the editors thought it would be useful and of unique interest to have several acknowledged and nationally known family therapy experts to react to this case report and to comment on how they might have treated this family similarly or differently.

M. Duncan Stanton is nationally recognized in the family therapy field as an expert on the strategic and structural models of family therapy, and for the application of a family therapy method for treatment of drug abuse and addiction. He is also well known for his research on the systematic evaluation of the effectiveness of family therapy. His book *The Family Therapy of Drug Abuse and Addiction* (New York: Guilford Press, 1982) is probably the best-known publication to date in this field. In a chapter he coauthored with H. Charles Fishman and Bernice L. Rosman in that book he provides a rationale for using structural family therapy methods in treating families of adolescent drug abusers:

The desired result is to bolster the family hierarchy while increasing members' repertoires so that they can respond more appropriately both to developmental needs and the vicissitudes of life. . . . Movement toward differentiation between parents and the adolescent is taken only to the edge of the family's outer boundary. . . . The family is kept intact, and shifts are effected within the given composition. This dictates the predominant use of techniques that are more typically structural in nature (e.g., enactment, unbalancing), in line with the structural emphasis on the developmental process in families with younger offspring . . . Great importance is attached to getting parents to work together, reinforcing the family's generational hierarchy . . . the goal with adolescent abusers is to achieve an intact, in-the-home hierarchy that remains in place at the end of therapy. . . . Consequently, interventions more in line with structural than strategic methodology are appropriate. (pp. 340, 357)

The reaction and comments by Dennis M. Reilly are quite comprehensive and include observations about the possible effects of various structural intervention procedures that may be conducted, on both the drug-abusing adolescents and their families. Reilly also offers some useful additional areas that are worth considering for the therapy of families with drug-abusing members. He has published several papers on family therapy for adolescent drug abuse, including "Drug Abusing Families: Intrafamilial Dynamics and Brief Triphasic Treatment" (in E. Kaufman and P.N. Kaufman, eds., *Family Therapy of Drug and Alcohol Abuse* [New York: Gardner Press, 1979]).

Ross V. Speck, M.D., is one of the early pioneers in the development of family therapy, having started to conduct family therapy in 1959. He was a founding member of the Clinical School of Family and Marital Therapy of the Family Institute of Philadelphia. His unique contribution, however, for which he is better known, is the creation of the network therapy model, which is based on an expansion of the family therapy concept. The treatment unit for this network therapy includes not only the nuclear family but all available relatives, close friends, and other figures (such as the employer, clergyman, teacher) in the life of the symptomatic family members who are in a position to provide support and are concerned about the family. Included in his publications are *Family Networks* (with C.L. Attneave; New York: Pantheon Books, 1973), and *The New Families: Youth, Communes, and the Politics of Drugs* (New York: Basic Books, 1972).

Comments on Frankel's Structural Family Therapy Chapter

M. Duncan Stanton

In chapter 13, Frankel has provided us with a comprehensive explication of structural therapy and its application with adolescent substance abusers and their families. Many helpful hints for beginning therapists are described and then shown in action through a case example. The case is handled skillfully, and the rationale for the interventions is presented clearly. The chapter serves as a useful guide for those who would undertake treatment with problems of this sort.

I find very little with which to take issue in Frankel's chapter. There are, however, a few points at which I either (*a*) differ in emphasis from the author, or (*b*) believe there are advances in the field that could further facilitate the treatment efficacy. These advances are in the areas of the treatment contract, the use of enactment, the involvement of grandparents, and the inclusion of death and bereavement issues in therapy.

The Contract for Number of Sessions. Rather than contracting up front with a family for twelve sessions, I find it less intimidating to the members to start "smaller." Whereas I believe twelve sessions is a reasonable and usually adequate schedule, I prefer initially to get an agreement for three or four meetings. At the same time, I arrange with the family to recontract for more sessions when we reach that point if it "makes sense." This provides the family with a more chewable bite that is generally easier to commit to. It can also work as a positive reframe, especially if they expected to get hit with an obligation for what they might see as "long-term" therapy. It conveys the message, "You're not so bad (or sick), and we may only need a few sessions to get this situation under control."

Enactment. Regarding the assignment of family homework tasks, Frankel observes that "more often than not the family will not adequately implement" such tasks. It is my experience that when this occurs it is commonly because the therapist did not bring about, in the session, an enactment of the pattern that the task is meant to establish. For instance, if a therapist wants a mother and daughter to spend more time together, the therapist must help them have a successful discussion within the session. If the first enactment attempt fails, it should be practiced again until it occurs without, for example, being detoured by another family member.

Such enactment may take the form of actually walking through the task in the session to see if it will hold up, and also to see who else might interfere with it. The point is that if the therapist helps to bring about the actual task experience in the session, it has a much greater chance of being carried out at home. If it is not enacted, the family members will be faced with having to initiate a totally new pattern on their own at home. For a family beset by such difficult problems as chemical dependency, the likelihood of their doing it on their own, without enactment, is even less.

Involvement of Grandparents. I was pleased and impressed by Frankel's inclusion of the maternal grandparents in the therapy of the Miller family. This was certainly important in the successful outcome that occurred with the case. However, this could be carried even further (Stanton and Landau-Stanton 1989). I would have wanted also to engage Mr. Miller's parents— the paternal grandparents—in the treatment. As I have stated elsewhere (Stanton 1981), adult alcoholics are often closely involved with their families of origin, and I would not be surprised if Mr. Miller were no exception. I would wonder in what ways, and to what degree, his parents (or the people who raised him) were involved both with him and with other family members, such as his children and grandchildren.

Pursuing this topic further, it is my preference when initially meeting a family, first to introduce myself to, and attempt to join, the most senior family member present. This might be a grandparent or even a great-grandparent. Such a tack honors the senior person's position in the family and is a subtle way of reinforcing the natural family hierarchy. Further, if I wish to have a senior member and a younger family member sit next to each other, and possibly converse, I would be very hesitant to move the elder person from his or her chair. Rather, I would ask the younger person to sit next to the elder. Asking someone to move from his or her seat has the effect of at least momentarily lowering that person's status in the group. If you are trying to elevate senior members, or at least support them in their proper position, you work against yourself by asking them to get up and seat themselves closer to someone else.

In terms of the treatment of the Miller family, there are two areas, in particular, in which I differ with the author. First, I would never have let the maternal grandfather "get away" so easily. For one thing, he was needed for his wife to turn to when she was being pressured to emancipate her daughter (Mrs. Miller). At the very least, the grandfather could have been telephoned from each session to get his opinion and blessing (along with the maternal grandmother's) about the decisions and tasks that were emerging in the session. I would also have made a greater effort to reenlist his expertise by trying to get him to return to the meetings. Not to make this effort would be to collude with the family in their idea that fathers aren't important and are to be excluded. While Frankel readily and aptly challenged the "useless father" idea in the nuclear family, I do not think she took it far enough in her handling of the extended family.

The second intervention that I would question was the task required of John, the son, that he keep tabs on his parents and report to the therapist on their progress—in a sense, serving as their evaluator. This move can introduce more problems than it solves. John was put in the terribly difficult position of overseeing his parents—the people who rightfully should have been overseeing him. He was thus given responsibility without authority—a predicament that any business manager knows minimally spells frustration and commonly can result in disaster. More to the point, however, it worked to overturn the family hierarchy in a family that was already having trouble maintaining an even keel. Further, if John acquiesced with the therapist and conscientiously reported on his parents, it could be expected that he would feel guilty. This might result in his later undoing his actions in some way, so that the net result would be no change. On the other hand, if the overseer's task were given to the *parents* of the parents—that is, John's grandparents—the task might have a better chance of being realized. Here is another example where grandparents can be incorporated into the treatment in such a way that the chances of success are enhanced (Boszormenyi-Nagy and Spark 1973; Landau-Stanton et al., in press).

Death and Bereavement Issues. As a number of colleagues and I have asserted (Coleman and Stanton 1978; Reilly 1975; Stanton 1977; Stanton and Coleman 1980), families of drug abusers are often upset by unexpected deaths and losses to which they have had difficulty adjusting. Although such issues are not touched upon in the Miller case, I would suspect that they are present. If I were treating the family, I would at least make some inquiries, perhaps while developing their genogram with them, as to who in the family died, when, and from what. Possibly nothing significant would turn up, but if so, the Miller family would be an exception. On the other hand, if important events of this sort are identified, they may need to be dealt with in order to ensure more complete and lasting improvement in both the index patient and the family.

A Response to Frankel's Report on Structural Family Therapy and the Miller Case

Dennis M. Reilly

It is possible to conceptualize drug dependence as a symptom of family system dysfunction, as a defect in the normal family process of adolescent separation and autonomy formation. To use a metaphor drawn from the space age, the drug abuser is unable to reach the "escape velocity" required to successfully overcome "family gravity" and leave the "home planet." A failure has occurred in the family's launching sequence and the identified client's drug abuse represents a "held countdown," "scrubbed mission" or "aborted launch." The drug abuser just cannot seem to achieve either the speed or the altitude necessary to break the invisible but powerful bonds tethering him to his family. He or she cannot "leave home"—at least not for long—emotionally, and often physically. Either he seems fated to "self-destruct on takeoff" or else he slips into a retrograde or decaying orbit, spiraling closer and closer, until he makes a fiery and frictional reentry into his family's atmosphere (Reilly 1984).

Frankel's case report on the Miller family, along with its description of structural family interventions, is an excellent introduction to family therapy with drug-abusing systems. The guidelines around engaging reluctant family members, empathizing with the family, proceeding at family's own pace, "joining" the system, and reaching out to all family members, especially the seemingly "peripheral" or isolated ones, represent valuable advice to a beginning family therapist. They are consistent with my own approach, as are the techniques of carefully observing nonverbal interactions, helping the family to set realistic change-oriented goals, widening the focus from the "symptom-bearer" to the whole family, and task-setting and "homework" assignments.

The importance of helping family members develop clear generational and subsystem boundaries is made clear in this chapter, and it cannot be overemphasized. These are families that are usually characterized by lack of consistent parental limit setting; by massive parental denial (even in the face of flagrant and dramatic exhibition of drug abuse symptoms and behaviors by the identified client); and by vicarious parental behavior in which parents gain covert gratification from their children's acting out. The children serve as impulse-ridden surrogates, as "foxy proxies," or "chips off the old block," on "secret missions" for their parents (Reilly 1975, 1979, 1984).

Children may be parentified or otherwise cast in inappropriate roles. The drug abuser may be delegated to "save" the parental marriage by distracting from marital conflicts or by regulating the marital homeostasis—his "problem" alternately allows parents to move toward or away from each other in a constant recalibration of spousal distance. Thus, delineating and strengthening appropriate subsystem boundaries becomes a vital part of therapy.

The author's emphasis upon "setting a time frame," perhaps twelve sessions, is well placed. Setting a time limit helps to maintain focus and motivation, aids in specification of goals, and also confronts the family with separation issues. Since drug-abusing families are often permeated with themes that involve loss and its denial, blocked mourning, and impacted grief, a therapy that induces or "surfaces" separation issues via time limits is particularly appropriate (Reilly 1975, 1978.)

I would agree that positive reframing is a key intervention. In these families that are so often characterized by angry, negative, critical, and blaming interactions, and by an absence of positive reinforcement for desired behavior, attention can too often be secured only by "making trouble" or "having a crisis." The "squeaky wheel gets the oil," and negative behaviors are unwittingly reinforced. For these reasons, it is very important to teach the family to "emphasize the positive." In fact, as early as the first session, I make it a point not only to ask what changes does the family want (as does Frankel), but also what would they *not* want to change about their family. Frequently, families who arrive ready to lay blame and point accusing fingers can be taken off balance with a "surprising" question—what do they like about each other family member and about themselves? Instead of asking them to identify problems, I ask them how family interactions could be "improved, made even better." I interpret their taking the time and effort to come to the session as evidence of family loyalty and love. Expressions of anger and criticism are swiftly relabeled as expressions of concern and caring. The family is retrained to attend to positive behaviors and incremental improvements, to reinforce them with praise, attention, and other rewards.

Frankel's approach as described in this chapter, is very congruent with my own. These are only a few things that I would change, add, conceptualize, or do differently.

1. *The provision of individual sessions.* Frankel notes that it is "often useful to alternate individual sessions with family sessions. Adolescents frequently need some sessions apart from their families." I would simply add that parents or other siblings may also benefit from their own individual sessions. In fact, I typically tell families at the first session that how I will see them will be flexible from visit to visit—one time I might see one of the parents or siblings alone, the next the parents together, just the siblings, or some other combinations of the subsystems. Offering the possibility of individual sessions to everyone also helps to redefine the family as "patient" and not just the drug abuser.

2. *Family of origin data.* One thing I missed about Frankel's description of the Miller family was some information about the father Dick's own family of origin. We learn about Betty's parents, but not about his. Since family or origin experiences, both past and present, can have a major impact upon family of procreation roles, behaviors, attitudes, and relationships, this information would have been helpful.

3. *"Splitting" the therapy.* Frankel states in the description of the Miller case, "Since it was important that Sharon get off drugs as soon as possible, she was told to make an appointment with the drug counselor"—detoxification was felt to be necessary. I am quite sure that it was—however, while I know it is a common practice in many programs to split off "drug counseling" from "family therapy," I am not convinced it is the best approach. For one thing, providing the drug abuser with a second counselor tends to reinforce the family idea that he alone is the "sick one," that drug abuse is an individual personal failing unrelated to the family. Once two counselors are involved, the possibility inevitably exists that the identified client or family may triangle one against the other, thus replicating pathological patterns of family relationships. Assigning the drug abuser to a drug counselor may put off the family therapist from important firsthand information about emotional, cognitive, situational, and relational triggers or antecedents of drug abuse episodes or relapses, as well as consequences and sequelae of such lapses. My own preference would be to make the drug counseling part of the family therapy. Certainly, individual sessions could be provided by the family therapist to the abuser to focus on issues such as detox, relapse prevention,

and so forth, using cognitive and behavioral techniques like those described by Marlatt and Gordon (1985). These discussions could also be held within conjoint family therapy sessions, thus helping all family members to become more aware of family relapse "triggers," of the ways *other* family members may be themselves "self-medicating" or abusing substances of various sorts, and of the ways they can best help the identified patient forestall a relapse, achieve and maintain sobriety, and so on.

4. *Griefwork.* Since noting that many drug-abusing families are families in mourning who have never recovered from a series of emotional losses, I have found that it is often helpful to ask about family losses and deaths, especially in the parental and grandparental generations. It is important to identify the "ghosts" haunting the family since, through parental projections, identifications, displacements, and expectations, the identified patient has often become the family's "reincarnation" or revenant of a lost, ambivalently regarded loved one. The drug user serves as the family's "melancholy baby" or "mourning star," as their grief-bearer. Thus, it often helps to ask whom children are "named after" or "take after" in order to trace family identifications, and to help the family express previously blocked emotions, belatedly to complete their griefwork (Reilly 1975, 1978, 1979, 1984).

5. *Paradoxical interventions.* Just as I have found that straightforward directives, commonsense homework assignments, and structural interventions may need to be supplemented with "griefwork" in certain families, so too I have discovered that "noncommonsensical" or "paradoxical" interventions might be necessary with particularly noncompliant or "resistant" family systems that have not responded to the more usual therapeutic techniques. With these families, one may need paradoxically to "prescribe" symptoms, "restrain" change, direct the family to vary the symptom in some way, and so on. Several authors give excellent descriptions of their systemic approach, including DeShazer (1985, 1988); O'Hanlon and Wilk (1987); Seltzer (1986); Watzlawick, Weakland, and Fisch (1974); and Weeks and L'Abate (1982).

In summary, I found Frankel's exposition of a structural approach to family therapy with drug-abusing families to be an elegant, concise, intelligent, and creative description of the state of the art. It will be of great value, to everyone in the field, especially to beginners, who will benefit greatly from Frankel's helpful explanation of the role of the therapist.

Lillian Frankel's Response to the Comments of Dennis M. Reilly

I agree with a number of statements in Mr. Reilly's critique. I could have provided more information about Mr. Miller's background, his parents, siblings and significant others; although they did not seem to play an active role in his current family turmoil, as far as I know. I admit it would still be essential in understanding Dick . . . who he is, where he comes from, etc., and its place in shaping his current family functioning.

The suggestion that the therapist ask the family members what they would *not* want to change about the family is a very good strategy, and I shall use it when appropriate. Also, Mr. Reilly's mention of griefwork is highly significant. I use it frequently but did not feel it was pertinent to the Miller case as I described it.

Comments on Frankel's Structural Family Therapy Chapter

Ross V. Speck, M.D.

The author of this paper and the course of the family therapy attest to very positive results using the structural family therapy approach, of which Minuchin is the father. Much was accomplished in twelve weekly sessions.

An important point is made that with adolescent drug abusers, it is often useful to alternate individual sessions with family sessions to allow the adolescent some separate and private time with the therapist.

Sharon brings the family into treatment when she shoplifts, but her acting-out behaviors are a "sick role" assignment as she colludes with and is encouraged by her mother and grandmother. Substance abuse is a shared family psychopathology, and the father's alcoholism is probably more serious than Sharon's substance abuse.

I was a little incredulous that so much happened in every family therapy session and that it all occurred so logically and predictably. It was all too idyllic for me. I would have liked to see more of the negative aspects of the treatment. Although the chapter is primarily for beginning family therapists, if this is the standard model, I think the beginner would feel defeated when the families did not behave like this one.

Since the Miller family has four generations in close contact, and obviously many friends and acquaintances, a network therapy approach might have been used. This would involve assembling support systems for each family member: father's buddies, Sharon's friends, grandparent's friends, mother's neighbors and friends, and Freddy's friends. One large assembly with forty to fifty persons meeting in a home with three network team members who catalyze the energy inherent in a large group might be sufficient. A second meeting in two weeks' time would be possible. The goals would be essentially the same as were outlined for the Millers.

All beginning therapists model themselves after mentors and supervisors who can support them in finding their own style. Finally, family therapy is a complex process and should not be sugar-coated for the beginning family therapist.

Lillian Frankel's Response to the Comments of Ross V. Speck

I respect many of the things Dr. Speck has to say about Structural Family Therapy, but I believe he is under the impression that in my chapter I tried to portray the Miller family as a successful case. He suggests I "sugar-coated" it for beginning family therapists to use as a model. That was hardly my intention. I was attempting to highlight the dynamics of SFT by compressing them into the twelve-session period.

As I say in the first paragraph of Chapter 13, "Starting with the initial meeting with the family, we move through the various procedures in family assessment and planning, therapist roles and behaviors, task assignments, and other stages of intervention inherent in structural family therapy." Further down, in the second paragraph of the same page, I also say that the chapter "does not presume to teach the reader to become a therapist. Even if one reads all the material listed in the references, learning how to become a family therapist would require a considerable amount of experience in working with real families. Some of the concepts presented in this chapter, however, will help make that experience somewhat easier and more meaningful."

Now, why didn't I have more negative material? After all, as a therapist, I know that movement towards health does not happen easily and quickly.

The reason is I was dealing with two constraints; one was to show the workings of all the pertinent dynamics of SFT in twelve sessions. The other was a more practical one; it pertained to space. My assignment called for a certain number of words and pages. If I were to discuss all the times the Millers did not follow through on their assignments or did not appear, or when Sharon regressed, the manuscript would have been over fifty pages long, describing the activity (or lack of it) in not twelve sessions, but 120 sessions.

I opted for showing the sequence of more positive events and interactions. It was as if I were saying to the beginning therapist, "This is how it could go if you are successful and lucky."

Notes

Boszormenyi-Nagy, I., and G.M. Spark. 1973. *Invisible Loyalties* (New York: Harper and Row).

Coleman, S.B., and M.D. Stanton. 1978. The role of death in the addict family. *Journal of Marriage and Family Counseling* 4: 79–91.

De Shazer, S. 1985. *Keys to Solution in Brief Therapy* (New York: Norton).

———.1988. *Clues: Investigating Solutions in Brief Therapy* (New York: W.W. Norton & Co.).

Landau-Stanton, J., P. le Roux, S.M. McDaniel, S. Baldwin, S. Horowitz, and M.D. Stanton. In press. Grandma, grandpa, come help. In T.S. Nelson and T.S. Trepper (eds.), *101 Family Therapy Interventions* (New York: Haworth Press).

Marlatt, A., and J.R. Gordon (eds.), 1985. *Relapse Prevention* (New York: Guilford Press).

O'Hanlon, B., and J. Wilk. 1987. *Shifting Contexts—The Generation of Effective Psychotherapy* (New York: Guilford Press).

Reilly, D.M. 1975. Family factors in the etiology and treatment of youthful drug abuse. *Family Therapy* 2: 149–71.

———. 1978. Death propensity, dying, and bereavement: A family systems perspective. *Family Therapy* 5 (1): 35–55.

———. 1979. Drug-abusing families: Intrafamilial dynamics and brief triphasic treatment. In E. Kaufman, and P.N. Kaufman (eds.), *Family Therapy of Drug and Alcohol Abuse* (New York: Gardner Press).

———. 1984. Family therapy with adolescent drug abusers and their families: Defying gravity and achieving escape velocity. *Journal of Drug Issues* Spring: 381–91.

Seltzer, L.F. 1986. *Paradoxical Strategies in Psychotherapy: A Comprehensive Overview and Guidebook* (New York: Wiley).

Stanton, M.D. 1977. The addict as savior: Heroin, death, and the family. *Family Process* 16: 191–7.

———. 1981. Marital therapy from a structural/strategic viewpoint. In G.P. Sholevar (ed.), *The Handbook of Marriage and Marital Therapy* (Jamaica, N.Y.: S.P. Medical and Scientific Books).

Stanton, M.D., and S.B. Coleman. 1980. The participatory aspects of indirect self-destructive behavior: The addict family as a model. In N. Farberow (ed.), *The Many Faces of Suicide* (New York: McGraw-Hill).

Stanton, M.D., and J. Landau-Stanton. 1989. Therapy with families of adolescent substance abusers. In H. Milkman, and L. Sederer (eds.), *Treatment Choices for Alcoholism and Substance Abusers.* (Lexington, Mass.: Lexington Books).

Watzlawick, P., J. Weakland, and R. Fisch. 1974. Change: *Principles of Problem-Formation and Problem-Resolution* (New York: Norton).

Weeks, G.R., and L. L'Abate. 1982. *Paradoxical Psychotherapy: Theory and Practice with Individuals, Couples, and Families* (New York: Brunner/Mazel).

15

Working with Black Families on Drug Problems

Gemencina Reed
S.J. Marks

Editors' Comment: We introduce this chapter on the treatment by a black family therapist of two black families with the following series of quotes from a book published in 1970, *Black Ghetto Family in Therapy* (Sager, Brayboy, and Waxenberg). The issues and problems referred to are still as relevant today for most poor black families who come to family therapy. The problems for the success of the therapy are even more relevant if the family therapist is white rather than black:

> It is essential that the therapist know, and, more importantly, want to know the living conditions, cultural patterns, and value systems of the people he seeks to help. Certain areas of sensitivity require an understanding and tact that can come only from intimate knowledge of black people and their culture.
>
> Methods of engagement which are more deeply rooted in the patient's world, and which reflect his priorities rather than the therapist's, need to be developed. To accomplish these aims, we must move into the community and earn a place in it.
>
> It is clear that the alleviation of the mental ills of a population rests first on the remedying of the social ills of the nation. Similarly, the treatment of the psychic pains of an individual or a family cannot be divorced from treatment of the conditions in which they live.
>
> When we consider the scarcity of alternatives available to black lower-class families, we can better understand the psychological effects of their oppressive living conditions. There is no place to go and few possibilities to choose from. If inner psychology is to be altered, outer life must change.
>
> Being understood and appreciated is the keystone to many forms of therapy, with this as with any other population.
>
> In general, in work in ghetto areas, one need not be so much concerned with sweeping modifications of technique as with avoiding manifestations of racism.
>
> The white therapist finds that his daily efforts to practice in accordance with the tenets of his training are unsuccessful with patients whose first priorities are the pressing and immediate concerns of survival.

A special feature of this chapter is the presentation of a verbatim transcript from a session with a family, with process commentary by one of the co-authors of the chapter and co-editor of this book.

Personal Statement (Gemencina Reed)

I am a black woman family therapist who has treated both black and white families. I am middle-aged and have been married for thirty-five years. I have a son who is thirty-three. I have sixteen years experience working primarily with the West Philadelphia black community on drug abuse problems with individuals as well as their families. I am a graduate of the Family Institute of Philadelphia and have been a family therapist for over ten years.

As a native Philadelphian, I draw on my experience and knowledge of the city. This has been an asset in my work, allowing me to network contacts from the many familiar resources in the various communities to assist my clients with suggestions about necessary supportive services. This has proved to be helpful for many reasons. For example, if the basic needs of the person are not met, my use of family therapy, however expert, is futile. If a client comes to me hungry and homeless, he or she cannot concentrate on the issues of intrapsychic and interpersonal functioning.

Some of the black families trace their lineage back four or five generations in the Philadelphia area. These families have a sense of stability and family pride. They feel they are the community. In most cases, that community centers around the church and has done so for generations. But there are also other kinds of social activities, such as fraternity and sorority groups, civic organizations, the Urban League, the NAACP, and the Black Professional Women's Organization.

The black population has contributed to the culture of Philadelphia since colonial days. Black family members in this area all have a similar history of racism and slavery, as do blacks across the country. What is unique for Philadelphia blacks is the spiritual foundation that began here with the black church. The church played a significant role for blacks in Philadelphia. It represented all that was left of African tribal life and was the sole expression of the organized efforts of the slaves. The church acted as an extended family system of the black family in colonial days; this remains constant today. The church is part of the black family system. As a family therapist, I am acutely aware of this. I assess all aspects of the family system, how it works and how it fails. The black clientele I treat in the clinic comes from a wide range of socioeconomic classes, ranging from the indigent poor family to the upper middle classes. These groups are generally harmonious in the basics of their value systems. Black parents encourage their children to strive for higher education and a stable work situation.

I feel connected with the black families I treat, beyond the initial journey of shared skin pigmentation and shared social experiences. I also find that our individual similarities and differences compare and contrast as occurs within all races; for example, in working either with a black or white family, I find that each member within the family has a unique personality, and that this family has a unique history and system of relationships that is different from that of any other family I have known.

The dynamics of transference know no racial boundaries; this is equally true of my own countertransference issues. My entrance into families whose ethnic background is different is simple and direct. I state my ignorance and curiosity about their overt and covert differences from me. I note my intrusion and strangeness as an active participant in their family. They usually invite me in as part of their need for help in their pain and confusion. For instance, with a Jewish family I treated, I asked them to make me a member of the family; I said I wanted to know what it feels like to feel what they feel and think.

The Impact of Church on the Black Family

In early America, the church was the center of life, the remaining element of black people's former life. The church of the Free African Society, as early as 1791 in Philadelphia, helped regular religious exercises. At the end of the eighteenth century Philadelphia had three Negro churches, two of which were independent black churches. As reported by W.E.B. DuBois (1899), there were in 1813 six Negro churches in Philadelphia. The extraordinary number of black churches was not just for religious reasons, but was also an indication of the increasing intricacy of black social life and the center of group life. The black church served several functions; so far-reaching are these functions that its organization is almost political. Other functions included social intercourse and amusements, the setting of moral standards, and efforts for social betterment.

The black church historically has always been an integrated part of the community. In colonial times, the church was the only institution that blacks could call their own, since they were excluded from most of the white institutions; the white power structures were not running the black churches. It was one of the few institutions that whites permitted blacks to have because the church was the moral and ethical authority figure for the community. It has a history of providing social service and cultural activities, such as giving shelter to the homeless, clothing to the poor, day care to the working class, and education to the parishioners. Culturally, the church provided the forum for musical and theatrical expression. This was the circuit whereby the world renowned contralta Marian Anderson got her start.

Today the church still functions in a similar capacity; however, it is more sophisticated in its multidimensional social service and social advocacy. For instance, the Reverend Leon Sullivan created O.I.C. to fill a perceived need in the community. It is very important for a family therapist to know the resources that are available in the community. As noted earlier, the therapist needs to understand the context of the client in treatment. For many addicts, the church serves as the extended family system. It offers guidelines, structure, and familiarity. The returning to church accomplishes two things: it fills the void that was once occupied by drugs and begins a healing process between past and present association with church and family.

Some observations relevant to the issue of spirituality, church, and religion that I have made in my work with black families with substance abuse problems are (1) religious people or people who are active in the church and who use drugs and/or alcohol tend to leave the church, not go, or become inactive; they stray away because their deviant behavior causes them shame and embarrassment; and (2) when religious substance-use clients diminish or eliminate their chemical use, they sometimes return to the church; when they give up their deviant behavior, they're ready to go back to church. Both are usually conscious decisions. In one case, a thirty-three-year-old man appealed to his mother to help him return to the church as a factor in helping him give up his drug use. His mother took him to the minister of her church. The church was sanctified (a church where people testified in front of the whole congregation), and the minister invited the man up to the altar to get on his knees before everyone in the congregation and ask for forgiveness. The client was upset and balked. He felt his privacy or confidentiality was being breached. In discussing the situation afterward with his therapist, the client mentioned that as a child he was more accustomed to going to his grandmother's church (which she'd attended with him). The therapist suggested that the client go back to his grandmother's church. He called his grandmother, and she said she'd go back to the church with him, though she was ill. They attended church together, and he began replacing his drug use with religion.

Some Further Ethnic Considerations (by S.J. Marks)

The family therapist treating black families needs an awareness that ethnicity affects family dynamics, nodal family processes, and life cycle rituals, as well as treatment issues—what people present for treatment, how they use the treatment services, and how they use methods of problem resolution.

Ethnicity is a sense of commonality and a blend of qualities of communal support and day-to-day concern derived from networks of families and from community, people, or system. It seems to be an essential determinant of values, perceptions, needs, modes of continuity, and connection with the past, and there's usually a transgenerational emotional language or phraseology of the family and its ethnic community.

Descriptions of individual problems, dysfunctionality, and conflicts are affected by the norms and frames of reference of families and communities. Symptoms and definitions of sickness differ greatly among differing ethnic groups.

How are individuals and families referred to treatment? Who seeks help and how? What are the clients' attitudes toward the helpers or therapists? How does an "outsider" family therapist handle a black family's distrust? For example, if I (Jeff Marks, a white male therapist) am referred or approached by a black family, I first try to engage a black female therapist to be a cotherapist with me; the way we relate as cotherapists to each other in the session provides, it is hoped, a sensitive resonance and a "holding" environment for them and a model of interethnic relating to them. Second (whether I have a black cotherapist or not), I ask the black family's members how they feel about being treated by me, a therapist of different color and ethos, and I point out to them (when appropriate) the differences in ethnic influences. If the prior experiences of some members of a black family with white people have been negative, the chances are that their feelings toward a white therapist will probably also be negative. A white therapist working with such a black family would be best advised to discuss any possible generalized attitudes toward white persons as related to the history of discrimination and oppression in the United States. However, I would not introduce such a sensitive issue in the first session. In my view, addressing how generalized attitudes toward whites and how other aspects of the family's value system toward white people affects this treatment in an ongoing way will aid the treatment process.

To my way of thinking, the family therapist (of any differing ethnic origin) must not hesitate to ask direct, forthright, probing questions and to promote family expressiveness and family interaction. Still, the family therapist must respect others' privacy and reserve, while not siding with the maintenance of family secrets, distortions, and evasions. However, similar ethnic life experiences may contribute to countertransference; for example, a therapist with a similar ethnic background who hesitates to ask questions in a direct, forthright manner may very well be in collusion with the family's trouble and dysfunctionality.

Knowledge of and sensitivity toward ethnic factors helps explore the family context and environment. By exploring and asking ethnic questions, the family therapist frees him- or herself to know and relate to the values of others and to gain important family information. For example, what is *this* black family's attitude toward black ethnic groups and their values?

Enabling family members to discuss and explore their cultural identities helps each one develop a more personal understanding of the issues and problems in the family. Seeing the problems and issues develop in the family history helps decrease the family's anxiety about current aspects of hopelessness, stuckness, helplessness, despair, and confusion. It shows a larger context, a macrosystem.

Third, I can ask them, "What do I need to know about your culture to treat you effectively?" Here, one needs an awareness of one's own ethnocentricity and a clarity and directness in talking about one's ethos (to be able to face and discuss one's own biases) in order to meet each new family and each new session freshly. (My assumption here is that to be able to use the self as a tool in working with crosscultural families, the therapist needs an internal gyroscope [one factor of which is one's ethnic grounding, as well as one's theoretical orientation to therapy, aspects of one's personal self and one's integrity and ethical self] while listening to and responding to differing [and similar] aspects of family interaction).

Fourth, I ask them to have an experience with me (and me with them), and discuss and explore our experience (of likeness and difference) together and whether it's been useful or helpful to them, and then to decide mutually what treatment course to pursue (that is, whether to see me or to get another, possibly black, therapist). "Can you work with me (and who I am)?"

The therapist treating families of differing transcultural or ethnic heritage needs to promote an effective joining and a high quality of rapport to establish and maintain a positive therapeutic alliance. However, the ingredients for therapeutic relating do not necessarily lie in similar backgrounds. Rather, they reside in the therapist's capacities for a rich understanding of the variability of human life: capacities of curiosity about other people; flexibility and adaptability in terms of a multicultural perspective, receptivity, and responsiveness to feelings (especially negative feelings, like pain, anguish, sadness, hunger, fear, anxiety, frustration, despair, hopelessness, helplessness, and hatred); an awareness of stressful events (that include death, war, unemployment and job loss, physical and emotional abuse in the family, severe physical injury or disease, illiteracy and poor schooling, and divorce); and a capacity to doubt and be perplexed and not have all the right answers. From my view, a perceptive, sensitive, and compassionate therapist can work with religious, ethnic, and racial differences in families and affect their lives in constructive and helpful ways. In response, the family says, in effect, "We're glad we got with you, we're comfortable with you, we can work with you." As Harry Stack Sullivan said, "We are more simply human than otherwise."

Reed's Theoretical Approach with Substance Abuse Families

The foundation of my treatment approach is an integration of Murray Bowen's and James Framo's family therapy theories and techniques (Bowen 1978; Framo 1970) with a few innovations of my own. The use of the Bowen and Framo family treatment practices represents a historical and intergenerational approach to family systems. In my work, I find that while family exploration with drug-abusing clients in the traditional Bowen framework (that is, voyaging into family systems to gather factual information) often opened up new areas of search and discovery, I also found that Framo's family of origin therapy (that is, preparing for and bringing together all the pieces of the whole to gather more data, to clarify distortions, to enable me to experience firsthand the family members interacting with each other [and with me], to use their energy to start the healing process) was a great asset in having more lasting impact on the family system. While using the concept of coaching individual members of the family to journey back into the family, (as described by Bowen, 1978), to ask questions and obtain public and private information and family stories, I also keep the family in ongoing treatment and explore the object-relations (as in Framo's use of these concepts in marital family therapy) as they are played out in the current family situations. The differentiation level in the addict family is extremely low. Sometimes, the slightest hint of an "I" stance can cause emotional repercussions within the family system (that is, raise the anxiety level to a point of intolerableness or panic). Also, some addict families tend to function at an "emergency ward" pitch. The acting out, often overdosing, behavior of the addict tends to trigger constant family crises. The emotional face of these families often seems flat and crushed, anxious and waiting (for tragic announcements). The reality of overdosing is a continual and readily identifiable possibility that presents a "house on fire" atmosphere—a drama in which the forces of life and death are tensely opposed, a turning point where terrible personal destruction can take place, or, paradoxically, where an abrupt desire to sustain and learn about life may occur. To ignore the threat of the presenting problem would be foolish and counterproductive, just as to ignore the multigenerational patterns might lead to an inadvertent collusion with the family pathology. Hence, while the stage may be set for family exploration, the abatement of life-threatening and manipulative behavior—that is, drug use—must remain the primary goal, which cannot always allow the luxury of a prolonged multigenerational "Bowen journey" (Bowen 1978). To use some of Framo's methods, in my treatment of drug abuse, is to attend to the immediacy of the presenting problem and to expand the family process by having all family members present access their resources, thereby addressing both the short- and long-term issues and goals in a practical way (Framo 1970). I intervene by seeing couples, subgroups of the family (parents, grandparents, siblings, and intergenerational dyads and triads, such as mother-son, father-daughter, mother-daughter-son, father-daughter-son, and so on), and extended family members (cousins, aunts, uncles, significant peripheral people) at their earliest convenience. Seeing the whole and partial families or structure that emphasizes a concept of balance—if I talk more with a wife in one marital session, I'll balance it by talking more with the husband in another session—in an ongoing therapeutic way allows me to observe the communication patterns among family members, including body language, and the manner in which words are used. The families are able to talk openly about it (this in itself is a notable change—in most substance-abuse families, there's little genuine, honest conversation, especially of an emotional nature) and attempt to resolve their problems in a nonthreatening atmosphere. My seeing various family groupings on an ongoing basis is an extension, as I see it, of Framo's theory of significant meetings with the family of origin. I find that the more family members I involve, the more intensive and direct the interrelating becomes. My primary goal is to engage the family in the healing process (through slowly developing trust that's been lost between family members) in order to help the drug abusers in the family eliminate their chemical usage.

Another of my goals in these cases is to realign the generational boundaries, with the mother-father dyad made primary or enhanced (that is, with clearer and more understandable communication between the mother and father) and the parent-child dyads diminished or nurtured in new ways (that is, the father-son alliance emotionally strengthened, or the father taking charge of his son to provide adequate controls and limits that were previously missing). The primary motivating force in these cases is the drug abuse. Under the drug-abuse umbrella are a host of underlying intrapsychic and interpersonal problems, with drug abuse as both the symptomatology of and the pseudo- or false solution to these problems. I use family therapy as the treatment of choice and my primary intervention with substance abusers. I observe progress with the substance-abusers who stay in long-term family therapy with me, the remedy being antithetical to the "feel better fast" symptomatology. The progress includes the realignment and strengthening of generational boundaries and limit setting in the family, more open, direct, and effective communication among family members, and a decrease in, and in many cases a cessation of, the substance abuser's drug use.

The Lewes Family

The following case was a referral from a high school psychologist. The family was referred to our clinic because Mark Lewes was abusing cocaine.

Present in the first interview was Alice Lewes, a fifty-one-year-old black female, her son, Mark, seventeen years old and in his senior year in high school, and myself. Alice describes a series of events that led her to seek treatment for the family. She cited several changes in Mark's behavior: he had become very short-tempered with his sister; he appeared to forget things, then got angry when the situations were brought to his attention, such as his forgetting to do his share of chores around the house. The symptom that triggered her awareness that something was upset in Mark was his grades dropping from A + 's to C − 's; Mark had been an honor roll student since he was in the seventh grade. Alice said, with a slight sob in her voice, "I need help for my son, I am afraid I'm going to lose him." I asked Mark if he had any feelings about coming to the clinic. Did he think he had a drug problem? Mark said he felt he had a problem and he did want help. I could sense that the mother and son were anxious—neither knew what to expect from our first interview. I tried to allay their fears by first directly addressing the drug-abuse issue and then by inviting them to talk about their family history in terms of family membership and of family hungers and needs—how members coped with difficult emotional issues, and whether anyone else in the family used chemical substances. This reframing was my way of defocusing the emotionally charged subject of the index client's illegal substance abuse. The tone was calmer and more relaxed at the end of the session. Alice agreed to have Mark's father, Raymond (age fifty-four) come to the next session because she worked at night. She would call from work during her lunch break and in that way would participate in the session; by using a conference call all present (mother, father, index patient, and therapist) could hear and respond to each other.

The next several sessions with the Lewes family were devoted to helping Mark establish a schedule of his activities and how to use his time constructively. In these sessions, it became apparent that Mark wasn't a typical "problem child." He had gotten involved in cocaine use with some school acquaintances over a dare. Both parents felt they had given Mark too much freedom. Alice said, "He has too much unaccounted time; idle hands are the devil's workshop." The parents and Mark, with my encouragement, developed a structure for him (time for study, for chores, for recreation). I noticed that Mark tended not to voice his opinion if it was different from his mother's. After my probing, Mark expressed some negative feelings about not being able to measure up to his mother's standards. "I think my mom wants me to be like my Uncle Tom, a doctor; I'm not interested in being a doctor." I asked Mark what his interests were. Mark was hesitant, but finally he answered, speaking slowly, "I would really like to do what my Uncle Ben does—sell real estate." Alice said she didn't know Mark was interested in selling real estate. She was concerned about his continuing his education and acquiring stable employment. In my opinion, this was a part of the "black prince legacy" from Alice's family of origin. My sense of the role of male supremacy, as enacted between Alice and Mark, was that she was heavily invested in his achieving academic excellence. The women in this family push the men to succeed in school. The women inhibit or sacrifice their own academic endeavors to guide, direct, and support the men in theirs. I pointed out to the family the importance of talking together and of listening to each other (in terms of each person's academic desires). I coached Alice on how to listen to her son. I said, "He has an opinion of his own. Let's listen to what he has to say; you don't necessarily have to agree with it." I also coached the son on how to describe his feelings in more appropriate ways, to make his statements directly, honestly, and fully.

One of the issues in these early sessions was the influence of Mark's friends. The parents both were adamant about Mark's not associating with his school friends, because, they said, his friends were all involved in drugs. I asked Mark was it possible for him to avoid some of his peers and would this be a real problem for him to tell his friends, "I don't want to do drugs anymore." Mark said, "I don't think I could tell my friends that, at least not now." In our fourth session, Mark initiated the conversation by saying he had used drugs over the weekend. He said he wanted to tell me first before he told his parents, but he hadn't. (His beginning the session by stating his actions and taking responsibility for them was a small step in taking an "I" stance [and individuating himself].) Mark also stated that he could go only five days without using: "I really couldn't control the urge to get high, so I did cocaine; I had a strange reaction, my body was nervous all over. I got frightened, and it was a very strange feeling. I didn't want to come home. I did not want to face my parents. I felt so ashamed and scared." The parents said they and many other friends and relatives had spent half the weekend driving around searching for Mark; both Alice and Raymond said they feared the worst: that he would overdose and die. Mark had never stayed away from home before. Mark's behavior threatened the existing family structure and its process; he'd never before defied his parents. I scheduled an extended family session, including all the siblings and the two maternal uncles.

Alice, the mother, had told me previously that her two brothers wanted to be included in the treatment. In this session, the sixth, Mark's siblings voiced their concern about their brother's welfare. The fourteen-year-old twins, Joy and Joyce said, "We love you, and we don't want to lose you. Just stop using. We are afraid you will kill yourself." The two older sisters, Mary (twenty-three) and Elizabeth (twenty), also expressed their fears of losing their brother to drugs. At this point, I interjected that I felt Mark was really struggling with trying to control his drug urge. However, he was in a very difficult position. Drugs were being sold in school, making it impossible for Mark to avoid the presence of drugs. Also, the peer pressure to use drugs as part of the group was intense. I suggested to the family that I felt Mark might benefit from a residential rehabilitation treatment facility. I told the family my reasoning and clinical opinion: there was no control over the environment, and it was difficult at this point for Mark to say no to his desire to use and to the temptation and pressure of his peers. I also said that I find it difficult to treat cocaine users unless they're "dry" (abstinent). The family collectively discussed the financial problem of paying for the cost of the rehab treatment, and the two maternal uncles both responded with a substantial amount of money to help finance it. Following this session, Mark was admitted to the rehab program and stayed there for four months. Treatment (including three sessions with Mark's parents) continued at the rehab; I discontinued family therapy during this period. After returning home, Mark was drug free at that time (several urinalyses were taken to monitor his abstinence), and he graduated with his high school class.

The family then resumed family therapy to work mostly on issues other than Mark's drug use. The father was concerned that the mother's high expectations for Mark's education and career might constitute too much pressure, and he wanted Mark to be free to do what he wanted. The mother was cautious and overprotective of Mark; she was overconcerned and anxious. Father was ready to risk giving Mark permission to do what he wanted to do with his free time when he went out (mother wanted him to account for all his activities and time) but also to give him concrete responsibilities and restrictions (in terms of what was expected of Mark while living in the Leweses' home). Mother indicated that she had been disappointed and hurt by Mark since she learned that he was using drugs. She felt that he violated the understanding and trust they had between them. Theirs was a close relationship in which she depended on him for some emotional support and to assist her around the house. Mark was indecisive about his career and expressed some guilt about not winning a four-year scholarship to college. He said he was angry at himself for dropping out of the competition due to using drugs.

Nine sessions followed which only Mark and his parents attended and in which the following issues were worked on: Mark's school situation and his schedule for the summer, Mark's relationship with his mother, and how mother's preoccupation and concern for Mark interfered with and intruded into the Leweses' marriage (as well as the father's excluding himself from the marriage). (Mark was encouraged to speak directly when he disagreed with his mother and not clam up.) Mark also announced that he had found a full-time job working in a stationery store. The parents suggested that Mark pay (on a sliding-scale basis) for his therapy sessions (as well as save some of his money). Mark was ambivalent about continuing his education, partly as resistance to pressure he felt from his mother to do so. He considered permanent full-time employment. After some questioning from me and further discussion, Mark decided he wanted to go back to school but felt it would be too much of a financial burden for his family. His father reassured him on this: "If you show me that you are really trying, your mother and I will help you."

In one of the family sessions (following the nine sessions with Mark and his parents) when the four siblings were in attendance, the twins and Mary expressed concern that their mother had become tense. Also, they stated that the parents played favorites. Mark of course was mother's favorite, and Mary (who lives at home with her two-year-old son in the parents' home) was the father's favorite. All four of the sisters agreed that Mark and the twins were expected to do too much in the house and that Mary was not expected to do as much. I suggested the siblings draft a petition to present to the parents outlining their proposal for an equal division of tasks and responsibilities. The parents accepted this proposal; they did not accept the siblings' statement that they had favorites and were not fair.

The next four sessions were used for the process of separation and termination. We reviewed the treatment (and whether their goals were realized—whether they'd gotten what they came for), we discussed Mark's future plans, we talked about saying goodbye to each other (I to the family, they to me) and how we felt about our time together, and about how losses were experienced and mourned in the family. Mark had been accepted at the local community college and his parents were agreeable to his decision. He also worked and was able to pay about half of the cost of his tuition. Mark's parents kept the promise to him and paid the rest of the tuition. This family entered treatment because of Mark's cocaine use and the family members' fear that he would kill himself if he continued using drugs, that he would become so dysfunctional (because of his involvement with drugs) he would have to alter or discontinue his educational goals. Therapy was successful in that Mark stayed alive, maintained a drug-free status, and continued his education.

In my view, one of the key factors that predicted or influenced a positive result in this case was the support and resource of a strong, active family network system (including relatives and friends). Many of these network members belonged to the family's church and others were members of the father's fraternal order. This family could rely on a deep source of nurturance and care. Another factor was the family's willingness to engage in open and honest talk about the problematic issues—they talked about their feelings directly and forthrightly. A third factor was the family's perseverance and determination to continue treatment until it worked (though it went through several phases or aspects). They had a lot of faith in themselves and their religion; there was a spirituality they expressed in their persistence and in their words—"Something led us to you to be our therapist." There were a number of other issues in this family which I pointed out that could be explored in depth, but it was the family's choice to remain with the presenting problem. For example, there was emotional distancing between father and mother (father was only included when there was a family crisis and was usually outside the family's daily functioning); "the twins" were excluded and seen as *only* a mutually self-nurturing subgroup; communication went only through the mother (as a switchboard) and became confused and distorted; women were devalued and they devalued themselves in pushing the men forward (education was the way to economic or financial stability and security). It is my opinion that a family having a positive experience with family therapy (and the Leweses said that they had benefited from the treatment) will probably engage in therapy again if and when another problem surfaces.

Family Therapy Session: The Johnson Family conducted by Gemencina Reed (Process Commentary of the Session by Samuel Granick and S.J. Marks)

First Contacts with the Family

The index patient was Anthony, a twenty-one-year-old single black male. He was brought into the Westminster Clinic by his mother, Lillian, and his older sister, Mimi. During the initial intake session, Mimi did most of the talking, stating that Anthony had been violent at home early that day. He had attacked several of his siblings with a butcher knife, which resulted in Anthony's right hand being seriously cut. The family was seeking treatment for Anthony because they believed his drug use was causing him to act violently. When Anthony was questioned, he admitted using methamphetamines, cocaine, and alcohol quite heavily. He also expressed feelings that everyone in the household was out to get him. Anthony agreed to attend the Westminster Clinic twice a week for individual therapy sessions and once a week for family therapy. A treatment contract was agreed upon during the first interview (that is, the family would come in for therapy once a week). Five days after the client's first therapy session, the client was brought into the clinic again by Mimi and her younger sister, Mary. Anthony's right arm was in a cast. Both sisters were extremely upset, and Mimi once again acted as the spokesperson for the family. She described a violent situation that had occurred the previous evening at home. Anthony had started wielding the butcher knife and slashing at everyone in the house. Mimi requested that I help her place Anthony in a psychiatric hospital. I suggested instead of hospitalization that the whole family come in for treatment. Mimi agreed to have the mother and all the siblings at the next session.

In the first scheduled family therapy session, the family agreed to come in for a series of eight sessions at the end of which they would decide whether they wanted to continue with family treatment. The Johnson family maintained their contractual agreement of eight sessions. The mother and eight siblings attended the first two sessions (the family had nine siblings). At the fifth session, two of the siblings stated they could not return because of their work schedules. The remaining sessions were attended by the mother and seven siblings. At the eighth session, Mimi announced that the family would not be continuing the sessions but Anthony would continue in treatment. Evelyn, the oldest sibling, requested individual treatment. George stated he was thinking about therapy for himself. He asked Anthony if he could come to several sessions with him to work on their differences, to which Anthony agreed.

Anthony, the index patient, remained in treatment for one and a half years. His drug usage decreased from daily to once a week. He also found part-time employment in a restaurant. Though he was working, Anthony was arrested for disturbing the peace. He'd been involved in a fight in a neighborhood bar. Mimi paid Anthony's fine after he promised to register with an inpatient rehabilitation program for three months. Anthony registered in the program and stayed one week. (Note Anthony's indirect invitation for strong limits and boundaries.)

George started individual sessions four months after the family terminated. He remained in treatment for six months until he was sent to prison. Evelyn has remained in treatment and has started a differentiating process from her family of origin. She is actively working on maintaining her "I" stance within the family. Evelyn is still being seen once a week for individual sessions and once a week in a family session with her children as this chapter is being written.

Brief Description of the Johnson Family Composition

Parents. *The mother,* Lillian, is a fifty-four-year-old black female. She is the second of five siblings born to Evelyn and Donald Green. Lillian Green married Horace Johnson when she was seventeen years old. At the time of the couple's marriage, Lillian was three months pregnant. Lillian stopped school at the tenth grade. She's been occupied mostly as a housewife; she worked one year before the death of her husband as a nursing assistant. Lillian is an alcoholic. She has been hospitalized three times for depression, once for one month when she was six months pregnant with her third child, a second time when she was three moths pregnant with her fourth child, and a third time two years after the death of her husband.

The father, Horace Johnson, is deceased. He was a black male. He was forty-nine years of age when he died in 1968 of lung cancer. He was the second oldest of seven siblings born to Rose and Horace Johnson. He was raised by foster parents, Mr. and Mrs. Jelton. A family myth is that Horace's mother gave all her children away for a bottle of wine. Horace completed high school. He was a civil service employee with the federal government of the United States. He had no record of any psychiatric history. He was an alcoholic.

Siblings. Evelyn is a thirty-six-year-old black female. She has been divorced for ten years. Evelyn has two children: one by her husband, a girl, thirteen years old; and a son, sixteen years old, from a prior relationship. Evelyn maintains her own home. Evelyn stopped school at the tenth grade. She is presently obtaining her GED and taking a creative writing course at one of the local colleges. She works in a day care center owned by her sister, Mimi. Evelyn was hospitalized when she was thirteen years old for psychotic trauma as a result of a gang rape. She was seen by a psychiatrist for two years at a community mental health center. Evelyn has hypertension. She was addicted to cocaine, methamphetamine, and alcohol. She has been drug free for a year and a half.

Horace Jr., is a thirty-five-year-old black male. He has been divorced for nine years and has one child, a daughter. For the past six years, he has been involved in an interracial relationship. The couple has been living together for five years. Horace stopped school in the tenth grade. He was involved with gangs during his adolescent years. Horace is a tractor-trailer driver. He was treated beginning at the age of ten for five years by a child psychiatrist. He was involved in a gang fight which resulted in the death of a ten-year-old boy. A month after the separation from his wife, Horace shot himself in the right lung with a shotgun. He was then hospitalized for three months in a psychiatric hospital. He has cancer of the ear and neck. He abuses cocaine and morphine.

Mimi is a thirty-three-year-old black female. She is married and has three children, two boys and a girl. She lives with her husband and children. Mimi stopped school in the tenth grade. She is presently the co-owner of a day care nursery. Mimi has some neurological problems. She smokes marijuana and has abused diet pills.

Donald is a thirty-year-old black male. He has been involved in an interracial relationship for six years. The couple has two children, a girl and a boy. Donald has a B.S. degree in biology. He teaches in a GED program at one of the local colleges. Donald is a bisexual. He has been involved in some form of psychotherapy since he was ten years old. In his early twenties, Donald's stomach was slashed from side to side and he was hospitalized for abdominal surgery. He abuses cocaine.

George is twenty-eight years old, a black male. He has two children, a girl and a boy, from two different relationships. He lives at home with his mother. George stopped school in the tenth grade. He has worked for one year in the maintenance department of a local hospital. George suffers from physical problems resulting from an old stab wound in his chest. He abuses heroin, cocaine, and alcohol. He is a dealer/user.

Mary is a twenty-five-year-old black female. She is a single parent, the mother of four children. Mary lives at home with her mother. She stopped school in the tenth grade. Mary has worked one year in a summer youth program at age fifteen. She has no history of psychiatric treatment. She has a number of gynecological problems. She uses cocaine, methamphetamine, and alcohol.

Anthony, the index patient, is a twenty-one-year-old single black male. He has two children, girls, from two different relationships. He lives at home with his mother. Anthony stopped school in the tenth grade. He has never been employed. He abuses methamphetamine, cocaine, and alcohol. Anthony had no prior treatment until he came to this drug treatment program. Anthony continues to become involved in situations that result in various kinds of medical injuries, such as broken arms, jaw and stab wounds.

John is an eighteen-year-old black male. He lives with his mother. John stopped his education at the tenth grade. John has never been employed. He has no history of psychiatric problems. His physical health is good. He uses alcohol and methamphetamine.

Diane is a seventeen-year-old single black female. She is presently living with her mother at home. She stopped school at the tenth grade. Diane has never been employed. She has no history of psychiatric or medical problems. She uses methamphetamine and cocaine.

The Session

The following is a verbatim transcript of part of a family therapy session with the Johnson family. This session (the fourth in the series of eight family sessions) demonstrates the underlying themes of love, attachment, deprivation, and rage in this family system; it also makes clear that the family members have never gotten what they needed (the emotional nourishment and intellectual stimulation and challenge) in their lives. There is a three-generational history of emotional instability in the Johnson family.

The mother, Lillian, had just finished saying she never argued with her husband because

It wasn't any need to say anything, there was no win with him. He would say, "Shut up."

Mimi (daughter): How come he did not want to sit with us that time?

"Don't talk, don't express feelings" and "it's hopeless, nothing can be explored and resolved" messages in the family. (S.J.M.)

Mother (Lillian): Because he always had that superior damn attitude that he was better than anybody else.

Horace, Jr. (son): You know who else got that attitudes? (Nodding his head toward sister, Evelyn).

Attitudes passed along in multigenerational transmission process. (S.J.M.)

Lillian: (Nods in agreement) Right.

Therapist (Gemencina Reed): I seem to be hearing that your husband liked to wear nice clothes. Was he always dressed up and you weren't?

Therapist encouraging family members to talk about father and others so as to clarify family attitudes and systems of functioning. (S.G.)

Horace, Jr.: Shit, yes!

Lillian: Well, he bought things for himself, but most of my money went for the kids and housewares; sometimes a couple of housedresses for myself.

Therapist: Did you and your husband ever go out together, just the two of you without the children?

Therapist exploring and emphasizing the importance of the marital relation. (S.J.M.)

Lillian: One time, we went to someone's house for a party. A housewarming, and we had our picture taken. He took a picture with me once. He took a picture with them three or four fucking times.

Therapist: When you say them, who do you mean?

Lillian: People at the party. I guess I did not look good enough.

Mother's acute and angry sense of rejection. (S.J.M.)

Children: (Comments about their father— protecting him) He was all right.

Horace, Jr.: Yeah, you still upset about that shit?

Children: That his woman being [*sic*] there.

Lillian: You're right. He was no damn saint. You think he was a saint. He was a phoney.

Mother expresses her differing view of their father. (S.J.M.)

Horace, Jr.: He worked. He is a ladies' man.

Note the justifying attitude toward father's betrayal of the marriage and his role as husband and father in the family. (S.J.M.)

Therapist: When did you start drinking, Lillian?

Lillian: I started a month after he died.

Therapist: Can you talk a little about how you were feeling when he died?

Changing the subject so that mother will talk about

Lillian: Because (pause), I couldn't—just missed him. I couldn't deal with it.

Therapist: I have a hunch that you were very angry with your husband for leaving you with all these children he never let you take care of.

Lillian: Yes, I remember I went around to his house (pointing to Horace, Jr.). The little fucker. He would not let me in.

Horace, Jr.: Mimi would not let you in either.

Lillian: I wanted to talk. Then I came home and I called this ass up (turning toward daughter, Mimi). She hung up on me. She did not want to talk to me. She said, "Don't be calling me up when you're drunk." So I sat there for about an hour, I think. When I realized what was going on it was about four days later. He (pointing to Horace, Jr.) was standing over me. He took care of me—gave me coffee.

Therapist: How did you feel when your husband died? Can you put yourself back at the time of his death?

Lillian: I stay back there. (Long pause, voice starts to tremble.) I felt resentful because I knew it when he died and I used to tell him that, and he never listened to me. "You know if anything ever happened to you, I have no control over these kids at all." I felt like I should just leave them there and keep going about my business and just because there was never going to be no control, no respect, no nothing. So what I did, I just turned to drinking instead. And then, if they had any respect for

herself instead of attacking father and then having one of the children defend him. (S.G.)

Therapist moves to the difficult and core issue of handling of the death of the husband/father. This is suggestive of how all separations and losses are coped with in the family. (S.J.M.)

This elicits the ambivalence mother feels about father, which is probably a reflection of the ambivalence each family member has toward the other family members. (S.G.)

Holding on to the anger acts as a cork preventing the grief and mourning from being thoroughly expressed. (S.J.M.)

Mother's desire to express herself and how she allows herself to be thwarted in the family. (S.J.M.)

Therapist's intervention encourages mother to become aware of her varied feelings—anger, compassion, fear, sense of inadequacy, and so forth. The mother shows her need to run or escape from the realities of her life, sensing her inability to cope with them. (S.G.)

Therapist establishes herself as a "good hands" person (people can put themselves me they lost it totally when I started drinking 'cause I was bitching.

Horace, Jr.: Sho' was.

Lillian: I didn't care what I said to them.

Horace, Jr.: Sho' didn't.

Lillian: All my anger came out when I drank.

Therapist: Have you ever really cried about your husband's death?

Horace, Jr.: Yes, she embarrassed people.

Therapist: Have you, Lillian, ever really cried about your husband's death?

Horace, Jr.: Yep! (The oldest son continues to speak for mother, protecting her.)

Lillian: Yep. Sat in that empty damn house and I cried for two solid days and I didn't like being by myself. I stayed out in the street. If there was nobody there, it wasn't going to matter that much anyway. And that dumb Donald, he wouldn't stay home. He was in the streets. Donald was into school. He (Horace, Jr.) was home in his house. She (Mimi) was in her house. He (Horace, Jr.) didn't want me in his house when I was drinking. He didn't want me in his house at all. I didn't go to her house too much, but I knew she couldn't deal with it. And Evelyn, she met this guy . . . and they used to call me up on my job and he used to tell me, "Them kids don't know," used to tell me, "You ain't got no business keeping that money, the money should go to your oldest daughter. Who the hell do you think you are and . . ."

Horace, Jr.: Who told you that shit?

in her hands) and her environment as a nourishing ground on which a deep focusing can take place. (S.J.M.)

Mother's powerlessness in setting controls, limits, and boundaries. She turns to chemical solutions to soothe herself. (S.J.M.)

The mother shows her self-destructiveness, which also seems to be an important characteristic of virtually all the family members. (S.G.)

Therapist is encouraging the mother to work through her mourning reaction and depression over being abandoned by her husband. (S.G.)

Mother talks about her own and others' isolation in the family—their inability to grieve together. (S.J.M.)

Lillian: I went through so much changes at that time that the woman refused to let their calls go through on my job. I quit my job 'cause they were calling me too much.

Therapist: What kind of work did you do?

Lillian: I was doing, I like it too, it was working with old people.

Horace, Jr.: Geriatrics.

Lillian: Yes, I used to work at the Scott House. I liked that. I like, even though he said his wife wouldn't work. But when he got sick, then he comes to tell me, "You know, I think you should get a job and try to take care of yourself. You never know what's going to happen and you're going to have to find some way of taking care of yourself." So I found a job. He took me to my first job six o'clock in the morning. (Looking at Horace, Jr., and giggling.) (Laughter follows.) I didn't know how to get there. I didn't know how to go around the corner. Yes, I used to be the . . . I called myself; remember I got mad (turning her head first toward Horace, Jr., and then Mimi) one time and was running away from home and they found me (again she gestures toward Horace, Jr., and Mimi). I was still on the corner crying. Grown woman crying and I was about four blocks from home. (Everybody laughs.)

Therapist: I still think you've got a lot of anger about being kept a child; and you're still angry.

Lillian: I am. You see, if he had let me grow up maybe I could deal with be them, you know, the young ones, you know. I couldn't do a thing with them. Horace, Jr., I couldn't do a thing with him. I would cry all the all the time for him. And then when I went down and seen him laying in this dirty, filthy, soiled bleeding and went to the hospital and seen this one (pointing to George) with his face opened up, I just, you know . . . they don't know.

There's work mother derives gratification from—a positive aspect of her parental modeling. (S.J.M.)

We see how despite the anger and disorganization in the family there is much mutual caring and protectiveness. This is evident in many parts of this session. (S.G.)

Therapist persists and perseveres; this is also a model of how to persevere. (S.J.M.)

Anger and depression dominate this woman's feelings. The therapist encourages her to express and externalize them. (S.G.)

The mother feels contained, imprisoned in the context of her situation. She feels powerless and externalizes and blames; she hasn't

It's so much inside of me that . . . (Begins sobbing.)

Therapist: Let it out.

Horace, Jr.: Go ahead, he said relax. I wish you would.

Lillian: Just to see him laying there (referring to when Horace, Jr., attempted suicide—shot himself in the right lung with a shotgun); that opened me up. I love my children, but I just been sitting back so long that I couldn't deal with them. And another thing hurt me when I gave them to Mimi. It just tears me up.

Therapist: What tears you up about it?

Lillian: They don't want to hear it.

Mimi: I want to hear it, Mommy, I'm listening to you.

Horace, Jr.: Me too, you can say what you want to say.

Lillian: It just tears me up. (Sobbing.)

Therapist: Let it go.

Lillian: I wanted you. I wanted you with me. I needed you with me but I was drinking too damn much. I would drink from the time I got up in the morning to the time I go to bed at night. And I knew there was always someone there taking care of them. I knew that they needed more than just me sitting there, you know, there . . . alone.

Therapist: Go on; take your time.

Lillian: I love them and the trouble with them, they had such a stormy look on their damn faces, you know? I love them. I love them.

Therapist: Who has a stormy look on their face?

Lillian: Like those. Like, like Mimi. Like those (pointing to her children). And like Horace, Jr. I just want to hug them sometimes and tell them I love them. And I look at them and I say, "Oh, no!"

Therapist: Do you think you can hug them now, here, with me?

Lillian: No.

taken her power in her hands, until now—the therapist empowers her. (S.J.M.)

Mother talks about how the family violence affected her—the personal human consequences, how it feels, how it hurts. (S.J.M.)

Again the indication of caring and mutuality. (S.G.)

Mother takes personal responsibility for her drinking and her turning away from family members and abdicating her parental role. (S.J.M.)
The therapist's acceptance—letting the person in pain in the family (the one who's ready to handle it) take the time to express it fully and thoroughly. The technique of emotion—exposing the deep wounds. (S.J.M.)
Love and anger—a basic characteristic of this family's system of functioning. Much of the anger, moreover, is self-hatred. (S.G.)

Therapist: You want to try it? Horace, do you think you can go over and hug your mother and tell her that you understand that she loves you?

Horace, Jr.: I don't have to do it, it ain't no thang.

Therapist: Can you get up and go over and do it now?

Horace, Jr.: It ain't no thang, shit, ain't no problem she got . . . (Mixed laughter follows.)

Therapist: Can you go over and hug your mother?

Horace, Jr.: Huh! (Diane goes over and hugs and kisses the mother. Mary and Anthony follow, except for John.)

Therapist: George, can you go over and hug your mother and tell her that you understand and that you know she loves you?

George: Oh, I know she loves me.

Therapist: George, can you go over and hug your mother and tell her you understand and that she loves you?

George: Oh, I know she . . .

Therapist: I asked you, could you get up now and go over and hug her?

George: Yeah, I can get up and go over. (Inaudible conversation follows.)

Therapist: John, how about you? Can you hug Mom?

John: I hug Mom all the time.

Therapist: I'm asking, can you do it now and tell her?

John: Sure.

Therapist: I would like for you to do it. (Indecipherable mumbling.)

Horace, Jr.: That's the one that should be killed (points to his sister, Mimi). (Laughter followed by mixed conversation.)

Mimi: First of all, my old lady knows how I feel about her.

Therapist: I'm asking you right now, can you turn and hug your mom and say, "I know you love me. I understand a little bit of your pain"?

It is so difficult for them to show love directly, even with the therapist's encouragement. (S.G.)

The therapist challenges and confronts each child. (S.J.M.)

Horace, Jr.: Git it, Mimi.

Mimi: I ain't no affectionate person.

Therapist: I asked you, can you hug her?

Horace Jr.: If she was in the graveyard, you'd try to pull her ass out of the graveyard.

Mimi: I'm not an affectionate person. I try to keep my emotions and everything under control.

Therapist: I think you need to hug your mom.

Mimi: I always kiss my mother. (Mixed conversations, laughter.) You are always saying, "I won't let her in the house" (pointing to Horace, Jr.).

Horace, Jr.: Neither one of you can whip her (points to George and Anthony, who're making fun of Mimi). (Mimi turns to hug her mother. Lillian stands up to receive the embrace from Mimi.)

Mimi (mumbling): We do not agree all the time, but I love you.

Therapist: Why did she have to get up for Mimi?

Mimi: No particular reason.

Therapist: Mom, why did you feel you had to get up for Mimi? What did you feel then? Why did you feel that you had to stand up? You didn't do it for anybody else.

Horace, Jr.: She ain't gonna hit you.

Lillian: I felt that's what I had to do right then.

Therapist: Or were you standing up to your husband?

(Silence.)

Mimi: You know what, Mommy, she just hit on something, because you know why?

Therapist: Let your mother respond, Mimi.

Lillian: She got a lot of Horace in her (referring to her husband). She is dominating and she's stronger than I am and I don't think . . . I envy it. I could cuss at her and get mad at her when I am drinking. But there's something about her I can't fight completely. I would like to. I would like to tell her sometimes.

Continuation of family message—stuckness about expressing positive emotion. The protectiveness has to do with vulnerability, disappointment, and further hurt. (S.J.M.)

The therapist's directiveness; she uses herself, puts her values on the line; she's direct, forthright, and has established rapport with them. (S.J.M.)

Therapist is quite forceful and persistent in getting the family members to break through their inhibitions and be more realistic about expressing their feelings, especially love. Also, therapist encourages family members to try to be aware of what they feel and why they do things. These are ways of encouraging social-emotional maturation. (S.G.)

Therapist: But are you really fighting Mimi or are you fighting your husband who you never stood up to?

Lillian: Fighting what I see in her.

Therapist: Is it Mimi or your husband?

Lillian: Yes, I see him in her.

Therapist: Mimi is your daughter, not your husband.

Lillian: Yes, but she still has that stand back (Mother's voice starts to break), stand 'hind me attitude. She still has it. She has that attitude that she is better than anybody else. She is goody, goody, good-shoe. Like you don't come before me unless you come right. Don't lay with a man and can't be married to him. She's so damn arrogant. That attitude he use to use when (Mother starts to cry) . . .

Therapist: Come, let it out.

Lillian: She got it more than any of them.

Horace, Jr.: Yeah, he should have took her ass with him.

Mary: I know why.

Horace, Jr.: He did not talk to anybody but her.

Lillian: She has it so strong until, you got to understand Mimi. She's so damn critical. I love her but she's so damn critical.

Therapist: Are you angry with Mimi or are you angry at your husband?

Lillian: It's . . . I don't know, it's him.

Therapist: I would like to try something, Lillian.

Lillian: I'll try.

Therapist: I want everybody to be quiet please. I want you (to mother) to imagine that your husband is sitting in this chair. I want you to tell him all the things you never told him before. And then, I would like for you to reverse roles and be your husband and say what he would say to you. Try it. Take a little bit of time to put yourself into that role.

Lillian: What he'd say to me?

Therapist: Yes. First, I want you to say all

This intervention is to help the mother see and experience her daughter more realistically rather than in terms of her transference reaction in which she equates her daughter with her dead husband. (S.G.)

Son comments on holding on of father-daughter dyad. (S.J.M.)

Therapist stays tenacious and persistent. (S.J.M.)

This is known as the "empty chair" technique, a procedure used extensively by Gestalt therapists to address split-off or divided aspects of the self and to address aspects of absent members which have been introjected or taken in by self. This technique is often those things that you felt you'd like to say before when he told you to get behind him, and he'd get dressed up in his suit and look all dapper and go out and leave you home. Say what you feel. I don't care what you say. Just let it all out. Then I want you to switch roles and be your husband and say what you think he might have said to you.

Lillian: First, be myself—tell him everything I feel.

Therapist: Yes, take your time.

Lillian: You know what, Horace? You only married me 'cause you had to. If I had had any damn sense, I ain't going to let somebody talk me into this. I don't like you. I don't know why that damn woman told you to marry me 'cause I wasn't going to marry you. I didn't want to marry you. I ain't never wanted to marry you. Since everybody told you that I ain't got no sense and I'm stupid and I don't have no education. They act like you got to marry me. You don't have to marry me. I don't want your pity. I don't want to marry you. You don't love me. You just marrying me to give Evelyn a name. Damn it, she could have had anybody's name. She could have had any name. She don't need yours. It ain't no damn good anyway. It ain't nothing but a bunch of faggot-ass bitches in your family anyway. I hate you. I hate all of yous. Don't . . . why you . . . why did you do this? You got drunk on your marry night and you went out to West Philadelphia to hang with your other damn women; you didn't care about me. You took your money and bought furniture for other babies. You didn't care about mine. Then your ass just died. You should have died years ago, you didn't want me. And I don't want you. (Crying.) Old bastard. No-good bastard. You had women, had other kids. You just used me. You didn't want me. I was too dumb for you. I was a good thing. Your day will come. You'll get yours. I'll fix your ass. I don't want nothing

used as practice or rehearsal for preparing to deal with relationships where one person finds it difficult to begin to address the problematic issues directly to the other. (S.G. and S.J.M.)

Therapist uses mother as a role model for children. Therapist asks mother to speak as if her husband were present (addressing introject of him in herself, freeing up locked-in aspects of herself and her energy) to provide help in the family grieving process. (S.J.M.)

to do with you. Take and take your sex back in West Philly where the hell you been taking it. I don't need you. I don't need you. You phoney ass. You get in front of people and all your friends and act like you like me. You know you don't like me. You put on a front, dragging me out to that Annie Lawrence's house and make me look like an ass in front of all her friends and your damn friends too. You treated me like shit, Horace. Ah, big shit Horace, big shit Horace. You marble-head "motha-fucka." You never wanted me. You never wanted me one bit. Long as I lay up there and have kids like a slut, an old low-lifed cat, alley cat. You take your money out there and give it to them bitches out there like they're Miss Joe Hall. You never wanted me. Oh, I hate you. I hate you for this. Then, you're going to tell me I'm no good. Well, maybe I'm not no damn good, but I wouldn't have done the things to you that you done to me. But I'm going to fix you. I'm going to hurt your fucking pride since you got so damn much. I'm going to make your manhood look like shit. And I'm going to do it to you (crying). (Pause.)

Therapist: Can you switch and be your husband and say what you think he would have said to you? Be him—take a minute or two before starting.

Lillian: Huh, huh, yeah. Marry you? I'm on my way to California. You ain't no damn good, you're just a good thing. Since Ms. Lawrence insisted that's why I married you. Since she said you wouldn't be capable of taking care of them children, 'cause you didn't have enough education to raise a baby. You wouldn't even know how to make a formula. You're so dumb. That's all right, soon they'll be old enough to start doing for themselves. So they don't need you anyway. You ain't shit and you know it.

Therapist: Can you tell me how you feel right now?

Expressing an oppositional dialogue within herself—a step toward healing split-off parts of self. (S.J.M.)

This exercise has the desired effect of providing a cathar-

Lillian: I feel good on one hand and angry on the other.

Therapist: Who are you angry at?

Lillian: Me, for being so dumb. I gone 'head.

Therapist: What are you going ahead with?

Lillian: Having all these kids. I never should have married.

Therapist: When are you going to stop hurting yourself?

Lillian: I'm going to stop. I should have been stopped. Shoulda stopped the day he died. I guess that's the reason I went off drinking. He loved his kids, but he didn't give a damn about me, though. They never knew it. He's a good fronter. Mimi worshipped the ground he walked on. Oh, he fronted for them like mad. I'm sorry to let you know he was no angel.

Mimi: I don't want to hear it.

Therapist: Why can't you hear it, Mimi?

Mimi: I don't want to talk about it.

Therapist: Why don't you want to talk about it?

Mimi: Just like she said, I worshipped the ground my father walked on. He was the most important thing to me and can't nobody in this room say nothing to me about him.

Therapist: Mimi, can you try to understand—your mother is talking about her relationship with your father.

Mimi: If that's the case, then that means that the childhood that I remember wasn't there.

Horace, Jr.: It wasn't.

Mimi: It ain't gone—fuck you, Horace. I ain't dealing with that shit.

Horace, Jr.: The truth is, it wasn't there.

Lillian: We couldn't sit down there and discuss how we actually detest each other in front of you kids.

Mimi: You mean to tell me you all weren't happy?

sis for the mother and of enabling her to be more realistic—to be more in touch with her emotions. (S.G.)

Therapist encourages self-respect and caring for herself, being a "good-enough mother" (in Winnicott's phrase) to herself. (S.G. and S.J.M.)

Mimi shows her escapist tendency but it's challenged by the therapist, so that she may try to be more mature. (S.G.)

Horace, Jr., in his way, also tries to help Mimi be more realistic. (S.G.) Horace, Jr.'s experience was different from Mimi's. (S.J.M.) Lillian acknowledges no open talk in the family. (S.J.M.)

Lillian: No! Where did he ever take me, Mimi?

Mimi: Nowhere.

Lillian: I was damn near thirty the first time I ever went to Atlantic City. Thirty years old, Mimi.

Mimi: I know, when I took you.

Lillian: I should have been to those places. I was only seventeen, Mimi, when I married him.

Mimi: You don't wait for no man to do nothing for you.

Lillian: In them days, when I was coming up, you did.

Therapist: Mimi, maybe you saw what you wanted to see. Sometimes, when things are very painful when we are children, we make them the way we want them to be.

Lillian: We didn't make it hard for you kids.

Mimi: I don't want it destroyed.

Lillian: And another thing, how can we destroy something between you and your father, when you did it yourself?

Mimi: Why, by getting pregnant?

Lillian: Yes.

Mimi: He forgave me for that. You know what, you know what that man said to me? I was the only one that he allowed to sit on his chair. He said that he was going to take care of me.

Horace, Jr.: He didn't though, did he? He scared the shit out of you. He didn't even tell you he was dying. He told me and begged me not to tell anyone. He made me promise to tell his other children when he died. Wanted me to see that they got to the funeral. You knew, Mimi, 'cause I told you.

Mimi: I knew.

Lillian: He would have took care of you. I know it. You and all the rest of them. And you know what, if he had lived, we wouldn't have

Mimi begins to realize others' experience in the family wasn't the same as hers; each person's experience in the family is different; her father and their father were different (though the same person); hence, the importance of sharing experiences of the family openly and directly. (S.J.M.)

What Mimi's learned from the family about taking her life in her own hands—she has to be active in getting what she wants. (S.J.M.)

Helping the family to separate early childhood wishful thinking from adult realities. (S.G.)

Repetition of like actions in next generation—teenage daughter getting pregnant (imitating mother's behavior). (S.J.M.)

been together because you all is grown, could
do for yourself.

    Therapist: Mimi, can you bring yourself to
try to have some of your mother's feelings
about her relationship with your father?

*Therapist making a contin-
ued effort to be empathic
and realistic. (S.G.)*

    Mimi: Yeah, but I still don't want my
memories destroyed.

*Therapist succeeds in part.
(S.G.)*

A Theoretical Note

This family fits some aspects of a pathological family system as described
by Claus Bahne Bahnson (1979). The parents and the three older children
regressed somatically and became ill physically under stress (a centrifugal
interactional pattern); there were invisible emotional walls and distance
between these family members. The younger children regress behaviorally
under stress (a centripetal pattern); here, between these family members,
individual barriers were low or nonexistent, and people overlapped with and
represented each other. The older generation and older children of the family
had internalizing, rather than externalizing, tendencies (that is, they were
withdrawn, introverted, and self-punitive in areas of medical sickness and
illness). The younger children of the family express an externalizing process
in which they act out their inner conflicts and problems through accidents,
illegal behavior, drug abuse, and acts of violence. There is a high probability
that the younger children will gravitate toward a more internalizing process.

Current Family Process

In the six-month period after the family sessions, almost every member of
the Johnson family had medical problems that required some form of
hospitalization. The family system appears to be plagued by somatic
symptoms and substance use behavior patterns that are psychologically
contagious and transmitted down the generations.

    A year after family treatment, within a three-month period, Lillian was
hospitalized twice. Both incidents were the result of her attempts to prevent
acts of violence between her children. Before the first hospitalization, Lillian
had a heart attack while trying to stop Anthony, John, and Diane from
fighting (they were all swinging bats at each other). After Lillian was
stabilized from this heart attack, the medical staff recommended that she be
transferred to the psychiatric unit in the hospital. One week after Lillian
was transferred, Mimi encouraged her mother to sign herself out of the
hospital against the advice of the medical staff. Mimi objected to the

hospital's rules about patients taking care of their personal needs—that is, making their beds and washing their clothes.

Two months later, in June 1985, Lillian's second hospitalization occurred while she was trying to stop Donald and Anthony from slashing each other with knives. Lillian had a stroke and remained in a coma for fourteen days.

During Lillian's first hospitalization, Mimi enrolled Anthony in an inpatient drug rehabilitation program. She felt Anthony was creating all the problems in the family because of his drug use.

Mimi herself was hospitalized in May 1985 because her doctor felt she was suffering from physical and mental exhaustion due to family problems.

In June, Horace Jr., announced he was discontinuing his radiation treatment for cancer. While Lillian was in a coma, Horace, Jr., threatened to kill his mother and himself. He told doctors and family members, "Mom and I both need to be taken out of our misery." The doctors referred Horace, Jr., to a staff psychiatrist, who hospitalized him for two weeks.

Mary was hospitalized in July for gynecological problems. Also, in late July, two weeks after Lillian came home from the hospital, Diane announced to the family that she was three months pregnant. She aborted spontaneously a week later because of untreated venereal disease.

In August, the three youngest Johnson children—Anthony, John, and Diane—started terrorizing their neighborhood, by verbally abusing people, breaking into homes and stealing radios, TVs, and stereos. Anthony was arrested for breaking into a variety store. Evelyn started complaining of chest pain (which the doctor stated was the result of emotional stress), and her blood pressure rose uncontrollably.

Therapeutic Interventions and Limitations

The first therapeutic intervention was to engage the entire family in the treatment process. The whole family was involved in negotiating the treatment goals and the treatment plans. This process allowed the therapist to observe the interaction between family members, which gave her a chance to gain a diagnostic picture of the family and the index patient.

Violence in the Johnson household among the younger siblings was the reason the family sought treatment. In treatment with this family, I initially assumed the task of controlling and limiting the physical fighting (as a kind of superparent) because the violence seemed to be escalating. The intervention used was a behavioral task with a paradoxical intent. I told the younger Johnson siblings it was all right to fight as long as they fought in a constructive, nonviolent way. I suggested that the family fights be scheduled at a certain time each day. Another function of the suggestion was to lessen the anxiety in the family system. Another intervention I used in the therapy was the Gestalt technique described in the verbatim transcript. I felt that if

Lillian could express some of her anger toward her husband with other family members present (to witness her release of anger in a responsible and therapeutic manner, and to resonate to their own anger), perhaps she could begin to function in the role of mother of the family.

Fighting among the Johnson family siblings had stopped by the end of the series of eight sessions, and for the first time in six months Lillian started to take control of her household. She came in for individual sessions several times after the family sessions to work on her parenting skills. The two young Johnson children started attending school regularly, as well as helping with chores around the house. The family system remained relatively calm for six months.

It was difficult working with the Johnsons—they were volatile and violent. However, I suggested that family treatment continue, but they declined to continue as a family. Mimi sabotaged her mother's continuing individual treatment with me. As far as I can tell, both Mimi and Lillian were afraid of further treatment revelations—that the actuality of their lives (both past and present) was too painful for them because of the possibility of old wounds and hurts being reopened.

Concluding Comments on Ethical Issues

The pathology in the Johnson family was traced back three generations during family treatment. The possibility for constructive change in the family system at this time is, in my opinion, limited. The oldest sibling, Evelyn, remains in treatment and continues to struggle to maintain a differentiated "I" stance in the family.

When treating families whose ethnic background is different, family therapists need to probe in order to stimulate their own curiosity about different cultures and to address the differences openly and directly. When we begin treatment with families of different races, we ask them if they have any feeling about the therapist being of a different racial or ethnic background (that is, black or Jewish, as in regard to us, the authors). Important here is that we are candid about our ethnic differences, and if the issue of race or ethnicity (or gender, for that matter) does surface during the course of treatment, we have opened the door for discussion. We recommend that the family therapist state his or her ignorance and curiosity about the clients' cultural differences and ask the family to help the therapist understand these from their own perspective and experience. We believe even families of the same background and ethnic affiliation need to be treated in a respectful and sensitive manner. Despite their perceived similarities each family system is unique. Our natural tendency is to uncover the individuality of each system.

This serves the function of keeping us alert and interested while at the same time igniting family members' interest in their own family constellation.

Most important, all families need to feel the therapist's warmth, genuineness, caring, and concern for them in order for them to let the therapist into their private domain. Black families, like many other families, enter treatment with apprehensions, defensiveness, anxiety, guilt, and shame. They need acceptance, reassurance, and understanding to help them, hopefully, to begin their journey of wonder and healing, which starts the moment the family enters treatment, and, if treatment works, spans a lifetime.

Notes

Bahnson, C.B. 1979. Dying, death and the family. *Interaction* 2(3): 155–64.

Bowen, M. 1978. *Family Therapy in Clinical Practice*. New York: Jason Aronson.

DuBois, W.E.B. 1889 (Reprinted in 1973). *The Philadelphia Negro: A Social Study* (New York: Schocken Books).

Framo, J. 1970. Symptoms from a family transactional viewpoint. In N.W. Ackerman and J. Leib, eds., *Family Therapy in Transition*. Boston: Little Brown.

Sager, C.J., T.L. Brayboy, and B.R. Waxenberg. 1970. *Black Ghetto Family in Therapy: A Laboratory Experience*. New York: Grove Press.

Additional Bibliography on Black History and Culture

DuBois, W.E.B. 1903 (Reprinted in 1986). *The Souls of Black Folk*. Chicago: McClurg.

Foley, V.D., 1975. Family therapy with black, disadvantaged families: Some observations on roles, communication and technique. *Journal of Marriage and Family Counseling* 1: 29–38.

Franklin, J.H. 1948. *From Slavery to Freedom*. New York: Knopf.

Franklin-Boyd, N. 1989. *Black Families in Therapy: A Multisystem Approach*. New York: Guilford Press.

Frazier, E.F. 1966. *The Negro Family in the United States*. Chicago: University of Chicago Press.

Frazier, F.F. 1963. *The Negro Church in America*. New York: Schocken Books.

Harding, V. 1981. *There Is a River*. New York: Harcourt Brace Jovanovich.

McGoldrick, M., J.K. Pearce, and J. Giordano. 1982. *Ethnicity and Family Therapy*. New York: Guilford Press.

16

I Am The Stranger Who Takes Their Lives Seriously

S.J. Marks

Introduction

My aim or intention, as I look back on it from a twelve-year perspective, in having the Gray family in was to have a series of experiences together that would be lively and mutually adventurous: to touch on unknown and unspoken of areas in the family and in me too; to promote a more honest, direct, and deep communication among all of us; to gather and discuss information and hear the several different points of view expressed and be part of how they relate to each other; to provide a safe, secure, and nurturing holding ground where family members would be able to focus on serious, threatening, "toxic" concerns (and I'd be the "good hands people"); and to promote a process of struggle and exploration (though this had begun with Carol individually, I wanted to engage the whole family in this venture). I wanted to stay respectful of their journeys in life and challenging in problematic and conflictual areas.

First Contact

I was in my office. The phone rang; I picked it up. "Hello," I said. A female voice said, "I've just had a leg out an eighth-floor window, then I pulled it back in and called you." "Why don't you come on over and let's talk," I said. I ascertained who she was and where she was, told her who I was and where I was (Wurzel Clinic at Philadelphia Psychiatric Center), and how to get to me.

First Interviews

Carol came to treatment frightened, confused, upset, dependent on drugs (she was a polydrug abuser), and suicidal. She was nineteen, two weeks away from being twenty. She felt insecure in life and empty within herself. She wanted therapy kept secret from her parents (though I told her that family therapy was part of my best prescription for her); she concealed much of her current life from her parents: "What they don't know won't hurt them," "They know I smoke cigarettes, they don't know anything about pot," "They would kick my ass in," "I don't want to talk to them, I don't want to be close," "I would rather go crazy or die—I'd shoot myself— rather than talk to my folks," "I want no part of communication with them," "I felt depressed and suicidal and sad before I came here."

Carol said she was referred to the Philadelphia Psychiatric Center Drug Treatment Program by a friend who knew of it. She was single, working as a secretary at a nearby psychiatric hospital (evidently seeking help in some sort of sideways fashion, as if by osmosis; she never sought help there in a straightforward and direct way), and living with a female housemate. Carol was of English/Irish descent; her mother's ancestors came from Ireland and Scotland, and her father's side was Canadian (originally from the British Isles)—both sides were Protestant.

Since Carol was reluctant to and resistant to having her family in treatment immediately, I offered and suggested to her the following architecture of treatment services: individual psychotherapy twice a week, and group therapy once a week. At the Wurzel Clinic, the staff considered multimodalities to be the treatment of choice for drug abusers. During her twelve years in treatment in the clinic, Carol also used educational counseling and psychological testing, as well as twelve-hour marathon groups (approximately once every four months for the first five years of treatment). In addition, Carol and the Grays participated in the clinic's ten "Family Days" (a once-a-year event) in which patient families and staff families engaged in a shared day of therapeutic and play endeavor (in simulated therapy sessions and games), educational and scientific pursuits (in workshops and group discussions), and ate a lunch (to which each family contributed its special dishes) together.

Carol

Her Face

The skin was stretched tight across her cheeks; it was stiff like porcelain. It was a face open, flat, and unknowable. Occasionally, in the individual treatment sessions, I'd ask Carol to close her eyes and, without touching it, to become aware of the skin of her face (for a few minutes).

Her Breasts

Carol developed breasts at eight years. She said she "hated" her body when she was thirteen. In therapy, she said she mostly hated her breasts now, and she still would have preferred not to have such appendages. I said that was fine with me. In order to get her to accept that part of her being that she had split off from herself, I wondered if she were curious what her breasts felt like. I said if she was curious she could hate her breasts for twenty-three hours and fifty-five minutes a day and that she could touch her breasts for five minutes a day (for example, lying in bed just before sleep) and touch her breasts all over, experiencing what her breasts felt like to her hands and what her hands felt like feeling and exploring her breasts. I said that from my point of view the only way the exercise would be effective was if she did it diligently and consistently for many, many months or years.

The Dark Blue Overcoat

One winter evening, Carol came to an individual appointment in an enormous dark blue overcoat. It reached the floor. She sat down in it without unbuttoning it and looked at me intensely and angrily. (She may only have been angry that she had to reveal part of her body, but I was not sure what it was at the time.) The coat covered her entire body. "I can still see your hands and head," I said. She rammed her arms into her sleeves. "There's nothing I can do about my head," she snapped. "I happen to have a blue towel here," I said reaching over to pick it up from atop some books on my desk and handing it to her. She wrapped her head completely in the towel, put her arms back into the opposite sleeves, and proceeded to talk to me shrouded in blue.

Carol and Addiction

Over the years of treatment, I came to view Carol as a borderline personality masquerading as a drug abuser. Carol used anything—drugs, alcohol, sex, food, cigarettes, obsessive fantasies, work, study—to fill the emptiness inside her.

The rhythm of addiction, if it becomes coupled to anxiety of sufficient intensity, can be enough to hook and contain the addict. The process of lifestyle, or the sequence of activities involved in obtaining the drug and preparing to take the drug and the setting in which it is taken, can be addictive, in addition to the physiological effects of the drug itself. There's a craving for a certain schedule of sensation, as well as for the substance itself. Carol's cycle of searching for these sensations, together with the anxiety, risk, pain, and uncertainty, had a force that the chemicals themselves sometimes tend to lose.

I tried to replace this schedule of experiences with another that was challenging and stimulating in different ways. I was close to her feelings (without taking on the emotional burdens or responsibilities of them), and I confronted her forthrightly and directly to make her accountable and responsible for what she did in her life and how she was with me. In response, I was accountable to her, in that I shared with her my feelings about what she was saying and about our interaction.

Carol had a diffused sense of herself; she's lose herself in bad parts of the self—in drug use, soothing fantasies of being attached to other people, drinking, and so on. As Loren Crabtree says in "The Borderline Person as a Patient" (Unpublished paper: for copies write Loren Crabtree, Jr., M.D., 408 Dresher Rd., Horsham, PA 19044):

> For many borderline persons, the "good" self is the public self. And the "bad" self is the private self. The good self, the public self, is what you think I'm like. It's what I put effort into being and appearing. But this, to me, is my phony self. It's not really me! "For me, the bad self is the real me. I'm going to be private about it. I'm going to try to conceal my real self. It is my true self."

Carol experienced a split, confused world interpersonally; she externalized in her behavior the splits she'd internalized from the family: who was good, who was bad, who was good and bad, and what parts of them were good or bad.

Five Symptomatic Aspects of Carol's Character

1. The presence of a smoldering, intense affect.
   a. A suppressed anger, a seething fury.
   b. A depressed loneliness—a sense of futility and isolation.
   c. A detachment from what she described as what had happened to her and a muteness—not talking about what she'd experienced (a sullen, flat silence, despite a sense of deep woundedness, the hatred and confusion peering out of her eyes).
2. A history of impulsive behavior: extensive polydrug use, indiscriminate promiscuity, episodes of self-lacerating and self-destructive behavior.
3. A seemingly socially adaptive surface (good achievement in school, though this was deteriorating—she'd dropped out of music school; appropriate appearance, though she looked doll-like, plastic), covering a disturbed confusion. Carol developed a rapid and superficial identification with others—mimicking, imitating—and talking about wanting to be like others (like the Woody Allen character in the movie *Zelig*).
4. Brief experiences of disorientation, fearful, suspicious.

5. Interpersonal relationships marked by transiency (few friends she could count on) and intense fantasy (for example, being attached to women—sitting in their laps, being held by them).

The Family

The Parents

At the time of Carol's admission to treatment, Grace Gray, the mother, was fifty, Gerald Gray, the father, was fifty-eight, and Sybil, the older daughter, was twenty-three. The father was a car insurance underwriter, and the mother, now a full-time housewife, had been a secretary and nursery school assistant. There seems to have been little talk or communication about deep feeling concerns when Sybil and Carol were growing up. The parents were often concerned with what their daughters wore and how they looked; their concern was about appearance, how things seemed to be on the surface or exterior. Sybil was the good girl—the white princess—Carol was the bad girl (though this was only surfacing as treatment commenced)—the dark princess.

The Sisters

Sybil (Carol's older sister, age twenty-three) and Carol were both musical. Carol was talented—she played an instrument in a local youth orchestra. She attended Peabody Conservatory before dropping out. Sybil married a young classical musician. He got a musical position in Chicago, Sybil got a job in a bank, and after a year or so, he auditioned for and got a job in England. He was uncertain whether it would last, and so Sybil stayed in Chicago. She liked her work; though not educated in finance or banking, she showed an aptitude and a reliability for it. Her husband stayed on in England, and eventually Sybil went to England on a trial basis. It didn't work out, and they separated. Sybil returned to Chicago and resumed working for her old employer; she rose to positions of greater responsibility. She and her husband divorced, and after a while, Sybil met another man she fell in love with and they married. She continued working for the bank and moving slowly up the executive ladder. They have no children of their own (though he has a child from a previous marriage who lives with them).

Carol's and Sybil's parents lived in Maryland at the time that the family session presented here in the transcript occurred. Later they moved to Missouri (because of the father's business), and when he retired, they moved to Michigan—to the small town where Sybil's present husband's parents have a summer home.

Carol in Relation to the Family

Her Expectations from Life

Though Carol had difficulty sustaining heterosexual dating (she and a young man would date two or three times, then he'd stop calling), she came in angry and upset one day saying, "I'm twenty now, I should be married and have a child when I'm twenty-one." This kind of unreal expectation of an external structure for her life, which she anticipated as providing internal meaning and satisfaction, was paralleled by the maintaining of a smooth surface appearance by the parents while the strong internal undercurrents (both intrapsychic and interpersonal) were left unspoken and undiscussed (leaving a sense of blurred confusion in both Carol and Sybil).

An episode apropos of this happened well into treatment when Grace was operated on to have some precancerous polyps removed from her intestines. She and Gerald called their daughters afterward to explain what had happened and to say that the operation had been successful; they were surprised both daughters were upset and angry. The parents assumed that everyone would be glad about what had happened. But Sybil and Carol felt that they had been bypassed, in not knowing what had been going on, and that their feelings had been coopted. They said they felt "empty," "lost," and "confused" since they had not shared in the experience (the worry, the support, a chance to be helpful and useful) with their parents. The parents were confused too—"We didn't want to worry them." Though I tried to get a family session together as soon as possible to discuss more fully what had happened, it was not seen as a desperate enough situation to reconvene the family (the parents were in Maryland, the father was ill with a flu, and Sybil was in Chicago); I did, however, send out (through Carol) an invitation for them to contact me so I could state my concerns, and Grace and Sybil called me and we talked about what had happened and how all of us (except Gerald—he was too sick to talk on the phone, I was told) felt about it (including my intervening in their family in this intrusive way). Though Grace said she understood what Carol and Sybil and I were talking about, neither she nor Gerald talked to either daughter about Gerald's illness.

An Aspect of the Family in an Individual

Carol felt empty inside. She couldn't consciously bear all the rage and murderousness she felt toward her mother and all the elderly, hated women relatives who lived with them while they were ill and dying (and who usurped her space). She feared her mother's rejection and desperately held on to her mother's closeness (whenever it was available). Carol felt unstable, only part of a person; she felt empty, vacant—as if she were only a husk.

"I'm twenty," Carol said, "when I'm twenty-one, I should be married and have a baby when I'm twenty-two." Carol felt emptiness all around her. ("A girl who longs for marriage longs for something she know nothing about," Milan Kundera says in *The Unbearable Lightness of Being.*) Carol longed to imitate the external order of her parent's life.

Later, after I had seen the family in session, I experienced a correspondence between Carol's life and the family's life. The family, to me, felt empty inside. People in it weren't able to talk openly of their expectations, losses, and deep disappointments. The interactions were hollow. There seemed to be a deep reluctance or fear of talking about one's inner experience in the family openly and directly.

Carol sought ways to fill her vacancy and feel the pain of her sorrow (as if I were the father she needed and didn't have, the lover she needed and didn't have, and I could do nothing but be with her and watch her suffer). One of my senses of her was that she was wounded without adequate preparation for learning from her hurts. The family (and each other member in it) was too.

Carol (and Her Mother) and Me

For Carol, life's been sucked out of her; her mother possesses her, she has no right to her own emotional life. Every attempt to get away from her mother leaves her with rage; she would tend to overeat at such times. Also, she likes to bite; presumably, the anger she had during the infantile (oral) period led her to develop these reaction tendencies. Further, her efforts to leave her mother stimulated the guilt that was associated with destroying (devouring) her mother. She can't escape. It's symbiotic. She's never openly angry at her mother. She feels empty. Her mother's inside her: she's guilty because she has ingested, sucked in her mother; she's cannibalized her. But she can't accept or digest her mother and so she feels empty. Everything she says of her mother is true of her too. (So she doesn't accuse her mother.) She's afraid of being abandoned, of disappearing. (She stated that at times she wanted to get into other women's bodies as well as her mother.)

Part of Carol wanted to be rejected (you can kill a patient out of countertransference), which was related to her guilt about wanting to totally take me over.

Part of my treating her was to respond as an emotional presence (to be fully there as a person), yet set limits, to be sensitive but firm. Separation is traumatic; the basic structures weren't there in her—out of sight, out of mind—I wanted frequent repetitions of our contact (to be kept in sight). To be present, to be there (metaphorically) with every step she takes (at her job, at her apartment, on a date). Every time she separates, she gets discouraged and feels more hopeless. (With all her hunger, her need to take in and to incorporate, which is merged with her mother's hunger, she still can't get her mother in.) People she wanted to be with is to be part of them.

In the mother, on an unconscious level, my hunch is that there were oedipal issues—"You want to kill me and have Dad"—so she (the mother) wasn't encouraging Carol's growth and development (that is, she was not supporting psychotherapy). For Carol, her sexual involvement with her father's boss and with the family minister probably had oedipal implications; the boss and minister could have been objects of displaced primitive sexual feelings toward her father. She had felt that she was the devil, in regard to her sexual episodes.

To enable Carol to discuss such difficult material, I tried to provide a background of safety and security with warm, consoling, maternal (but no seductive) aspects of myself.

Rationale for Family Therapy with the Gray Family

Family therapy would provide a step toward each member's differentiating him- or herself within the family of origin. These sessions would provide an opportunity or ground for open talk between the daughter and the parents. Here, the daughters could each model taking a stance with the parents in the presence of a therapist who was uncluttered with the expectations and complex loyalties of the Gray family system. The parents would be able to respond or initiate freely, individually or together, in an uncritical atmosphere. The daughters could challenge and test the parents, and the parents could firmly exemplify their values and the purpose and meaning of their lives. Adolescents have one foot in the family and one foot out with friends and new associates, hearing and trying on new and different ideas, experiencing new behaviors and feelings. The daughters could deepen themselves talking with their parents about their new and controversial experiences outside the family (and experiencing the parents' strength through their denials and acceptances). The occasion of Carol's threats to her own life and her drug use (and her concomitant distrust of other human beings) would provide a beginning for talking about unpleasant aspects of family life. The structure of family therapy would provide a safe holding environment where the members of the Gray family could experience themselves in new ways.

A Glimmer of Family Therapy—First Appearance of a Family Member in Therapy

Carol's mother, Grace, came to therapy for the first time four months after Carol entered treatment. This session preceded the family session, the verbatim transcript of which follows in this chapter. In that session, Grace talked about how much of the hurt, sadness, pain, and pressure in the family was on her. She talked about how "nice" Carol was until two years ago. She also talked about how she wanted to protect her daughters, how both grandmothers domineered and dictated how the family should be. Carol deferred to her mother in the session (sometimes, she appeared scared); Grace dominated the session—in a sense, she cowed Carol. Carol said she wanted to part from her mother, but to part with good feelings. Grace didn't object; she listened and nodded. Carol also said she was "deathly afraid of being smothered." It wasn't clear that the mother was really so overwhelming or intrusive, or whether Carol was supersensitive or overreacting. However, Carol was caught in a contradiction: she wanted to be attached to her mother and other mother-substitutes (in a symbiotic manner), and she wanted to be independent too—"If I could part with my mother, I might be able to have a good sex life and marriage." Grace presented herself as having rigid ideas with little give and take, and she engaged at times in an extreme degree of denial. After I mentioned Carol had had suicidal thoughts, Grace responded as if she hadn't heard me. She talked about Carol's clothes (how she shouldn't wear jeans in public), how Carol ought to behave, and about Carol's friends (how she couldn't understand most of them.)

Some Therapist Impressions of Other Family Members

Mother (Grace): Strong-willed and self-determined, assertive, opinionated. Though we tangled and disputed, I admired her strength of character (which I had a hunch was to make up for and cope with the hurts and deprivations she'd suffered). She did not want to talk about her illness or surgery (the illness that would develop into the malignancy that would kill her thirteen years later).

Sybil: A directness in speaking to whomever in the session she was addressing, and a directedness in her life—going toward marriage, going toward a career. There was a definiteness to her manner. She also had a vibrancy, an aliveness, a veiled erotic energy, an intensity of affect; yet I also experienced her as hiding and distrustful, with no open, frank talk about herself personally.

Father (Gerald): Hungry for male contact; friendly; a man who needed to adapt to and depend on structures and procedures for his security; a follower; he was quiet and went along with things. He had bursts of righteous anger but was essentially confused about how to deal with conflictual emotional issues between people, which appeared to be out of his ken, out of his domain of understanding; he was neglected and pacified in the marriage.

The Gray family: Frightened of a stranger (me) helping, exploring.

Two Exemplary Tales in the Gray Family

Gerald, the father, as a college student, was out on a date with a young woman librarian. Coming back to her place after the evening out, she invited him up to her lodging. Though he found her attractive, he declined, and, in telling the story, he's proud of his resolve.

Grace fell in love with a medical student. He wanted to marry her; she wanted to wait until he became a doctor. (She was fearful he'd never finish medical school if they married; she feared the loss of the expected external security.) They broke off. He eventually fell in love with another young woman while he was still in medical school and they married; he did finish medical school. Grace waited and then Gerald appeared.

A Hint of Emotional Digestion in the Family

Well along in the third year of treatment, Carol said her mother had called her and said that she, the mother, had to talk to me as soon as possible (note that she didn't call me directly). I replied in kind, giving Grace an appointment through Carol. She drove up the next day from Maryland alone (saying her husband had to work). She told me a story about a neighbor's eighteen-year-old son who'd been acting strangely and seemed depressed. The parents had scheduled an appointment with a psychiatrist but it was a month off. One night in the interim, the son had closed the garage door, sealed the openings, turned the car motor on, and asphyxiated himself. His death, Grace said, stunned her, how, she said, she understood in her grief what I'd said about Carol's being suicidal. Somehow, she'd needed a similar event, outside the family but close to them, to bring my words home to her, to rechew and digest them differently and more personally. Note, though, that she wanted to talk to me alone (and I'd permitted it too), left her husband in Maryland, and didn't want her daughters present. Of course, I encouraged her discussing her new awareness with Gerald, Sybil, and Carol (which was subsequently done; but, as I found out later, in a desultory fashion).

The Therapy Session

The clinical work that I recount in the session transcript to follow has no pretensions to offering a scientific explication of the difficulties of the solutions for this family. It is an attempt to share our experience together on this particular evening, where each of us made his or her contributions and abstentions, and what we were unable to say as well. Here, in this (transitional) ground, a meeting took place that eased only gradually the distrust of each one of us and enabled an occasional sharing of each's hidden, clouded self with the others. In this context, one learns to hold back the anxiety related to unknowing and uncertainty, or to bear the uncertainty so as to facilitate conversation (talk) and thus empower the means to that unpredictable journey we call healing. Reconciliation and growth in family life entail living and learning the hard work and deep joy of those tasks. If we succeed in this therapeutic work in time (for me, over the long haul), we part in a state of mutual respect and with a fresh sense of the formerly hidden or only partly sensed aspects of ourselves and our families which we previously found unpleasant and were afraid of.

During the day before the family session reported here in the transcript (which was the third occasion on which I was going to see the family, and which I had asked for), I began to feel anxious, apprehensive and full of misgivings and uncertainties, and lacking in self-confidence with respect to being able to make a clinically positive encounter with the expected family (though I'd met with them in family therapy previously for two sessions). I felt self-critical, that I didn't have any authoritative reasons and purposes in a clearly elaborated order for inviting them in. (It's not my style of clinical work to plan a session in advance in any detail, and instead of helping me, such reasons probably would have left me dull, boring, and somewhat emotionally paralyzed. Clinically, I've never found prior conceptualizations as such to be of the slightest use.) Yet I sensed I was right to rely on my therapeutic intuition in asking for them all to come in (regarding mother's forthcoming operation and my hunch that physical problems and emotional dysfunction were somehow related in this family and needed an open forum of discussion).

Transcript of the Third Session With the Family

Ther.: I am in the worst position that a therapist can be in therapy right now with you.
I asked you to come tonight.
    Mother: Yeah.

These comments represent not only the therapist's interpretations and view of the interactions in the session, but also represent the impressions and critique of another family therapist (Alfred S. Friedman) who read the transcript and collaborated.

The author wishes to thank Donna McCardell for her diligence and persistence in transcribing the audiotape of the Gray family session and Harriet M. Schwartz for retyping the transcript and the session notes.

Ther.: This is the worst position a therapist can be in.

Mother: Well, Gerald said he would.

Father: We made the appointment.

Ther.: Yeah, but you made the appointment for the whole family.

Mother: But we did not realize that. We thought last time you said that Sybil is fine—I just assumed that you did not need to see her again.

Ther.: . . . a need of mine? I will tell you what a need of mine is: to have the whole family here, to work together. (1)

Father: I did not even know Carol was to be in on it.

Mother: I knew Carol was to be, but I didn't realize Sybil was to be.

Ther.: I understand you are going in the hospital. (2)

(1) The therapist was referring here to having the whole family in (which he had been trying for a long time), to get more information from the family, their various perceptions, points of view, etc.

(2) Therapist introduces an important impending event in the family, for further discussion and to let the family know what the information is that he already has about them—so, they can clarify it, and respond to it.

Mother: Next Wednesday.

Ther.: Next Wednesday, and that Sybil and her husband are leaving the area.

Mother and Father: The end of May.

Ther.: The end of May—that is later than what you said.

Carol: I thought she said the beginning of May.

Mother: Well maybe they are—as soon as graduation is over.

Carol: I think she said about the beginning of May—but I am not all that positive.

Father: They are going to look around Cook Country for an apartment—and be there for the summer before he starts school in the fall.

Ther.: I was thinking of the family—the breaking apart—that whenever somebody goes in the hospital it is important to talk about it.

Mother: Maybe I am only going to be there for the day. (3)

(3) Mother immediately and automatically denies the seriousness, minimizes the problem.

Ther.: Carol told me what you are going in the hospital for. I do not know how you feel about her telling me. I think it is important that she told me—I probably would not have seen you tonight without knowing that.

Carol: We would have come—we planned to come.

Father: We planned to come.

Ther.: My plans were to see the whole family. (4)

Father: Except for an emergency—*she wasn't called in on an emergency*—she has a regular appointment at the hospital.

Mother: Next week I cannot.

Father: What is it, a week from tomorrow?

Mother: Yes.

Ther.: We are also late in starting the session, and I know you are irritated about it. (5) Do you want to yell at me a little?

Father: No. I am not happy about getting home later and I am not going to say that I'm smiling about it.

Ther.: You can get angry at me. It's OK. Carol has gotten angry at me often enough. I can handle the anger.

Father: It (anger) will take me a little longer, a little more to get me to blow my lid.

Ther.: Do you smoke cigars?

Father: Yes, I do.

Ther.: I will make you a peace offering.

Father: Thank you.

Ther.: I think you will like these. They are 1959 Havana tobacco.

Mother: 1959. (6)

Ther.: Yes, they are. If you like them, I have a couple more you can have.

Father: Thank you. The only time I had one is when somebody has a baby and they

(4) Therapist means he would not have seen them without the whole family present, with Sybil absent.

(5) Therapist sets a tone that "anything goes" in the session, including negative expressions toward him.

(6) This was during the period when smoking was considered more socially acceptable. Possibly the therapist meant literally what he said, that he was making a "peace offering," since he had kept the family waiting. Like indians smoked a peace pipe together. Also, the therapist already had evidence that the father was somewhat of an outsider in the family and wanted to make him more welcome. (The therapist now reflects that it was also his way of conveying "I have good stuff to offer you.")

(7) Mother interrupts therapist's alliance with Father. This is consistent with her having tried to influence

hand them out in the office. No, I was not too angry about it. It will take more to blow my lid.

Mother: Jeff, I really don't know how much more you think we can accomplish because . . .

Ther.: It depends on how much you want to accomplish. (7)

Mother: I feel the past few weeks Carol and I have gotten along pretty well together. I think we all had a good day Sunday—Sybil, Carol, Eddie, Gerald, and I.

Ther.: The whole family was together.

Mother: Yes.

Ther.: In Elkton.

Father: No, here—in Sybil's apartment. We came up—so they are coming down in about a week or two.

Mother: Carol and I had a real long talk all day Friday. I hope she understands that we are sympathetic to whatever she wants to do.

Ther.: Up to a point.

Mother: No. She talked about her plans and what she thinks she would like to accomplish, and this is fine. I mean the sex bit I do not approve of and she knows I do not approve of it. As far as having it just promiscuously I think this is the most foolish thing she could possible do—but I think . . .

Ther.: Does Carol tell you much about her sex life? (8)

Carol to terminate therapy. Both parents had earlier said to Carol, "Why do you have to go talk to him? You can talk to us in the family" (meaning to keep it all in the family). This reflects the family focus on and concern with surface issues and appearances; to maintain a facade of surface amiability and to give the impression that nothing is wrong underneath the surface—a fairly common attitude of a WASP family. Consistent with this, Carol was still, at this point, withholding from her family that she had a drug problem and had been suicidal, has been abused sexually, etc.

(8) Carol had earlier reported to the therapist that she actually didn't enjoy sex very much. She more likely had given her mother the impression that she wants to do what she wants to do, in spite of mother's disapproval, and thus led mother to believe that she actually enjoyed sex. Probably Carol enjoyed the opportunity to experiment, to have the experience, and to talk to her mother about it to provoke her.

Mother: No, not much. She just says she likes to have it and that is that. I don't know how much there is to tell. I don't really know.

Ther.: I think you kind of let it go at that. (9)

Mother: No, I tried to find out, but she just doesn't want to talk about it. Now I don't know how you find out—when somebody won't talk about it. Maybe when she trusts us more she will tell us. I don't know.

Ther.: Maybe she will.

Mother: . . . and maybe she won't.

Ther.: This much I will tell you because I think it is important that the interaction, the transaction, the nearness, the closeness of people is what she wants, what she enjoys. The actual sex isn't enjoyed as much.

Carol: Sometimes I do.

Ther.: Sometimes you do and sometimes you don't. It is mostly not.

Mother: Well, that is good! This relieves my mind. (10)

Carol: There are some cases that I do, though . . .

Ther.: I know. We talked about that. I think that is important to know about your different associations with people.

Father: Is your definition of intimacy physically, psychologically, socially, and . . . I mean what is your definition of it? (11)

(9) Therapist indicates that mother wants to keep things on the surface, and that she "puts a lid" on her curiosity. She doesn't want to look into herself or into others.

(10) Mother is satisfied her daughter's sexuality is OK. Once again, it's a surface acceptance, with little or no evidence of what's actually going on with her daughter; as long as her daughter says she's OK, she is. The daughter, however, is responding to an unspoken invitation in the family to make everything appear to be OK. The daughter's sexuality is problematic—she's described sexual situations where she's treated in hurtful and dismissive ways and has responded in emotionally and physically paralyzed ways.

(11) Father doesn't address the question of sex directly but only indirectly and tentatively, referring to some sort of "intimacy." He addressed his question to the therapist as if he is more hesitant to talk to females, or to talk within the family, about sex. He may be asking the therapist's approval or encouragement to talk more directly about physical sex, and asking for "definition" as an aid or support for entering into an area

Ther.: What is the "it"?

Father: The closeness of people—your statement.

Ther.: Being held, being touched. Somebody you can just feel comfortable with being held by or holding. Although there are more ramifications.

Father: Sure.

Ther.: People who can talk to each other about how they feel about each other. (12)

Father: That is the reason I asked you to define it. (13)

Ther.: I think we had an experiment here last night where people—one guy has great difficulty getting close to people and so what he did was to just sit in front of someone who agreed to do this with him, and they just looked at each other for a few minutes. We had them close their eyes and explore each other's hand for a few minutes, then look in each other's eyes again for a few minutes without saying anything and then when that series of six or seven minutes was done, they shared their feelings about what had happened, and that I call closeness. How you feel in the moment about what you do with somebody else—that I call closeness. (14)

Father: That's a good definition.

Ther.: That is important. This is something you develop and it takes time.

Mother: Well, I wonder if the closeness has not been satisfying because she is afraid of people. Can this be?

Carol: What? (15)

that is unspoken between him and his wife and his daughters, as if to speak about it is like entering an unknown area.

(12) (See comment [11] above)

(13) This response may fit with the therapist's hunch that father and mother did not talk to each other about sex, or other intimate feelings.

(14) The therapist tells an exemplary story of an incident that happened in a treatment situation to emphasize the importance, in his view, of closeness and intimacy in life.

(15) Mother apparently is right on target here, regarding Carol. Carol's responses indicate that she is almost rendered speechless at her mother's accuracy and incisiveness. Presumably, she had never talked directly to mother about her considerable fears and terrors, which in certain situations had immobilized her.

Mother: Are you afraid of people? I mean your peers?

Carol: My peers?

Mother: I am not speaking of us because I think we would expect that being the same kind of closeness. (16)

(16) Mother appears to be saying that closeness within the family is assumed, and doesn't leave an opening for Carol to express any ambivalence about closeness within the family.

Carol: I'd say to a certain extent I am afraid of my peers. I do not think that I am afraid of closeness as some other people are—because after being in the group for a while I realize that everybody in the group is afraid of closeness—I don't feel that it is all that abnormal.

Ther.: (To mother) What did you mean that you expect things to be different in the family when it is evident that some part of Carol doesn't feel it can open up?

Mother: I am not talking about that kind of closeness. I am talking about this touching closeness that you are talking about now. I think the other closeness maybe will come. (17a)

(17a) Mother acknowledges that emotional closeness is lacking in the family.

Ther.: When you said that—you know what I thought about? I had a brief flash about the times I said goodbye to my dad and we hugged and kissed—and what a nice feeling that is.

Mother: We have *just never done that.* This goes back. I mean—I can remember the look on my father's face when I was leaving for my honeymoon and I forgot to kiss him goodbye. He said "Didn't you forget something?" and I said, "What did I forget?" We have just never done much of this stuff. (17b)

(17b) An example again of the lack of expressiveness and of demonstration of affection, typical of WASP culture.

Ther.: That is a very special kiss, isn't it?

Mother: Yes, it was.

Ther.: You are kissing your father goodbye for all time in a certain kind of relationship and leaving with another man—he is giving you away.

Mother: . . . and I could tell by the hurt look on his face that this was something that I really shouldn't have done. We were *just never a real close family.* I would not say that he was a very close man physically with us.

Carol: I feel to a certain extent that we are a close family. I feel that there is love and things like that. I mean really I do.

Mother: I think your father's family is very affectionate (in the closeness bit).

Carol: I have thought about it and I see how lucky I really am because there really has been a lot of love in the family. Sybil and I were talking about it today and you can't really expect miracles of any family. I think in our family there has been a lot of love, more in the care and concern people have for each other. I don't think it has been in the physical closeness, and I feel that for my own life this is just something that I have to continue to work on. (18)

Carol: . . . and I feel good about saying it. I feel that nobody can really help me with it. I have got to do it myself.

Father: That's logical.

Mother: I think this is something that comes with growing up.

Father: You are an adult now, honey. (19)

Mother: As I said the other day, growing up is not easy and it never was. This is where I think so many young people are wrong. You seem to think that you have a copyright on an easy way out—there just isn't. (20)

(18) She expresses her loyalty to her parents here. (The intense anger and rage toward her mother which she later expressed may have been suppressed and not available to her at this time.)

(19) Both parents are here reinforcing Carol's need to deny her need for nurturance.

(20) Mother criticizes Carol and her generation. This is in spite of the fact that Carol just expressed love and loyalty to her parents, and indicated that she has been changing from her earlier behavior and attitude. Father expresses support for Carol, saying she is behaving in a mature way, thus disagreeing with mother, but only in an indirect way.

Father: Whether the commonwealth makes it eighteen or twenty-one it makes no difference. You are an adult now and that is it.

Mother: . . . years beyond high school are

different from the safety of your home and going back and forth to school every day.

Carol: Yeah, I know. I just feel that I am to the point now where I have to work a lot of things out on my own. There are things that people really cannot help me with. I have to do them myself.

Mother: I know, I know—we talked about that on Friday.

Father: There is only one person that can make that decision—you, personally. (21)

Mother: I think as far as we are concerned, unless Jeff thinks we need a lot more, I feel that Friday was a real good day, and I said to Carol the last few times I have seen her and I want you to tell me if I am right.

Father: . . . or wrong.

Ther.: Did you hear that sigh? (22)

Mother: I know, but I want you to tell me whether I am right or wrong. You see her in one way and I see her in another. What I said when she hopped off the bus—what was it—two weeks ago, three weeks ago, or whenever—she was like an entirely different person and I was real anxious to see her this weekend to see if she was the same person and her eyes had such a peaceful look. She looked as though she had felt satisfied; that was the first time in a long time she had a peaceful face, as far as I was concerned. (23)

Ther.: Did you tell her that?

Mother: I told her that on Friday. I'm just telling you.

Ther.: Did your mom say that just like that? How did you feel when she said that?

Carol: It felt pretty good.

Mother: But what I want to know is, am I right? I think I'm right. (24)

(21) For some reason, Father has the need to reiterate several times that Carol is an adult and is on her own now. He seems to want her to individuate (and she does too) before she's ready to. Also, there seems to be some prohibition about asking for help from others.

(22) Therapist calls attention to the deeper needs and affects in the family that parents are denying (possibly that father's sigh indicates some feeling of hopelessness or inability to do anything about the problems in the family).

(23) Mother again is trying to prove that all is well, and that neither Carol nor the family needs help or therapy, and everything is nice and in order, and she and Carol are reconciled.

(24) A family theme, which is implied also in the WASP cultural pattern, is that there is a right way and a wrong way to do things. This ignores the need for struggle, where there is doubt about right and wrong, or how to go about solving problematic issues.

Ther.: Carol is the only one who knows.

Carol: I feel pretty good about it. I feel that it is pretty right because now I realize that there is a lot I have to do on my own and I am ready to work on it. (25)

Ther.: Let me ask you something. Have you ever told your parents how you playact? How you used to playact in the family? You used to put on a good front. (26)

Mother: Well, this is what I wondered about, whether she was playacting again. No, I did not know that.

Carol: I don't think that I was playacting.

Ther.: That is what I want to know. You are the only one who knows that.

Mother: Now wait a minute—playacting?

Ther.: I think the only way you will get anywhere is to be honest one way or another. If you have some anxiety and you are not talking about it . . .

Carol: I don't feel that I was playacting, Jeff.

Mother: . . . you mean playacting?

Ther.: She puts on a role for you.

Mother: This is what you told us the first time we came.

Ther.: She put on a role. She was obedient. She did what she was told. She had a social role that she played.

(25) While Mother is saying that Carol has arrived, is all OK and doesn't need any more therapy, Carol is also saying, "I am ready to work on it, on my own", meaning without depending on parents or on a therapist. She is responding to the major family message of being stoic and solving all of one's problems by oneself, and not asking for help.

(26) Therapist confronts Carol, that she may be putting on a false front, acting compliant and telling her parents (and others) what she thinks they want to hear from her; she tries to please them to avoid conflict and rejection.

Mother: . . . but we knew there was something wrong.

Ther.: Underneath she felt she could not talk, could not say . . .

Mother: . . . it was not because we didn't ask her.

Ther.: Maybe you asked—and she was afraid to. . . .

Mother: She would not talk.

Ther.: She had reasons.

Father: She would put on a show.

Ther.: So if that is disappearing, also Carol sometimes wears a mask. I don't know whether you can see it—I can see it. When Carol wears a mask her face is tight. You can see the skin being tightened—her face is blank.

Mother: I know.

Carol: I don't think this has any importance because my family are not psychiatrists.

Mother: When her face is blank, her eyes are too.

Ther.: I think it is terrific that your family is sensitive to you and that you are sensitive to your family. You are sensitive to Sybil, and Sybil is sensitive to you parents.

Carol: I feel good about my family and I feel that I want my problems to be my own problems. (27)

Ther.: . . . they are.

Mother: They are. Nobody can work them out but you—but don't keep them a secret if they are upsetting you.

Ther.: (To Carol) I didn't ask for the family to come in tonight because of you or to talk about you.

  (To mother) My concern was with you and your feelings about going into the hospital; your feelings about having a D and C; your feelings about possibly having a hysterectomy. I want to know your feelings about this. (28)

(27) She may mean that she doesn't want to share her problems and her real feelings with her parents. This assertion by her, implying some rejection of parents, may be partly related to the fact that her mother has just agreed with the therapist that she is not open about her real feelings. She may feel somewhat threatened by their agreement about her.

(28) Therapist here refocuses and breaks the tone and the pattern of the session. He had the information on mother's hospitalization and assumed that it was being avoided and minimized by the family. Possibly he chose this moment to introduce the problem because Carol has been the focus (the target? the scapegoat?) of the session thus far. Therapist also shows a milder side of himself, and his concern.

Mother: My feelings are great because I found out that the Pap test was negative and I'm not afraid of anything. You can believe that or not. I feel completely relaxed about the whole thing because I know it was a shock (to me) for him to find anything. (29)

Ther.: What could he have found? Was it a routine check?

Mother: No, I am diabetic, and I went to see him about my hand and then he decided that I needed a complete physical—then he found trouble.

Ther.: Trouble . . . what did he find?

Mother: Polyps, and he said that when I—when he goes in to remove that he would like to do a D and C. If there is too much hemorrhaging, then he will go ahead and take everything. I was worried until I got those Pap tests results.

Ther.: They are nonmalignant?

Mother: Yes, they are.

Ther.: (*To father*) I guess you were pretty worried for a while.

Father: Oh yes.

Mother: Until I got the results of that—but I still don't know what he is going to do—whether I will be laid up for days or for a couple weeks. (30)

Ther.: Have you ever had a D and C before?

Mother: I have never been in the hospital except to have the girls.

Ther.: How do you feel about going into a hospital? (31)

Mother: Well, I worked in one for four and a half years. I am really not afraid of hospitals. I am not afraid of doctors as long as I know I have a good doctor. When things happen you have to go through with things—that is all. You just can't worry about them. (32)

Ther.: I am not talking about going through—I am talking about your feelings.

Mother: What do you mean, my feelings? Do you mean "am I afraid?"

(29) *This is an example of the mother's personal strength, which she showed in some aspect of her life (but didn't succeed in conveying to her daughters).*

(30) *Feeling is not allowed (i.e., anxiety is suppressed) until some certainty is established (that she will be laid up for two weeks for a hysterectomy). Then she can worry.*

(31) *Therapist is more sensitive than earlier.*

(32) *As clear an expression as possible of the WASP tendency to deny problems and to tough them out.*

Ther.: Whatever your feelings are—I don't know what they are, I just wanted to give you a chance to talk about them.

Mother: Well, it is just a nuisance, but . . .

Ther.: Do you have any fantasies? People sometimes have fantasies that there is something wrong or they may find something wrong. They may find out there is in fact cancer. People have fantasies like this. They may be feelings that you suppress or put down.

Mother: The only fear I had was before I got the Pap test back; and once I got the results on that I did not worry. Now maybe it is (malignant)—who knows; but I certainly cannot worry about something that might not be. (33)

Ther.: I just wanted to know what your feelings are. (34)

Mother: I lived with an aunt—don't forget, we talked about this many times—who was worried about things that she shouldn't have been worried about, and I'm not like that. I think I am more like my mother. (35)

Father: She never worried about anything.

Mother: If the doctor said so, she does it. I don't care what it is.

Ther.: I assume you are going to do it one way or another—the doctor says so—so you would go in the hospital even if you had apprehensions—or fears or some nervousness— you would still go. (36)

Mother: Yes, but I do not feel nervous about it. I asked several people who have lived in the community for a year if this man is a good doctor, and they said yes, and I said to the doctor that I also want an M.D. to administer the anesthetic, I do not want a nurse, and he made arrangements for that—and that is it. You cannot take any more precautions than that.

Carol: Then you don't know whether you are going to get a D and C or whether you are getting a hysterectomy?

(33) Again, she refuses to worry unless a serious problem is absolutely established. Feelings or doubts are seen as not useful— also, note her strength of will.

(34) Note the quiet relentless persistence of the therapist.

(35) A family-of-origin trait.

(36) Therapist tries to make her aware that there could be another human level to her experience.

Mother: I will not know until I wake up what I have had. They put you under the anesthetic and they do an instant biopsy—a sectional biopsy—and you do not wake up until they find out whether that is all right. The Pap test is all right, so probably the biopsy will be all right. (37)

Father: What is the anesthetic? Sodium pen? (38)

Mother: I don't know what it is.

Ther.: Do you have any apprehensions about being under an anesthetic?

Mother: Only with somebody who is not skilled. My sister died under an anesthetic, so I asked for supervision.

Ther.: How did she die?

Mother: She went into shock at Bryn Mawr Hospital with a doctor who said he had never lost a patient. So my cousin, who is a doctor, said never go under an anesthetic unless there is an M.D. there. So I have never let the girls— well, I guess Carol has never been under it. I have never been in the hospital, period. I guess Sybil then. I insisted that she have a doctor too. He explained what he was going to do.

Carol: Sybil has been in the hospital about three times, hasn't she?

Mother: I figure once you take the precaution then he just does it—that's all.

Father: . . . as long as an M.D. does it. (39)

Mother: . . . as long as a good M.D. does it—let's put it that way.

Father: Most M.D.s . . .

Mother: No, not most M.D.s. I worked in a hospital . . .

Father: . . . are equipped to handle anesthetic procedure.

Carol: I am glad that you are not letting a nurse give you the anesthetic. It is good to have somebody who knows what he is doing.

Mother: Do you want to see us again or not? (40)

(37) She is optimistic.

(38) Father's focus on concrete details may be a way to handle his anxiety.

(39) Father's repetitions and parroting are ways to feel secure, and a way of entering and participating. (40) Mother's question here, which appears somewhat abrupt, may indicate that she wants to change the subject, or she is uncomfortable, or she didn't intend to stay any longer. Her question also suggested to the therapist that Carol's comment "somebody who knows what he is doing" may have led mother to

question the therapist's competence and the efficacy of the family sessions.

Ther.: I am going to put that back on you—but I am not going to do that for a few minutes. (41) I just thought of something you said—if you do not have a D and C, he might take everything.

Mother: . . . then he will do a hysterectomy.

Ther.: How do you feel about that?

Mother: It doesn't bother me. If I were twenty-five it might, but it doesn't now. I know this—that whatever the trouble a person has they are better off without it, if it is going to give them pain. I cannot see worrying about it. If you had a toothache and the dentist said the tooth was bad and had to come out, you would have it pulled.

Ther.: . . . Yeah, but it is different.

Mother: . . . Not really.

Father: . . . You are just taking it as it comes. (42)

Mother: . . . Right.

Ther.: It is a different part of your body.

Mother: Well, that may be, but still if it is not any good—you know I always figure you go along with what the doctor says—if you feel that he is a good doctor.

Ther.: You can still have feelings about parts of the body—losing parts of it.

Mother: Well, I can, but sometimes if you don't lose the parts you are six feet under—then what good does it do to have everything?

Ther.: I know, but you can still have feelings about this part. (43)

(41) The decision whether to continue in family therapy is the family's choice.

(42) Father, while agreeing with mother as usual, is also pointing out her process of accepting everything in life, pleasant or unpleasant, as it comes.

(43) The therapist persists in trying to get to any underlying apprehensions (concerns about losing parts of the body or about death). Some therapists, after establishing an atmosphere for anxieties to be expressed, might desist from the engagement and the struggle with this mother. They might think that if she can manage to suppress her anxiety—if that is her style, her way of coping—let her do it her way; if she has a hysterectomy or if malignancy is found, she will cope with whatever feelings she has about it at that time. This therapist,

Mother: Well, maybe I will have more feelings when I come through.

Ther.: . . . Well, maybe so.

Mother: Let's put it that way. I am certainly not going to worry about it between now and next Wednesday. There is no point. I will tell you one thing, I was not more worried about *this* than I was when I heard I was a diabetic. I was much more concerned about this than I was that. It is not anything now, but it was— it looked like an awful dose of poison ivy— thick scabs—this was so sensitive I nearly lost my mind.

Ther.: . . . Painful?

Mother: It itched and it was painful at the same time. That scared me. It may not sound rational to you but it was much more frightening to me.

Ther.: What scared you about it? What did you think about?

Mother: Well, I know sometimes those things just don't heal. That is what scared me about it.

Ther.: Will it spread?

Mother: Well, sometimes they just remove a part of your body.

Ther.: They might wind up taking your hand. (44)

Mother: . . . That is right. This is much more frightening to me than that. Maybe that is why I am so relaxed because I have more to worry about than that. (45)

Carol: What did they say about that? Are you OK now?

Mother: It healed.

Carol: It won't spread to another part of your body?

Mother: . . . Oh, it could.

Ther.: Your fantasies were that they would amputate your hand or your arm.

Mother: I would not say that they were fantasies. I just went to a good doctor and said, "What can you do?" and he is a real honest

however, believes in a style of engaging family members in a struggle to enlarge and deepen their experience together, with each other and with him. Here, he's contending with her about feelings of loss associated with the amputation of a body part (or of a shared human experience).

(44) Therapist joined mother by repeating what she said, but with greater emphasis on the threat at a serious loss, in his effort to evoke some real feelings. He is using the threat of loss of her hand, which is not imminent, to get to her suppressed anxiety regarding the hysterectomy and the possibility of having cancer. (45) Mother apparently was able to resonate to the more distant threat and to express her fear.

guy and he said, "I cannot tell yet. It might heal in two weeks or it might take six months." But I do like an honest doctor. I don't like somebody who is going to kid me and not tell me the truth.

Father: Put it on the line. (46)

Mother: . . . Right.

Ther.: I guess I have put things on the line.

Father: I think you are honest. If I have a condition like cancer or something, I want to know about it.

Mother: He was worse than I was. (47)

Ther.: (To Father) It took you a long time to face up to your hearing (problem).

Father: That took me a long time.

Ther.: Maybe just having the facts and digesting them may take some time. (48)

Father: You are right; it took time.

Ther.: Not everything gets swallowed. You may have the facts and then it takes some time to work it out emotionally.

Father: The remarkable part about this is I understand every single word you say, even to an *a*. Before, everybody seemed to be blurred.

Mother: We never thought we would hear that, did we?

Carol: . . . No.

Father: (Laughs) It was well worth the $437 I paid for it.

Mother: Wait until you find out you need one in another few years.

Father: Well, I will have to get it. Almost four hundred bucks by that time.

Mother: It will be more than that.

Carol: That is a lot of money.

Mother: It is your life now.

Ther.: (To father) Are you aware of the importance of hearing?

Father: Oh yes. It is very important in social contact.

Ther.: (To mother) I guess you became aware (very conscious) of the importance of your hand, your right hand. (49)

(46) Father "parrots" mother again.

(47) That he was worse in denying. It took him a longer time to accept that he had a problem.

(48) Therapist is acknowledging that each person's emotional digestive process is different and takes its own time.

(49) Therapist returns again and again to the main purpose of the session, his original "intuition" that physical problems and emotional dysfunction are related in this family.

Mother: You can believe it. I couldn't do anything, could I? Rubber gloves for about how many weeks . . . about six.

Father: Even to wash the dishes you had to put them on.

Mother: Scrub the floor and everything with rubber gloves. It is a pressure situation and the doctor said that it took something to trigger it off; and I kind of think it was the light on my sewing machine—I think I burned it. I couldn't remember when he told me. It happened so gradually.

Ther.: Did your doctor talk about any of the emotional things that go along with a hysterectomy; they're emotional.

Mother: No, but I think I have read enough to know that there are emotional problems that go along with it. I don't intend to worry about them unless I have to—because sometimes they just *never* happen. (50)

(50) As usual, she denies all negative affects. This is an extreme example of denial.

Carol: (To mother) You told me that there is a depression.

Mother: Well, there is sometimes, and if there is, then you see the doctor.

Ther.: You keep talking about wanting to end, which I think is fine. However, I would like to leave the door open. (51)

(51) Therapist answers her earlier question. He had deferred the answer, but now feels that there has been a thorough enough discussion of the main immediate issue (mother's scheduled operation). He is ready to end any time that they are. (This therapist believes that one should always be able to say goodbye, while stating his continuing availability.)

Mother: Well, I think we would like that.

Ther.: If you do have feelings that you want to talk about, or you want a place to talk about them with the whole family or with me, I will just leave an open invitation to you.

Father: OK, we have your phone number.

Ther.: The only other thought I had was that I think it would be appropriate to have one more session with the whole family—with Sybil before she leaves. (52)

(52) Therapist realizes that the business he engaged in at the beginning of this session, of getting the whole family together, in a session, is still unfinished.

Mother: . . . Before she leaves?

Father: We will have to find out the date. It is in May, I know that.

Ther.: How do you feel about that? You don't have to do anything.

Father: Well, it is all right.

Ther.: You're not doing it for me. This is the main point I wanted to say. That is a suggestion of mine, but whether you accept it or decide to act on it or not, is your decision, not mine. (53)

Father: We will if she will go along with it.

Carol: I think she would come up here.

Mother: Well, she didn't expect to come tonight, that was the problem; she didn't have it planned.

Father: I don't know exactly what time in May they are going.

Mother: . . . Well, I don't know when Eddie graduates.

Carol: They are going to leave right after Eddie gets out.

Mother: They are real anxious to escape for the summer.

Ther.: It is a really nice place.

Father: The cost of living is high there. (54)

Mother: They know someone out there who is going to line up a few places for them, which will help. I am very glad they are doing this, because I think Eddie has to be the breadwinner. I think he should be able to do what he wants to do.

Ther.: Nonetheless, they are traveling a long way. (55)

Mother: That is true. This is the way it happens. (56)

Father: It is just one of those things.

Ther.: . . . Which, again, you have feelings about.

Mother: Well, only in that I think that they have done a lot of growing up and I am not

(53) Therapist emphasizes the throwaway nature of his suggestion for another session. He says it is the family's decision; they do not have to do it for him.

(54) Father's recurring concern about money.

(55) Perhaps they are dwelling on this because of their concern or feeling of loss because the daughter will be a long way from home.

(56) So, don't worry about it.

worried about them because I think they are able to make their own decision.

Ther.: Well, anytime a part of the family leaves, it is a sad feeling.

Mother: Oh well, yes. (57)

Father: He is a guy who under no circumstance will be pushed around; he is a very nice fellow, I think. Mild spoken. (58)

Mother: I think their biggest problems were the fact that they were so young. I think they have done a lot of growing up and I think they are going to be fine.

Father: They are more interesting to talk to than they used to be.

Ther.: Well, maybe you would like to invite him too.

Mother: Well, we will see. We better let Carol make a date, though, because we don't know—(59)

Father: As I said, we don't know exactly when they are going to go. Because PMA may have its commencement early in May; I thought it was late May.

Carol: The grad students always have their commencements early, about a month earlier than anybody else.

Father: He is finishing his fifth year. (60)

Ther.: I wondered another thing. I wondered if when the family all got together whether you talked about what went on here last session with Carol and Sybil.

Father: We did somewhat in the car—or did we or didn't we? (61)

Mother: You mean yesterday, Sunday, when we were together?

Ther.: Any of the time in the last month.

(57) *Ping pong over the main theme between mother and therapist.*

(58) *The way he would like to be himself but probably doesn't feel able to be.*

(59) *The responsibility for this therapy is being put back on Carol. Mother is disowning this therapy?*

(60) *The family is taking a lot of time with this. It may be that they need to stay on, although told they could leave at any time, because something has been stirred up in them, or because Sybil's move is a major event and a loss for them.*

(61) *Father isn't into the therapy in any way meaningful or serious. He may have wanted to please the therapist, but couldn't remember whether the last session had been talked about. He apparently isn't a deeply thoughtful or analytical person, and tends to be concrete.*

Mother: We really haven't even seen each other. (62)

Carol: (To therapist) You suggested that Sybil and I get together for lunch someday, and she is all for that. She thinks it is a good idea too. You said, "Why don't you go out to lunch sometime and talk about things?" I asked her today about when I get a little bit better if she would like to go out to lunch and she said that she would. (63)

(62) A real close family!
(63) In order to facilitate more contact and relationship with her family, the therapist had suggested that Carol have regular brief and casual meetings with each member of her family, separately, on neutral turf (e.g., to go for lunch, go for a walk, etc.). The dyadic meetings are for avoiding triangulation, and getting to know each other as separate, autonomous individuals. This therapist has found this treatment exercise to be very useful for some families.

Mother: Well, you have been there (at Sybil's house).

Carol: I have been going—I'd say in the past month. I feel really good about it because we have gotten together a lot and have had some really good times and we are going to go to a Phillies game.

Father: Yes we are.

Carol: I have never seen a Phillies game before.

Father: I hope they win.

Carol: That sounds really good.

Father: Don't forget about the Baltimore Orioles. (64)

Carol: I mean I will come—if everybody wants to come one more time—I will be glad to. (65)

(64) The surfaciness of this family discussion suggests a vacuousness in the family interactions, and reminds the therapist of a visceral feeling of emptiness that Carol has expressed to him. It is not a resistance. It also shows a way in which the family has fun together.
(65) Carol's specifying only one family session at a time may be out of loyalty to her mother, who obviously wasn't wanting very much to return for family sessions.

Mother: All right, you better make the date—because of next week—we'll see how things work out.

Carol: We will see how you are too.

Mother: That is what I mean. Find out when I can come.

Father: (To therapist) I will even light your cigar. (66)

Ther.: Have I seduced you? (67)

Mother: Yes, I think you've made it.

Father: They are good.

Mother: What time is it? (68)

Ther.: Eight forty-five.

Father: I don't have the finesse Groucho Marx has. (In lighting a cigar.) (69)

Ther.: You look good with it, though.

Carol: Groucho Marx puffs all that smoke right onto the screen. That is all you see when he gets a cigar. You see all this smoke all over the place. (70)

Father: He was on a Washington channel at 11:00 P.M.

Carol: I smoked a cigar once, Jeff. I never told you about that. I was with my friend when I was in Rochester. She is like 85 percent blind. We got really friendly and everything. (71)

Mother: When you traveled with the high school orchestra . . .

(66) *A very positive transference in a dependent way, and with deference, to the therapist.*

(67) *This therapist can be provocative.*

(68) *She has been ready to leave. She has been uncomfortable about all the focus on her in this session.*

(69) *Note the similarity to the therapist's name (Marks). Is father aware that sounds like he is saying he does not have the therapist's finesse?*

(70) *Carol's talking about the screen may reflect some of the confusion she feels in her life. She may be implying in an indirect and symbolic way that the therapist, in refocusing the session and dealing with mother's problem, talking about things other than her problems and what she wants to talk about, is creating confusion for her.*

(71) *She is jealous of the pleasant and playful relationship between therapist and father. She needs the therapist's attention focused back on her. It is related to or part of her need to be targeted; it is a return to the familiar, where she's the index patient in the family as she's known it.*

Carol: Yeah! I didn't like her because I always thought she was conservative and straightlaced, but I got to be really friendly with her and we decided when I was in Rochester what could we do that was really crazy, and we couldn't think of anything so she suggested that we go out and buy two huge Dutch Master cigars and walk around the street smoking them. That was the only time I ever smoked a cigar. It tasted awful, but we got stares from people (laughter).

Ther.: Is that what you wanted, the attention?

Carol: Yeah.

Ther.: Did you inhale them?

Carol: I inhaled it the first time I puffed it and I got sick, so I figured I would just smoke it but not inhale it.

Mother: I think we better get on our way.

Father: I think so, also. We have got the dog down there to put out. She still misses you (to Carol). (72)

Carol: I will be down soon.

Father: She gives us a hard time after you leave every Monday.

Mother: She ran off to your door yesterday and waited. Nothing happened.

Father: She still misses you.

Carol: Mary has a cat now. It is really crazy. This cat that Mary has is about this big, it is so tiny; it is absolutely crazy. I didn't like it.

Mother: What is it, about three weeks?

Carol: I was really irritated when I saw it Sunday because I told her, "If you get a cat, you take care of it yourself." I want no parts of cats, but this cat is so adorable I have just fallen in love with it.

Mother: When you leave there, leave the cat.

Carol: It is her cat. I don't want to take it with me.

Father: She probably wouldn't let you anyway.

(72) Since these parents don't express their feelings directly, they are expressing their feelings of missing Carol and about the distance between them in an indirect and symbolic way by talking about the dog's feelings.

Mother: Well, do you want to go get back in bed? (73)

Father: We are still available for you. I will get my sleep on the way down. "Mother" will drive the car.

Mother: You got it on the way up.

Carol: I hope everything goes OK in the hospital.

Mother: I do too.

Carol: You are going in a week from tomorrow.

Father: . . . Eight in the morning.

Mother: . . . Six in the morning.

Father: . . . Six in the morning.

Mother: That will be a new thing.

Father: Yeah, to get you up.

Mother: No. I have never been in the hospital. (74)

Father: I was sick once.

Ther.: (To father) Well, were you in the hospital?

Father: . . . Adenoid operation, tonsils. Back in those days, before you appeared on the scene, I think they gave you ether. There was nothing so sickening afterwards—sick. I have been very fortunate.

Carol: I remember one time you came out of the dentist's office—you had a tooth pulled. They put novocaine on the side of your mouth and you came out like a gangster. You could only smile on one side of your mouth. Remember that?

Father: I remember that.

Carol: You have had a lot of problems with your teeth.

Father: I need a good set of teeth. That is about the only thing on my mind.

Mother: He (the therapist) doesn't need a rundown on our health, I guess. (75)

Ther.: That is it. (76)

(73) Apparently referring to his sleeping in the car while she drives.

(74) Mother has now suggested ending the session several times and leaving. The therapist hasn't questioned this, but the family still doesn't leave, for some reason.

(75) Mother may really want to leave. Possibly she is waiting for the therapist to adjourn the meeting out of a formal respect for authority.

(76) He apparently means that that completes the review of the father's health problems.

Mother: OK.

Ther.: It is nice to listen to you talk about it.

Mother: Well . . .

Ther.: There is a different flavor to your talk than there was a few months ago.

Mother: We were all scared, I guess. (77)

Father: . . . Scared, I guess—fear. I don't know. I think things have worked out for the better.

Ther.: Have you talked about some of your devils? (78)

Father: . . . Some of my what?

Ther.: Devils.

Father: Did we develop—

Mother: You mean here? I guess we have.

Father: . . . a good portion of it. I can only say that it has been in details. I might not have entirely agreed with you, but basically I have all the way through, although I have argued (with the therapist).

Ther.: I think it is great that you argued. I hope you know how to argue with Grace (wife). (79)

Father: . . . We do.

Ther.: (To mother) Can you argue with Gerald? (husband).

Mother: Oh, I do.

Father: It does a world of good. (80)

Mother: That is what upsets Carol. (81)

(77) Mother finally expresses a negative affect directly, though tentatively. It comes right after the therapist's approving of the family's effort.

(78) Therapist persists, continues to bring up issues.

(79) Therapist encourages struggle and contending between himself and family members, and between one family member and another. In the process of his conducting therapy, he encourages facing, describing, and resolving the impasses and disagreements between people.

(80) Father may only be identifying with the therapist. The therapist isn't convinced that the father and mother confront each other in vigorous and meaningful ways, and is not impressed with father's implying that he is assertive in disagreeing with his wife.

(81) The therapist was asking about husband and wife arguing with each other, and mother isn't discussing

Father: As far as I'm concerned, a world of good has come out of it, fortunately.

Mother: I think things look a lot better than they did six months ago. Unless you say we are still looking through rose-colored glasses.

Ther.: (To parents) As long as you deal with your feelings, I don't think that you are looking through rose-colored glasses, as long as you are able to deal with the feeling, deal with your fantasies, and talk them over. I think I would suggest that kind of thing that I was suggesting with Sybil and Carol—that you spend an hour or two with Carol sometime; maybe you could come up alone on the train and see Carol alone—spend a couple of hours with her. Spend some time with either Carol or Sybil alone. I think that parents have a lot to share with their children. Not collectively— individually. I think that that is important. There are things that you can relate as a man, Gerald—your growing up and your life—to Carol, that are unique. And there are things, Grace, that you can talk about that are unique to you. The more that you can talk and get things out and share them, the more it will promote open communication and a lack of secrecy. (82)

Carol: I just want to mention one thing

it. She sidetracks the issue by referring to and triangulating Carol.

(82) *Therapist is indicating behavioral tasks that they can do to promote more interaction between them as they explore relationships, and not just continue to gloss over situations as if everything is OK. If they will meet and continue to talk with each other frequently, they will get to a deeper level of relationship (but this process, which is similar to Bowen's "coaching," needs to be monitored by at least one member, if not the whole family, continuing in therapy.) The reason for suggesting the dyadic meetings (e.g., for one parent to meet separately with Carol) is that it might lead to a more intensive experience. This type of coaching is an effort to move away from the distractions and triangulations that occur when more than two family members meet. This particular family therapist views these dyadic exercises (which are not therapy sessions) as adjunctive to the main family therapy approach, which involves full family meetings (of two or more generations).*

(83) *Therapist sees this as*

before the evening is over—that is, that I want to and will continue coming here individually, and as I mentioned to you Friday (to therapist), I do not think that it means that I am having any kind of crisis or any really depressing problems. I feel good about coming here; I want to continue mainly because there are new discoveries that I want to find out about myself. (83)

mainly a positive, healthy assertion by Carol, that she states in the presence of her parents that she wants to continue to try to differentiate herself and to individuate. More typically, in the past, Carol felt she was in a powerless position, and closed-up emotionally, and presented a surface appearance of attempting to please others, whereas her resentments seethed and festered underneath.

Ther.: We touched on one of those earlier; we talked about a fuller exploration of sexuality. We just kind of skimmed the surface of it. (Carol starts to interject here) Excuse me, Carol, some of that can go on as you suggested. It depends on how frank you want to be. Two of the areas are sex and death—how people in the family have handled death. I'm not just talking about you, I'm talking about your families. (84)

Mother: I think Carol has seen some of this. (Referring to loss and death in the family) (85)

(84) The therapist's reference to death here is not only because he believes it is really important to face and discuss, but also because of mother's imminent surgery and Carol's suicidal tendency.

(85) Mother is probably referring here to losses and death that Carol experienced when the two grandmothers and a great-aunt were taken into the Gray home. They displaced Carol from her room. Carol had to move into Sybil's room. Sybil resented the intrusion and punched Carol in the stomach. One of the grandmothers and the great-aunt died while living in the family's home. Carol had earlier reported this to the therapist. She had not complained or protested at the

time about the displacement. Although she felt disregarded as a person, that her parents had not acknowledged her or handled her in a sensitive way, she suppressed this (as described in comment number 83 above).

Ther.: Well, some of it she hasn't seen—when you (father) were a little boy and you (mother) were a little girl—what was happening in your families and how people handled it. These issues are important. Loss, violence, and anger, and how people handled them; and dependency—how people have hung on in (the family) in various ways. I'm not just necessarily talking about living together, but also emotional dependency—when somebody cannot leave, emotionally leave, another person. That's what Sybil is beginning to do—she's beginning to leave geographically and maybe that has something to do with her taking some of her independence. At any rate, that's something we explored a little bit the last time. A lot of these things will go on, depending on how frank you want to be. I happen to be a believer in a great deal of frankness. (86)

Mother: This is what we talked about on Friday too. I did say that I hope that Carol will come to us if she has problems and . . .

Ther.: *Why* does it have to be problems?

Mother: OK—problems or anything she wants to talk about—I don't care—anything.

Ther.: The last time my father was in town we got to talking—we were just sitting there. He began to talk about a part of his life when he was in his early twenties—what was happening with him and his mother—incidents that happened and where his father was and what he was doing—and this is something that he had never mentioned to me. It had to do with a samovar and how his mother had to go in the

(86) Therapist is describing or setting up a schema or architecture or map of the territory (after summarizing what has already been discussed) of the direction that the therapy (both family and individual) will generally take. More specifically, he focuses on separation, loss, the dependency-independency struggle because he realizes the difficult and complex process Carol will have in separating appropriately from her mother.

(87) The therapist shares a personal anecdote from his family life. This therapist tends, as other therapists may be less likely to do, to share his own process with the families he treats. His notion is that "we are all in this together," and that his struggles and explorations may provide a model for openness of expression of feelings, and identifying with their journey together. This type of sharing also

hospital. His mother had to go in the hospital, and friends were packing their things and it was a very emotionally-laden article, a samovar which had been in the family for generations and brought over from Russia. These things were lost, and my father was talking about how he missed some of those things and they were important to him. I had bought a samovar and it was sitting there and that's what triggered it. This was new and it was nice to hear—it was nice to hear about him and his mother in a little different context and what happened when she got out of the hospital and how she was OK, but she missed these objects. They never got them back, because their friends had packed them in storage, and they never remembered what storage company they had taken them to. He'd made a search and now, when I am talking about it, I thought—I was just thinking about how, when my own mother died, a similar thing happened. My mother put some fur coats and some other things in storage and we never found the ticket, we never found what happened to it. (87)

(Response from the family in the background): Hmm-m.

    Ther.: . . . which makes me think of all the things I wanted to say to my mother that I never got a chance to when she was dying. It is not necessarily problems—that is a long way around saying that the conversations need not necessarily be based around problems. (88)

enhances the family's positive transference to the therapist, and serves as one part of balancing the therapist's tendency to confront the family in a direct and aggressive way in particular situations. The therapist's telling of the samovar incident from his own life and about his relationship with his father (which he probably associated to at an unconscious level) appears to be very appropriate at this juncture in the session. It exemplifies (1) sharing within a family, (2) a time of impending loss (when a mother figure is going into the hospital), and (3) the desire to hold on to the love object, and the positive aspect of the family relationships, through the symbolic representation of special family possessions or heirlooms. (This appears to be a very rich association of the therapist's, and resonates well with the family's emotional state at the time.) (88) While the therapist's associations have to do with problematic areas (i.e., the therapist's loss of his mother), he emphasizes the positive aspect of family members sharing the problems together. The therapist's association to his relation with his mother had to do with his own "unfinished business" (his not fully expressed grief). (The therapist had not reviewed or explored his relation to his mother or shared his feelings about her illness and dying out of his loyalty to his father, who had asked all the children to not talk about her dying to her.)

Mother: . . . No, no—I know.

Ther.: People getting together in the family—just sharing. It is nice to do because you like doing it. (89)

(89) This is one of the therapist's theories about family therapy—that it is not just to solve problems, but that the sharing of an experience with the family is an important part of it.

Father: . . . Share her pleasant experiences as well as the unpleasant ones.

Mother: Right.

Ther.: Just what it was like.

Father: Well.

Mother: I think we better leave. I have to drive home. He may take the wheel before we get there, though. (90)

(90) She finally takes responsibility to end the session. She had started to do this much earlier, when only about half of the scheduled time had elapsed; and the therapist had left it open for the family to decide when to end the session.

Carol: . . . This weather makes you sleepy.

Mother: . . . So we thank you and we may see you before Sybil leaves. Carol can let you know how things go and whether we can do it. (91)

Ther.: I hope the operation works out well.

Mother: I do too.

Father: I am glad that we're not more than eighty miles away. (To therapist) Thank you very kindly.

Mother: OK, thanks a lot, Jeff. We might see you once more.

Father: When we find out, we may see you again once more, before Sybil leaves. (92)

(91) She is still not totally comfortable with the idea of coming to therapy and has a tendency to end the process or to run away from it.

(92) Although it has become clear that he has a positive transference to the therapist and probably wants to return, he repeats what mother has just said and is careful not to disagree with her.

Mother: I guess she (Sybil) will be back.
Father: . . . She will be back.
Ther.: See you Monday (to Carol).
Father: Thanks an awful lot, Jeff.
   Carol: Should I make an individual appointment Monday night? (93, 94)
   Ther.: Yes.

(93) This question of Carol's appears to reflect her dependency on the therapist and the deferential quality of her transference to a parent-authority figure. Possibly, also, she needs to doublecheck on this, due to her general tendency to feel uncertain.

(94) For this treatment situation, as for many other cases of serious drug abuse, the therapist planned to conduct multimodal therapy. He did not believe that family therapy, without intensive individual therapy, would be as effective. He saw the individual therapy as providing a secure frame for developing a relationship of trust and for the "staying and holding" operation that such young adult clients often require. (This was not one of the cases in the systematic research demonstration study of family therapy referred to elsewhere in this book. For those cases, either the family therapy or parent group modality was the primary method of treatment.)

Factors in the Successful Possibility of Treatment

This is a selective description of therapist factors in the twelve-year treatment of a drug-using borderline patient and her family. Three major factors come readily to mind:

1. I had to establish active constructive contact with Carol and the other members of the Gray family. I had to join them. We had to "get engaged," so to speak. There had to be a likability between us. I have a hunger for closeness with others—I want in; I also have a capacity for flexibility, to move in and out of the family system, to be close and to be distant, to care and to be uncaring (to be responsive and attentive in the session and to say goodbye and forget them when they're gone). Essentially, I was saying to them, "When we're together, you'll get what I have to give, when you're not with me, nothing; but you can carry me with you."

2. There was a part of Carol's neediness that was consuming and devouring of people and relationships—she could eat me up. Her need was endless and draining. I could give and give and she would never be quite satisfied. I had to keep a relative peace of mind or calmness. How could I survive? How would I take care of myself? How could I be attentive and sensitive? I had to keep my emotional gyroscope or rudder steady. I did this mainly by speaking my mind openly and directly (as to what I saw and experienced with Carol and her family), and by working at resolving impasses, and clarifying misunderstandings and distortions. Also, I found that which was positive and life affirming, and was able to face unpleasant aspects of myself and state them forthrightly and clearly.

3. We all needed staying power—the capacity to develop and sustain an enduring stable therapeutic relationship: Carol and the Gray family and I would return to the situation of therapy again and again (through persistence and tenaciousness, with stubbornness and sheer pigheadedness). Psychotherapy can be difficult, tormenting (in facing aspects of self and family that are unpleasant or loathsome and disgusting to oneself); we needed perseverance to struggle, to wrestle, to contend, to disagree and to agree to go on talking.

What I brought to the experience was a multiplicity of self and consciousness (the many aspects of myself), my flexibility of self, and that which is affirming to me (the way I live my life); humor, an appreciation of the outrageous and the positive (to kid with them about what they do), playfulness (including rebelliousness, defiance, and brinkmanship), respect for their journey (as Edward Albee has a character in his play *Zoo Story* say, "Sometimes, a person has to go a very long distance out of his way to come back a short distance correctly"); irony (that is, to explicate projective identifications and make them absurd); capacities for empathy, confrontation and directness, and compassion; a capacity to reframe their experience—to see into them (both personally and interpersonally) and to hold their defenses and fears up to them in ways that were palatable and digestible to them; a sensitivity and empathy for their stuckness, bewilderment, and failure as a family; an awareness that the psychotherapy I practice is limited by and mirrors my personality and my biases; an ability to face my inability to know and solve everything for myself and others; and an ability to handle failure (not to blame them or myself if our endeavor didn't work out); and a capacity to bear failure, not to do well. In my view, basic change in individuals and families takes place over a long period of time.

I'm challenging, provocative, arrogant at times. At other times, for example, when there are deficits in the patient's introjects, I can fill in with a soothing presence. I look for similarities and differences, a way to connect with others. I have two tendencies: a need to be sensitive and feel close to the basic and primitive conflicts and the pain; and also a need for confrontation and bluntness about the emotional consequences of people's behavior; I like to move between these two.

On Psychotherapeutic Tracking in Family Therapy

You've got to wander around a little. You look for your chance. Details, clues. If you're not having a little ramble with them, you're not in touch with reality.

Notes to an Afterward

1. Carol was reluctant and resistant to having her family in as part of the treatment process; she kept much of her life a secret (that is, her drug taking, her being abused and victimized sexually), though she'd made life-threatening gestures. It took three months to convince Carol that it would be helpful and useful to have them in, that they would still relate to and care for her though they'd know her "awful" secrets. (To Carol, hers was an unspeakable situation.)

2. It's difficult recapitulating and explaining what I did intuitively; I did not plan my interventions. (The purpose of these family therapy meetings is to gather information, to clarify distortions and conflictual or problematic issues, to hear family members express their unique and individual points of view and to have other family members respond to them, and to have an experience together.)

3. Carol's drug taking and passionless sexual behavior masks her feelings of emptiness and isolation. She doesn't enjoy the drugs or the sex—she just wants the space and freedom to experiment, to do what she hears about from others as to what life is. Her life is filled with uneasiness, uncertainty, pain, and doubt. She enjoys the chance or opportunity to do what she wants or what she thinks she wants to do (in a counterdependent or rebellious manner in relation to what she's been told in a parental way she should do).

4. There's satisfaction in the family with a surface placidity—therapy was to help each of them look deeply into themselves and into each one's

relationships in the family. There was little curiosity for such exploration in this family; one could be appalled at what swims under the surface.

5. Carol had a symbiotic relation with her mother (Carol was the unconscious or id aspects of the symbiotic entity, being acted out; her mother was the conscious, determined, intentional, superego aspects). Carol, understandably, had contradictory or ambivalent feelings about her relationship with her mother. Carol feared expressing the negative side of her ambivalence, she feared being disloyal and losing her mother as a part of the symbiotic self—an amputation or separation might mean each would die—and losing her mother as an ally.

6. There was a "you have to do it yourself" message from the parents, in the family. Though there was evidence in other family sessions of other family problems (for example, Grace's cancer, Sybil's estrangement and divorce from her first husband), no one asked for emotional help or brought up these issues for thorough discussion.

7. At one point, about two years into treatment, Carol reported a provocative and illustrative episode. Her mother had left to take her mother (Carol's grandmother) to her sister and brother-in-law's in Florida. She (Grace) left instructions for Carol to come home (from Philadelphia to Maryland) on the weekend to cook for her father. Carol went home; her father invited his boss, a younger man, home for dinner; Carol cooked dinner and they all ate. After dinner, the father's boss and Carol went off for a motorcycle ride and, during the evening, engaged in a sexual relationship. Apparently, Carol and her father colluded, wittingly or unwittingly, in this incident, which was provocative but also had self-destructive implications for both of them. It could also be seen as a displacement and acting out of an incestual wish.

8. According to the parents, there are clear right and wrong ways to do things in life. The parents ignore the need for struggle where there's doubt about right and wrong or how to go about solving problematic areas of their lives. As Grace, the mother, says, "There's no easy way out" (that is, you have to do it the "right way," regardless of how difficult it is).

9. Carol's compliant—she tells her parents (and others) what she thinks they want to hear from her. She tries to please them, to avoid conflict and rejection. I was contentious with her; we'd fight and battle, disagree and agree.

10. Carol's rejecting and despairing about resolving anything with her family. She offers herself as target, victim, scapegoat (the "problem"), and martyr.

11. Carol's drug use isn't mentioned in this session—her drug use is an expression or a facade, masking her borderline personality.

12. Sybil was an absent member in most of the family therapy; the parents minimized the importance and necessity for her attendance, though

I continually pointed out the void and loss of information and point of view left by her absence. The distance of Sybil's going away (moving to a large midwestern city) creates a sense of anxiety and loss in the family. Her absence in the family sessions points to the parents' anxiety related to Sybil's problems and issues (such as her divorce). They wanted to see Carol as the only problem. The family talked about their underlying anxieties in blurry or indirect symbolic terms.

13. There was a vacuousness in the interactions between family members—there was little play or fun in the beginning of treatment. They were overserious—the forbiddenness and difficulty of accepting or coping with negative affect.

14. Emotional digestion for each person in the family takes its own time; each person has his or her own internal process.

15. Family strengths: Mother's personal strength throughout the therapy. Carol's persistence and tenaciousness in treatment.

16. My asking originally for the family therapy session was aggressive, intrusive, and somewhat disruptive to the Grays in their usual manner of handling physical illness. Another part was that my providing a transitional time and space for discussion of this problem was a way of my caring for them. I was available to them and for them in new ways. I was opening up new opportunities and possibilities for them. Still, meeting the family was in my mind, to fight fire with fire.

17. The therapist as curious nonexpert (like Columbo, the television detective: "I was just wondering . . .") The use of a hunch, a "gut feeling," a speculation, to discover the true, especially the hidden or disguised character of . . . to discover or determine the existence, presence, or fact of . . .

18. The therapist's sense of not being heard by the family—in one ear and out the other—and his need to be heard.

19. Therapist's flexibility—capacity to join family system and to move away, to get close and become distant. My own life is at stake in each treatment hour as well as theirs, at least on a symbolic level. It feels that way to me at the time, whether it is actually true or not. Also, I break the current of family interaction in the session, to refocus and reframe. This restructuring may serve a useful purpose for the family; but I need to do it for myself, to maintain my own identity.

It's been a lifetime struggle for me to learn to articulate myself—to name, to gain control, to know, to express, to share. It's a continual struggle to grow. I've lived in a lot of confusion, pain, and not knowing. No one, including my parents, seemed able to clarify or explain the emotional world to me. Looking back now, I think books (novels, stories, plays, poems) were my first therapist; they showed people in their lives talking, acting, struggling, trying to understand themselves, figuring out their problems and conflicts, trying to live happier and more satisfying lives, accepting their imperfections, their humanness. As I struggled with my parents and later with therapists and teachers, I began to trust my perceptions. Though I'm essentially hesitant, fearful, and shy, I'm capable of being contentious, arrogant, and provocative.

The Grays and I shared a stubbornness, a tenaciousness, a stick-to-itiveness, a pigheadness, an obstinacy in returning to the situation of treatment over and over for twelve years.

It is through resolving the disagreements and impasses as they develop between the psychotherapist and the patient or members of the patient family (or the family itself) that trust develops. It is not just freely given; it must be earned and learned interpersonally; it happens between us.

What's Happened in the Family Since Treatment with Me Ended Three Years Ago

Carol completed her B.A. She's currently in her third year of law school at a large midwestern state university. When she recently visited Philadelphia, she contacted me. I'm in private practice in the Philadelphia area. Personally, Carol appeared relaxed; the skin of her face was softer (not stiff), and there was a sparkle of excitement in her eyes. She seemed more relaxed in herself and more accepting of herself. She said she's able to ask for help directly and forthrightly. For example, she said she's used individual psychotherapy intermittently at school—it's a frame or structure she can count on. She said she's aware of a need for balance in her life: study, food, work, play, family, sleep, exercise, socializing. Her mother died a year and a half after treatment ended. Carol took a year's break from classes, worked, and stabilized herself. "I said goodbye to my mother" (both actually and in therapy). "It made me aware of my own death, how short life is. I'm communicating to people, enjoying my life more. My dating is more successful. I don't sit around and fantasize about guys anymore. I don't get high or drink, I know when to stop. I have tighter controls on myself now. I'm better at controlling my impulsiveness. I know I still have it."

Carol talked about a trip her parents took to visit her at school shortly before her mother's death: "It was at spring break and my mother was dying, but she was worried about me and the trip reassured her I was okay." Carol and I talked of her mother's strength and her acceptance of her approaching death, and that Carol had inherited some of her mother's strength: "It was a stressful time. I needed something [Carol needs regeneration] too. I felt guilty [about her parents traveling to see her while her mother's health was deteriorating], it was a strain for all of us, but it worked out, and I remember something you [S.J.M.] said: 'Infinity is in people, eternity is in the moment.' "

Carol said Sybil's second marriage is stable and fulfilling. She and her husband live in Milwaukee and both are successful in the financial field. They have no children, though he has a child from a previous marriage.

Grace, the mother, died in the spring of 1987; her cancer had metastasized. Gerald, the father, lives in a small town in Michigan. He's retired, has a dog, and socializes with friends and neighbors. Carol said she and her father "have gotten closer."

17
The Therapy of
The Schmidt Family

Michael Falzone

Editors' note: This is a case in which an adolescent's misbehavior and involvement with drugs displays a clear message that the family as a whole is experiencing great difficulty in maintaining its integrity. Within the chaos shown by the family during the early sessions, the therapist could perceive basically positive qualities, particularly the mutual caring and desire for order and control. The crucial element of parental cooperation and mutuality in enabling the children to achieve self control and constructive behavior is well illustrated in this case. Also demonstrated is the therapist's effective handling of his own countertransference reactions. In addition, flexibility in managing intervention strategies is well illustrated.

Meeting the Family

Sitting in the waiting room were three stone-faced people. My first thought was, I was expecting the child and parents, not the grandparents. Mary, age fourteen, looked like eighteen years old and was very pretty, with long brunette hair hanging down over her shoulders; she was the index patient. Mom and Dad, who I thought were grandma and granddad, were sitting there looking old, depressed, disgusted, and noncommunicative.

I asked them to come into my office. At that moment, Mrs. Schmidt grabbed Mary's arm, pulled her out of the seat, and pushed her into the office. It was apparent that the index patient did not want to be here. It immediately became apparent that Dad also was not pleased about coming to therapy. Mrs. S. was the spokesperson for the family. She began with a rough, brash voice, accusingly talking at her daughter. As she continued to talk, Mary slumped down more in her chair until I could no longer see her face. Mr. Schmidt's face was at the same time becoming strained and agitated. At the same time, my stomach was becoming sick. Mrs. S., who is fifty-one years old (and looks at least sixty-three) was coming across as abrasive and offensive. I had a flash of my stepmother. Mrs. S. not only talked like my stepmother but looked like her. She also had similar mannerisms. Oddly enough, at age forty-two, I still have an ambivalent relationship with my stepmother. I began to realize why I was getting the sick feeling in my gut.

After I let her talk a little, I interrupted and asked why they came. Mr. S. said, "I am here only because the judge ordered it." Mrs. S. said, "Something has to change, I am sick and tired of the shit that is going on in our family." I asked Mary, "How come the judge ordered you to come for counseling?" As this point she sat up and said she got into trouble with two friends. I asked what had happened, and she proceeded to tell me that this girl in her town was causing a lot of problems for her at school, was talking against her and turning other friends away from her. So Mary and two friends beat her up, which sent her to the hospital. Mom interrupted and said that they also got caught with drugs on them. Mom said, "I don't know what happened to her, she was so good. These friends she hangs around with are changing her!" I asked Mom, if being here could be helpful to the family. She said at this point anything could help. Dad said it was useless, and Mary said, "I don't know."

There was about twenty minutes left in the session. I proceeded to get a genogram of the family. Mary has a twin brother, Ralph, and a cousin, Sally, age fourteen, who has been living with them for two years. Mr. and Mrs. S. told me that their oldest son, Tony, age twenty-two, is also living in the house, along with two sons of Mr. S.'s deceased brother. There were also five dogs and three cats. As the session was ending, it was getting confusing and mind boggling just keeping track of the household.

I ended the first session by reiterating the importance of all the family being here to work the problems out together. I asked them to bring Ralph, Sally, and Mary back next week. Their older son, Tony, was going to be away for three weeks. When he returned, I said I would like to see him also. At this point, I did not have a feel for the situation of the two nephews that would be sufficient to ask them to come in right away.

The Calm Before the Storm

In the second session there was the calm before the storm. In my office is a couch that comfortably seats four people. On it were the bold-faced mom; her son Ralph, age thirteen; Mary, age fourteen, the index patient; and the niece, Sally. On a chair in front of Sally and across from me was Dad, leg over leg, looking angrily at the opposite wall. Not a word was said for the first three minutes. I kept looking from Mom down the couch to Dad. I caught Ralph fidgeting in his seat, and finally with an anxious laugh and a wave of his hand he said "Hi." I responded, "Hi, I'm Mike; you are Ralph?" He smiled. Then I turned to Sally and said, "You are Sally?" She said nothing. Mom said in a rough, harsh, very loud voice, "Answer him, he's speaking to you!" Sally turned and gave her a look that could send shivers up and down one's spine.

Then came the storm—they all started screaming at each other. Dad was telling them all to "shut up." The walls were vibrating. I got up out of my seat and left the room. I closed the door behind me. I heard it clearly for about two minutes more. Then it became silent. I opened the door and returned to my chair. Ralph and Mary, the twins, were laughing. Sally was angry, with her arms folded in front of her. Mom and Dad were looking at me inquisitively. I said in a calm, low voice, but sternly, "I hope that will be the last time that happens." The twins were still laughing. I looked at them and said, "I mean it. You could do it all you like at home, but not here. I am confused, I do not understand what caused such a commotion." Mom and Dad immediately proceeded to talk to me about it at the same time. My right hand went up to stop them, and I said, "Please, one at a time." This became a phrase I used at least twenty times for the next six sessions. It took me a whole hour just to get them to try to talk one at a time. I saw through this chaos the two adults—Mom and Dad—acting like the children and using their children, including their niece Sally, to take their sides. I pointed this out to them. As the session was drawing to a close and my confusion remained with me, I shared it with them. Mr. S. started to say, "This is getting nowhere and it's hopeless. This is going to do nothing." The kids sided with him. Mom gave them all a dirty look and put her head down. I took the opportunity to say, "It took years to get to this point; it is going to take time to communicate better. Furthermore, at this point, you do not have a choice. The judge ordered it, and it's up to me to decide if it will work or not. I cannot make that decision yet. I will see you all next week at the same time."

In working with the judicial system, I once in a while use the leverage of the courts, especially since some of the families need to be told to do things because they lack motivation in the beginning.

Further Sessions

In the next two sessions, three and four, I continued to stop them in midpoint, asking them to "please talk one at a time." The seating arrangement always stayed the same. Mom and Dad always distanced themselves from each other as far as they could. The twins always sat next to each other, and Sally always managed to be near her uncle.

In these two hours, I managed through the loud shouts and mish-mash to get a sense of this family. They live in a fairly nice section of a suburb in Pennsylvania "on the right side of the tracks." Mom and Dad both work and bring home a middle-class income. Mr. S. has been in a managerial position for twenty-five years. He rose to the top level and manages a department of forty people. Mrs. S. works in a factory setting and enjoys it. She claims she is out of the house and has made some good friends. The children lack nothing materially. Mr. S. boasted about his political influence with top government officials in the area. Both parents have completed twelfth grade. They do stress to the children the importance of education. Mrs. S.'s daughter Arlene, age thirty, from a previous marriage, is a registered nurse and supervisor of nursing at one of the local hospitals. Mrs. S. beams ear to ear when addressing her daughter.

I sensed after the fourth hour that this family was proud of their industriousness. They know that if you want something it isn't going to be handed to you—you have to work for it.

What they learned in the two sessions is debatable. I encouraged them to talk to each other, not through me. I constantly pointed out how they all talk at the same time. I do believe after the fourth hour that Mr. S. was hooked into therapy. Since I connected with him in the work force and honestly praised him for his years of accomplishment, he felt affirmed. As the fourth session was drawing to a close, I asked them to bring in their son Tony, age twenty-four, for the next session, since he had returned from vacation. They agreed.

As the fifth session unfolded, I felt I was interviewing a frustrated rock star with five of his most loyal subjects around him. Tony was dressed in a leather jacket and leather boots. His hairline was receding. He looked like Ralph's twin brother, only ten years older. When Tony's face was serious, he looked passable for a rock idol; however, when he smiled, he looked as if he came to the interview from the bowery, missing his front teeth.

Mr. S. was very proud that he had Tony working with him at the same firm: "He is my second in command." "How do the two of you like working together?" I asked. Tony said, "Fine. What I really like is the money." Dad laughed and said, "Yeah, and I wonder what he does with it, he always asks me to buy him cigarettes and lunch." I asked Tony if he pays board. Mrs. S. laughed. Tony said no but angrily said "I bring them TVs, toasters, and last month a refrigerator."

Tony proceeded to tell me that he had been living at home for six months. He left his wife and daughter, age two, and supports them: "My wife is on welfare and I pay welfare." I asked if he was moving toward divorce. Mom and Dad both said that's why he was always over at her apartment. He said she was pregnant and blaming him: "I'm not going to support another child." I asked him if it were his. He said, "I don't know." "Have you slept with her since you've been separated?" "Oh sure."

The younger guys were mesmerized by Tony's every word. They said he is "cool." As the session continued, I noticed that he was calming for them. They gave him the floor a lot and did not interrupt. At one point when Mom and Dad were going at it, I asked if this was the way it was growing up. He said he noticed a difference when he came back home to live. It doesn't get to him "because I'm not home much."

As the session was ending, I said to the family, "You all seem to be on good behavior. Maybe Tony should try to be home more and there would be less arguing and fighting." They all laughed. I also thanked them for bringing Tony. I asked to meet their other daughter, Susan, who lives with her boyfriend. She left the house about six months ago. It was discussed that she and Mary were very close until she moved out. Now they hardly talk to each other.

It was beginning to become apparent that there had been a lot of changes about six months ago. Tony came back into the house, Susan left the house. It was also the time that the nephews moved in because they had no place to stay. Mary's acting out became meaningful, especially since prior to this Mom and Dad claimed they had no serious problems with her. In fact she was an A student and never hung around with the "wrong crowd."

When they arrived for the sixth session, Mom said she talked to Susan, who had agreed to come next week, provided we could make it a different day. I agreed. The session began as usual; they were all arguing about what I do not know. I asked, "What are you fighting about? I can never make heads or tails because you always argue at the same time." Sally did not want to come; she did not think it was her problem. Mrs. S. said that she had a lot to do with it. She and Mary were always fighting, and Sally always goes to her uncle for protection. Mrs. S. said, "I punish Sally and say no to her, and he [the uncle] always says it's OK and lets her do what she wants." Mary, very upset, agreed and said, "I can't do anything." Mr. S. said, "That's because you are on probation and are not allowed to be with your friends." At this point I found out her probation officer's name and asked Mary permission to be in touch with her. Mary agreed. Mary reports to her each week. I thought it would be good to inform the authorities that the family is cooperating; they also might have some useful information for me.

This was the session I pulled up some real alliances. Dad and Sally were together. Mom and Ralph stuck together. Mary, interestingly enough, swayed back and forth. She played them against each other. She sided with the twosome that benefited her at the time. It was noticed that Mr. S. felt sorry for Sally because of all she had been through. She had been placed in foster homes every time her mother was hospitalized. Sally also saw her mother kill a boyfriend she was living with, and she had to testify in court. As a result her mother was sent to prison for two years. Sally grew up streetwise and took care of herself and her mother in her younger years when she herself needed nurturance. It was obvious that Sally resists authority. However, it was also evident that these last two years with the Schmidts have been the most stabilizing for her. Sally is doing average work in school and has not been a behavioral problem, as in the past. Sally has two older brothers, Wayne, age twenty-five, who is borderline retarded and cannot take care of himself. He was in a couple of institutions before he moved in with the Schmidts. Joseph, age twenty-two, was raised by foster parents, and he was heavily into drugs. He ran away from the foster parents and lives now with the Schmidts. Mr. S. feels responsible and sorry for them because his brother married their mother and died. On some level he is trying to repay his brother. It is causing Mr. and Mrs. S.'s relationship to become more strained than ever. As the session was ending, I pointed out the sides being taken and the breakdown of the parental boundaries. I began to sense that they were able to hear me for the first time since they began. I told them I would be looking forward to meeting with them and Susan next week.

When Susan showed up the following week, she came with her mother, father, and Mary. Both Ralph and Sally were sick with the flu. Interestingly enough, Susan looked like Mary's twin. As a matter of fact they looked the same age, though Susan was twenty-two. Mary had been wearing a lot of make-up and looking older.

Mom and Dad sat on either end of the room facing each other. Susan sat nearer to Mom on the couch, and Mary nearer to Dad on the opposite end of the couch. There was a big span between the sisters.

I told Susan I appreciated her coming to the session to shed more light on her family. She proceeded to tell me, "I'm not sure I could, I haven't been living home for a while." I asked, "How long?" She said about six months. I said, "Prior to that were you living at home?" She said yes. I then mentioned that the time before she left home would be helpful to talk about. She proceeded to tell me that the year before she was engaged to be married but that that ended when she found out her fiancé was involved with her girlfriend. She claimed she was not too upset because she was not in love with him. She "just wanted to get out of the house." I asked, "How come?" "With all of my friends married I thought I should be too. I realize now that was immature." I said, "It turned out for the best that your fiancé did what he did—you could be married now to a man you didn't love." She agreed. Both Mom and Dad also agreed.

I was watching Mary, who kept her head down during this dialogue. I then turned to her and asked if she thought Susan was leaving the house for the right reason. "No, I wish she were still home," Mary said and started crying. Susan turned to her and said, "What's the matter?" Mary did not answer. I then turned to Mom and Dad and asked them why Mary was crying. Mom said, "Probably 'cause Susan is not around much." I asked Mary if that was correct. No answer. Susan turned to me and said, "We were very close before I left. I would share and do everything with Mary."

I said, "Like best friends." Mary cried more and I gave her a tissue to use. I asked Mary if she missed Susan, and she continued to cry and nod her head affirmatively. I asked Susan if she realized how much Mary missed her and loved her. Susan said, "I miss her too, but I had to leave to find myself. I could not do it at home." "So you didn't leave to hurt the family but to find yourself," I said. Mary started crying and Susan said, "I had to depend on myself for a while; I still need to do that. I know everyone, Mom and Dad included, did not want me to leave, but I felt and still do that I need my space."

Susan works for a department store, part-time. She is also taking a couple of courses at the community college. She met her boyfriend where she works; he is the manager. They moved in together in an apartment, and she claims it is working out well.

Dad voiced his concern about the boyfriend: he does not seem to like his lack of industriousness. As manager of the store, he does not make a great salary, and there is no advancement for him. Mr. S. comes from a position in which he climbed the ladder in the last twenty-five years and received good monetary compensation for it. I used this to let Susan know that Dad "wants to make sure you are financially taken care of out of love for you."

The session was a fairly quiet one that had some healing of rejection and loss feelings. Susan felt good about it because she said she would be glad to come back again. I thanked her.

A Turning Point

This was a turning point for me. I really began to like this family a lot and understand them better. After the first session my sick feeling disappeared because I brought to consciousness the feeling I have toward my stepmother. This, I believe, helped free me up to see Mrs. S. as an individual who had traits similar to those of my stepmother, but was not my stepmother. I also sensed on some level that this family was experiencing a great deal of pain, loss, and rejection. They hid this in their chaotic behavior, as well as in their many distractions. When they lose someone or something, they replace that person with someone else. For example, they have five dogs and three cats; this I believe has symbolic meaning in that the animal takes the place of a lost one.

I contracted for Mr. and Mrs. S. to come to the eighth session themselves. I felt that they were hooked and in fact enjoyed coming. This also was a turning point in therapy. Mr. S. no longer felt obligated to come. In this session, Mr. and Mrs. S. sat on the couch but with a whole space between them. Mrs. S. had had her hair done. She looked nice, and I complimented her. She beamed from ear to ear. I also asked Mr. S. if he had told her how nice she looked. He looked away, embarrassed. Mrs. S. said, "He hasn't said a nice thing to me in a long time." Mr. S. said, "Yes, I did, I told you how good dinner was." "She's a good cook?" I said. He said, "Yeah, when she cooks."

This started World War Three. They were again talking at the same time. I had to raise my voice and ask them to speak one at a time. "Wait a minute, Jane [Mrs. S.'s first name]. Tell me about your Mom and Dad. Are they still living?" She proceeded to say that she and her parents have an ambivalent relationship. They argue with her a lot. They do not like Mr. S., and she feels they still treat her like a child. She has an older brother and sister to whom Mom and Dad do not give any problems. She does not see her brother and sister much, and she has a distant relationship with them and their families. Her parents she sees consistently at least once a week. Mr. S. has fights with his father-in-law: "He thinks he knows it all."

I then asked Mr. S. about his family of origin. He lost his mother and father within a year of each other about twenty-five years ago. He lost his two older brothers, one ten years ago and the other four years ago. He began to get teary-eyed. He was very close to his brother, who is the father of Sally and the nephews living with him, and who died of a heart attack at age sixty-three. Mr. S. is coming close to age sixty-three himself, and I asked him, "Are you concerned about dying too?" "Hell no," he said. I said, "Good—but if you keep up with this stressfulness at home, I'd be worried you might not live too long." Mrs. S. said, "I keep telling him the same thing." I said, "See how much she really cares. It seems she doesn't want to lose you." I then said to Mr. S., "There have been a lot of losses in your life. Is this why it is important to have Sally, Wayne, and people around to keep a sense of family together?" He said, "I feel responsible because their mother is not fit to take care of them." "I understand, but you may have to weigh out what it could be doing to your own family." Mrs. S. agreed by saying, "I do not know if I can take it anymore. With them [the nephews and nieces] and the animals the house is like a zoo." He said, "Well, if you didn't drink so much, maybe there would not be the problems and fights with everyone." She retorted, "I drink because I come home to the madhouse and filth that's always there. No one does anything around the house."

The session was drawing to an end. I said, "I appreciated how open you two were about your families." This was helpful to me in understanding things better. "I could be wrong but I have a feeling that your families of origin interfere with your relationship." They said, "What do you mean?" "Well, you [Mr. S.] always fight with your father-in-law and that upsets you [Mrs. S.]; and you [turning toward Mrs. S.] are upset because your husband has his brother's children living with you." They were quiet. I told them to think about that and see if maybe that interferes with their having a better relationship between them. I told them I would like to see everyone next week.

The Approach of a Holiday

The ninth session took place the first week of November. The reason I mention this is because Thanksgiving has a significant and symbolic message for this family. The session began almost like the first one, except that along with Mary, her mother, and father were also Ralph and Sally. They were all carrying on at each other. I said, "It seems we are back to square one." Dad said again that this was going nowhere. The kids agreed with him. I at this point was thinking, "I wonder if last week got too close to home." I asked what happened. Sally was placed on the hot seat. "She [Sally] is causing trouble. I'm sick and tired of it. I don't want her in the house if she is going to continue to disobey and cause trouble," Mom said. I asked Mr. S. what his wife was referring to. He answered, "I guess the way Sally and Mary are fighting over their room and wearing each other's clothes." Both Sally and Mary verbally went at each other. Ralph stood up and walked around the room nervously. I said to Ralph, "This is upsetting you!" "They always do this. When I am home I just go out and get away from it," he replied. I turned to Mom and Dad and asked them if they realized how upset Ralph gets with the fighting. Mom said, "He gets that way when I fight with his father too." Dad said, "He is too sensitive." I said to Ralph, "Are you worried your family is going to split up?" He did not answer. I then asked Mom and Dad if they thought he was afraid the family was going to fall apart. They did not know. The session continued with more accusations. Finally, Mom said, "I've had it," and turned to me and said, "You wonder why I drink." I turned to her and said, "Well, why do you take it, why don't you leave and maybe they will see what they are missing?" "I left once before and they could not care less." When? "Three years ago, I stayed overnight at my married daughter's house. When I came home, things were the same, and they didn't even ask where I was." Dad said, "I knew you were with Arlene [the married daughter]." "See," I said, "He [Mr. S.] was worried about you." She snickered.

The day before the tenth session, I received a phone call from Mrs. S. She was calling from her daughter Arlene's home. She informed me that she had moved out yesterday and told her husband she was not returning until he got rid of his nephews, his niece Sally, and all the animals. I was pleasantly surprised but concerned she was calling to say it was quits with therapy. I asked her if she was going to return with the family. She said, "I will pick up the kids, but I am not sure my husband will come." I told her,

"I hope so. It is especially important now to see what is going to be done. I'll see you all tomorrow night."

The next night came, and Mrs. S. showed up with the twins. Sally claimed she was sick, and her husband had kicked out the nephews and was staying around to make sure they would not sneak back into the house. I asked her if she seemed interested in returning. She said yes. I also voiced my opinion about how quickly Mr. S. had moved to have his nephews leave. Mrs. S. said, "He knows I mean business. I will not return until he gets rid of the animals and does something about Sally."

Mary began to talk about Sally, saying, "When my mother left, Sally went to her guidance counselor and said some things. He called the Division of Youth and Family Services and the representative from the service called the house." After hearing this I became curious. I said, "Why would he call protective services?" Mary said, "I think she thought they would remove her from our house because my mom left." I seemed puzzled. Mary turned toward her mother and said, "Sally thinks she's pregnant." I asked, "Has she been sexually active?" Mary said, "She told me she has been having sex since she was six years old." Her mom made a concerned face and said, "What!" "Mom, she told me she was also having sex with Wayne [the twenty-five-year-old nephew]." I asked Mary if she shared this information with her father. She answered no. I turned to the mother and said that these accusations were serious and that I was concerned. We spent the rest of the session discussing the immediacy of what needed to be done. I informed Mrs. S. that protective services should come to the house immediately: "It is good to know that Wayne was kicked out of the house. Your husband should be informed of the seriousness of this matter. If this is true about Sally's activity since age six, then protective services needs to evaluate her." I told Mom I would be happy to release information to protective services. I also told her to give my name to the representative there. I ended the session by telling them all to be present next week: "We need to clear up some of the accusations heard about tonight."

On the night before Thanksgiving, the eleventh session occurred. It was a session in which Mrs. S. left her car at their home and drove with Mr. S., Mary, Ralph, and Sally. When they arrived for the session, Mrs. S. had been out of the house for a week and a day. In the beginning of the session it seemed as if Mr. S. were giving his wife the "silent treatment." I did not address myself to this and instead moved quickly to the issues and accusations brought up in the previous session. I asked the family whether protective services had been in contact with them. Mr. S. replied, "She [the caseworker] was out to the house and reopened the case." I asked Mrs. S., "Were you aware of the caseworker being at the house?" "I went to the house when she came, when Mary told me she was coming." I continued to ask Mrs. S. whether the caseworker was aware that she was living elsewhere at this time.

Mrs. S. claimed she was more concerned with the abuse—that she did not offer that information. I asked Sally if she knew what we were talking about. She thought so. I turned to Mr. S. and asked him if he were aware of what was happening. "Mary told me and I am glad I kicked those bastards out [the nephews]." Turning to Sally, I said, "Mary mentioned last week that you told her you think you are pregnant?" She replied, "Yeah, but I'm not. I got my period." "Oh good, you must be relieved?" She nodded her head affirmatively. I continued gently to question Sally about her sexual activity, and she did not deny it. She claimed she slept around with a lot of guys. I then asked her about having sexual contact with her brother. She denied it. She said she told Mary that he tried it but nothing happened. I informed the family that I am bringing these things out in the open because they are serious matters and because I am obliged to do so. I told them that this will be explored with protective services in great detail. Mrs. S. informed me that she gave my name and phone number to the caseworker. I proceeded to have them sign a release of information, since they were the appointed guardians.

We had about fifteen minutes left in the session. Ralph informed me that his father had given away all the pets, except for one dog they had had for ten years. I turned to Mrs. S. and asked, "Did you know that?" She said the children had informed her. "It seems your demands were pretty much met." There was no reply. After a few minutes of silence, Mr. S. said, "We got a turkey with the stuffing, and Mary is going to make pumpkin pie." Ralph shouted, "I already made the pie crust." "You know how to bake," I said. Mom beamed and said, "Ralph is a good cook." I said, "That's great, and I bet he learned from his dad." Mom laughed, and Dad smiled. I asked Mrs. S. what her plans for Thanksgiving were going to be. "I probably will have dinner with my daughter, Susan." I turned to the other four members of the family. "You guys going to have dinner with your mom?" No reply. I asked Mr. S., "Was that your invitation to your wife to join you for dinner by telling her what you were preparing?" Both Mary and Ralph turned to their mom and asked her to come to dinner. The session was ending, and I said, "Well, Mom, you got an invitation. I will see all of you next week, and I will follow through with the worker at protective services."

Continuing Therapy

During the week after Thanksgiving, I received a phone call from the Division of Youth and Family Services worker. She informed me that she had reopened the case and had gone to their home for an investigative study. She voiced her concern and asked me to submit a report to the division. I.

sent out a report on the progress of the Schmidt family and voiced my concerns that Sally might need some individual attention.

At this point in the therapeutic process, I discussed this case with the staff on the research project and with my supervisor, Dr. Alfred Friedman. They felt that some good progress was being made with the family. They also suggested that I think about having a session between Mrs. S. and her married daughter Arlene, who was born from Mrs. S.'s first marriage. Arlene lives in another suburb in Pennsylvania with her husband and two sons. Mrs. S. had spent the previous week and a half with her daughter and family. I also learned that the prior two times when Mrs. S. left the house, which was only overnight, she went to her daughter's home.

In the twelfth session, I learned from Mr. S. that Thanksgiving was good "until she got drunk," referring to his wife. Mrs. S. replied to the accusation with "He brought me the bottle of wine." Before the session could get out of hand, I asked, "I guess you went home for Thanksgiving dinner?" Mrs. S. said, "I went home right after the session and asked my daughter Arlene to bring my clothes home." I turned to the children, Mary, Ralph and Sally, and asked them if they enjoyed their Thanksgiving. They all responded in the affirmative. Ralph said, "My dad gave my mom the bottle of wine, and then they started fighting the rest of the night." "What did you do," I asked. "I went over my friend's house," Ralph replied. I turned to Mary and Sally and asked the same question. Mary was the spokesperson for them and said, "We cleaned the dishes and went to our bedroom to listen to music." Mrs. S. turned to me and started defending herself: "I was at my daughter's all week and I didn't drink a thing." I asked her if she was telling me she does not need to drink. She informed me she only drinks on weekends, and she reiterated that when she is living in her household it is a way to escape this "craziness." I asked Mr. S. how come he waited until after dinner to bring out the wine. He informed me that he forgot he got it for her (her favorite kind). "You were pleased she was home and gave her this because you knew she would appreciate it." He replied in the affirmative. I asked him if he drank with her. He does not like to drink. Mrs. S. replied, "He likes to gamble and I'm not supposed to get upset at that." "I'm entitled to it, it's my spending money. I give you my whole paycheck." They started going at each other. It seems that they get a little closer and then fight and argue to distant themselves.

At this point, to have explored their relationship and the dysfunctional patterns with the drinking and gambling would have, I believe, prematurely interrupted the therapeutic process. I began to talk about Mrs. S.'s daughter, Arlene. The children seemed to be fond of her and had a nice relationship with her and her children. Mr. S. also spoke fondly of her, even though she was not his biological daughter. I asked Mrs. S. if Arlene would come in with her to have a session. I told her I felt she seemed to be a source of strength to her. I also stated that she must have felt very close to Arlene to go and spend a week with her and her family. We discussed the possibility and set up a tentative appointment for next week. Arlene is a teacher at one of the local schools and at times she works overtime. I asked Mrs. S. to call to confirm after she found out her schedule. Mrs. S. called two days before and confirmed that she and her daughter would be present for the thirteenth session.

Arlene and her mother were in the waiting room five minutes before the session. Arlene had come directly from work. I opened the session by asking Arlene if she knew why she was here with her mother. Arlene replied, "My mother told me I might shed some light on the family." I asked her if she felt she could. She informed me that she has been away for ten years but does talk to her mom almost every day and frequents the family. I was observing Mrs. S., who seemed very relaxed, delighted, and proud to be there. This was a changed posture for Mrs. S. Normally she was more anxious with the other family members and smoked cigarettes one after the other. I asked Mrs. S., "Why are you smoking less? Is it because your daughter is a teacher?" At that point, her daughter lit a cigarette. "No, I just do not feel a need to smoke so much," Mrs. S. replied. "It seems Arlene has a soothing effect on you." Mrs. S. smiled. Arlene spoke: "It comes with the job. I work with children and after a while you get excited about very little." As the session proceeded, it was quite evident that Mom and Arlene had a very close and healthy relationship. Arlene claimed that her mom shares openly with her. She also informed me that she listens and offers little advice. "I have learned to stay out of the middle between my mom and dad." Arlene was raised by Mr. S. since she was three, and he is the only father she knows. She speaks of him fondly and had some insight into his behavior. She claimed, "His bark is worse than his bite." Arlene loves her work and gets a great deal of satisfaction from it. She also supervises other teachers. She shared that her marriage had its ups and downs. Her husband was out of a job for one year, and they were struggling. She had worked all during their marriage except when her sons, nine and eight, were born. Grandma indicated that the grandchildren are a handful. Arlene agreed. Arlene was glad that her mom had gone home and that the family is in counseling. Arlene indicated that she has been more like a mother to Mary and Ralph. They were four years old when she left the house. She tried to talk to Mary: "When she just got in trouble she wouldn't listen to me. She tells me I'm not her mother." As the session was drawing to a close, I thanked Arlene for sharing her feelings and concerns. I told her she certainly had some good insight into her family. Mom felt supported and affirmed by her daughter. It was therapeutic in that Mrs. S. knows she has her daughter to turn to in good times and bad. I told Mrs. S. I would see her and the family next week.

In the fourteenth session, Mr. and Mrs. S. seemed to be very friendly. The children, Mary, Ralph, and Sally, were quiet. I said to them, "This is a switch. Usually you guys are talking and Mom and Dad are quiet. It is the other way around." Mom said that Mary was just getting over a cold and Sally was coming down with one. I told Mrs. S. she should have left Sally home. "I told her she could stay home but she wanted to come." Mrs. S. said she was probably afraid to stay there. I asked why. Mr. S. informed me that the other night his nephew Joseph came into the house and slept behind the couch in the family room. He is living out in the street, as far as Mr. S. knew, and needed a place to stay. Mr. S. told Joseph if he came back he would call the police. He also informed me that he had changed the locks on the door. They remained quiet and I asked Sally if she was worried her brothers would come back into the house. She did not answer. Mrs. S. turned to Sally and said, "If they come near the house, I will call the cops." I asked them if Tony, their oldest, was sleeping in the house these days. Mom claimed he is in and out and "we never know when to expect him home." I said it might be a good idea to ask him to be home for a while until this blew over. "Is he aware of what has been happening?" Mr. S. said, "I see him at work every day, and I tell him what's happening." I asked the family to bring Tony with them next week: "Maybe we can discuss this together as a family."

Next week came, and Tony was with the family. Sally was feeling better, and so was Mary. I asked Tony what he thought about his cousins leaving the house and about Joseph attempting to sneak into the house last week. He said, "If I see either of them, I'll break their legs." "Tony, you sound angry," I said. "You are damn right I am—especially with what I heard they did." Sally shouted, "They didn't do anything, leave them alone." "That's not what I heard, Sally," Tony said. "Joseph didn't do anything, and Wayne just asked me to," Sally said. "Asked you to what?" "Okay, nothing," and she put her head down. It got quiet in the room. Ralph said, "Maybe he didn't do anything, but he's a pothead and acts crazy." I asked Ralph what he meant by "crazy." He described him as looking into space and not responding to people when they talked to him. Everyone concurred. I asked Tony, since he was concerned for Sally, why he didn't come home at night. He mentioned that he would meet some girls and stay with them. I asked him until things settled down around the house if he could make an effort to come home at night. He thought he could. "It seems like your brother, sister, and cousin Sally are concerned about being in the house alone." The three of them did not disagree. I told Tony I felt that the family looked up to him as the oldest and that his concern and protection would be appreciated. He seemed pleased with the statement. I also told him that making an effort to come on short notice was also a sign of caring. As the session was drawing to a close, I saw Mom and Dad jelling together better.

I asked them to come next week together. I wanted to reinforce their efforts at working together on parenting skills.

Both Mr. and Mrs. S. were joking with each other in the waiting room, as I approached them for the sixteenth session. I noticed both of them smiling, and I was happy to see this. I even said then that both of them had million-dollar smiles, and they should do it more often—"It's contagious!"

I asked them how they thought things were going at home. They claimed that they had really noticed a change in Mary—she was staying out of trouble. She and Sally were getting along a lot better. I wondered if it had anything to do with the "two of you." They asked me what I meant. I said, "You seem to be getting along better, especially since you moved back into the house." Mrs. S. said, "He is not on me." I asked what she meant. "Well, he doesn't nag me. As a matter of fact, he is even helping me with the housework." I said, "That's wonderful!" He said, "I am close to the house, and I started to come home for lunch and clean a little." I said, "That is really nice, and your wife seems to really appreciate it." Mrs. S. said, "I can get to supper right away when I get home. Before, I used to clean up after everyone." I asked them if they were together more to discipline. Mrs. S. claims that she says no, but he still gives in to the children. I told them, "The more you allow that, the more the children will manipulate and play you against each other." I asked them to work on that skill. I praised them a lot for the progress they had made and how this helps cause the children to work together. They added that Sally helps with the supper dishes and Mary helps with the cooking.

In the seventeenth session, I met a while with the three children. I told them how their parents praised them for their cooperation, saying that things had been going better at home. I asked the children whether they agreed with this. They said they had been getting along better. They said that "Mary still gets mad whenever she fights with her boyfriend." I asked Mary if that were so. Mary agreed: "I do take my anger out on anybody who is around." I asked her what she and boyfriend fight about. She claims he doesn't always want to be with her. Sometimes she finds out he is with his friends and she gets mad. I asked her, "Do you want him to be with you all the time?" She said yes: "I always want to be with him." "Do you ever want to be with your friends?" Sally answered, "She is losing her friends because she never wants to go out with them." I asked Mary, "Is that true?" "I want to be with Johnny [her boyfriend]." I talked to her about being exclusive and how that could stifle a relationship. I also talked about having other friends at her age. I brought Mom and Dad back for the last fifteen minutes. I told them what we had talked about. I also mentioned to Mom and Dad that they should have a talk with Mary about her boyfriend and about the importance of sharing with others, not just with Johnny. I ended the session by reinforcing their positive behavior. I felt they were making some good movement forward.

Finishing the Therapy

The last phase of treatment began with session eighteen. It was after the Christmas holidays and the situation at the Schmidts' house was relatively tranquil, considering what it had been like prior to the holidays. At this point in therapy, I evaluated my feelings concerning this family. I found myself liking them very much and understanding them a lot. Up to this point, I felt they made some real strides and were committed to therapy, liked me, and wanted to be in family therapy.

From session eighteen to twenty-five, Mom, Dad, Mary, Ralph, and Sally were always present. These sessions were used to point out concerns from previous sessions. I felt now that they were able to hear some of the issues better, and were motivated enough to change their chaotic and enmeshed behaviors to more flexible and connected behavioral patterns. They fell back into old patterns of behavior when they all talked at once and would take sides with either parent. However, the children avoided setting Mr. and Mrs. S. against each other. Sally seemed to be less depressed and was relieved that her brothers were out of the household. She and Mary seemed to be getting along better and were sharing a bedroom together more peacefully. I praised them for their positive behaviors and pointed out ways they could function better as a family, for example, by Mr. and Mrs. S. mutually deciding on punishments for the children and sticking to them. Both parents began to see how this created a united front and less manipulation could go on.

In the session before the last, I prepared the family for termination by informing them that the six months in which they contracted for treatment under the research grant was coming to a close. As I was saying this, it felt right. It was not premature, for they accepted it well and problems that brought them into therapy were resolved.

In the last session, I asked the family whether this past six months of counseling had been helpful to them. Mrs. S. responded, "The family is getting along better." Mr. S. nodded his head affirmatively. Ralph said, "There are a lot less arguments going on between my Mom and Dad." They informed me that Mary was doing better in school and was staying out of trouble in the community. I asked both Mary and Sally, "Is your relationship with each other better? It seems to be, from the way the two of you relate to each other here." They both agreed and smiled at each other. I ended by telling them I really liked them and how well they are doing as a family. I also told them I would miss them: "The door is always open if you ever need to talk or come back for a session or two." They thanked me, and we parted.

Conclusion

In my opinion, this family has other issues that need to be addressed. The marriage contract and the drinking problem alluded to previously need to be looked at more closely. However, I believe at this time that the family members were not ready to be pushed in that direction. I also believe that they gained enough trust and a sense of being comfortable that they might seek help in those areas in the future.

18

Case Study: The "G" Family (An Intense Conflictual Mother-Son Relationship)

Anthony Errichetti

Editors' note: What happens to a family when the mother is immature and emotionally needy, relating to her children very much as if to siblings? How is the family system affected when the father, on whom all depended for stability and control, dies? What function does drug abuse have for the child whose acting-out behavior led to the initiation of family therapy? These are but a few of the issues dealt with by the family therapist whose involvement with this challenging case extended over several years.

Family therapy rarely offers a permanent cure to chronically dysfunctional families. At best it offers a family the chance to right itself, pick up the pieces, and go on with its life. If the family is resilient, and perhaps a bit lucky, it will have other experiences besides therapy that will help it to grow.

The following family case history illustrates the tendency for dysfunctional symptoms to fluctuate between the manageable and the impossible. During times of high stress in a family life—a birth, death, illness, a departure—symptoms of dysfunctional family behavior flare up. I've had contact with the "G." family for over five years. The first year was during therapy and then I've gotten periodic updates from the mother. This case illustrates the tendency for symptoms to disappear and reemerge during times of crisis.

Vinnie G., seventeen years old, had come to the attention of Tom, the local juvenile detective, a number of times over the previous five years. The detective, expressing what appeared to be genuine concern, grabbed my attention before I was to begin my first session with Vinnie and his mother Betty, forty-five years old. He told me that since Vinnie's father died, five years before, he had noticed a pattern of trouble in the G. family and with Vinnie in particular.

The family had been referred for treatment following Vinnie's recent charge of possession of a small amount of marijuana on school property with some other boys. The action was overt, as if the intent by all was to get caught. This was Vinnie's first charge. It was a rather minor charge but representative of a pattern of overt behaviors that seemed to be a cry for help.

Vinnie had two older sisters, Cindy, twenty-five, and Lori, twenty-three. Cindy was a registered nurse and lived with a roommate. Lori was an aspiring actress living in New York. Betty's mother, Martha, sixty-six, lived nearby.

The detective gave me a short history of Vinnie and his family since the father's death. Shortly after the funeral Vinnie set fire to a neighbor's fence. He had temper tantrums and sometimes threatened physically to attack his mother and two older sisters. Vinnie occasionally vandalized property, and he was getting a reputation as a "hothead" and neighborhood nuisance. Tom described the family atmosphere as volatile, and he suspected the women in the family "ganged up" on Vinnie. Several times over the past five years Betty had called police to the house to restore order following heated family arguments.

Problems at home had intensified recently. Betty had been leaving Vinnie at home alone on weekends for the last couple of months while she went to the seashore with her boyfriend, Jim. Vinnie took the opportunity to host noisy, brawling parties at the family's suburban tract home, with the result that neighbors were complaining to police. The possession charge was predictable, Tom thought. Indeed, everyone expected Vinnie to act out. Tom made it clear he felt Betty was acting irresponsibly for leaving him home alone.

The First Session

The first three evaluation sessions contained most of the themes and interactional patterns of their therapy, so I will describe those sessions in some detail. The first session was especially rich in content.

Betty and Vinnie were seated quietly in the waiting area, silently leafing through magazines when I arrived. Both shook my hand firmly when I introduced myself, but Vinnie avoided eye contact. Once inside my office Betty immediately broke the silence. She was a striking brunette, forty-five years old, with a rather cool demeanor. My immediate impression was that she was strong and self-assured. Her bearing contrasted sharply with her self-description, which poured out immediately after our introductions. She said, "I'm hurting, I'm vulnerable, and I'm angry." She repeated a number of times that she needed help, not only with raising Vinnie but also in coping with the grief over the loss of her husband which had begun to surface over the past year. More than once she repeated that she needed help, wanted desperately to rely on someone, and was bitterly disappointed that Vinnie would not provide the support she needed. She described Vinnie as inordinately dependent on her, demanding, and physically threatening when he did not get his own way. She complained that he demanded money, refused to do simple chores around the house in return, and, when frustrated, would wreck parts of the house with his fist and threaten her with his karate weapons. She also suspected he was abusing drugs and alcohol.

Betty suspected Vinnie hated her, and she wanted him to stop being angry and hostile to her. She demanded that he help out by being more responsible and less conspicuous if he could not be more loving toward her. Betty accused him of never talking to her, never listening, but instead acting out his thoughts and feelings. The new school year, his last, was to begin in six weeks, and she feared he might purposely fail summer school as a strategy to avoid graduating. Within the first five minutes Betty made it very clear she was unhappy, felt drained by the demands of the last five years, and wanted to start a new life for herself without Vinnie as soon as he graduated the following year.

Betty had been working as a physician's receptionist but was being terminated because she had recently been unable to carry out her responsibilities. For the past six months she had started feeling depressed for the first time about the death of her husband. Feelings of grief were gradually paralyzing her, while Vinnie's behavior, she felt, was getting worse. She was bitter that Vinnie would not acknowledge all she had done for the family following her husband's death. She wanted him to take care of her, mostly by taking care of himself, until she worked through her depression. She blamed Vinnie for her depression.

Betty had had individual counseling with someone who specialized in Transactional Analysis. She found TA a rather concrete way of understanding how she was interacting with people in her life. The counseling, however, avoided dealing with the grief of her loss.

Vinnie was a very muscular and attractive young man who stood six-foot-one and weighed 165 pounds. Betty pointed out that he resembled his father. He could easily have passed for being in his early twenties. He was dressed in designer athletic wear and flexed his muscles impassively as he pretended not to hear what his mother said about him. He then coolly contradicted his mother's accusations and said he was coming to therapy not because the juvenile authorities had ordered him to, but because his mother was sick: "I'm here because she needs help." He described Betty as "weak" as he continued to touch and flex his muscles. He accused her of overreacting and distorting the facts about his problems with the police and with school. He attended summer school but stopped going, claiming he had been excused from the remainder of classes and had not simply dropped out, as Betty had thought. He denied he had actually been charged with possession. He told Betty, "You're not around, so what do you know?" Finally, he complained that his mother was forever humiliating and berating him. He accused her of having problems with men and described her boyfriend Jim as a "wimp." Betty defended herself by portraying Vinnie as a potential woman abuser. Both claimed that they simply wanted respect from each other.

Vinnie was a very bright young man, but his school performance was marginal. Teachers reported he did things in class that drew attention to himself. He sometimes argued with teachers and other students but was often able to charm his way out of trouble. He had been smoking marijuana and drinking for several years but claimed his mother exaggerated his use. If she found rolling papers or other drug paraphernalia, he claimed to be simply holding them for his friends. He worked infrequently, preferring instead to extract money from his mother through threats or promises. When she refused he would sometimes wreck parts of the house. He admitted being angry with her because "she doesn't accept me for who I am," and he tried to give the impression that Betty simply imagined his threats. He consistently characterized his mother as an "emotional wreck" who exaggerated his behaviors. Vinnie was a master at turning the tables and Betty spent a great deal of time justifying her own behavior during the session. She expressed guilt for not being a better mother but realized this made her easy prey for his manipulations.

It seemed she wanted Vinnie either to take care of her like a good husband, or, more accurately, a good father, or get out. I spoke to her in the language of TA to try to get her to understand how their roles had somehow gotten reversed. This temporarily halted their cycle of accusation and counteraccusation. She recalled how childlike she used to feel in the presence of her deceased husband, Paul. This prompted Vinnie to complain bitterly that he was the kid, not his mother, and that he wasn't ready to grow up just yet. My impression at this point in the session was that they were also interacting on the level of competing children, each complaining that the other was a bad parent who was not satisfying his or her needs, and yet they were unwilling to cooperate to help each other.

During that first session I took some family history and tried to determine who in the family might be important to include in therapy. Vinnie had two older sisters. Lori, several years older than Vinnie, was living in New York and was trying to get an acting job. She had difficulty holding jobs and had been under the care of a psychiatrist intermittently after the death of their father. Betty described Lori as excessively dependent and demanding. She felt Lori feigned emotional problems as a ploy to stay financially dependent. Cindy, the eldest child, was described as the most responsible of the three children. She worked as a registered nurse in a city hospital and was taking on ever increasing responsibilities.

Betty described her marriage to Paul. While she talked, Vinnie lounged on the couch, which he occupied alone, and feigned disinterest while correcting his mother on various points of the family story. Her husband was a "pillar of strength" throughout the marriage. Using the language of Transactional Analysis, she said, "I was a child to Paul's adult." She was a housewife with three children and never had to work since her husband made a good living as an engineer. They married after she became pregnant at age eighteen. In the early years she found the marriage emotionally unsatisfying. Betty grew up as an only child without a father and had high hopes that her husband could provide the love she missed. The marriage began to feel like a recreation of her childhood as she realized her husband was not as emotionally giving as she expected. He spent long hours away from home, and being "stuck" at home with three children made her feel as lonely as she had as a child.

During this time she experienced periods of extreme depression and withdrew from the family by staying in bed. Vinnie would come into her room to check on her. She admitted that staying in bed was sometimes a ploy to get Paul to pay attention to her and that it often worked. But her husband would once more distance himself from her through his work, and she would respond by getting depressed again.

She described being in competition with her children for her husband's attention. The children often fought at the dinner table, and only Paul would be able to intervene. She felt resentful toward the children because their behavior made it difficult for her to have a loving relationship with Paul. Being a "child" herself she did not know how, or even want, to control her children. She wondered if the children were driving him away. Betty considered separating from Paul, but the couple instead entered Marriage Encounter. Thus began a happy period of her married life. Paul, perhaps realizing their marriage was in jeopardy, made an emotional turnabout and became the kind of man Betty had always longed for. The couple became group leaders in Marriage Encounter and counseled other troubled couples. Problems with the children continued, but her marriage now seemed happy. Vinnie at this time was about eight years old.

During this period Paul developed terminal lung cancer. Ironically, this began, from Betty's point of view, the happiest period of her marriage because his illness intensified their emotional connection. For two years the couple shared every emotion by talking, writing down their feelings, and helping other cancer victims. I said to her that I got the impression that Paul's dying made her come alive. She admitted that sadly this was true.

After Paul's death Betty went immediately to work and began dating within the year. Paul had encouraged her to start her life over again. He gave her permission to see other men, and she began dating within several months after his death. The family's grieving process, then, was interrupted. Betty worked in part to block out the pain of the loss, and until the past six months before entering treatment she functioned adequately. The children, however, competed for her attention, and she was at a loss to know how to handle them.

Betty went into great detail about her own pain and loss, and I became aware that she was talking about the experience as if she had gone through it alone. During this part of the session Vinnie listened carefully to his mother without interrupting. When I pushed her to think about who else in the family was hurt by the death, she revealed that her eldest child, Lori, was hospitalized following her father's death. Lori and her father never got along, and his death threw her into a major depression.

Vinnie remembered his father being sick but couldn't remember feeling anything after the death. Betty reminded him of the time he burned a neighbor's fence, and he commented that it probably was a difficult time for him. This comment about his pain shifted to an accusation: his mother was a weak imitation of his father. Thus began another round of arguing and bickering, with Betty begging Vinnie to understand she had tried her best to play both mother and father.

The session ended on a conciliatory note, with Vinnie giving credit to his mother for trying to help him while expressing some anger that Betty was trying to get him to be something he wasn't. I contracted with them to come in for at least two more evaluation sessions, after which we could determine whether or not we could all work together. I also mentioned that it would be important to bring in other family members, including Betty's mother. Betty and Vinnie agreed to continue.

My hypothesis at this time was that both mother and son were angry at Paul for dying and were still in the grieving process but could not express it directly. Paul had given the family instructions to forget about him and go on with their lives. Betty was trying to carry out his wishes but it was not working. She said things to Vinnie that I imagined she wanted to say to her husband, like "Vinnie, why don't you support me? I need your help but you're not there for me. You're weak and you disappoint me. You're the reason I'm so depressed." Vinnie, I imagined, was also quite angry with his father, perhaps for abandoning him in a household of women. But he was taking on the role of the father as he imagined it to be: strong, angry, oppositional, distant. Betty alluded to problems in the marriage, but Paul's death seemed to canonize him in her eyes. I suspected that Betty and Vinnie were acting out scenes from the marriage, but it was too early in the therapy to make this interpretation. Their interaction was the evidence I was gathering that they were acting out themes of dependency, abandonment, and rage.

Reviewing this session I noted that my interventions took two basic forms. First, I continually pointed out their repetitive, nonproductive behaviors. For example, there were moments of tenderness and caring between Vinnie and Betty, but these moments were usually shattered with

acceptable emotion in this family than sadness. When I tried to get him to stay with the sadness, he started fighting with Betty.

Vinnie talked about his male friends and their need to "live on the edge." He viewed drinking and drug taking as a normal part of growing up in his town. He found he could distinguish himself among his peers by taking risks and acting "crazy." He antagonized Betty by labeling her concerns as understandable but misguided because he could handle himself.

The session ended with Betty's expressing confusion about his behavior. She didn't understand his need to act crazy and macho. I pointed out that her not understanding Vinnie made sense, given her history with men. I suggested to Vinnie that he was attempting to teach his mother about men but that she was only getting part of the picture. He simply reinforced her idea that men in this family were flawed. I also pointed out that they seemed to be responding to the sadness in the family with anger, and I wondered out loud how this was helping them cope with their grief.

My impression at this point was that Vinnie's macho behavior was an attempt to appear lively but was in part a reaction to his fear that men in his family were really weak, both emotionally and physically, and died young. He played into his mother's fear of men but was also being told, on some level, to act out the role of the threatening male. His only reaction to my comment was to say that he didn't think his mother liked him very much, but that it really didn't matter that much to him.

Third Session

The session dealt with a crisis that came up over the weekend. While Betty was away for the weekend with Jim, Vinnie had a party at their home. The house was damaged, and the police had to be called. When Vinnie minimized the seriousness of the incident, Betty lost control and blasted him, calling him a "manipulative bastard." He responded in kind by calling her a "bitch." For about five minutes the two argued bitterly, and there was no stopping them. Vinnie threatened to leave the session several times, a stance that only served to give his mother more ammunition to use against him. I intervened by demanding they stop the "dirty fighting." This scene—the unproductive arguing, the name calling, and threats to leave—repeated itself many times during the course of treatment. These two were volatile, and I learned to intervene earlier in the arguments, but I always had the sense that I was breaking up two children. The theme, expressed again and again, was "you let me down, and now you're going to pay for it." I held back this interpretation until they were calm enough to hear it.

After the two had calmed down a bit, Betty responded to my remark about dirty fighting. She complained that Vinnie's attempt to deny or downplay his behavior made her so angry she wanted to hurt him back. She said over and over how powerless she felt with Vinnie and that she had felt powerless and insecure since Paul's death. She talked about how her husband controlled Vinnie and how she felt like a failure. Vinnie said he liked his father because he indeed was strong, unlike his mother, who was a weak imitation. He resented the control his mother was attempting to exert on him now, especially since she had given him almost unlimited freedom. For the past five years mother and son had often gone their separate ways. He had gotten used to this situation but often found the home a lonely place. His sisters, like his mother, either ignored him or gave him a hard time.

The session dealt with a recurring problem: Betty was trying to have a relationship with a man and Vinnie was undermining it. This echoed Betty's marriage to Paul and her resentment of her own children. Their needs got in the way of her having her husband for herself. She was quite frank in admitting her ambivalence, both then and now, about having children, and the guilt she felt made her especially prone to manipulation. The problem now was that Vinnie's manipulations were becoming more serious. She found it quite difficult to feel affection for him.

We worked on the function of Vinnie's acting-out behavior. He acted out the role of the swaggering male but still needed his mother. He accomplished this by getting in trouble and drawing her in. He was getting in more trouble lately, I thought, because Betty made it clear she wanted him to leave home after he graduated from high school. He complained that his mother was trying to get rid of him and then denied that he felt hurt or angry about this. "I'll leave when I'm ready," he said. "I just don't think it's right to be thrown out of my own house, do you?" Betty was thinking of moving in with Jim but couldn't do this if Vinnie was around.

Betty demanded that Vinnie act like a man as a price for her affection, and I pointed out that that was exactly what he thought he was doing. Men, from his perspective, got drunk and rowdy, never asked for love, and remained elusive. When they tried getting closer, they usually ended up arguing and fighting for greater distance. I suggested that their love for each other was conditional and based on a strong feeling of entitlement.

Betty had felt emotionally deprived from childhood, and she tried to get her husband to make up for her losses. She realized she couldn't give to Vinnie because she felt so needy herself. When both responded that they just wanted to get away from each other, I pointed out their behavior was saying the exact opposite.

They had several routines for acting out their mutual ambivalence. One variation was that Betty would distance herself from Vinnie—through dating or work—and he would get her back through acting out. If he got in trouble, she would bail him out. She simultaneously felt guilty for being an inadequate mother and furious with herself because she was once again being manipulated.

This would cause her to distance herself emotionally from Vinnie, and the cycle would begin again. She talked about her need to get away from Vinnie. She had been angry with him since Paul's death because he made it so difficult for her to feel like a good mother. His emotional needs were as great as hers, and she had no way of fulfilling them.

I suggested that perhaps they should consider finding more positive ways of staying dependent on one another as a way to preserve their relationship, but that their task was also to find positive ways of separating. I expressed my concern that they were heading toward the type of messy "divorce" I'd seen in bad marriages and that they could perhaps prevent this from happening by denying their mutual dependence. This remark seemed to confuse them because I was suggesting they consider doing two contradictory things—that is, stay dependent while separating. This gave them permission to continue doing the very thing they had been doing all along. The intervention was not "paradoxical intention" but rather my accepting their family system for what it was.

The session ended with my asking Betty to get her daughters and her mother in to the treatment. My sense was that any efforts to improve their relationship could be undermined by other family members who might also be feeling abandoned.

Later Sessions

After the first three sessions things calmed down at home, but Betty continued to feel depressed. Shortly before our first session Betty was fired from her job as a medical receptionist. She was paralyzed with depression and unable to carry out her responsibilities. She realized that the depression was to some degree a delayed reaction. For the last five years she had been too busy raising the children to grieve. Now she wanted time, as she said, "to heal myself." She had asked Vinnie to give her a chance to feel her pain by not getting in trouble, and he seemed to be respecting her wishes. I gave her the name of a psychiatrist to contact if the depression continued, but I felt confident Vinnie would find a way to "cure" his mother's depression.

He did this during the session by incurring her wrath. He accused her of being weak and said that her depression "proved" that it was she who was sick and not he. She reacted to this by screaming at him and vowing to throw him out by age eighteen so that she could get on with her life. After she calmed down, I asked Vinnie how his mother's depression affected him.

Vinnie: Sometimes I think she'll go off the deep end.
Therapist: Sometimes it looks like you want to give her a little shove.
Betty: Exactly!

Vinnie: No, no, it's not like that at all. I just get tired of hearing her complain. She complains about me, but I get sick of her too.
Therapist: You ever worry about her?
Vinnie: Sure. Why not?
Therapist: Now?
Vinnie: Sure.
Therapist: But whenever she talks like this in here you say things that make her go crazy.
Vinnie: Well, better crazy than lying around in bed all day.

I asked him to tell her what he worried about. He told her he didn't like seeing her sick and wanted her to stop beating herself up for being a bad mother to him.

Vinnie: Look, I'm okay, all right? You didn't do such a bad job.
Betty: But you're a mess, Vinnie.
Vinnie: I am not a mess. If I'm a mess, it's not your fault, okay?

It was difficult for Vinnie to talk for long about his fears without getting a sarcastic remark from Betty. It became clearer to me, and eventually to both of them, that her depression both frightened and angered him. If he acted out, she got angry, which he found more comforting than her depression. I have seen this pattern of behavior between severely depressed mothers and acting-out children many times before in treatment. The mother gets depressed and withdrawn, and the child, fearing for its own well-being, does something to "jump start" the mother. Moving one's mother from a deadly depression to a lively anger through negative or self-destructive behavior is a form of parentification: the child takes care of the parent at its own expense. My impression is that the fear the child experiences beholding a depressed parent turns to rage if the pattern continues and the child feels abandoned.

I pointed out that their fighting kept them connected over the years because they didn't seem to know any other way. They reacted by lamenting the family's losses caused by Paul's death. The rest of this session also dealt with the family process and how they were locked in a repetitive cycle. Accusation and counteraccusation produced alternating cycles of depression and anger that kept the sadness buried while making them feel alive with rage. My intervention was to connect them to their shared sadness and loss.

Over several months the family seemed to calm down. Vinnie was back in school, and Betty was home most weekends. They were fighting less, but she was still feeling depressed. She had decided not to seek a psychiatric consultation since her depression was manageable. She was troubled by her relationship with Lori, who was living in New York. Lori was described as a "carbon copy" of Vinnie—that is, manipulative and angry. Both of these children seemed intent on draining her of the remainder of Paul's life insurance money. Lori had had psychiatric treatment intermittently since her father's death, but Betty felt she was feigning illness to get attention. She agreed to bring Lori in for a session with Vinnie and Cindy.

One session Betty came alone. Vinnie refused to come, saying that because their relationship seemed to be improving the counseling no longer concerned him. She felt there was really no basis for his believing this, but she also felt powerless to get him to attend the session. Because she had been complaining of depression I asked if she really wanted the session for herself. How hard, I asked, did she try to get Vinnie to come to the session? She admitted that she did not try very hard to get him to come because she wanted to talk about herself and not work on Vinnie's never ending problems. I made the judgment call to see her without Vinnie because she seemed very depressed but ready to work. In situations like this, where a member comes alone, I maintain a family systems perspective.

Betty started by saying she was feeling very fatigued and sad. She felt the therapy had started to open up old wounds. Her way of dealing with the grief up to this point was to feign cheerfulness and concentrate on her career and supporting the family. This never worked because her children did nothing but complain and fight with each other. Vinnie especially made her feel like a failure as a mother, which in turn brought her loss into sharp focus.

Betty: Vinnie is making it more difficult for me to let go of my husband because only Paul would be able to keep him under control.

Therapist: How does holding on to Paul, not letting him die, help you with Vinnie?

Betty: Well, it helps me to not feel so alone. I'm trying to take Paul's place with Vinnie because he needs a father as well as a mother.

Therapist: But you're not a man.

Betty: I don't know the first thing about men. But I don't feel that what I am is good enough. My kids keep reminding me in so many ways what a failure I am. Paul really had them under control.

Therapist: Are you sure? You said that the kids always fought, especially around the dinner table, when he was alive. Where did you get this idea that Paul had everything under control and you were, and are, just one of the kids?

Betty: Those last couple of years with Paul were so special. There was so much talking and sharing. The kids were upset, probably because we were so close there wasn't much room for them. It's terrible to admit that you're jealous of your kids because they demand so much there isn't much left over. They wanted so much of Paul. Now I have Jim, and Vinnie is causing trouble there. I just want to start a new life for myself so I can have something before it's too late for me. Is that too much to ask?

Therapist: You know you all got gypped when Paul died. The marriage was just getting to the point where you always wanted it and then your husband gets sick and dies. Everyone is still hurting from this. You want to start your life all over again, but Vinnie won't let you. He's not ready. What do you think he wants from you before he's ready to get on with his life?

Betty: He says he just wants to be left alone, which would be fine, except that he keeps doing things that make that impossible. If he can't abide by the rules of the house, then he should leave when he turns eighteen.

She repeated many times that she wanted Vinnie out so she could start her life over again. I questioned the stance that she was taking with Vinnie, that he should shape up or leave by his eighteenth birthday:

Betty: I think I'm just pushing him away again, the way I've always pushed him away. He was always difficult for me, and Paul was good with him. Also, the more he says he wants to leave the more I want him to leave. I told him he could stay if he was good. He makes promises, and I believe him and then he does whatever the hell he wants.

Therapist: Not very reliable. Just like all the men in your family.

Betty expressed guilt for being a cold mother who was calculating to reject her child, but she rationalized that Vinnie was really the one doing the rejecting. She seemed to want my permission or approval to ask Vinnie to leave when he was eighteen.

Therapist: If what you say is true, that pushing him away really encourages his dependence, then you're going to have to try something else with him. Unless you really don't want him to leave.

Betty: But what if he doesn't want to come in?

Therapist: Make him. Drag him in here. It's your house. I give you permission to throw him out at age eighteen, if that's what you need. But I don't think you're going to be able to do it unless you work on the relationship with him. But maybe you don't want him to come in. Like today. This reminds me of what you were saying about being jealous of the kids because they took time away from you and your husband. Maybe you want me for yourself.

Betty admitted that this might be true, that she wanted someone who could help her understand her feelings. Vinnie was a bitter disappointment because he was so insensitive and demanding. She again repeated that she wanted to get on with her life and that she expected Vinnie either to cooperate at home or leave when he was eighteen. This stance, however, made her feel guilty because she realized Vinnie still needed her. She vacillated between overindulgence and aloofness, and she came to realize this inconsistency was a reaction to her guilt. She also began to realize that her inconsistency made her vulnerable to manipulation. She complained that Vinnie also manipulated her daughter Cindy and her mother.

Together we worked on a list of priorities for her. She wanted Vinnie out on his own, and she wanted to start a new life and career for herself. We then discussed the major obstacles to her getting what she wanted. She thought that Vinnie might try a delaying tactic, like failing school or getting arrested again for drug possession. She thought that if this happened she would be overcome with guilt and would be manipulated into rescuing him once more. When asked to construct a different scenario, she visualized herself as impervious to his manipulations. She would have to make some decisions about the kind of life she wanted for herself and then take concrete steps toward her goals.

My strategy for the remainder of therapy was to unbalance the system and change the relationship by supporting Betty's stated goal of starting a new life and by supporting her competence as a mother. Because of her history of depression and her tendency to overprocess her feelings, I decided to try to get her to take some action that might help her gain more control.

She felt both guilty and liberated by the thought of living on her own. Betty knew intellectually that the guilt paralyzed her and made her vulnerable to manipulation. She knew this intellectually but couldn't stop the feeling. My stance was that she couldn't wait to feel better before taking action. She would have to take some action with Vinnie and the rest of her family and then sort out the feelings later. She could not permanently repress her conflicts, but I explained she would have to put them on hold for a while if she wanted to make some changes. She could avoid feeling the guilt, I explained, if she began acting like a competent mother even if she didn't feel like one.

At my urging, Betty's mother and oldest daughter Cindy came to the session. I explained to Betty that her decisions could be undermined by others in the family besides Vinnie. She talked often about her feelings of being an inadequate mother and sometimes compensated at home by enlisting the support of Cindy and her mother in her ongoing struggle with Vinnie. She started the session by asking Cindy, "Will you share an incident with Tony [the therapist] that happened on Sunday?" Cindy dutifully recounted how Vinnie was ruining the fireplace at home because he kept dropping his weights on the bricks. She described how he was making his mother "crazy" because he denied doing the damage. She added that Vinnie hated her when all she ever wanted to do was help him. His grandmother tried to help out by taking Betty's side against Vinnie. She had the reputation for talking tough with Vinnie but rescuing him when he got in trouble.

The session demonstrated how the women in this family, when provoked, ganged up on Vinnie. This then gave him the excuse to feel victimized and justified in provoking them. I attempted to get the three to begin relating to Vinnie, and to each other, as individuals and started by suggesting that Cindy and Vinnie go out for lunch and talk by themselves. They reported later that they tried this and that it was moderately successful. Problems came up when Cindy began relating to Vinnie not as a sister but as a surrogate mother. She had become a parentified child after her father's death and often looked after her brother. She was a very responsible nurse and remarked that "it came natural to me." Vinnie both resented her and expected her to take care of him, and the relationship was strained by his excessive demands.

The second child, Lori, came in for a session with Vinnie and Betty. Vinnie and his sister spent a large part of the time blaming each other for taking more than each deserved of their father's insurance money. Several years before, Betty had tried to stop the arguing by giving them each a portion of whatever money remained. Vinnie felt that his sister had taken more than her share and that there was less for him. He sometimes stole money from his mother, rationalizing that he was owed the money. Betty felt frustrated and angry with both of them because she needed the money herself to live on but often gave in to their demands because of guilt.

This was a family with unresolved issues of entitlement. Betty had a rather emotionally impoverished childhood and looked to her husband to satisfy her needs. She was in direct competition with her children and sometimes sacrificed their needs to satisfy her own. Although this became increasingly evident to her in therapy, she did not know exactly how to reverse the damage. With the two neediest children present I noted that they all got cheated by fate and that perhaps it was no one's fault. They had a choice to make: they could either continue to blame each other for their misfortunes, or they could take responsibility for their own action. As it was, the family was not growing. The sessions, like the family's time together, were often spent in nonproductive bickering, and I offered to continue working with the family only if they wanted to work.

I continued working with Betty and Vinnie over the next several months. I continued to support Betty's competence as a mother by validating her wish to stop handing money to Vinnie or rescuing him when he got into trouble. Though he felt this was a kind of abandonment, I explained it was simply a push from the nest.

I referred Betty to a vocational counselor who helped her define her career interests. She enrolled in a business school to learn advertising but dropped out after a short while for medical reasons. She took some action she considered positive. She got a job and eventually left her boyfriend, Jim. She met another man, Tom, and fell in love. The two began making plans to live together, but Betty felt that she should probably live on her own for a while before committing to this relationship. Vinnie continued in school, and when it was apparent that he'd probably graduate, the family stopped therapy. It had been ten months since they had started family therapy. They were not cured, but they were working again.

About a year later I ran into Betty at a community theater production. Her daughter Lori had a part in the play and was reportedly doing much better. She was no longer under the care of a psychiatrist. Vinnie had finished high school, joined the Navy, and was stationed in California. He was getting married and appeared to be doing quite well. Betty was living on her own for the first time in her life but was still seeing Tom. She thanked me for my help, and I was gratified to think my work got the family back on track.

Two years after this meeting, Betty came in for a session in a crisis. Vinnie was having some mysterious medical problems that were causing him to regress emotionally. She recalled that his father had died of cancer, and now Vinnie was afraid he was going to die. She was uncertain about the problem, but he was calling her from California asking for money for medical treatment. She suspected that he was manipulating her again and reasoned that the Navy should be paying his medical expenses. She needed the session for a "reality check," which I provided. She was living with Tom and was very happy with their relationship. Lori had become a born-again Christian and disapproved of her mother's life-style. Betty felt that every time she found happiness with a man, one of the children would try to ruin it. During the session she declared her intention not to be manipulated but yet not cut Vinnie off completely.

One year after this, Betty came in for a session in crisis. Vinnie's marriage had broken up, he had received a medical discharge from the Navy, and he was living nearby but was being evicted from his apartment for not paying rent. He had gotten fired from his job several months before and was not seriously looking for work. His lungs had been damaged in the Navy, and he was awaiting compensation. She felt he was both frightened about the possibility of getting lung cancer like his father but was using his disability to get the family to take care of him. He had resources he could have been using through the Veterans Administration, but instead he went to Betty and his grandmother for financial assistance. Betty was angry with herself for giving in to his manipulations. She was still very happy with Tom, but the situation with Vinnie was threatening the relationship. She wanted help in controlling the situation, and we made an appointment for her, Tom, Vinnie, and the rest of the family.

The next week Betty came to the session alone, claiming that she didn't realize I wanted the rest of the family in. I reminded her that it was her wish, not mine, to work with Vinnie and the rest of the family, and we explored this distortion. Within the past week the situation with Vinnie had "resolved" itself when he moved in with her mother. She had made progress over the past week, she felt, in distancing herself from Vinnie. She realized, however, that it was only a matter of time before Vinnie wore out his welcome at his grandmother's. I interpreted her behavior, and that of her mother's, as a covert wish to keep Vinnie dependent. I recommended that she work on this issue, but pointed out that her mother and the rest of the family were part of the conspiracy. If she wanted to break this cycle of dependency/counterdependency, I advised her to bring in the rest of the family for therapy. She agreed, and we made a contract to continue working together.

Conclusion

This case demonstrates what I have found in many families like this one—that the overall emotional health of chronically dysfunctional families rarely improves dramatically. Some of the individuals may do well in their personal lives, but they seem to deteriorate in the presence of other family members. With persistent treatment, some symptoms disappear altogether, while others go into remission. The symptoms may reemerge in times of crisis but perhaps with not the same intensity. Some family members benefit more from treatment than others. Betty was ready for treatment when she came in, Vinnie less so. I have found that it is important to keep in mind that family members are individuals and want different things from treatment.

I was not successful in completely "curing" this family. Their ambivalence was such that they didn't know whether they even wanted to be a family. Betty held on to the idea that their family really died with Paul, and this myth had affected the family for years. My success, however, was in forging a working relationship with Betty that continued over some years. Betty said she wanted answers from me but I kept telling her that I didn't have any. All I had to offer her was therapy, a relationship that guaranteed nothing but my presence and my attention. Perhaps this is a relationship that, for a time, she can live with.

19

Ned: A Case of Drug Abuse in a Middle-Class Jewish Family

Nancy Casella

Editors' note: Nancy Casella's chapter presents a multigenerational orientation to the treatment of a family, three generations of family members having been actively involved. A detailed family history is presented (and much of this history is used by the therapist during the treatment) by pointing to the historical antecedents of current family relationships.

Ned Green was a twenty-one-year-old member of a middle-class Jewish family in Philadelphia when I had my initial contact with him in June 1973. He was referred by the Community Mental Health Center in his neighborhood to our psychiatric hospital's drug abuse treatment unit for inpatient treatment for detoxification for Demerol addiction, for depression, and for suicidal ideation. His family experienced this situation as an acute crisis. Earlier, Ned had used and abused other drugs such as amphetamines, Quaaludes, and Valium and had been very involved in dealing drugs as a teenager.

The Treatment of Ned and His Family

As part of his initial treatment he was assigned to an inpatient drug treatment group and to an individual therapist in the program. Ned quickly became known to hospital personnel as a result of the furor he was stirring in the hospital. Though he was initially depressed, he was now expressing a great deal of anger, particularly toward those in authority, such as head nurses, doctors, and others. Some of his anger took the form of advising other patients about their medications. Since he was quite well versed in pharmacology, fellow patients were inclined to listen and then question their doctors and nurses. At the same time he questioned his own doctor's detox schedule and generally provoked considerable irritation and annoyance on the part of the hospital staff. The more the response to his behavior, the more grandiose he became (much like his behavior with his parents). They were partly naive about his knowledge and often let him go on without placing any limits on him.

One of the first things to be done with Ned was to provide and enforce limits. We were going to be parent figures who provided limits; Ned was told that his pharmacy texts were inappropriate reading and resources while he was in the hospital. He had placed himself in our hands, and we expected him to follow our prescriptions. His attempts at medicating himself were ineffective and inadequate and would not be acceptable while he was in our program.

At the same time he was told what was expected of him while he was in the program: daily attendance in group therapy, individual sessions with his assigned therapist, family involvement in the treatment process, and general compliance with the rules of the hospital and the program. Ned was resistant to the demands initially. He was encouraged to express his discontent with the group therapy sessions, which he began to see as an opportunity to do battle with the staff within a structured framework. He vacillated between being very depressed and being openly grandiose and hostile. In the group sessions where there was a male and female cotherapist team he was confronted with his hostility and grandiosity and realistic limits. Until he felt the control of the therapy structures, he could not get into his depression and suicidal ideation.

For several weeks, he vacillated and tested out the situation until he could talk somewhat about his feelings of low self-esteem dating back to early childhood. This was not a consistent focus, but it was a beginning at dealing with the real pain in his life. While he was in the hospital, family therapy was initiated within a few weeks. Ned's parents, his older brother, and his fiancée were invited to participate. His parents were quite willing to do this. His older brother had many excuses or reasons for not being able to attend. His girlfriend, while not eager, did come in for some sessions.

If one views substance abuse as symptomatic of family dysfunction, it is extremely important that the family patterns of interaction and communication be explored and that this occur relatively early in the family treatment. In the beginning of Ned's individual, group, and family therapy this premise of treatment was verbalized—that drug abuse is symptomatic of family dysfunction and that along with changing Ned's drug behavior, we would help the family to change the patterns of behavior that reinforced the substance abuse behavior. In the beginning of family treatment, the main focus of the family was Ned and his various encounters with his family relating to his drug abuse and dealing, his hostility and rage toward the family, and the great amount of energy that was poured into Ned's activities. It was difficult, for example, for Mrs. G. to talk about anything but Ned. It seemed as if the main part of her life centered about Ned, what he was, is, and will be doing to himself and to her. At times she did express some concern about her husband's heart condition and the effect of Ned's activities on Mr. G., but generally her focus was on Ned. Ned and his mother were a dyad, while his father was an outsider.

An example of this early interaction appeared in the second session. Mr. G., Mrs. G., Ned, and his girlfriend were present. Paul, the brother, was absent, working on his second job. Mother starts off the session by asking Ned what he is going to do constructively for himself. She pounds him with pointed questions. Are you still using drugs? Why haven't you gotten a job yet? And so on. Ned eventually explodes angrily, and the mother responds by pointing out how sick he is. Ned's anger increases.

At that point the therapist talks about the idea that the whole family is in treatment, suggesting that this kind of mother-son interaction is an example of the family "sickness." From there, the therapists begin to explore the mother-son interaction and the function it serves in the family—for example, how the mother's behavior reinforces negative activity in the son, such as drug abuse, rages, and tantrums; and how the father is a passive participant in the same situation.

Later in the session, the mother tells Ned, "You are aggravating me, I'll have a heart attack," when he is expressing angry feelings appropriately. The mother thus attempts to reconnect with Ned through guilt. Ned becomes depressed and starts to recall other episodes where he felt guilty regarding interaction with his mother. The therapist points out the "racket" involved in this, how each hooks the other and how at any point either could own his or her own feelings. At the same time it is noted that the father is an outsider and excluded.

An initial objective of therapy was to defocus Ned and explore the family patterns that reinforce the drug abuse, to get a family history over several generations that would allow a picture of family messages that lead to and reinforce drug abuse and suicidal thinking and behavior. It is important to get at issues of the past that have remained alive and contaminate the present interactions. A considerable amount of time in the early family sessions was spent obtaining this historical family information, as well as in confronting the present interactions in the family. It was evident right from the beginning that work needed to be done in the present within the intergenerational framework. Early on issues around limit setting and separation and loss were obvious, both historically and in the current interaction.

During this initial phase Ned was in the hospital for approximately three weeks. The multimodality treatment (that is, detoxification, and individual, group, and family therapy) was intensive. From the onset the therapists stated that treatment was not over once Ned left the hospital but that outpatient treatment should continue for at least a two-year period. Ned and his family were free to choose where to obtain their treatment, but this was our prescription.

During his inpatient stay, Ned had a taste of some limits that were structured by the staff, and he later expressed a sense of security that the staff did not bend or fold when he tested these limits. As an outpatient, limit setting became a somewhat different matter. Ned was left more to his own structures. He was encouraged to become involved with structures that would work for him (such as his network of friends, settings, school). He and his family continued to come in for family therapy, with the exception of Paul, the older brother. It is important to note that Paul used work the way Ned used drugs—to avoid pain and conflict.

As mentioned previously, much of the initial family treatment focused on the antecedents in their families of origin. The issues of separation and individuation were primary for a fairly long time. While Ned and his mother both complained of their involvement with each other in terms of nagging, arguing, and cursing by Ned, they both seemed to need its presence as did Mr. G., who jumped in only to defend his wife. He and his wife rarely argued, and Ned's interaction with his mother provided a great deal of excitement and passion in the family. The therapists speculated that one of Ned's functions was to provide passion and excitement for the parental couple.

During the course of treatment the parents tended to focus on Ned's drug activity when stuck on issues about their own lives. In one such session the therapists talked about drugs that Ned was using as medication to blunt emotional pain. Mrs. G. commented that Mr. G. used sleep in the same way. Mr. G. started talking about his childhood, relating the pain he felt as a result of the lack of emotional support he experienced from his mother. As he talked, Ned seemed to become more attentive and willing to talk about his own painful feelings. On several occasions during the session, Mrs. G. interrupted while her husband was talking, attempting to refocus on Ned. Mrs. G. was unable to give her husband emotional support, much like her mother-in-law. The therapists pointed out what she was doing and refocused on the father. Mother's main complaint about father was that "he does not talk . . . to me . . . to Ned."

In the individual and group sessions as well, focus was on the issues of limit setting and separation. Ned got a great deal of feedback from group members about his grandiose presentation of himself and his inability actually to function on his own. Ned had dropped out of school and was living at home, dependent on his parents but expressing a great deal of resentment about it. Also he openly flouted his parents' rules about sex with his girlfriend in the house, pot smoking, and so forth. The parents were having difficulty maintaining a structure with Ned, and without the external structure of an institution they all floundered. The therapists also suggested exploration of the need to give in to Ned and not to set limits on their own.

Mr. and Mrs. G. had difficulty reaching agreements with each other regarding how to react to and deal with Ned's activities. In the family sessions Mr. G. tended to sit back and encourage arguments between Mrs.

G. and Ned. The more silence on the part of Mr. G. the more intense the arguing between Mrs. G. and Ned. Ned becomes so angry that he storms out of the office, slamming the door. The male therapist tells Ned that his outbursts will not be permitted in the office. Mrs. G. expresses her anger with Mr. G. for his silence. The therapists encourage Mr. G. to talk and explore his lack of talk. The male therapist also provides an *in vivo* model for the father, who begins to talk to mother. Mr. G. begins to talk about how talking had no value or meaning in his family. He learned at a young age that he couldn't get what he wanted, and so he turned to work in order to get by.

Ned had some contact with the vocational psychologist in the program, taking a series of aptitude and interest tests that suggested areas other than pharmacology. Ned thought that psychology would be a primary choice. He reenrolled in school, taking a few psychology courses, but then quickly returned to employment in a pharmacy. For several months this position seemed to work out well, since the head pharmacist was a very strong, limit-setting person. Ned came in consistently for treatment both alone and with his family. He got an apartment of his own, was working, and going to school part-time. Near his apartment, however, he soon found a pharmacy where he was offered more money, and he quickly changed jobs. He continued to see his grandfather.

Within months, his attendance at individual sessions became increasingly sporadic, and he missed family sessions as well. When the therapists confronted him with this situation, he denied any problems. The parents, who had been focusing more on their own relationship and feelings within themselves, quickly refocused as Ned became more symptomatic.

Little pieces of information about problems in his present employment situation and increased drug taking on his part became evident. His new employer was involved in illegal activity related to the manufacture and sale of drugs and had enlisted Ned's aid in this endeavor. Ned saw no way out, and in his impulsivity and hopelessness he overdosed and was rehospitalized, expressing suicidal thoughts and feelings. At that time he verbalized being under constant pressure and said that he was fearful that he had gotten in over his head with criminals who were reported to deal in violence. He had not talked about the situation but had acted out against himself instead. (Much like his father, he didn't talk.)

During this hospitalization he was less grandiose than previously and more willing to talk about his feelings. Therapy focused in on these feelings and their antecedents in his early family life. Work with the parents focused on letting go, allowing Ned to make his own mistakes and refocusing on their own lives while learning to weather the uncertainty about Ned's behavior. It became evident that the loss of Mrs. G.'s father was related to her enmeshment with Ned, and she began to talk about her earlier loss.

It was revealed that Mrs. G. was pregnant with Ned when her father died, and she was unable to see her father before he died. Her sisters had kept her from the hospital because they feared her loss of the pregnancy. She had lost a baby prior to Ned. She had not mourned her father, and each time Ned flirted with death these old feelings about the loss of her father were stirred up inside her.

The therapists helped the family to see how Mrs. G.'s father's unmourned death was contaminating her relationship with Ned, and they suggested that she needed to work on her own issues of loss and mourning as these related to her father.

Having left the hospital, Ned was living in his maternal aunt's basement. She was protective of him, much as she had been with her sister. As his mother was beginning to work on her issues with her father's death, Ned began to be resistant to leaving the basement and became depressed.

The family became concerned about a relapse, and the therapists felt that a rehospitalization would not be in the family's best interest. A network was offered in lieu of hospitalization, and the family got together fifty people at Mrs. G.'s younger sister's home in an attempt to use the resources of the family and revitalize the system. Family and friends alike attended, and new information was revealed, family secrets were blown out in the open, and support systems were formed for each of the family members, except for Paul, who stated that he didn't need any.

Three weeks later the network again met and was able to help the family use its resources in a more effective way via its support systems—for example, Ned's support system began to meet with his therapist in order to develop strategies for providing support and confrontation for Ned.

It is important to note that although there was an overall trend for progress to be made in treatment, the treatment process had its ups and downs. While Ned became more consistent in his attendance, his acting out behavior—that is, drug taking, criminal activity—became more sporadic. His father, however, had several heart attacks, and the therapists focused in on the family's fear of the father's death as well as the father's failure to take care of himself (through overwork and tension). The mother expressed a great deal of concern about her husband and related earlier losses, particularly the death of her father, for whom she continued to grieve.

Treatment continued for several years. At different points in time problems arose in the family but to a less intense degree. For example, Ned was arrested for driving while intoxicated, and he received probation with a mandate for treatment. He talked about the situation and what was going on with him at the time. Shortly afterward, however, he made a decision to go to California without informing probation. The therapists pointed out to him and his family that he was breaking probation (a limit), but he left anyway. While away he broke his arm in several places. When he returned from his six-month stay, his arm had not yet healed and his probation was not yet completed. Breaking his arm was interpreted to him as his self-destructive behavior that takes place when he breaks limits. The therapists recommended that he ask for six months more of probation and ask that the probation officer check on his attendance in treatment on a monthly basis. Ned was willing to explore his self-destructiveness as well as to ask for a continuance of his probation. It is important to note that Ned's parents were in favor of his trip to California: he would be away from his "drug friends." They reinforced his breaking of the probation limit in spite of their verbal assertions to the contrary.

Upon returning from California and asking for additional probation, Ned came back into treatment on a regular basis. He took a counselor training position with another drug program where he successfully completed his training and worked for a year. He continued in therapy, talking about the issues that arose for him as an "ex-addict" counselor, since many of his clients had problems that stirred up old feelings in him. He moved into an apartment with his old girlfriend, to whom he became engaged, and worked steadfastly on issues in separation and differentiation in the family.

Ned's family was in treatment while he was in California, and they came in for some sessions with him upon his return. Ned's parents were doing more things alone: taking vacations and trips, and having less involvement in Ned's activities. Paul and his wife had another child, Paul began to lose weight, and he quit one of his jobs.

Mrs. G. brought her sisters in for a session in order to talk about her father's death and her impaired mourning process. All of the sisters except Rita came. She was regarded as the family scapegoat.

Follow-up two years later found Ned married, working as a counselor, and finishing his degree. His parents were retired and traveling.

Follow-up five years later found Ned with a wife and two children and applying to medical school. His parents were living in Florida. His father had lost his pension following an investigation into illegal activities on the job. His brother, Paul, was fired and indicted for theft of a similar nature. Neither father nor older son was able to see alternative options for living and had shortcut in the work situation the way Ned had with drugs.

A Three-Generation History of the G. Family

For the purpose of understanding the treatment process within an intergenerational context, I would now like to present some of the family history.

Mr. G., Ned's father, was a fifty-two-year-old, conservatively attired, fatigued looking man, who appeared rather quiet, tense, and serious. He was hardworking and, at the time of the contact, was employed by a state agency after having many years of self-employment. During his self-employment he had had several heart attacks as a result of overworking and tension. He was now employed in a situation where no physical labor was involved. However, there was considerable emotional tension as a result of his feeling unappreciated for his efforts at the agency. He seemed to feel embattled.

Mr. G. was very angry with his youngest son, Ned, whose behavior was said to "aggravate his wife's heart condition." He tended to show more concern about his wife than about his own heart problems, which were compounded by "back trouble." He denied any concern about his own health and minimized the concerns of his family about the possibility of his own death in spite of having had several heart attacks.

Mrs. G. was a friendly, outgoing, fifty-year-old woman, who was protective of her husband. She was generally depressed about the condition of her son, in whom she was obviously invested. She alternated in action between outbursts of anger and sadness—showing more affect in her relationship with her son than she did with her husband. Mrs. G. had worked as a bookkeeper during the time her children were in school, but she had given up her employment (which she enjoyed) after several serious heart attacks. Mrs. G. talked about the seriousness of her health problems and the possibility of her death. At times in her exchanges with her youngest son, she alluded to the possibility of her death as a result of his behavior— that is drug abuse and involvement in illegal activities.

Paul G., the eldest son in the family, was a grossly overweight, overworked young man who held down three jobs at once. One of his jobs was with his father's agency. He was married and had been living out of the family home for several years. He had one small daughter and spent most of his waking hours at work and with his daughter when possible. He spent little time with his wife because of his work (much like his father in his earlier years). Paul was described by his parents as a worker. He had had difficulty in school with reading and was not interested in intellectual pursuits. He liked working with his hands (like his father). His main employment was as a mechanic.

Paul denied any concerns about his parents' health problems and tended to focus his energies on his brother, whom he saw as upsetting his parents. While he expressed genuine concern for his brother, he tended to give advice to him and expect his brother to change his behavior. He had difficulty expressing anger toward Ned and was inclined to avoid passionate interchanges in the family whenever possible. Working at three jobs a week allowed for the physical and emotional distance he wanted. In spite of his protestations of concern about Ned's behavior, he was generally unavailable until a crisis involving the possibility of a death occurred. Generally he denied any concern about his parents' deaths, in spite of their serious illnesses.

Ned was a very bright, highly intellectualized "know-it-all" who was seen as the family superstar. He was considered to be the brain in the family and had been accepted at several prestigious schools. He was enrolled in a pharmacy program, where he achieved high grades when he completed the course work. He had difficulty finishing his work. He was employed in a pharmacy on a part-time basis and was known to steal drugs from his place of employment as well as from the school setting.

Twenty years old, Ned alternated between being very depressed and suicidal, and furiously sarcastic, provocative, and hostile. He engaged in frequent verbal battles with his mother and at times seemed deliberately to attempt to agitate her. He was preoccupied with his own situation, particularly his embarrassment as a result of being caught in his illegal affairs. The pharmacy was not pressing charges against him, but he felt that he had ruined his career in pharmacy and possibly medicine. Mr. G. had studied pharmacy for a brief period but had given up his goal when an uncle offered him an opportunity in his business with the promise that a partnership was eminent. The promise was not kept, leading to a great deal of disappointment and bitterness in Mr. G.

Ned's present turmoil was not a new situation for him. He had been involved in the drug scene for at least five years and had abused and sold drugs over that time. His parents had sent him for psychiatric help for several years, but Ned had expended his energies in seducing the psychiatrist with his intellectual understandings and intentions to go to medical school. During this therapy he precipitated several emergencies and was able to avoid negative legal consequences because of his therapist's investment in him. At the time of my contact with him, Ned had escalated the danger of the situation a hundredfold. He was extremely grandiose, involving himself in the manufacture of drugs with known criminals who were under surveillance by the FBI. Ned seemed to ignore the possibilities of being arrested and/or killed, perceiving himself as superior and able to outwit anyone who might limit him.

The G. family was in treatment at our agency for four years. During that time we began to explore the family patterns over three generations and to see some of the multigenerational contributions that resulted in the present drug abuse symptomatology. In an effort to understand the impact of intergenerational messages, it is helpful to look at the grandparent generation, and at the family messages that resulted in the present-day crisis, since it is thought that the present symptomatology represents an expression of these intergenerational messages.

Mr. G. was the eldest of three children who were born in Philadelphia. His father, Paul, was born in South Philadelphia, though his family had emigrated from Austria. His mother, an immigrant from the same town in Austria, had met and married Paul in Philadelphia. Both families were regarded by Ned as money and security conscious, although Mr. G.'s father was described quite differently by Mr. G. and his wife. He was viewed as fun loving, quick witted, and a somewhat irresponsible man who was dependent on his own father, a successful bakery owner, for financial support. He tended to spend money without concern for security and at times was thought to be a gambler and womanizer.

Mr. G.'s mother, however, was a rather cold, self-indulgent woman, quite concerned with financial status. She was inclined to value others on the basis of income, title, and possessions. While her husband seemed to waste and spend money, running through the financial resources of his family of origin, she pressed on for the material symbols of wealth that helped her feel more secure. The more she pressed, the less she got from her husband. She was forced to take up sewing to help with financial obligations.

Because of his parents' differences, Mr. G. grew up in the midst of a great deal of arguing about money. His father was absent much of the time, while his mother, though present, was unable to provide much in the way of emotional warmth and support. She was a rather needy, insecure woman whose main concern was herself. She was jealous of her sisters, who seemed to have more than she did. She spent a good deal of her time and energy competing with her sisters who also emphasized money as a basis for security and worth. She dwelt on the injustices that life and her husband had dealt her. She was known in the family to bear grudges against her sisters who achieved financial security and would refuse to speak to them over a period of years.

Mr. G. was unable to rely on his parents for consistent nurturance and limit setting. He felt a lack of interest and concern on the part of his parents, and as a youngster he went toward his paternal grandfather and paternal aunts who were able to provide him with some sense of security. He spent as much time out of the home as possible, involving himself in sports and other activities as soon as he became old enough to do so. He felt he could not rely on his mother for care as she was quite mistrustful of others, frequently refusing to engage in obvious child care activities because she did not trust the judgment of doctors and would not face the realities of illness, both physical and emotional. At one time in his early life, Mr. G. almost died, save for the intervention of his paternal aunts. Mr. G.'s mother, who felt that she could not rely on his father for the security she needed, turned to her older brother Nate, who appeared to be the source of security and success in her family. She did not trust the women in her family. In times of crisis she turned to Nate and her father-in-law rather, than deal with her husband, whom she regarded as a wastrel. When they married, Mr. G.'s father was considered a good prospect since he was handsome and came from a wealthy family. He seemed to have little regard for the money, as it came from his parents, particularly his mother, who would encourage his father to bail him out of debt.

Concerning issues of the children, Mr. G.'s mother had a great deal of difficulty. She often denied the reality of situations, particularly in relation to physical illness. On several occasions Mr. G. was physically symptomatic and near death while his mother chose to deny and ignore the signs. In later years during his marriage to Mrs. G., he had a variety of physical problems to which she responded readily. He married a woman who seemed able to give him some of the care that he was unable to get from his mother. Little information about the childhood of Mr. G.'s siblings is known. Mr. G. stated that he was out of the house playing baseball and basketball as soon as he was able to play (his maternal uncle Nate was a well-known basketball player and coach). He remembers little about his sister, who was four years younger, and recalls that his brother, who was twelve years younger, "had it much better" than he. He felt that his mother put more caring and energy into raising his younger brother, and he expressed resentment that she made sure he went to college while she showed no concern about Mr. G.'s career.

At the time of our contact with the G. family, Mr. G.'s younger brother was a rather successful electrical supply dealer in partnership with his father-in-law. Both of his children were experimenting with drugs. Mr. G.'s younger brother and his wife used marijuana and cocaine occasionally, but denied their use to the rest of the family, with the exception of Ned, with whom the brother had exchanged drugs. One might suggest that Mr. G.'s brother broke an intergenerational boundary—making his credibility as an adult authority figure suspect.

Mr. G.'s sister had moved several thousand miles away and worked with her husband in their own modestly successful business. She had four children, one of whom was a girl and one of the few grandchildren who could get along with Mr. G.'s mother.

Mrs. G. is the fourth of five surviving children. A girl twin of her eldest sister died at eighteen months, and the first-born children were male and female twins who died at birth. Mrs. G.'s parents emigrated from eastern Lithuania. Her father as a youth had run away or had been sent to the Black Forest where he worked as a lumberjack. He was regarded by his daughter as a bold, hardy, down-to-earth man who was gentle and soft-spoken. Although physically short, he was rather powerful. As a young man he was reported to have been in conflict with his own father, who was alleged to have been physically abusive. Stories in the family differ regarding his leaving home. Some say he left of his own accord, others suggest he was forced to leave. Once he left home, however, he never saw his nuclear family again.

Mrs. G.'s father came to the United States when he was in his early twenties. Through relatives he met Mrs. G.'s mother, who had come from Lithuania via England to live with her cousin in the United States. Mrs. G.'s mother had lost her own mother at the very early age of two years. Her father remarried to a second cousin to ensure that he would have a mother to take care of his children. Mrs. G.'s mother and her stepmother did not get along well. Mrs. G.'s mother felt little love, caring, or affection from her stepmother. Her father was rather peripheral in the relation and gave Mrs. G.'s mother and her two brothers little support. One of her brothers left for England and sent for his sister soon after he arrived. Mrs. G.'s mother was unhappy in England and moved to the United States to be with a maternal cousin. She met and married her husband, Nathan, who was a hard-working tool-and-die worker who invested most of his energy in his new family. He put his wife on a pedestal and doted on her throughout the marriage. He was protective of her. She was known to be an apprehensive and fearful person. Mrs. G. remembered her father making great efforts to protect his wife from pain and suffering, and catering to her every need. She remembers her mother as a feeder—a woman who continuously cooked and fed her family and indulged in a great deal of overprotection in relation to her children. Ned recollects his maternal grandmother as a "tough old bird—a woman who cooked and fed others a lot, but rather cold, demanding, and difficult to feel close to." The daughters all revered their father, whom they described as a deeply religious and kind man. Mrs. G. has been known to say of her father, "No man could ever equal him." Her sisters agreed wholeheartedly.

It is important to note that Ned expended considerable energy in trying to live up to his grandfather, yet managing to fail to live up to his mother's statement, as did most of the men in the family who had married the daughters. Mrs. G.'s father died while she was carrying Ned, and in some ways Ned was seen as a replacement for his maternal grandfather (he was named for him). At the same time, Mrs. G.'s pregnancy with Ned was difficult and did not allow for her to take care of her father during his illness. She bore sad and angry feelings for years. Many of these feelings were unconsciously directed toward Ned. She was never able to grieve successfully the loss of her father, so Ned's frequent attempts at trying to live up to his grandfather provided the opportunity for getting in touch with her old feelings of loss. When Mrs. G. talked about her father, she would become very sad and would cry.

Mrs. G. had four surviving sisters, the oldest of whom was married but unable to have children. Her major concern was the welfare of her nieces and nephews, particularly Ned. She was a rather overprotective, controlling woman who had taken Ned into her home in an effort to "straighten him out." At one point he was living in her basement where her mother had lived until she died. Her husband was a rather passive man whom she was reported to belittle and control. He seemed to go along with it. He was a successful businessman who enjoyed his work.

Mrs. G.'s second-oldest sister had been estranged from the family and designated the family black sheep. She had married and divorced before her father's death and felt very attached to her father. She was and is the most attractive of the sisters but is suspicious and mistrustful of her family. Mrs. G. refuses to deal with her, saying that a psychiatrist over twenty years ago told her she should stay away because she could do nothing for her. There is a great deal of feeling between Mrs. G. and this sister, who is seen by the family as a paranoid schizophrenic. This sister was reported to be close to her father, spending time with him especially around problems in her life.

The third sister, a teacher, was married to an "intellectual." She had two sons, both of whom are fully employed in professional work. One is thought to be a genius and is compared to Ned. She appears to be the only sister with some emotional individuation in the family, although she feels left out and rejected by her siblings.

Mrs. G. is the fourth sister in line. She was regarded as the most lively and risk taking. Her mother frequently attempted to prohibit her from activities such as biking and skating when she was a child, expressing a fear that she would get hurt or killed. Mrs. G. would go against her mother's prohibitions and often be in trouble with her mother because of her "spirit." Mrs. G. was attractive as a young woman and dated a lot. Her mother was happy when she married.

The fifth sister and the youngest is married and had three children. She lost her eldest son (the same age as Ned) as a result of heart surgery when he was twelve years old. She is a very depressed person, has had considerable marital stress, and her youngest son has been treated for hyperactivity. The second son has had emotional conflicts and has sought out treatment. He has considered rabbinical schools as an escape from the family but is encountering a great deal of emotional stress.

Mr. and Mrs. G. met in the early forties while Mr. G. was in the service. They married during the war. Mrs. G. stayed with her family while Mr. G. was in the Navy. He was both on the Atlantic and Pacific fronts working as a corpsman and pharmacist's mate. He was the only survivor of a group of corpsmen who landed on Normandy beach. He was very moved by the death around him and experienced some guilt about being the sole survivor. He was recommended for honor and valor. When transferred to the Pacific front, Mr. G. recollects that he was one of the few Jews stationed aboard ship. When he was commended for his action on Normandy beach, he never received the medals promised him. He felt that this situation was a result of discrimination because he was a Jew. He felt a great deal of discrimination while in the Navy. He felt bitter and unappreciated there, much as he did in his family of origin. Strangely enough, Ned became actively involved in the more radical activities of the Jewish Defense League in high school and was known to threaten those who discriminated against other Jews in the school. He saw himself as affording protection. His father felt he had no such advocate in his family or in the service. While Mr. G. was in the service, Mrs. G. lived with her parents as she worked and worried. When Mr. G. returned from the service at the end of the war, the couple arranged to move out on their own.

About a year later their first son was born. He was the first grandchild on each side. He was named for his paternal grandfather who had died before Mr. G. went into the service. Mr. G. spent more time with his father as he grew older, especially in relation to work.

Paul was his father's son. He grew up learning to do the things his father valued—that is, hard work, working with his hands, and sports. He expressed little interest in academic areas, and as a child was diagnosed as having a reading disability. From the time he was quite young he spent considerable time with his father who frequently worked around the clock to keep his business going. Paul worked side by side with him while Mrs. G. stayed home with Ned. Ned occasionally attempted to help out in the business but felt rejected by his father. Mr. G. stated that Ned's attitude toward business and him was one of belittling others and being a "know-it-all."

During those years Mrs. G. bore a great deal of resentment toward her husband's work. He was out of the home a great deal of the time. For all the labor, there was little financial reward. After his first heart attack, Mr. G. was forced to give up his business and work for someone else. Long before that Mrs. G. went to work herself. It is a matter of interest in regard to Ned's problems that she went to work when Ned started school. Ned frequently became ill at school and needed his mother. Separation from her was difficult for him. This was not the first separation, for Ned had had several hospitalizations as a child for physical problems. Ned had to struggle with his dependency on his mother during the first two years of her employment and frequently called his mother to come home from work and be with him.

Times were difficult for the G.s. Working constantly, Mr. G. spent little time in the family home. No matter what he did, financial success was not forthcoming. His complaints were similar to those of his mother, who constantly harped on the bad deal she had gotten in life. Mr. G.'s overwork resulted in considerable tension. Even his elder son's assistance did not lessen the tension. Ned began to spend some time in the business but was generally regarded as more of a pest than helpful. When Ned was in his early teens his father had a severe heart attack and was near death. For Mrs. G. this was a sign that her husband should give in to her long-standing wishes—to give up the endless work and take a job working for someone else.

Mrs. G. recalled vividly the deaths of her father and second son. She felt she could not endure another loss. At the same time her mother had become ill and was being cared for day and night by Mrs. G.'s oldest sister. Mrs. G.'s mother had become ill after the death of her youngest daughter's eldest son, and she seemed to go downhill thereafter.

In the midst of the tension and turmoil Ned had begun to "feel his oats." He was a very bright boy, and he began to find ways to use his intelligence to get some of the attention from his parents that he so desperately wanted. He began to experiment and deal in drugs, yet maintained his grades and the appearance of doing well. Money began to come into the G. home in the form of expensive clothes, motorcycles, and so forth. While Mrs. G. was preoccupied with the illnesses in her family, her son was setting out to obtain the financial gains that his father and parental grandmother had so longed for. The parents did not seem aware of Ned's growing problems.

Eventually Ned had to use more of the drugs that he was dealing, and he flaunted this use in the face of the family. When his drug abuse became obvious to her, his mother took him to a psychiatrist at the age of sixteen. Ned saw the psychiatrist individually for several years; the psychiatrist then required that Ned take care of the bill. Ned then quit treatment. During the four years, Ned armed himself with psychiatric terminology and pharmacology information so that he could engage in an intellectual understanding of his problems. His therapist, a supportive parent figure, was available to Ned both emotionally and intellectually and tended to foster Ned's interest in the intellectual with the hope that he might gain more control. He encouraged Ned to read about his emotional condition. Ned took his readings seriously and used them to outmaneuver the therapist.

At the time of our meeting in 1973, Ned had run the gamut. While he had managed to survive physically and function well enough to get into pharmacy training (his therapist functioned as a support for his survival), his failure to obtain limits on his grandiosity had resulted in several suicide attempts and an escalation of his drug abuse.

Mr. and Mrs. G., who had managed to survive physically in spite of the recent loss of Mrs. G.'s mother and their own heart attacks, were asking for help with the situation with Ned and were willing to come in for family sessions.

What intergenerational family messages contributed to that stressful circumstances was the meat of the family sessions. The unresolved loss and grief over the generations, the unresolved dependency and separation issues, the lack of limit setting, the unexpressed anger and hurt over deprivation, and lack of attention and nurturance could be traced back over four generations on both sides of the family.

The values of the cultures whence the grandparents had come were expressed in the present generation with regard to security, wealth, hard work, and feeding and caring. The overprotectiveness toward Ned could be seen in his mother as a result of her not feeling protected and nurtured by her own parents (her mother had died when she was three, her father married a cousin who deprived her emotionally while the father tacitly agreed to it). Ned's maternal grandmother had to travel two continents to find some sense of nurturance and protection from a husband who reportedly admired her and shielded her from pain. Ned's maternal grandfather too traveled across continents to find a woman who needed him and daughters who served him (unlike the situation with his own father, who did not regard him well and with whom he had no contact before his death).

The need for wealth and material symbols therefore was evidenced in the G. family's endless striving for money and a sense of accomplishment, no matter the means. Hard work had not resulted in financial success for Mr. G. or his eldest son. Irresponsibility had not accomplished it for Mr. G.'s father, although his paternal grandfather had become very successful through hard work. Using his intellect and deviousness, Ned had been able to develop a sizable income but paid the price emotionally, ending up very depressed and near death. Ned thwarted his own intellectual ambitions in the world by jeopardizing himself and by being discovered for his illegal behavior. The intergenerational reinforcement of these behaviors became the center of treatment. The emotional energy that had been devoted to the old intergenerational family issues by the G. family had contributed to their giving up their lives in the present.

20

Breaking Homeostasis: The Treatment of Prolonged Adolescence

Norma Lefkovitz
Leslie Daroff

Editors' note: This chapter reports on the family therapy process as it was conducted with a family that had a number of confusing and severe problems—both offspring, a son and a daughter, having been seriously involved in drug abuse over a period of years. The therapy reported here is actually the second course of family therapy that this family participated in. The first course, which is briefly reviewed, occurred when the son and daughter were adolescent drug abusers (approximately eight years earlier); and they were now perceived in some important respects still to be in a state of continued adolescence. A unique feature of the report is a series of statements made by each of the four family members over a period of years, indicating the changes and the inconsistencies that occurred in their perceptions of their respective situations.

The Berk family consists of the parents, Ed and Elinor, and the two children, Evan and Judi. The family therapy that we are about to present here is treatment that we began with the Berk family when the children were both adults. However, the presenting problems, as well as the treatments for these problems, began years earlier when both the children were still adolescents. In order to give the reader an overview of the chronology of the events that preceded our treating the Berk family, we will begin with their first experience with family therapy.

Dr. H., a well-known family therapist, began working with the Berk family when Evan was fifteen and a half and his sister, Judi, was thirteen and a half. Elinor described the situation: "Ed and I were living separately under the same roof and the children were just falling apart. Evan had already been arrested at least once. I had gotten calls from [private] school about him and about Judi, who was starting to fail one subject after another. I had never had any problems like that with my children." The parents were both unaware that their children were experimenting with drugs, primarily marijuana, at the time they began therapy.

During the next seven years, the therapy with Dr. H. was a combination of couples and family sessions, with some individual sessions with one or the other teenager. That therapy ended when Judi married and Evan went away to college.

The question of why family therapy with adult drug abusers is being presented in a book about adolescent treatment might well be asked. Seemingly both teenagers were on their way to adult functioning after lengthy therapy. However, it became increasingly apparent that their strategies for coping with the demands of adult life were inadequate and that the adolescent therapy had not succeeded with some of the underlying and pervasive problems. The homeostasis of the family's dysfunctional communication systems, coping mechanisms, and maturation abilities had not been broken. The family was still stuck and had made only surface changes in its system. George Santayana many years ago said it best: "Those who cannot remember the past are condemned to repeat it." (We don't doubt, however, that the family would have even more severe problems without the prior therapy. All we have is their appraisal of the earlier therapy. It could be that they benefited more from it than they realized.)

In retrospect, Elinor and Ed said that "we worked things out in our relationship, but the children weren't getting anywhere. If anything, they were being very secretive." Evan was often absent from sessions and said, "I don't remember much of the therapy itself. I have a feeling I didn't obtain a lot at the time."

While in college, Evan used pot and said that he was a fairly successful dealer. He began individual and group therapy as "the alternative to suicide . . . I think that the group therapy actually did more in a lot of ways than individual therapy, but I didn't feel that we got to the core."

Judi used opiates when she was in college and had to drop out; while in college she started in individual therapy with Dr. I. When she came home, she began to see Dr. H. by herself.

> I had reapplied to college, and I was accepted. I really didn't know what I wanted to do. I had already kicked drugs once. When I came back to this city I stayed clean for a while, and then it started over. I was kinda tired of the whole thing. Bobby offered me a future and painted a picture of a way out. He was very insistent on getting married, and I was swept away by that. I was really down, and I didn't want to start again with drugs."

After a few years of marriage and one child, Judi began individual therapy with a new psychiatrist, Dr. A., seeing him for about three years.

After Evan graduated from college, Ed asked him if he wanted to move back and join his business.

It was very difficult. He wanted me to come back very much . . . One of
the main things in my life that I always thought about first before I ever
made a major decision was how it would affect my father. I mean I had
opportunities to do things in life that, when I look back, it is amazing to
me that I didn't take advantage of them. But it would have meant doing
something that would have hurt him, and I wouldn't do it. I would have
always come back to face accusations that I was disloyal.

So Evan began working for his father. As the situation deteriorated, he
began to get depressed, "fooled around with narcotics but not enough to be
addicted," and sought therapy at a clinic specializing in depression. At the
clinic, he saw his first female therapist and also participated in group
therapy. Evan said that this treatment experience ended disastrously when
the therapist encouraged him to participate in an experimental trial of
naltrexone. The drug caused a frightening LSD-like trip, ending in a suicide
attempt and severing therapy.

The parents' concern about Evan brought them back to Dr. H., who
was unable to be the therapist since he was going away. Dr. H. referred the
family to Dr. G., who saw the family for a few sessions. When Evan needed
to be hospitalized, Dr. G. was out of town, and Evan saw his colleague, Dr.
B., who initiated Evan's first hospitalization. Ed continued to see Dr. G. on
an individual basis and began using an antidepressant as part of his treatment.

Our seven-year therapy relationship with the Berk family began when
Evan, then thirty years old, was admitted by Dr. B. to the drug unit of a
private psychiatric hospital for his first inpatient detoxification from opiates.
Evan continued to see Dr. B. as an outpatient, and our next meeting with
Evan occurred two years later when he readmitted himself to the hospital.
This time Evan agreed to ask his parents and his sister, who lived two hours
away, to become involved in family therapy.

Although Elinor, his mother, believed that previous therapy had been
harmful, that the "kids were overprotected by therapists," she was willing
to participate actively in the sessions. Several years later, Elinor was more
revealing about how she had felt at the initial family session:

> I remember really feeling forced. I was so fed up with the whole idea of
> listening to all the therapy and all the therapists with whom we were
> involved while my kids went from bad to really worse—drugs to suicide
> attempts, divorce, drinking, everything, police . . . I felt that I had raised
> the kids as best I could and that it was time that they stand on their own
> and let me live my own life . . . But you know, I'm still a mother, and
> you certainly can't turn your back on your kids.

When the family began therapy with us, Evan was no longer working for
his father, and his major source of income was from narcotic sales. During

this time, Judi's marriage, which had been quite unhappy, ended. She was hospitalized twice, once for an alcohol detoxification and once for a suicide attempt. Her relations with her ex-husband continued to be strained. Since she was not employed, her parents helped her financially.

Ed has always been an exceptionally energetic and successful businessman who "worked very long hours and came home late many times—days on end—after the kids had gone to bed." He was able, in his early sixties, to continue with a rigorous business, athletic, and social life. Ed, as well as Dr. H., encouraged Elinor to begin a life outside her own business, which she continues to run quite successfully. Both Ed and Elinor are well educated, attractive, engaging people, with varied interests.

Evan characteristically spoke in a quiet, flat, almost expressionless voice. When asked about his expectations of family therapy, he said, "When I started, I don't think I thought anything. You [Les] suggested it. It sounded like it might work and maybe I could get something out of it. I just did it." Judi voiced her hopes with a great deal of animation and intensity: "I wanted to feel loved and accepted. I wanted very much to be heard, and I felt it gave me an opportunity to be heard." Ed's major goal was "to get the kids back in the family and get them off drugs and suicidal feelings. Elinor and I had pretty much worked out our problems. We thought we had to do something to get the kids normalized." Although Elinor didn't reveal her ambivalence about getting involved in therapy again, she did say that "I never had any faith in individual therapy. With Dr. H., I was convinced that the only way that you could make things better was that you got everybody together."

Having introduced the Berks, let us introduce ourselves and present an outline of the rest of the chapter. Les Daroff, thirty-four when therapy began, had graduated from a family therapy training institute two years before and had been working for twelve years in the field of substance abuse, eight of them at the clinic. Norma Lefkovitz, then forty-one, was a student at the same training institute and came to the clinic as an intern. Since training students was part of the clinic's purpose, we made no attempt to hide the differences in our training and experience. As we will explain toward the end of the chapter when we discuss our personal reactions, the differences may indeed have been beneficial.

Although families are often given descriptive labels, such as "enmeshed" or "skewed," which are intended to clarify the family dynamics, we believe that the interlocking, and sometimes contradictory, dynamics of some families are too complex to be labeled easily. Such complexity can be both a serious problem and a challenge for the therapist, since an intervention in one area may be colluding with the family pathology in another. By giving family members their own voice, using quotations from family sessions, we hope to convey to the reader the complexity of the therapy with this family that had such complicated and enduring problems. Following the quotations, we shall discuss the major themes that emerged and the interventions we made.

People in therapy often make definite and unconditional statements, partly because they sincerely believe what they're saying at that moment and partly because they wish that what they're saying were and would continue to be true. Both the family and the therapists can feel confused when serious contradictory feelings and ideas become apparent over time. The following dated quotations from family members will help the reader to see the complexity of the family problems and struggles as they became evident over time.

Starting with the first family session, Elinor talked about her relationship with her husband:

9/25/81 "We got along fine once the kids grew up and left the house."

10/31/81 "Until recently Ed would deny feelings. I don't see him that way now."

6/14/82 "Ed denies my point of view and my feelings."

6/28/82 "Ed and I spend less time together than most married couples. I haven't thought much about it. If he were around all the time, I'd be annoyed. He wants me to do things his way."

4/14/83 "If something happened to either child, more Evan, I don't think Ed and I could stay together. We've got roots together—we've been married thirty-five years—but I don't know how deep the roots are."

3/29/84 "I get angry at Ed for not telling me when he has contact with Evan. I tell Ed when I talk to Evan."

1/21/85 "Ed's and my relationship has improved. I don't feel a need for therapy. I can talk to Ed and my sister."

2/11/85 "I don't think Ed sees us as two parents."

2/18/85 "You [Ed] dismiss me and I feel hurt and angry. It's no wonder the children don't pay attention to me."

10/28/85 "I told Evan that if he didn't want to come to family therapy, it was okay. Ed and I might continue because we got a lot out of it."

8/4/86 "It's like I'm dead for this family. Ed didn't tell me that Judi had moved into her house and that he talked to Evan's probation officer."

The following quotations reflect Ed's attitudes toward his marriage:

9/25/81 "I feel so bad about Evan's picture of us. We're proud of our marriage and we work at it."

6/14/82 "Judi, you and I practice communication. Elinor and I have a truce."

9/23/85 "Last year Elinor said she would leave me if something happened to Evan because she blamed me. I think she's changed."

Here are Evan's statements about his relationship with Jane, with whom he has been living for four years:

12/28/81 "Having a relationship with Jane is a tremendous help."

11/8/82 "I may break up with Jane."

1/3/83 "Jane and I haven't had our talk. I haven't had the time."

11/26/84 "Jane threatened to throw me out this morning."

7/8/85 "Jane is ready to put the house up for sale. We're ready to split."

Elinor talks about her feelings toward the children:

10/7/81 "I've sort of gotten over the what-did-I-do-wrong."

12/4/81 "I'm still afraid to call you [Evan]. Your voice sounded slurred and I got hysterical. I can't go through this again."

3/15/82 "Evan and Judi have controlled more of our lives than we have controlled theirs."

3/29/82 "I feel hopeless about this. I'd like to quit therapy."

4/19/82 "Why don't the kids know I'd do anything for them?"

6/7/82 "When Judi is in the city, I'm not as anxious because I can do something. I haven't been sleeping well. I think about Judi and I get sick to my stomach. Evan is just hopeless; he's like trying to get hold of mercury."

8/13/82 "Evan has moved into adulthood. Judi still talks to me as if she were an angry child. With Evan I can talk as an adult."

4/14/83 "I've been hurt by them and gave up on them. If something happened to Evan, I don't think I could stay together with Ed."

5/2/83 "I think an altercation could send him over the brink. I feel so hopeless about Evan."

5/31/83 "I used to be more bothered, used to be afraid that what I would say would make you suicidal."

5/10/84 "The children are taking me out for Mother's Day, and I'm really pleased."

7/5/84 "We want to spend more time with the children."

1/7/85 "I feel down [about Evan] but he is talking in a different way now—not like everything is okay."

1/21/85 "We're afraid to stop coming. This place is like a lifeline. We might not see Evan again. I feel like a failure as a mother [to Evan]."

4/22/85 "I'm very angry with Judi. She called me and really berated me and hung up on me."

5/13/85 "I've given up on Evan. I only invite Judi to dinner because she's responsive and responsible."

9/23/85 "I let Evan placate me. I don't want to see the truth. In the last week I've seen him differently—not a poet collecting first editions but streetwise, a man in trouble. I can distance myself because I see him as a grown man, not a kid."

11/11/85 "I want to break from worrying about Evan."

11/18/85 "I cried all night. We're afraid Evan will kill himself."

12/2/85 "Judi had us for Thanksgiving dinner. It's the first time we felt welcome there. She said we were doing so much for her child's confirmation that she owed it to us. It was nice."

12/23/85 "Judi's tone of voice with Ed is so nasty. I felt like smacking her."

2/17/86 "You [Evan] don't control part of my life anymore. My life is my own."

5/8/86 "I have a special connection to Evan, like an umbilical cord. I'd like to break it."

This section documents the changes in Judi's outlook.

10/7/81 "I really do respect you two for coming [to family therapy]. It can be uncomfortable."

2/5/82 "I'm thinking of dropping out. It's a waste of time and money. I've personally benefited but not as a family unit."

6/14/82 "Dad, you took the first step."

12/27/82 "I feel more sure about it [family] than I did in the past. I noticed you've [Ed] been more human and fallible and I appreciate that. I don't have to be perfect to be accepted in this family."

1/10/83 "I'll have to take care of myself; you [Ed] could have been more supportive." Ed replies, "I started giving you $200 a week seven years ago."

1/24/83 "Both of my parents have been easier to get along with."

2/14/83 "I'm leaving. I don't know why I come to family sessions."

6/21/84 "My father gives me more latitude than he gives Evan."

8/30/84 "I couldn't have gone through this [child custody battle] alone."

11/1/84 "The family bailed Evan out. I need help."

5/13/85 "I don't have any relationship with Evan because he won't allow one. I've been able to establish a good one with my parents because they want it."

7/1/85 "Nobody in this family cares about me. You only care about Evan. I'm having a nervous breakdown from overwork. Why don't you [Ed] give me money and property the way you did Evan?"

1/20/86 "It was too much for me. I don't want to get involved with Evan's problems. You don't want to hear about it. I'm leaving."

4/14/86 "I'm glad my parents supported me through my child custody problems."

Ed's statements about his children:

11/29/81 "I don't want anything for myself. I want them to be self-sufficient."

2/12/82 "As far as Evan is concerned, we're beginning to have a better relationship. What are we trying to accomplish with Judi?"

5/3/82 "Judi needs to learn to respect money, so I'm not giving her any more. I'm tired of linking to people to carry them on my back."

6/3/82 "Judi has changed very fast. She has run out of money so she has to do something adult. She can't spit in my face and expect help. We've changed."

6/7/82 "Judi is more intransigent than Evan."

6/21/82 "You [Judi] treat me like shit."

7/9/82 "I'm absolutely crushed [Evan is using drugs]."

7/26/82 "If the kids were off our back, we'd be fine."

9/13/82 "I feel able to talk to Evan."

10/18/82 "I keep thinking something's going to change."

2/7/83 "I'm tired of my kids."

2/21/83 "I'm beginning to feel that what I give is not appreciated."

4/14/83 "I want my kids to understand me, that I'm really a good person. Judi seems to be seeing that now."

5/2/83 "I get fed up with Evan, but I keep it to myself. I'm afraid to start a confrontation with him."

3/29/84 "I've given up on Evan."

8/30/84 "I feel a rapport with Judi. There's giving back and forth."

3/18/85 "I saw Evan on Sunday, dopey. When will I stop fantasizing that he'll be living a normal life? Judi did take what I offered."

10/28/85 "I'm fed up with offering and giving and being turned down."

1/20/86 "We've been here four years and you're [Evan] still in hospitals and Judi's jumping around."

2/24/86 "How we can get Evan on the right track? It kills me to see what he's doing to his life. I can't let go of that."

5/8/86 "I don't want to face the possibility that Evan will kill himself."

7/7/86 "We're very unhappy when he's unhappy. I started crying when I talked to him."

9/4/86 "I'll be sixty-five in a few months, and I'm going to retire from parenting."

9/11/86 "I'm sore as hell and I told Judi that if she cursed at me again, I'd never talk to her."

Evan's relationship with his parents:

10/1/81 "My perception of both of you has changed."

12/27/82 "I'm not harboring any resentments toward my parents."

2/21/83 "At this moment, I believe Dad wouldn't screw me. But it has happened in the past."

7/18/83 "I'm doing a project with him right now. Things have changed. I feel he listens to me. There are still some problems but nothing that can't be worked out."

7/19/85 "I'm worried that my father might steal my money."

10/28/85 "The family has been supportive. I've seen some changes."

11/18/85 "I've been wrapped up in my own experience. My parents' recent feelings have been a revelation to me."

Evan's statements about his substance abuse:

11/6/81 "Life seems different, a qualitative change."

6/15/85 "I've gone to NA but didn't find it helpful."

7/22/85 "I'm not going into the hospital. The only time I ever stayed off drugs was when I did it myself. I'm thinking of going to NA."

9/2/85 "Now that I'm using NA and therapy, I'll never go back to drugs."

3/17/86 "This is the end. This is the culmination of years that this [substance abuse] has been going on."

4/7/86 "I'm taking more drugs. I almost see myself as a chemical laboratory. I administer various drugs to create my moods."

The expression of so many conflicting feelings and actions may at first seem overwhelming and confusing. How can we make sense out of this mass of contradictions? Why do people continue to use old coping behaviors that are clearly ineffective? It is often difficult to give up old ways of thinking, feeling, or coping because the old ways are familiar and comfortable. To give up old ways involves a leap into the fearful unknown, to live in uncertainty. It also means moving away from what your parents taught you to do, possibly resulting in strong feelings of disloyalty and fear of disapproval that conflict with the desire to change.

This picture is further complicated by the fact that family members with feelings of resentment and hatred toward each other can inflict wounds on each other, even though the one doing the inflicting may suffer the most.

Our primary goal as family therapists was to bring the family members into the present so that they could learn to treat each other as adults rather than as "parents" and "children." The family seemed to be stuck in the past despite many years of competent help.

An overriding theme that emerged during the course of therapy was the need for closeness and dependency. The children behaved in dangerous ways, implicitly or explicitly asking their parents for help, while at the same time saying that they wanted to be independent. Both parents said they wished to be relieved of their parental burden, but both nevertheless responded in ways that seemed to maintain their children's dependency. There were several ways in which we tried to help the family members understand how they were working at cross-purposes and how they might change.

One way was to look at how the parents were repeating their past. We explored what they brought into the new marriage from their own families of origin. Ed's father was a quiet, emotionally reserved man, who had not had a close relationship with his father. It is no coincidence, then, that he maintained an emotionally distant relationship with Ed, who describes him as "living by axioms, cast-iron in his beliefs." In fact, as a hard-working, conservative businessman, he spent most of his time out of the home. Ed's mother, a beautiful but narcissistic woman, was an entertainer whose career kept her busy. She had little emotional contact with her husband—they seemed to run on "parallel tracks"—and left Ed and his younger sister, with whom he was not close, to be looked after by a maid.

Elinor's parents, on the other hand, had many violent collisions. Her father, an alcoholic, could be painfully sarcastic to his wife and children. At times he physically abused his wife, who never complained and sent the children to get groceries and avoided going out so that the neighbors wouldn't see her bruises. Elinor was close to her mother but felt a certain amount of disdain for her mother's passivity. Her father was a successful businessman, a bon vivant, who had extramarital affairs. In surface ways the marriages of both sets of grandparents seemed quite dissimilar, yet both lacked an emotional closeness.

In the beginning of their marriage, Elinor devoted herself to the children, while Ed devoted himself to making money. He could be aggressive and demanding, and Elinor feared that he would hurt the children if she didn't protect them. She saw Ed as being like her father, but she chose not to react passively like her mother. As she continued to protect the children from Ed's aggressiveness, he felt excluded, but rather than discuss his feelings he "shut up like a clam" and withdrew, as his father had done.

Evan grew up with conflicting messages: if you want your mother's love, don't be an aggressive, threatening man; if you want your father's approval, be tough and aggressive. But the conflict is complicated further by his mother's loving this aggressive man, in effect telling Evan both to be and not to be aggressive. How did Evan solve the conflict? He alternated between passivity and aggression, unable to integrate the two. An example of the aggressive side is his fascination with guns which began when he was a teenager and joined the rifle club at school, shooting at the windows of a neighbor's house. It ended at age thirty-seven when he turned in his submachine gun to the local police, was charged with federal firearms violations, and received five years probation. But while he was collecting guns, Evan was also using narcotics to put himself into a state of passive inertia.

Judi also grew up fearful of her father and close to her mother. However, she was not expected to be aggressive. Her parents expected her to marry and be taken care of by her husband. She fulfilled these parental expectations but chose to marry a man who could not meet the emotional needs of a dependent wife and child. Judi's choice of an emotionally detached but volatile husband repeated a pattern that apparently went back for several generations on both sides of her family.

Both Elinor and Ed had parents who were emotionally distant. Ed's considerable business activities kept him emotionally aloof from Elinor, as her father had been. In Evan, Elinor found a sensitive, nonaggressive, kindred spirit with whom she shared a love of books and ideas. Unconsciously this gave her hope that she could get love and approval from a man.

Ed's mother was less emotionally involved with Ed than was his father. Even when the children became adults, she favored Ed's sister. By investing time and emotional energy in Judi, Ed unconsciously tried to gain appreciation and emotional closeness from his daughter, whose personality had many similarities to his mother's.

Thus both parents, each unable to meet certain emotional needs of the other, turned to their children to fill the emptiness and loneliness. This made it difficult for the parents to permit, much less promote, their children's independence. They found it extremely difficult to let the children suffer the consequences of their immature behavior. As Elinor pointed out, "If Evan hadn't had this kind of family, he'd have been in jail by now."

Ed was now the powerful parent, and he had an opportunity to prove to Elinor and to his children that he was truly a good person, a good parent, and not the fearsome ogre of their childhood. Ed's need for proving his worth, coupled with Elinor's guilt for having previously excluded him, prevented them from acting together to set reasonable, age-appropriate limits on their children's behavior and demands. Their competitive, disunited style of parenting and their own immaturity fostered an immature detachment between parents and children.

Substance abuse was also a multigenerational problem. Elinor's father and his two brothers were alcoholics. Elinor was not aware that her own drinking had become immoderate until friends told her that her tennis would improve if she gave up alcohol. At that point, realizing that she could not be a moderate drinker, she stopped drinking.

As family therapists, we view substance abuse as a self-destructive coping mechanism some of the roots of which can often be found in the dysfunctional coping and communication behaviors in one's family of origin. If these patterns remain unchanged, they will be passed through the generations. Drugs and alcohol served several functions for this family. It was a familiar way to cope with daily stress and unpleasant feelings. Ed had used antidepressants for several years, only stopping after beginning family therapy. Substance abuse gave Judi and Evan a special bond, with much of their relationship revolving around drugs. In fact, the arrest that brought Judi into individual treatment at the clinic a few months after beginning family therapy resulted from her bungled attempt to fill a forged prescription that she had gotten from Evan.

Evan denied being dependent on his parents, claiming that he had lived on his own and had not accepted help from them since college graduation. But as the pattern of crises—arrests, overdoses, confused mental states—that coincided with his parents' vacations became obvious, Evan acknowledged that he was indeed fearful that he would not be able to survive emotionally without them. Since dependency feelings could not be openly talked about and needs for closeness and intimacy could not be met in more constructive ways, Evan and Judi created crises to bring the family together. Judi openly asked for financial help from her parents, angrily telling them they owed it to her as compensation for a crippling childhood.

Both children used substance abuse as emotional blackmail, holding out death as the ultimate threat. Thus they were able to punish their parents for the past and (paradoxically) at the same time emotionally nurture their parents by remaining dependent.

But drug use served other functions. It provided Evan and Judi with relief from unbearable feelings. Both suffered from periods of paralyzing depression. Even when not immobilized by their depression, they both felt an inner deadness and detachment from other people and ordinary pleasures. Drugs could then give them an artificial sense of well-being. For both, depression alternated with intense anxiety and panicky feelings about falling apart or exploding into pieces. In these periods, drugs had a calming effect.

The pattern of the alternation of opposites—for example, depression and anxious anxiety, aggression and passivity—permeated much of the family interaction. It was difficult for members of the family to deal with both emotions and facts at the same time. This phenomenon of splitting was very evident with the roles that Judi and Evan usually took. Judi had the emotional role, and Evan the intellectual one. At times the roles would flip, with Judi calmly taking care of Evan during one of his crises. But neither could have feelings and be reflective at the same time.

Another example is the split in the parenting roles. Elinor had the major role when the children were young, and Ed took that role when the children were adults. In neither period were the parents able to work effectively together for any length of time.

This inability to integrate smoothly different aspects of the self had a number of consequences. Family members found it difficult to understand one another, to see things from the other person's perspective, because they split themselves into opposites. Although Elinor and Ed had personally experienced depression, they could not understand how their children could be depressed when they stopped using drugs. It was as if the parents had "forgotten" and therefore could not use their knowledge of how it felt to be depressed to react empathetically. Judi, with her own child, and Evan, with his girlfriend's child, had experience in being parents, but they had great difficulty in putting themselves in their parents' place; they were often stuck entirely in the child role.

Communication also suffered from the phenomenon of splitting. Because it was hard to see someone else's perspective, family members often assumed incorrectly that they understood the other person and were themselves understood by the other. Factual information was often incompletely communicated, and no one asked for clarification. It was even more difficult to explain feelings to one another for there was the added fear of being vulnerable to hurt. Consequently the family felt a great deal of uneasiness and tension when they were together and often felt like "strangers in each others' lives."

In the beginning of therapy, family members communicated through us because they did not really trust each other. At this stage, we allowed ourselves to be used as mediators. We focused first on improving communication of factual information by asking questions to clarify what we didn't understand and pointing out how no one in the family had asked any questions even though they too were confused. We were supportive, and protective when necessary, of each member and helped each to communicate more fully and more honestly what he or she was thinking and feeling. Judi's individual sessions with Leslie Daroff were often used to go over the previous family therapy session and to role-play what she might say in the next family therapy session. Slowly trust increased, and the family members began to talk more often directly to each other. But it remained difficult for them to talk about their feelings unless they were extremely angry, and throughout therapy we needed to remind them that feelings, not just facts, influenced how people acted.

In fact much of the children's behavior could be seen as a way of forcing their parents to feel, not just think, and to express their feelings. During the first two months of therapy, Judi was often angry and verbally abusive to Ed, her father, who remained calm and rational. He finally got angry himself and screamed at her, "Don't ever curse at me. It hurts me. I feel sick to my stomach." His outburst seemed to allow Judi to see her father as a vulnerable, rather than invincible, person, and her verbal abusiveness markedly decreased.

Elinor allowed herself to express anger in a restrained way, often sarcastically. But she found it very difficult to reveal her deep feelings of despair. When she first allowed herself to cry, the other family members appeared uneasy and unable to approach her to offer comfort. Yet her crying was important to Evan and Judi in the same way Ed's display of anger had been.

Elinor and Ed had not realized how little known they were to their children. And not only unknown in an emotional sense; there were important parts of the family history that had been discreetly screened, and neither the parents nor the children had chosen to open the past. One untouched area was the parents' two-year separation; they lived in the same house but lived separate lives. Although family therapy with Dr. C. began in this period, the children had "amnesia" about the separation. And the parents were still reluctant to explain their feelings about the separation and what brought them back together. As a result there were many distortions about people's feelings and also about factual events.

In the first few years of therapy, there were many evening phone calls and emergency sessions to handle the crises that occurred. Our goal was to be supportive but not to be substitute parents. We tried to help the family understand both the reason for "needing" the "crises" and their reaction to them. The crises seemed to be a covert way of asking for closeness, while the family's reaction to them was the unconscious attempt to resist change, to keep things the same. Sometimes we used an intellectual approach, explaining family dynamics using the concepts of Transactional Analysis. At other times we worked in a more emotional way, occasionally using experiential, gestalt techniques. Evan and Judi were able to reenact their childhood desires for emotional closeness with their father by being held while he told them that he loved them for themselves, not for their achievements.

Initially only Judi responded to her father's overtures. She moved back to the city, detoxified herself from drugs at her parents' home, and found a job during the first year of therapy. When she was laid off and had a hard time finding another job, Ed brought her into the family business, giving her an opportunity as he had given Evan. However, during the same period, she sporadically used codeine and Valium, her driver's license was suspended, and she was unable to make ends meet even though her father provided her with an apartment, a car and insurance, and a moderate salary. Ed and Elinor focused on how much improvement Judi had made toward a "normal" life-style and tended to shrug off her failings. This was another important example of how the family was able to split off two contradictory aspects of the same situation.

They continued to support Judi financially and emotionally; but rather than becoming increasingly independent, she seemed to find it more and more difficult to stand on her own. She felt overwhelmed by the responsibilities of being a single, working parent. Although lonely and feeling depressed, she resisted any suggestions for socializing or resuming old interests in music and dancing. After reading a book about "burnout," she consulted the author and decided that he was better able to understand her problem and help her. She discontinued individual sessions but remained in family therapy. Over the next two years, she began using drugs again and finally decided to hospitalize herself in the same twenty-eight day program that Evan had been in a number of times. She was drug free for several months and living with a man she met in the hospital but then started using again.

Judi's initial improvement and subsequent regression is an example of how an intervention in one area can affect another area. The family support, particularly Ed's, seemed to help Judi to become less self-destructive, to become more competent at managing her life, and to find more interests in life than only drugs. However, the core of emptiness and worthlessness was not touched but rather covered over; and such a core could not, and did not, provide a solid foundation for independent, adult functioning.

For the first few years of therapy, Evan came to the family sessions sporadically. He had several arrests, was still stealing and using drugs, and intermittently trying to detoxify from drugs, either by himself, by using methadone, or through seven hospitalizations. In the second year of family therapy, Dr. B. ended Evan's individual therapy because he had illegally used his own muscle relaxants while in the hospital and was consequently discharged. Evan was offered individual therapy with either one of us, but he refused. There were some small but in retrospect significant changes in the next year or two. Evan communicated more openly about his feelings, was drug free for two months, his longest period of abstinence in many years, and was honest about his on and off again drug use. After four years of family therapy, Evan decided that he would risk trusting someone and began individual therapy with one of us, Norma Lefkovitz. He also began coming regularly to family sessions. In the same year, after a serious arrest on federal charges and the breakup of his relationship with Jane, he went to live with his parents and, with some assistance from his father, started his own business. A year later he moved into an apartment and began dating. Although he was not using narcotics, he did have several periods of heavy alcohol use. When confronted about his problem with alcohol, he refused to acknowledge its severity until two years later when he used alcohol and antidepressants to overdose. After he took this almost lethal combination of drugs, he called his mother, who rushed to his apartment and brought him to the nearest hospital. He was comatose and spent several days in the intensive care unit but recovered without impairment.

By this time the family had officially stopped therapy, but we talked on the phone or had an occasional session when there was a crises. Evan continued with his individual therapy and was more revealing about himself—

his fears, conflicts, inadequacies. It seemed that he was now more able to use his self-created crises to understand and change himself. In the past, he had tended to attribute much of his stress to the environment or to his relationship with his parents and had felt incapable of making changes.

Thus far we have not talked about our personal reactions. Our therapeutic stance was one in which we presented ourselves not as having "the answers" for the family, but rather as "knowing a process" by which open, direct communication could lead to resolution of old resentments and solutions to current problems, a process in which the family heals itself, thus empowering itself.

Being therapists for (and in!) this family was often difficult and frustrating as we saw the behaviors we had earlier believed to be stable, crumble under stress. How did we cope? We reminded ourselves that we were not members of the family and could not be responsible for making anyone change. We also consulted regularly with more experienced colleagues. We reviewed the sessions to see if there were more effective interventions that we could make.

But two other factors were more important. One was the family itself. They are people we like. We enjoyed their humor. We admired their perseverance, their willingness to struggle. The other factor was our cotherapy relationship. As Norma Lefkovitz became more experienced, the relationship became more equal so that the stress and responsibility were more evenly distributed. But just as we had become more accustomed to relying on each other, Les had an accident. His absence for a six-month period, about three years into therapy, caused a significant change. Up to this point, the males in the family had paid little attention to Norma, but they were now forced to work with a woman therapist. And Norma, for her part, was forced to stand on her own. When Les returned, it became obvious that Norma had become more forceful and direct, especially with the men. Evan later said that he had decided to see Norma for individual therapy because she "had the guts to tell me I was grandiose." We think that watching Les support and encourage Norma's growth from a novice to an equal had a beneficial effect for some of the family. Our cotherapy relationship provided a model for the possibility of growth, but also one for acceptance of conflict as Les and Norma openly disagreed with each other. Elinor became more open and direct in stating her feelings and needs. Ed seemed to have more regard for a woman's opinion. Perhaps Evan saw that it was possible to become more competent and independent without losing support and affection.

As a whole, the family has had to cope with enormous stress. The course for Judi and Evan in the past few years has been an uncertain one. Within the past two years, Elinor had an operation for cancer and Ed for a stomach ailment. The children now have to face the reality of their parents' aging and mortality in all its starkness and terror. The many twists and turns that we have experienced with the family leave us unable to predict how each family member will cope with the future.

Index

About the Contributors

James F. Alexander, Ph.D., is past president of division 43 (Family Psychology) of the American Psychological Association. He received the American Family Therapy Association (AFTA) award for Distinguished Contribution to Family Therapy Research and has been a "Live Master" presenter to the American Association for Marriage and Family Therapy (AAMFT). His Function of Family Therapy model has been widely researched and identified in numerous reviews as a preeminent interventional approach with acting-out youth.

George M. Beschner, MSW, formerly with the National Institute on Drug Abuse, has conducted studies on adolescent drug abuse, heroin addiction, phencyclidine abuse, cocaine use, AIDS, intravenous drug abuse, and drug abuse treatment. He is the co-author of seven books based on research findings, and he has published numerous articles on these topics in professional journals.

Nancy T. Casella, M.Ed., C.A.C., is a licensed psychologist and family therapist with nineteen years of experience in addictions treatment. The former director of the PCP Outpatient Drug Treatment Program, she is currently in private practice with the Suburban Diagnostic and Treatment Group and is a faculty member of the Family Institute of Philadelphia.

Leslie H. Daroff, M.Ed., has been practicing in the Philadelphia area for the past twenty years. He is currently in private practice providing psychotherapy, clinical supervision, consultation, and training services.

Anthony M. Errichetti, M.A., is a graduate and faculty member of the Family Institute of Philadelphia. He is presently a Ph.D. candidate in the Department of Psychoeducational Processes at Temple University, Philadelphia.

S. Michael Falzone, M.Ed., is a graduate of the Family Institute of

Philadelphia, Iona Graduate School of Pastoral Counseling, and Seton Hall University. He has been in private practice for ten years; presently, he is also part-time substance abuse coordinator at Lenape High School, Medford, New Jersey, and adjunct associate professor in the Humanities departments at Camden and Burlington county colleges. Mr. Falzone is a co-director of *Kaleidoscope*, a psychoeducational troop that addresses the issues of alcoholism, drugs, and the family.

Lillian Frankel began her career as a documentary radio and motion-picture writer. Later, after becoming involved with the topics of her scripts, she became a psychiatric social worker. Ms. Frankel, recently retired after thirty years of social work, is writing poetry and short fiction.

Nita W. Glickman, M.A., M.Ph., has a diverse educational background including master's degrees in computer science and public health. She is currently employed as a research coordinator/computer programmer at the School of Veterinary Medicine, Purdue University, West Lafayette, Indiana.

Edward Kaufman is professor of Psychiatry and Human Behavior at the University of California at Irvine and director of the University Chemical Dependency Program at Capistrano-by-the-Sea Hospital. He is an international authority in the field of drug and alcohol abuse who has authored and co-authored more than one-hundred publications. In addition to his research, teaching, and clinical work in substance abuse, the family, and family therapy, Dr. Kaufman has served on national government committees since 1982; as president of the American Academy of Psychiatrists in Alcoholism and Addictions since May of 1989; and as editor-in-chief of the *American Journal of Drug and Alcohol Abuse* since 1974.

Norma Lefkovitz, M.A., is a licensed psychologist and program director of the Career Program on the Woodside Hall Addictions Unit at the Philadelphia Psychiatric Center. A graduate of the Philadelphia Clinical School of Marital and Family Therapy, Ms. Lefkovitz is a family therapist with nine years of experience in drug abuse treatment.

S.J. Marks, M.F.A., C.A.C., is a psychotherapist and family therapist in private practice with GKSW/Crystal Group Associates in Wyndmoor, Pennsylvania. A former director of training (1980–1986) at the Clinical School of Marital and Family Therapy at the Family Institute of Philadelphia, Mr. Marks is currently a faculty member and supervisor at both the Family Institute and the Hahnemann University Master of Family Therapy programs. He is co-editor with Stephen Berg of *About Women* (Fawcett 1973), and a co-editor with Stephen Berg and J. Michael Pilz of *Between People* (Scott, Foresman, and Co. 1972). He is married and the father of four daughters.

Margaret R. Morrissey, formerly a research associate with the Philadelphia Psychiatric Center, is a clinical data assistant with Clinical Data Management of Wyeth-Ayerst Laboratories. Prior to her association with the Philadelphia Psychiatric Center, Ms. Morrissey taught junior high school in Philadelphia and in Palisades Park, New Jersey.

Gemencina Reed has a master's degree in counseling psychology from Norwich University. She is a faculty member of the Clinical School for Marital and Family Therapy of the Family Institute of Philadelphia. Ms. Reed is the senior family therapist for the Woodside Hall Outpatient Drug Program of the Philadelphia Psychiatric Center.

Dennis M. Reilly, M.S.W., C.S.W., A.C.S.W., is the director of Clinical Services at Southeast Nassau Guidance Center, a community mental health clinic in Seaford; and a clinical supervisor of the Guidance Center's Counseling Service, an outpatient drug-abuse treatment program in Wantagh, Long Island, New York. A board-certified diplomat in clinical social work, he is the author of numerous journal articles and other publications.

Ross V. Speck, M.D., is a clinical professor of Psychiatry at Jefferson Memorial Medical College in Philadelphia. A lifetime fellow of the American Psychiatric Association and a foundation fellow of the Royal College of Psychiatrists, London, Dr. Speck currently maintains a private practice in the Lancaster, Pennsylvania area.

M. Duncan Stanton, Ph.D., is professor of Psychiatry and director of the Division of Family Programs, Department of Psychiatry, University of Rochester Medical Center. As a clinician and researcher, Dr. Stanton has been working with addicted patients and the family treatment thereof for over twenty years.

Arlene T. Utada, M.Ed., has worked as a research psychologist at the Philadelphia Psychiatric Center since 1975, where she coordinated data collection for *Assessment of Family Therapy for Adolescent Drug Abuse* and *Diagnostic Strategies for Treatment of Drug Abuse Youth,* among others. Ms. Utada will complete doctoral studies at Temple University in mid-1990.

About the Editors

Alfred S. Friedman, Ph.D., was formerly director of drug treatment programs (1972–1983) and is now director of research at the Philadelphia Psychiatric Center. He is emeritus director of the Clinical School of Marital and Family Therapy at the Family Institute of Philadelphia and honorary full professor in the Department of Psychiatry at Thomas Jefferson University Hospital. He has been director or principle investigator of numerous federally funded treatment demonstration and research projects on adolescent drug abuse. One of these, a project entitled "Family Therapy for Adolescent Drug Abusers" supported by the National Institute on Drug Abuse, was the source for the research findings and family therapy case studies presented in this book; another was the first federally funded project for demonstrating family therapy, conducted from 1958 to 1965. He received the Distinguished Service award of the Pennsylvania Psychological Association in 1988. Dr. Friedman has published six books on family therapy and on treatment for adolescent drug abuse.

Samuel Granick received a Ph.D. in psychology from Columbia University in 1950. Throughout his professional career, he has divided his work equally between research and clinical practice. He currently serves as senior research psychologist at the Philadelphia Psychiatric Center, and he maintains a private clinical practice largely devoted to couple and family therapy. He has served as president of the Family Institute of Philadelphia and as director of its family therapy clinical training program. Other affiliations include AAMFT, the American Psychological Association, and the Philadelphia Society of Clinical Psychologists, of which Dr. Granick is a past president.